THE CONCEPT IN CRISIS

THE CONCEPT IN CRISIS

Reading Capital Today

NICK NESBITT, EDITOR

DUKE UNIVERSITY PRESS
Durham and London
2017

Typeset in Minion Pro by Westchester Publishing Services

Library of Congress Cataloging-in-Publication Data
Names: Nesbitt, Nick, [date]– editor.
Title: The concept in crisis : Reading Capital today /
    Nick Nesbitt, editor.
Description: Durham : Duke University Press, 2017. |
    Includes bibliographical references and index.
Identifiers: LCCN 2017004438 (print) | LCCN 2017007848
    (ebook)
ISBN 9780822369622 (hardcover : alk. paper)
ISBN 9780822369073 (pbk. : alk. paper)
ISBN 9780822372905 (ebook)
Subjects: LCSH: Althusser, Louis, 1918–1990. Lire
    "le capital." | Marx, Karl, 1818–1883. Kapital. | Marxian
    economics. | Philosophy, Marxist.
Classification: LCC HB50.A563 C66 2017 (print) |
    LCC HB50.A563 (ebook) | DDC 335.4/12—dc23
LC record available at https://lccn.loc.gov/2017004438

Cover art: Gareth James, *Money stands for limitlessness.
Art will too if it lasts too long*, 2009. Photo courtesy of the
artist.

CONTENTS

ACKNOWLEDGMENTS

The chapters by Alain Badiou, Étienne Balibar, Bruno Bosteels, Emily Apter, and Robert J. C. Young were all initially presented at the conference "Reading Capital: 1965–2015" on December 6, 2013, at Princeton University; each contribution has subsequently been revised for this volume. All chapters appear here for the first time. The editor wishes to thank all the contributors for their enthusiastic support and generous contributions to this project. Further thanks as well goes to the sponsors of the original conference: Verso Books and the Departments of French and Italian, German, and Comparative Literature at Princeton University, and to Peter Thomas, Alberto Toscano, and anonymous readers of these materials at *Historical Materialism*. Courtney Berger, Sandra Korn, and Susan Albury at Duke University Press guided the manuscript through the production process with enthusiasm and careful attention to detail, while two readers for Duke proved immensely helpful in reviewing the manuscript. A sabbatical leave from Princeton University allowed the editor to complete work on the manuscript. Princeton students in our seminar on *Reading Capital* contributed immeasurably to my own understanding of the volume's arguments, and Nicolas L'Hermitte in particular assisted with the initial transcription of what would eventually become Alain Badiou's chapter below.

Rereading *Reading Capital*

I do not believe there can be "Althusserians" in the strict sense of disciples of Althusser. One can only reiterate the questions he asked, and from them, fabricate others.

—YVES DUROUX

As he prepared his own contribution to the seminar that would become *Lire le Capital,* on October 2, 1963, Althusser wrote to Franca Madonia: "I'm working hard, and with good results; I'm reading *Capital* closely. Finally, I'm entering the citadel" (*Lettres à Franca* 459). After a period of intensive, even manic productivity in August–September 1962, in which he wrote many of the texts that would comprise *Pour Marx* in the span of a few weeks (and which Franca would translate in 1965), in the fall of 1964 Althusser set course with his "jeunes chiens," the precocious group of students at the École normale supérieure de la rue d'Ulm gathered around him for a seminar in spring term 1965, undertaking the philosophical reading of Marx's *Capital* that Althusser himself had previously called for in *Pour Marx*. The result, for the first time in Althusser's experience, was a truly "collective work, a collective project in which each working on his own reaches the same results by the most unexpected paths" (*Lettres à Franca* 605). The seminar, collectively organized by Althusser, Étienne Balibar, Yves Duroux, Jacques Rancière, and Jean-Claude Milner, culminated in texts by Althusser, Balibar, Rancière, and Pierre Macherey (Roger Establet, absent from the École, would later submit a text on the structure of *Capital*). Working again at a frenetic pace by November 1963, Althusser could rightfully observe: "What I'm producing," he wrote to Franca, "is incredible both in quantity and quality. I have so much to write, so much to say! . . . I've never been so conscious of the terrible danger contact with ideas represents—and at the same time the extraordinary power that it gives" (*Lettres à Franca* 482, 518). Each of the contributors produced works that, in their originality, timeliness, and vitality, would come on the publication of *Lire le Capital* in 1965 to comprise one of the key interventions in twentieth-century critical theory.

Reading Capital marked a watershed in Marxist philosophy and critical theory more generally, constructing a dazzling array of concepts that still today can be said to constitute the syntax of radical philosophy and that continue to inspire philosophical reflection of the highest order. The volume constructed powerful critiques of Hegel, of expressive totality, of teleologies, of humanism, of empiricism understood in its broadest sense, of causality, of phenomenologies and psychologistic philosophies of conscious intentionality, of historicisms, historiographies, and historians of every stripe and color and their reliance on mere methodology; pursuing the path of philosophical orientation first delineated in Jean Cavaillès's *On the Logic and Theory of Science* (1942), it undertook a Spinozist critique of phenomenology to pursue instead the construction of *concepts*, including the symptomatic reading, mode of production, overdetermination, the conjuncture, abstraction, structural causality, that of knowledge work as a form of production, of the necessity of contingency, of the very act of reading itself, and—in distinction to decades of reflexive and clichéd condemnation of Althusser's philosophy as somehow unable to think historical change—the construction of an array of critical concepts of a history with neither subject nor transcendental logic of transition.[1]

In 1961, there occurred an encounter between a young, largely unknown philosophy professor, born in 1918, and a small group of apprentice philosophers, who were in search of theoretical guidance at the rue d'Ulm in order to pursue new directions in philosophy. The political conjuncture of the climax of the Algerian war pushed these students toward both a theoretical and political passion. Given their political militancy, they were particularly happy to discover in Althusser a Marxist philosopher in their midst at the rue d'Ulm. Duroux, Jacques Rancière, Balibar, and Macherey thus together first approached Althusser in 1961, intrigued by his first articles on Marx, to ask for guidance in their readings. They constructed a *plan de travail* for the next three years, a research project that would culminate in *Lire le Capital*. Among the crucial absences or gaps in the final product that is *Lire le Capital*, Balibar has noted that of Duroux, who never actually wrote up a contribution of his own following the end of the seminar, yet who was an essential participant at every stage of the seminar.[2]

Following close on the seminar itself, by March 1965, Althusser had decided to publish the volume with François Maspero, and in November 1965,

Maspero duly published *Lire le Capital* (*Reading Capital*) in two volumes, simultaneously with Althusser's collection of earlier essays from 1961 to 1965 as *Pour Marx*. By the standards of French academic publishing at the time, it was an immense and immediate hit, vaulting Althusser and his collaborators to prominence in Parisian circles of philosophical academia and communism, both within and without the Parti Communiste Français (PCF).

In early 1968, before the events of May, François Maspero approached Althusser with the idea of a second, abridged, more "accessible" paperback edition of *Lire le Capital*. At this point, the decision was made to eliminate fully half of the contributions from the original volume: those of Establet and Macherey, as well as Rancière's chapter "The Concept of Critique and the Critique of Political Economy from 'The 1844 Manuscripts' to *Capital*." This decision would fundamentally alter the reception of the book, as this second edition in fact served as the basis for the foreign translations of *Reading Capital*, including the Italian, Spanish, German, and English editions.[3]

The consequences, for those concerned, are evident: to mention only the most obvious, Rancière was ineluctably pushed in the direction his thought had already taken of a free-flowing critique of all intellectual Masters and inequality, the direct result of which was the brilliant and devastating polemic of his first book, *Althusser's Lesson*. Balibar, on the other hand, was confirmed and encouraged in his allegiance and fidelity to the Althusserian theoretical line, becoming, as he has stated, the "porte-parole" of Althusserian thought through the 1970s and 1980s.[4]

Subsequently, in 1973, this truncated second edition of *Lire le Capital* was augmented in the *Petite collection Maspero* with two further volumes: volume 3, containing Rancière's chapter "Le concept de critique et la critique de l'économie politique des 'Manuscrits de 1844' au 'Capital'" (unrevised, but without the autocritique entitled "Mode d'emploi" Rancière had wished to append to it), and volume 4, containing Macherey's "A propos du processus d'exposition du 'Capital': Le travail des concepts" (revised) and Roger Establet's "Présentation du plan du 'Capital'" (unrevised). If this late rectification restored the totality of *Lire le Capital*, if only for Francophone readers, in those waning days of Althusserian Marxism and the rise of a poststructuralist politics of desire, how many beyond a few specialists and unreformed structuralists can have made it through a text that Rancière himself had virtually disowned, to press on through that final, obscure volume 4? This complete 1973 edition would then be reprinted in 1996 by PUF in their Quadrige series (and which is still in print as of this writing), with a new introduction by Étienne Balibar and Pierre Bravo Gala (with the collaboration of Yves Duroux), a list of errata from the 1968–1973 edition, along with an appendix listing the variations between the first and second editions. Finally, more than a half-century after the initial publication of this central text of critical theory, complete editions of *Lire le Capital* have as of this writing been published in English and German editions in addition to the original French.[5]

We thus find ourselves in a moment of rediscovery of *Lire le Capital*, at least in the Anglophone world. For a number of reasons, the historical diffusion and reception of *Reading Capital* since the 1970s was decisively inflected by the altered state of the abridged second edition. By 1967, the brief formalist, theoreticist moment in Marxist philosophy in France explosively initiated by *Reading Capital*, and that would culminate in the *Cahiers pour l'analyse*, had passed. Reception and discussion of Althusser since the 1970s has arguably been linked above all to the critique of *ideology*, with the theoreticist, epistemological focus of 1965–1967 (itself developed from the antiphenomenological tradition of Cavaillès, Bachelard, and Canguilhem) largely dismissed as wrong-headed or simply ignored.[6] To cite only the most immanent and well-known critique of Althusser, it is astounding to witness how Rancière's 1973 book *Althusser's Lesson* reduces the array of critiques and concepts listed a moment ago to the following statement of the central proposition of *Reading Capital*: "The major thesis of *Reading Capital* [is] the manipulation of the blind subjects of social practice," writes Rancière in his devastating polemic (53).

In fact, in the Anglophone world, *Reading Capital* is increasingly coming to be appreciated not so much as ideology critique but as a culminating moment in the twentieth-century French tradition of epistemology that extends from Bachelard, Cavaillès, and Albert Lautman to Canguilhem, and Foucault and Althusser. This was a tradition of thought that always and explicitly placed itself in opposition to all phenomenologies of consciousness. It seems that we are rediscovering this tradition, finally refusing all anti-intellectual disparagement of so-called theoreticism.[7] A raft of recent publications—from Warren Montag's *Althusser and His Contemporaries*, to Peter Hallward and Knox Peden's two-volume critical edition and translation of the *Cahiers pour l'analyse*, to Peden's *Spinoza contra Phenomenology: French Rationalism from Cavaillès to Deleuze*—have undertaken a critical revalorization and exploration of this epistemological tradition in which *Reading Capital* stands as one of the key and indeed culminating interventions.

Though this introduction can only hope to invoke a few of the key elements of this tradition set forth in Althusser's introductory essay on the Marxian epistemology of science, the key intertext with which Althusser remains in covert dialogue is clearly Jean Cavaillès's magnum opus, *Sur la logique et la théorie de la science*.[8] While Althusser rarely mentions Cavaillès in his writings, Knox Peden has shown that he took notes on the latter as a student after the war, becoming intimately familiar with Cavaillès's thought through the influence of his close friend and mentor Jacques Martin, "to whom," Althusser wrote, "I owe practically everything."[9] Warren Montag has argued that, more generally, "Althusser, fascinated by what he would later call 'philosophical strategy,' chose . . . to pursue something like a guerrilla war in the realm of theory, that is, a strategy of infiltration and impersonation that would allow him to gain a position within its walls from which an effective attack could be launched."[10] If this is the case for Althusser's Lenin (to whom Montag here refers), for his Spinoza, Mao, and countless other figures and interlocuters, I would argue that Althusser's attack on the citadel of existentialist phenomenology is waged above all with the arms Cavaillès had forged.[11]

Even more perhaps than his famous invocation of the necessity of a "lecture symptomale" (symptomatic reading) of *Capital* or Bachelard's "epistemological rupture," the fundamental ambition set forth in this text is to articulate a novel conception of the object of science, via the Spinozist distinction between the "object of knowledge" and the "real object."[12] "The production process of the object of knowledge," Althusser writes, "takes place entirely in knowledge" (RCC 41). While Althusser holds rigorously to Cavaillès's Spinozist epistemology, distinguishing between these two objects which nonetheless remain "modes" (43) of a single, material substance, his signal innovation is to introduce Marx within this Spinozist lineage of the philosophy of science, drawing upon the 1857 introduction to the *Grundrisse*. Science, in this view, is characterized not by the (empiricist) "reproduction" or representation of a truth "abstracted" from a real object in which it is held to exist, but instead is "produced" (38–41). While some eight pages from Marx's voluminous notebooks undoubtedly constitutes a flimsy basis for inducting Marx within the pantheon of Spinozist rationalism, this in a sense is Althusser's point; Marx's *scientific* critique of political economy still awaits the construction of the constellation of *philosophical* concepts adequate to its analysis.[13]

The scientific process of the exposition of a proof of necessity must in this view hold to two criteria: Spinoza's axiom of autonomy and adequacy (*verum index sui et falsi*) and Bolzano's assertion of *demonstration* as the proper apodictic procedure to substantiate this indexification.[14] In Cavaillès's terms, "There is only one means of imposing an authority that borrows nothing from outside itself, there is only one unconditional mode of affirmation, demonstration . . . Science, if it is to be, consists entirely in demonstration" (39, 40).[15] Althusser, following Cavaillès's critique of Bolzano, adds to this assertion the problematic of history, of the relation, in other words, between the demonstration of an adequate and self-sufficient scientific truth and the norms of the demonstration of necessity holding at any moment in the history of thought: "The essential problem presupposed by the question of the existing type of *demonstrativity* is the problem of the history of the production of different forms in which theoretical practice . . . recognizes the validating norms it demands, [. . . norms that] at a given moment in the history of knowledge constitute the theoretical problematic . . . and hence the *forms* required to give the order of theoretical discourse *the force and value of a proof [démonstration]*" (RCC 50).[16] For Cavaillès and Althusser alike, the production and development of ideas is an infinite, nonteleological process. As a "structure of openness," the production of knowledge occurs necessarily, without ground or reference to consciousness (RCC 57).[17]

The key distinction inhering between Cavaillès's and Althusser's epistemologies, however, centers on the relation of the object of thought to the "real" object. For Cavaillès, focusing on mathematics as the paradigmatic instance of a post-Kantian, post-Husserlian science, the Cantorian revolution of set theory forces the construction of objects of knowledge that are inherently unimaginable, concepts (such as that of infinite sets) that bear no basis in empirical reality, yet which are rationally demonstrable.[18] Althusser's focus on Marx's critique of political economy, in contrast, necessitates full consideration of the relation inhering between these two objects (of thought and the real). This problem forms the object of Althusser's critique of the Cartesian "closure of the ideological circle" in the concluding sections of his essay (53–73).

To carry through this critique, Althusser specifies the question to which his inquiry necessarily leads—"By what mechanism does the production of the object of knowledge produce the cognitive appropriation of the real object [*par quel mécanisme la production de l'objet de la connaissance produit-elle l'appropriation cognitive de l'objet réel*]" (58 [61])—but does so in terms that threaten to lead straight back into the empiricism he has just critiqued so powerfully. The term "appropriation," which Althusser takes directly from Marx's *1857 Introduction*, clearly indicates a property-based relation between the object of knowledge and a knowing subject who takes possession over a truth.[19] This regression to an epistemological model of "appropriation" in the culminating sections of Althusser's introduction makes it impossible for him to provide a substantial response to the Spinozist directive he has put forward: to "exclude any recourse to the ideological solution contained in the ideological characters Subject and Object." This is clearly the case, insofar as the juridical category of appropriation remains ineluctably ideological, symptomatic of the "legal instance," "laws," and "legal recognition" he rejects on the very same page (58). Given this contradiction, it is hardly surprising that the final sections of Althusser's text simply repeat this question ("by what mechanism . . . ?") without offering anything approaching a substantial response.[20]

That said, it is clear that a Spinozist, Cavaillèsian construction of such a response would necessarily remain in the modality of knowledge and the production of concepts, even in demonstrating the structure of capitalism. It would presumably conclude that the concept of this structure is not "appropriated" from the empirical, from what Althusser terms its "raw material [matière première]," but is instead itself, like any concept, constructed or, more strongly, produced "entirely in knowledge [tout entier dans la connaissance]" (RCC 42).[21] In this view, to pass between the Scylla of empiricism and the Charybdis of Idealism, knowledge of capitalism, as a complexly structured concept, could bear no recourse to a Subject of knowledge, but would refer instead to the development of apodictic knowledge as the open-ended, infinite construction of "new thought objects, 'ideas'" (62), the production of the concept of capitalism as the idea of the idea (of capitalism), from Smith and Ricardo to Marx and beyond, but also, for example, conceptualizing such seemingly empirical categories as the idea of the historical condition of the English working class that Marx develops from Engels or the idea of the Commune.[22] The subject of this knowledge, in turn, would not be attributable to a productive consciousness or even a transcendental subject, but would instead refer to the real materiality of a general intellect, to adopt Marx's famous concept. One might interpret Alain Badiou's fidelity to and development of the Cavaillèsian epistemology of Reading Capital in precisely such terms, extending the compass of Althusser's epistemology of the critique of political economy to include the domain of politics as an axiomatic logic of equality, one as devoid of moralistic guarantees and empiricism as it is to the empirical guarantee or foundation of "class struggle."[23]

In any case, and despite this significant difference in objects, Althusser and Cavaillès's texts share a final and preordinate imperative: the logical critique and displacement of the founding role of consciousness in post-Husserlian phenomenology.[24] For Cavaillès, it is always the case for phenomenology that "the reference to the primacy of consciousness permits in the end the suppression of [logical] difficulties. . . . It is the intentionality of consciousness—that is to say the 'experience of having something in consciousness'—that explains and *guarantees* the duality between the intended object and the act that intends."[25] Althusser, in turn, argues powerfully against any interpretation of *Capital* that would have recourse to "an idealism of consciousness, mind or thought" (RCC 41). Against post-Husserlian invocations of a "transcendental subject or absolute consciousness confronted by the real world as matter" or as "the faculty of a psychological subject," Althusser understands knowledge itself as a structure [*Gliederung*], "the historically constituted system of an apparatus of thought" (RCC 42).[26] In this mode of production (of knowledge), the system "assigns [the] thinking subject (individual), its place and function in the production of knowledges" (RCC 42). The production of knowledge, in this view, is not the attribute of a phenomenological, productive subjectivity (whether Kantian, Hegelian, or Husserlian), but the unfolding of the autonomous movement of ideas.[27]

The phenomenological attempt to extract a core of truth from the objective world ("to abstract from the real object its essence," in Althusser's words), the attempt to "to know the world, to understand the world" is for Cavaillès nothing less than a "renunciation of a necessity that links itself to nothing other than itself" (RCC 35; *Sur la logique* 34).[28] Cavaillès's summary final judgment regarding phenomenology in the closing pages of *Sur la logique* draws together the strands of his critique to underscore the fundamental subjective interiority in terms that Althusser will pursue in his critique of the Cartesian "vicious circle" of Reason (RCC 54):

> The phenomenological method and point of view limits itself to analysing the acts and constitutive intentions of transcendental subjectivity, that is to say, to decomposing the complex of elementary subjective motivations and actions, without the logical entity itself being interrogated. It is evident, moreover, that it cannot be, since no consciousness is witness by an act to the production of its content.[29]

In contrast to this interiority of the intentional, productive subject, the construction of a rationalist epistemology, understood as the production of an "absolute logic . . . can only draw its authority from itself, it is not transcendental" (Cavaillès 78).[30] Althusser's own directive "to exclude any recourse to the ideological characters Subject and Object" (RCC 57) in the construction of the concept demands nothing less.

Nietzsche, in one of the final aphorisms of *The Gay Science*, writes:

Prophetic human beings are full of suffering . . . Certain species, for example monkeys, have a prophetic insight about the weather . . . But we don't think of the fact that for them, their pains are prophets for them! When under the influence of an approaching, as yet far from visible cloud a strong positive electrical charge suddenly turns into negative electricity and a change of weather is impending, these animals act as if an enemy were approaching and prepare for defence or escape.[31]

In more than one respect, Louis Althusser was a Nietzschean genius of Marxist persuasion.[32] Althusser registered with prophetic and anguished intensity in the years prior to 1968, I would argue, the imminent waning of the proletarian politics to which he had committed himself unreservedly since 1948, a decline—however one may judge and react to it—that has become ever more evident since 1989. The heresy of this "prophetic insight," to borrow Nietzsche's phrase, is expressed in the fundamental distinction in Althusser's Marxist writings between two registers or modes of analysis: on the one hand, the antiempiricist, antiphenomenological rationalism of the purely Spinozist, depoliticized critique of capitalism articulated in *Reading Capital*, and a countervailing auto-critique and accompanying espousal of a Leninist politics of the class struggle and dictatorship of the proletariat in texts such as "Marxism and Humanism" and "The Historical Task of Marxist Philosophy," where Althusser first theorizes "the primacy of the class struggle in theory."

From the first essay of *For Marx*[33] through its culmination in the essays of *Reading Capital*, this process, in other words, became manifest not as a historical claim or analysis of the waning of traditional Marxism-Leninism— to the contrary, Althusser famously struggled to remain faithful to the PCF, proletarian class struggle, and socialism through the 1970s—but rather as an unyielding axiomatic decision in favor of the pure, Spinozist truth of rational thought over the lived experience affirmed by empiricism and phenomenology alike, regardless of the consequences or implications for political practice as it had been understood in traditional Marxism.

This commitment to rational theory over the contingency of the political, a commitment to what was in essence a rigorous development and extrapolation to Marx of Cavaillès's famous call for a "philosophy of the concept,"[34] reached its highest point of development in *Reading Capital*. It is not by studying the phenomenal, empirical facts of history that we will understand capitalism, Althusser argues, but by reading *Capital* and comprehending the conceptual apparatus Marx develops therein, at once out of and against the empiricist, bourgeois ideology of Smith and Ricardo. This commitment culminates in Althusser's rigorous and provocative distinction between a generic "practice" that is abstractly opposed to so-called theory, each mere ideological categories—and the specificity of an infinite plurality of practices: "There is no practice in general, but only *distinct practices* . . . This dichotomy [between theory and practice] is merely an ideological myth in which a 'theory of knowledge' reflects many 'interests' other than those of reason." Althusser explicitly draws the manifest implication of this claim: that any political claim such as "the workers' cause" or "egalitarian communism," no matter its degree of "revolutionary vision," necessarily "remains ideological" (RCC 60).

With this, Althusser neatly eviscerates the relevance of political judgments and practice to the verification of a scientific practice including and above all the critique of political economy. Althusser's Cavaillès-inflected Spinozism here rises to its highest, most heterodox pitch: "Theoretical practice is indeed its own criterion, and contains in itself definite protocols with which to validate the quality of its product, i.e., the criteria of the scientificity of the products of scientific practice" (RCC 61). Althusser assuredly confronts the implications of this Spinozist argument for traditional Marxism: against all pragmatism, all justification and guarantee by ideological categories such class struggle, the dictatorship of the proletariat, or any other political warrant, "the criterion of 'truth' of the knowledges produced by Marx's theoretical practice is provided by his theoretical practice itself, i.e., by the proof-value, by the scientific status of the *forms* which ensured the production of those knowledges. Marx's theoretical practice is the criterion of the 'truth' of the knowledges that Marx produced" (RCC 62).

When Althusser decisively (if briefly) bracketed the political teleology of socialism celebrated in the panegyrics of "Marxism and Humanism" to explicate Marx's *Capital* (and to delineate what he saw as the proper modality for this explication), he was roundly judged to have committed the cardinal sin of "theoreticism." For this, he was virulently proscribed by traditional Marxists of all stripes, in the face of which criticism he largely abandoned philosophical analysis of Marx's critique of political economy to (re)assert the "primacy of politics" and the intimate relation of philosophy and politics as "class struggle in theory."

What could possibly have been so upsetting to an entire generation of Marxists in the 1960s and 1970s, in Althusser's having produced an explication of Marx that Peden has called "the cumulative point of a trajectory of French Spinozism that has its roots in [Jean] Cavaillès"?[35] What made it imperative to vilify and denigrate this undertaking rather than critiquing it ("scientifically") or simply ignoring it? Perry Anderson, in his critique of Althusser in *Arguments with English Marxism* (1980), describes what was at stake under the stigmata "theoreticism" with stark simplicity: "Althusser's unilateral and remorseless stress on the overpowering weight of structural necessity in history corresponds more faithfully to the central tenets of historical materialism, and to the actual lessons of scientific study of the past—but at the price of obscuring the novelty of the modern labor movement and attenuating the vocation of revolutionary socialism."[36]

To be sure, each of the contributors to this volume has articulated singular notions of the political and its relation to the categories essential to Althusser—the critique of political economy, Marxism, history, science, ideology, the contemporary world, and, of course, philosophy itself. That said—this at least is the conviction of this reader of Althusser and Marx—"the novelty of the modern labor movement" and "the vocation of revolutionary socialism"[37] no longer adequately define the subject of progressive politics, in the wake of the global events of 1968, the decline of trade unions and nominally "communist" political parties such as the PCF, the globalization and automation of production since the 1980s, the end of state socialism in 1989, and the exponential expansion of financialization, to name only the most obvious factors. At the same time, the various forms of "local" and "micro"-politics that took the place of proletarian class struggle on the post-'68 Left, for all their real accomplishments, have been largely unable to mount a consequential offensive against the ever-more-dominant structures of global capitalism, which has constantly proven capable of absorbing the assertion of difference as the repetition of subsumption to the objective demands of valorization. At the very moment when human misery and subjection to the obligation to valorize value has reached unparalleled extremities in a "planet of slums" (Mike Davis), when the need for an effective anticapitalist politics is felt more strongly than ever, both traditional Marxist-proletarian and multicultural political formations and tactics arguably remain inadequate to combat the distressing scope of global desolation.[38]

That said, this attention to the separation between the conceptual analysis of capitalism in *Reading Capital* and Althusser's various philosophical excurses on political subjectivity is, I would argue, no mere retrospective speculation on my part regarding the destiny of Leninist class politics. It points as well to an exacting analytical distinction that traverses Althusser's writings, a distinction implying that not only history, as Althusser famously claimed, but capitalism, and, above all, its critique, are a processes without a (political) subject, if by "subject" we understand the singular support (*Träger*) for a process in exception or excess to a given state of affairs or situation.[39] Any critique of political economy must, in this view, be meticulously distinguished from the analysis and conceptualization of political subjectivities and processes—though the outcome of such analysis must in turn inform any truly "anti-capitalist" politics. Marx himself maintained such a distinction in his late writings (witness the warrant of *Capital* versus that of *The Civil War in France* or the "Critique of the Gotha Program"), and the absence of a philosophy of political subjectivity in *Reading Capital* rigorously adheres to this fundamental analytical distinction, to its utmost advantage.

It is more urgent than ever to carry forward Marx's conceptual, categorial critique of capitalism and to move beyond the superficial empiricism and subjectivism of neoliberal economics as a prolegomenon to the invention of contemporary politics adequate to the realities of contemporary capitalism. "It is precisely," Althusser argues, "this *Gliederung*, this articulated-thought-totality which has to be produced in knowledge as an object of knowledge in order to reach a knowledge of the real *Gliederung*, of the real articulated-totality which constitutes the existence of bourgeois society" (RCC 49).[40] For this process, the singular arsenal of critical concepts and methodologies forged by *Reading Capital* offer essential purchase for the invention of new political practices for the twenty-first century.

Althusser and his students' 1965 volume effectively, if briefly, disregarded the Leninist problem of the seizure of political power by the proletariat and the struggle for socialism, to engage—at the most rigorous level demanded by the ideas of Spinoza, Bachelard, and Cavaillès—Marx's conceptual critique of the political economy of capitalism. This move appears today not as mistaken lapse but as truly prophetic. If in the 1970s "Althusser's effort appeared hermetic, idiosyncratic, and to many downright bizarre,"[41] today *Reading Capital* offers a protean theoretical vocabulary for the categorial critique of the structure and limits of capitalism as a mode of production dedicated to the ever-expanding valorization of value.[42] In radical subtraction from all traces of neoliberal empiricism and phenomenological vitalism, *Reading Capital* articulates the promise for contemporary critique of the "idea of the idea" (Spinoza), that of a philosophy of the concept (of capital) that is arguably the necessary condition for any exit from capitalism itself.

The promise of rediscovering today the powerful theoretical and conceptual tools invented by *Reading Capital* lies far beyond mere antiquarian and scholastic curiosity. The real question is whether *Reading Capital* continues to allow for the production of new concepts, and whether, ultimately, it is possible and even essential today, after what Badiou has called the "obscure disasters" of the twentieth century, as postsocialist, neoliberal capital lunges in ever greater exhaustion from one crisis to the next, finally to read Marx's *Capital* as *Reading Capital* was the first to insist upon: as the systematic, conceptual, and, yes, scientific exposition and critique of the capitalist mode of production. The answer the essays collected in this volume propose is a resounding yes, reinventing *Reading Capital* for a renewed communist philosophy and critique of political economy in the twenty-first century. Speaking with Badiou, is it not the case that *Lire le Capital*, like the prodigious masterwork that is its object of investigation, proves itself timeless in the truths it continues to interject into an infinite multiplicity of worlds, to be grasped, critiqued, and relayed in the endless movement of thought itself?

Notes

1. See François Regnault's comments on the Althusserian critique of phenomenology in Aliocha Wald Lasowski, *Althusser et nous* (Paris: PUF, 2016), 255.

2. In conversation with the editor, New York, December 4, 2013.

3. Étienne Balibar, "Althusser," in *The Columbia History of Twentieth-Century French Thought*, ed. Lawrence D. Kritzman, 380–84 (New York: Columbia University Press, 2006); "A Philosophical Conjuncture: An Interview with Étienne Balibar and Yves Duroux," in *Concept and Form, vol. 2: Interviews and Essays on the Cahiers pour l'analyse*, ed. Peter Hallward and Knox Peden (London: Verso, 2012), 169–86; Étienne Balibar, "Althusser and the rue d'Ulm," trans. David Fernbach, *New Left Review* 58 (July–August 2009). See also the descriptions of the seminar in the interviews with Balibar, Duroux, Rancière, and Macherey in Lasowski, *Althusser et nous*, as well as the outstanding dossier on Althusser in *Viewpoint Magazine*, "A Struggle without End: Althusser's Interventions," and in particular contributions from William S. Lewis discussing the newly available digitized recordings of the 1964–65 seminar held at the IMEC and an extensive and meticulously detailed and knowledgeable interview with the figure perhaps most responsible for the recent revival of editorial interest in Althusser, G. M. Goshgarian. Accessed August 29, 2016, https://viewpointmag.com /2016/07/18/a-struggle-without-end-althussers-interventions/.

4. In conversation with the editor, New York, December 4, 2013.

5. See Louis Althusser, Étienne Balibar, Roger Establet, Pierre Macherey, and Jacques Rancière, *Reading Capital: The Complete Edition*, trans. Ben Brewster and David Fernbach (London: Verso, 2016); *Das Kapital lesen* (Münster: Westfälisches

Dampfboot, 2014). Though the studies in this volume predate the publication of the new, complete English-language edition of *Reading Capital* by Verso in spring 2016, it has been possible to update the majority of the chapters in reference to what is henceforth the standard English language reference.

6. This disparagement of a conceptual reading of Marx's *Capital* such as that first proposed by Althusser remains in force today. Witness the manner in which Gareth Stedman Jones, in his otherwise well-documented discussion of Marx, offhandedly dismisses *Capital* with the mistaken and simplistic claim that Marx directly "attempted to employ Ricardo's concept of value" in an effort, by Marx, "to make the value of labor measurable" (379). Bemoaning the increasingly objective and scientific character of Marx's various drafts of *Capital* and their increasing focus on "impersonal and inevitable processes, detached from the actions of human agents," Stedman Jones offers in conclusion the seemingly absurd judgment that the work's "most distinctive and lasting [quality is *Capital*'s] fact-based depiction of the development . . . of the relations between capital and labor, mainly in England" (428). In his summary description of Marx's magnum opus, Stedman Jones assures readers that Marx did not "succeed in identifying the 'laws of motion' of capital," and instead reduces the value of its four-volume analysis to a mere descriptive compendium of nineteenth-century (English) working conditions (429). See Gareth Stedman Jones, *Karl Marx: Greatness and Illusion* (Cambridge, MA: Harvard University Press, 2016).

7. See the comments of Pierre Macherey and Jean-Claude Milner on Althusser's so-called theoreticism in Lasowski, *Althusser et nous*, 189–90, 220. Peter Osborne has written more generally of a "reproach of abstraction," by which he refers to both a sense of melancholic despair over the lost real object, along with a feeling of shame accompanying the repression of a putatively more vital lived experience. Peter Osborne, "The Reproach of Abstraction," *Radical Philosophy* 127 (September/October 2004), cited in Mark Abel, "Radical Openness: Chord Symbols, Musical Abstraction, and Modernism," *Radical Philosophy* 195 (January/February 2016): 30.

8. Jean Cavaillès, *Sur la logique et la théorie de la science* (1942; reprint, Paris: Vrin, 2008). Althusser only mentions Cavaillès once in *Lire le Capital*, in a brief note listing the "few remarkable exceptions" to what he sees as the dominant "ideological conception of history": "Koyré, Bachelard, Cavaillès, Canguilhem, and Foucault" (2016: 529). Peden, however, demonstrates how Althusser's philosophy forms the pinnacle of a rationalist Spinozist tradition of antiempiricist, antiphenomenological epistemology extending from Spinoza and Bolzano through Léon Brunschvicg, Cavaillès, Martial Gueroult, and ultimately Althusser, Deleuze, and (I would add) Badiou, a tradition in which Cavaillès's thought articulates the fundamental problematic. Peden argues, furthermore, that the entirety of Althusser's philosophy remains faithful to this imperative to develop a "philosophy of the concept" (Cavaillès) in opposition to post-Husserlian phenomenology. See Knox Peden, *Spinoza contra Phenomenology: French Rationalism from Cavaillès to Deleuze* (Stanford, CA: Stanford University Press, 2014).

9. Cited in Peden, *Spinoza contra Phenomenology*, 139.

10. Warren Montag, *Althusser and His Contemporaries* (Durham, NC: Duke University Press, 2013), 50.

11. In *Althusser and His Contemporaries*, Warren Montag discusses the multitude of figures of thought with whom Althusser engaged. These were intellectual personae whose ideas he variously attacked, ventriloquized, and contorted to his own ends, or whose preexisting bastions of thought he willfully occupied (in the sense in which one occupies a territory in battle). Cavaillès, I am arguing, was for Althusser a figure of the latter type: to sustain Althusser's and Montag's bellicose imagery, the theoretical armature the philosopher-Résistant had forged was left abandoned by his untimely death, and Althusser readily took up these arms in his wake under the influence of Jacques Martin. Montag, *Althusser and His Contemporaries*.

12. "Spinoza warned us that the object of knowledge or essence was in itself absolutely distinct from the real object, for, to repeat his famous aphorism, the two objects must not be confused: the idea of a circle, which is the object of knowledge must not be confused with the circle which is the real object" (RCC 40). For Cavaillès, the object of knowledge is "un objet sui generis, original dans son essence, autonome dans son movement. Elle n'est pas plus un absolu qu'un élément dans le système des existants . . . La science est un volume riemmannien qui peut-être à la fois fermé et sans extérieur à lui" (*Sur la logique*, 36, 38). In contrast to Cavaillès's and Althusser's radical Spinozism, Bachelard's related defense of constructed concepts and corresponding critique of empiricism remains a logic of the "abstraction" of concepts from the real. See Gaston Bachelard, *La formation de l'esprit scientifique* (1938; reprint, Paris: Vrin, 2011), 8–11. See also Dominique Lecourt, *Marxism and Epistemology: Bachelard, Canguilhem, Foucault* (New York: New Left Books, 1975).

13. Althusser's analysis in fact focuses on a single section of the Grundrisse's 1857 introduction, constituting a mere 8 pages out of 882 in the English edition (101–8).

14. See Bernard Bolzano, *Théorie de la science* (1837; reprint, Paris: Gallimard, 2011). See also Léon Brunschvicg, *Les étapes de la philosophie mathématique* (1930; reprint, Paris: PUF, 1947).

15. "Il n'est qu'une façon de s'imposer par une autorité qui n'emprunte rien au dehors, il n'est qu'un mode d'affirmation inconditionelle, la démonstration . . . La science, si elle est, est toute entière demonstration." Cavaillès goes on to specify the characteristics of any apodictic demonstration: "unité, progression nécessaire et indéfinie, enfin fermature sur soi" (*Sur la logique*, 39).

16. Compare with Cavaillès on Bolzano: If "la véritable science ne quitte pas le démontré, . . . le problème qui se pose alors est d'appréhender ce principe dans son movement générateur, de retrouver cette structure non par description mais apodictiquement en tant qu'elle se déroule et se démontre elle-même" (*Sur la logique*, 40). In his discussion of "scientific rigour," Pierre Macherey places a similar emphasis on the demonstrable: "Making a science of economic reality means constructing an exposition by way of concepts; a theory is an arrangement of concepts into propositions, and of propositions into chains of propositions in a form of demonstration" (2016, 182, my emphasis). If in "A propos du processus d'exposition du Capital,"

Macherey's argument for the radical distinction of the real and conceptual orders is essentially identical to Althusser's, of the two Macherey's is the analytically more rigorous, developed, and penetrating exposition of this problem. I discuss Althusser's introduction here because it is by far the better-known and influential text, while I discuss Macherey's analysis in my contribution below.

17. "L'incomplétude et l'exigence de progrès [de la science] font partie de [sa] définition. Seulement progrès autonome, dynamisme fermé sur lui-même, sans commencement absolu ni terme, la science se meut hors du temps—si le temps signifie référence au vécu d'une conscience" (*Sur la logique*, 37).

18. "Avec l'infini commence la véritable mathématique" (*Sur la logique*, 85).

19. The *Robert* defines *s'approprier* as "s'attribuer la propriété de quelquechose," while the German term Marx uses, *aneignet*, is closely related to terms such as the juridical *Aneignungsrecht* (right of appropriation).

20. Alberto Toscano analyzes the degree to which this critique of bourgeois juridical ideology will become predominant in Althusser's later texts *Être marxiste en philosophie* (2015 [1976]) and *Initiation à la philosophie pour les non-philosophes* (2014 [1978]), both recently edited by G. M. Goshgarian and forthcoming in English translation. Alberto Toscano, "The Detour of Abstraction," *Diacritics* 43, no. 2 (2015): 68–90. Henryk Grossman, in his remarkable interpretation of the reproduction or "value" schema of volume 2 of *Capital*—though hindered, like Althusser, by a precritical distinction between the conceptual order and so-called economic reality— proposes precisely such a theory of the schema as conceptual "mediators" between the structural abstractions of volume 1 and Marx's objective phenomenology of the various forms of appearance of capital developed in volume 3. "We have surplus values in the reproduction schema," Grossman writes, "but not in reality. Surplus value is 'invisible,' while in the reality of capitalism only different forms of profit such as profit of enterprise, interest, commercial profit, and ground rent occur" (110). See Henryk Grossman, "The Value-Price Transformation in Marx and the Problem of Crisis" [1932]. *Historical Materialism* 24, no. 1 (2016): 105–34. On the concept of an "objective phenomenology," which I would argue constitutes—as opposed to Grossman's crude references to "the reality of capitalism"—the appropriate mode for understanding the conceptual categories of *Capital* volume 3, see Alain Badiou, *Logics of Worlds: Being and Event*, trans. Bruno Bosteels (London: Continuum, 2009).

21. Alain Badiou investigates this problematic in Althusser's introduction in his contribution below.

22. Cavaillès formulates this imperative to grasp conceptual production unfolding entirely within the realm of ideas in typically stark terms: "Il faut soit l'absolu d'intelligibilité qui légitime la superposition spinoziste de l'idée de l'idée, soit la référence à une conscience génératrice dont c'est la propriété de se saisir immédiatement dans ses actes authentiques" (*Sur la logique*, 34, my emphasis).

23. Alain Badiou, *Logics of Worlds: Being and Event II* (London: Continuum, 2013).

24. Étienne Balibar has recently described the critical project of *Capital* as one in which "an analysis of objective categories and a phenomenology of lived experience are

combined and complete each other [such that] the articulation of surplus-labor with surplus-value (with the antagonism it engenders) must be thinkable at once on the level of the society as a whole . . . and at the level of the smallest unit of exploitation" ("Critique in the 21st century: Political economy still, and religion again," Radical Philosophy 200 [November–December 2016]): 18. While this is undoubtedly an accurate description of Marx's project, I am arguing here that while analysis and discussion of the lived experience of capitalist exploitation has never abated since Marx's time, Althusser's emphasis on the antiphenomenological structuralism of Capital identifies a contemporary critical imperative demanding development at the level of rigor Marx first formulated.

25. "La référence au primat de la conscience en fin de compte permet de supprimer les difficultés [logiques . . .] C'est l'intentionalité de la conscience—c'est à dire 'l'expérience d'avoir quelquechose dans la conscience'—qui explique et garantit la dualité entre l'objet vise et l'acte qui le vise" (Sur la logique, 69, 70, my emphasis).

26. Cavaillès's understanding of structure is perfectly Spinozist, defined in terms that clearly announce Althusser's concept of structural causality: "En définissant une structure de la science qui n'est que manifestation à elle-même de ce qu'elle est, on précise et justifie les caractères [théoriques] precedents . . . par une revelation qui n'est pas distinct du révélé, présente dans son mouvement, principe de sa nécessité. La structure parle sur elle-même" (Sur la logique, 39).

27. "Pour la phénoménologie, . . . le moteur de la recherche et le fondement des objectivités sont la relation à une subjectivité créatrice" (Cavaillès, Sur la logique, 78).

28. For Husserlian phenomenology, Cavaillès continues, "entre l'évidence rationnelle d'une demonstration mathématique et l'évidence sensible de la perception historique d'un objet il y a l'homogénéité profonde qu'elles sont l'une et l'autre pleine lumière de la même conscience, que, par suite, des relations de conditionnement mutuel sont possibles et justifiables par une analyse des actes qui procurent l'une et l'autre. A la fois légitimité des rapports et le moyen de leur découverte se trouvent dans une prise de conscience par la conscience même de ce qu'elle accomplit. La vérité est une [pour Husserl] sous ses aspects multiples, parce qu'il n'y a fondamentalement qu'une connaissance qui est la conscience" (Sur la logique, 70).

29. "Avec la méthode et le point de vue phénoménologique, elle se borne à analyser actes et intentions constitutifs de la subjectivité transcendentale, c'est à dire à décomposer des enchevêtrements de motivations et d'actions élémentaires subjectives sans que l'entité logique elle-même soit interrogée. Il est evident qu'elle ne peut l'être puisque aucune conscience n'est témoin de la production de son contenu par un acte" (Sur la logique, 87).

30. Cavaillès's critiques of Kant and Husserl are in this sense analogous. In the Kantian concept of the faculties, "interviennent fondamentalement les notions d'action, de pouvoir, qui n'ont de sens que par référence à une conscience concrète . . . La nécessité des règles—c'est à dire leur caractère normative inconditionné—reste donc subordonnée à l'absolu d'une conscience dont la presence et la structure essentielle—ce qu'est la conscience en soi—sont un irréductible qu'aucun contenu rationnel ne définit . . . [Pour Kant,] il n'y a pas de science en tant que réalité autonome et caractérisable come telle, mais

une unification rationelle, suivant un type fixe, d'un divers organisé par l'entendement" (*Sur la logique*, 18, 30). Similarly for Husserl, reference to consciousness, like that of the "world," remains unable to "rendre compte ni du progrès effectif [de la science] ni des structures et des entités qui le jalonnent ... Le point de vue phénoménologique ... se borne à analyser les actes et intentions constitutifs de la subjectivité transcendentale ... sans que l'entité logique elle-même soit interrogée" (*Sur la logique*, 87).

31. Friedrich Nietzsche, *The Gay Science: With a Prelude in German Rhymes and an Appendix of Songs*, ed. Bernard Williams (Cambridge: Cambridge University Press, 2001), 178.

32. On Nietzsche's reactionary antipolitics, see Dominico Losurdo, *Nietzsche, philosophe réactionnaire: Pour une biographie politique* (Paris: Delga, 2008).

33. "Those of us who were the most militant and the most generous tended towards an interpretation of the 'end of philosophy' as its 'realization' and celebrated the death of philosophy in action, in its political realization and proletarian consummation, unreservedly endorsing the famous Thesis on Feuerbach which, in theoretically ambiguous words, counterposes the transformation of the world to its interpretation. It was, and always will be, only a short step from here to theoretical pragmatism" (*For Marx*, cited in Peden, *Spinoza contra Phenomenology*, 144).

34. Cavaillès, *Sur la logique et la theorie de la science*, 90.

35. Peden, *Spinoza contra Phenomenology*, 145.

36. Cited in Peden, *Spinoza contra Phenomenology*, 142.

37. Cited in Peden, *Spinoza contra Phenomenology*, 142.

38. Kurz, Lahoff, and Trenkle's despondent critique of this paradox is characteristically ironic and unsparing: "Class struggle is finished because the society of work is as well. As the system [of valorization] implodes, the classes reveal themselves as the mere sociofunctional categories of a single fetishistic system ... It only remains for people to humbly propose their services as ultra-cheap workers and democratic slaves to the fortunate winners of globalization. These 'working poor' are thus free to shine the shoes of the last surviving businessmen, to sell them contaminated hamburgers or guard the shopping centers of a moribund work society." Robert Kurz, Ernst Lahoff, and Norbert Trenkle, *Manifeste contre le travail* (Paris: Editions Léo Scheer, 2002), 56, 19.

39. Étienne Balibar says as much when he writes that "the social process of production [is] a process without a subject" (RCC 2016, 439). On such a notion of political subjectivity and its distinction from critique, which relies upon the philosophy of the subject that traverses the entirety of Badiou's thought, see in particular Badiou (2016).

40. Althusser continues, justifying precisely this necessity of a return to reading *Capital*: "The order in which the thought Gliederung is produced is a specific order, precisely the order of the theoretical analysis Marx performed in *Capital*, the order of the liaison and 'synthesis' of the concepts necessary for the production of a thought-whole, a thought-concrete, the theory of *Capital*" (RCC 49).

41. Peden, *Spinoza contra Phenomenology*, 174.

42. I develop this point in relation to *Reading Capital* in my essay below.

PART I

Reading *Reading Capital*

CHAPTER I

The Althusserian Definition of "Theory"

ALAIN BADIOU

What does Althusser have in mind when he uses the word *theory*? This word, in some sense, in *Reading Capital*, is what I would call a "master-word." The exact intention of Louis Althusser is to formulate a proof that *Capital* is, I quote, "the absolute beginning of the history of a science" (RCC 13).[1] And the provisional definition of "science," the absolute beginning of which he speaks, is the "theory of history." So, the problem is to give a proof that, reading *Capital*, we can identify the absolute beginning of the theory of history. And so, we find the word *theory* present at the very beginning of Althusser's investigation, as he summarizes the intellectual strategy of *Reading Capital*. But, immediately, we run into difficulties . . .

First, what exactly constitutes the absolute beginning of a science? The absolute beginning of a science is not the same thing as the pure apparition of something of theoretical value. Why? Because the birth of a theory is very often, perhaps always, the revolution of a preexistent theory: a theory comes, in general, not in the void but by revolution, as the transformation of an old or preexistent theory. Engels explains this point in the preface of the second volume of *Capital*, which is a very important reference for Althusser himself: a new theory is not the creation *ex nihilo* of a new theoretical dimension. In the best case, it is a complete revolution of an old theory . . . that is, in the case of *Capital*, a complete revolution of classical economic theory. So, and this is my first point, theory is not the name of newness as such; it is not pure invention. Its value is a differential one. It is the distance—the *écart*—between two different theories. This point will be a *constance*, a sort of fixed point in *Reading Capital*. All beginnings and also all contradictions must be reduced to differences. All that really exists is an articulated complex of differences.

This is the principal idea of the end of Althusser's introduction, at the beginning of *Reading Capital* . . . the text that announces the passage from *Capital* to Marx's philosophy.

Any theory possesses its discursive order, and thus the effective existence of a theory is always the immanent organization of concepts in the system. This is the last word of Althusser's text, "system," and we shall see much more *systématicité* of the system in the chapters that follow (RCC 72). But of what system does Althusser speak? Of the system of thinking as a *totalité*, of the thinking of *totalité*. So, *theory*, as a word, becomes in the end what Althusser names quite precisely the *systematicité* of the system. Theory thus occurs alongside other words like *totalité*, thinking, and concept, while system, as *systematicité*, is dissolved in a complex of differences. The word *theory* is not a stable word, and the history of the word in Althusser's text is much more the history of a sort of vanishing, of its *décomposition*. So, my argument here will be something like the story of the vanishing of theory; the theoretical vanishing of theory.

Theory cannot be understood, in the context of the Althusserian text, from the point of view of the dialectical relationship between theory and practice. This is a significant change from the Marxist tradition. In a common Marxist tradition, the relation between theory and practice is a very important one. Althusser is constantly attempting, in fact, to destroy this opposition between theory and practice. Why is this point so important? Why is it so important for Althusser to explain that the word *theory* cannot be understood from the point of view of its relationship to practice? I think it is because this constitutes the definition of the immanent materialism of Althusser, its general definition. Althusser always wants to replace the guarantee of relation by the real of production: this is the crux of Althusser's intervention. And if, after all, a dialectical relationship is a relation, it is not by itself a production. So we cannot understand clearly what constitutes a theory only by its dialectical relationship to practice. We must observe and determine to what extent that theory must also be a production, and must be by itself a production, and not in an external relationship to its opposite.

Althusser affirms a new form of materialism by the destruction of the dialectical relationship between theory and practice: not a materialism of relations but a materialism of production. And this is a very important point. Consequently, we also have the impossibility of determining theory, not only as the opposite term of practice, but as a result of practices, as something which is the abstract result of concrete practices. In a common vision of the relationship between practices and theory, theory is a sort of abstract synthesis, the origin of which is practice. For Althusser, we encounter what he named "pragmatism." Pragmatism is precisely defined by the idea that the verification of the truth of a theory lies in practice. Althusser affirms that a true understanding of theory must be the discovery of an immanent guarantee of truth, and not its external guarantee verified in the field of practices. Althusser is truly an *immanentist* thinker, at every level of its determination. A truth of a theory—if truth exists, if there is something like truth—lies purely within the theoretical process, inside the process of scientific theory and not in the form of an external guarantee. And this, naturally, introduces the question of theory as production and not as an expression, a theory which is not a result of some complex of social or historical practices. And this leads finally to the question, which will be my final question, as it is in the text of Althusser himself: the question of the productive mechanism, the productive apparatus, the materiality of production itself in the case of theory.

Althusser refuses any dialectical vision of the pair *theory-practice*. Theory cannot be understood by its relationship with practice; not only can theory not be verified by its application in practice, but we must, in fact, destroy the very correlation between theory and practice. This is certainly a very important point of all Althusserian constructions. It constitutes not the refusal of the *dialecticité* of the relationship between theory and practice but the destruction of the dialectical couple itself. What then are the means of this destruction?

This destruction of the dialectical pair theory-practice occurs via the affirmation that theory is a name for some particular practices. So the very opposition of the two terms is destroyed by the affirmation that theory itself must be understood as a practice. "Theory is, in the strict sense of the term, a practice, a scientific or theoretical practice" (RCC 61). It is clear that when you say that theory is a practice, you destroy the *classical* relationship between theory and practice, but when you say that, as a sort of verbal definition of theory, theory is a theoretical practice, this is hardly very interesting or novel. So the point is thus to understand, not the noun "theory," but the adjective "theoretical." And I think that Althusser's text orchestrates a movement, the transition from the noun "theory" to the adjective "theoretical." And this passage is also in some sense materialist. It is materialist because it is founded by a radical assertion, which can be formulated as the statement: "Only practices really exist." So Althusser's idea is that the relationship of theory to practice by dialectical opposition is not really radical from the point of view of materialism. The only radical solution to this problem is to affirm that theory itself is a practice; because in a materialist vision we must assume that what exists is always so in some form of practice. And it is also an anti-dialectical passage—from the noun to the adjective—because if all that exists, exists in the form of practices, the question becomes that of the differential multiplicity of practices; and this differential multiplicity of practices, the difference between all forms of practice is practically summarized by a certain number of adjectives: for example, "theoretical practices," "technical practices," or "scientific practices." So the nominal field of materialism is really the demand to transform certain nouns into adjectives. This is truly a materialist necessity, from the point of view of Althusser himself and from the point of view of the destruction of the dialectical relationship between abstraction and concrete. This is so because if you maintain the dialectical relationship between theory and practice in the form of an opposition, you naturally sustain the opposition between something concrete (the practice) and something abstract (the theory). At the same time, this opposition is not a materialist one: what is materialist is to affirm that only practices exist. But if there exist a multiplicity of different practices, we return to the idea of a complex of different differences, if you will, and theory must also be one form of practice. And so, the provisional name for this is, precisely, "theoretical practices."

This whole materialist vision is opposed to the idea that the Marxist theory of history is or proposes something like a hypothesis. The reason why is clear: if the Marxist theory of history proposes a hypothesis, we are in the field of pragmatism. Hypotheses must be verified by historical practices. If we don't accept that sort of pragmatism, we also refuse to say that the Marxist theory of history occurs in the form of a hypothesis. Hypothesis is, in fact, a pragmatist vision of theory; hypotheses must be verified by the concrete realization of history itself, by the concretization of history. And in some sense, history is also of a dialectical nature because it opens the field of the possibility of negation, the falsity of the hypothesis and, in some sense, the struggle between the possibility of the validity of the hypothesis and the possibility of its negation. All that is perfectly clear and explicit in Althusser's text: Althusser writes that it is impossible to understand the Marxist theory of history as form of hypothesis.

I have written a small book under the title *The Communist Hypothesis*, and it puts forward a radical point of opposition to the Althusserian vision.[2] I just want to say, in my defensive position, that the word *communism*, in the *Communist Hypothesis*, is not taken here as a category of the Marxist theory of history. It is not the signification of the word *communism* that is in question concerning the communist hypothesis. Rather, it is what I name an "idea," the "idea" of communism. An idea is not a concept: so "communist" here is not a scientific concept in the field of the Marxist theory of history. This then reminds me of an intense moment in my personal relationship with Althusser. It was in the brief sequence between 1967 and 1969, with 1968 just in the middle. Before and after, things were not exactly the same in regard to my relationship to Althusser. This was also the moment of existence of the Groupe Spinoza. The Groupe Spinoza was a group composed by Althusser, with some friends of Althusser, all precisely reading *Capital* practically, engaged in the project to write a sort of synthesis of our epistemological convictions. The idea was to produce a fundamental book concerning theory: concerning what theory is, what constitutes an epistemological rupture and so on; to propose something like an educational book concerning all these sorts of themes. All that was destroyed by 1968 and, after that, by very strong political differences and struggles.

But in discussions with Althusser at the time, I proposed—it was a part of my contribution to this inexistent book—to distinguish "concept," "notion," and "category." And there is an echo of that in my work concerning the concept of "model."[3] The idea was to reserve the use of "concept" for scientific discourse. So, the semantic unities of a scientific construction would be named "concept," in order to reserve the use of "notion" for ideological discourse. So we would have scientific concepts and ideological notions. And, finally, I proposed to reserve "category" for philosophical unities. And so my conclusion concerning the "communist hypothesis" is that, in this expression, "communism" cannot be a concept but "communism" can be a category. And, in fact, it remains to be shown that the word *communism* is and must be all at once a concept, a notion, and a category and this is in fact the case: communism is a concept as possible category of history; it is a notion because it has a very strong ideological value, a subjective value; and finally, it is a category in its more general and abstract philosophical meaning.

I agree with Althusser's critique of the idea of the Marxist theory of history as a hypothesis, while I maintain in contrast that we can speak of a communist hypothesis. Allow me then to return to the passage from theory to theoretical practices, or to the "adjectivization" of the question of theory. Naturally, we have many theoretical practices. This adjectivization is also a pluralization, it is also the affirmation of the multiplicity of differences as such, which is substituted for the pair theory-practice. Finally, all that is absorbed in the field of the multiplicity of different practices. Is this affirmation, this adjectivization in the form of the recognition of existence of a multiplicity of theoretical practices, the disappearance of a unified use of the word *theory*? And finally, is theory, as a concept, a possible concept, a name, a word, a category completely dissolved in the pure multiplicity of different practices? I think this is not exactly the case. And my reading of this text that is *Reading Capital* is to observe that this materialist movement, which is in fact the practical pluralization of the word *theory*, this "materialist gesture," is not absolutely the *disparition* (disappearance) or destruction of some form of unity in the word *theory*. There is a trace of the vanishing of the word *theory* in the multiplicity of theoretical practices. This trace is the apparition and the use, in Althusser's text, of many classical terms of an epistemological nature.

A sort of *retour du refoulé* (return of the repressed), the disparition of the unity of the word of the "theory" is paid for by the appearance of many words that lie within the vocabulary of the philosophy of science. And the most important of these appearances is that of "knowledge." "Knowledge" appears as the name of what is produced by theoretical practice: because, naturally, if you have the transformation of the opposition theory/practice into "theoretical practice," you must name the specific production of theoretical practice, and the specific production of theoretical practice is knowledge of some sort. So, finally, the definition of a "theoretical practice" is that it is the production, or rather the field of production, of knowledge: "The production of knowledge is the hallmark of theoretical practice." The characteristic activity of theoretical practice is the production of knowledge. But to completely understand knowledge, we find the more surprising return of "thinking." After the disparition of theory, we have the appearance of knowledge, and with the appearance of knowledge, we have the appearance of thinking, and thinking is the name for the element or the space of the process of the production of knowledge. It is the topological nature of the process of the production of knowledge.

Where do we encounter this process of production, the production of knowledge? The answer is: this production of knowledge occurs in thinking. Thinking is, in some sense, the common characteristic of all theoretical practices, the common element, the common place. I quote: "The production of knowledge . . . [the production of knowledge is, in fact, the materialist definition of theoretical practice; a theoretical practice is, in fact, a production of knowledge] constitutes a process [naturally, a 'process' and not an 'entity'] that takes place entirely in thought" (RCC 42, emphasis in original).

"To take place entirely in thought" is a very dangerous expression: because to be "entirely in thought" is to be outside the Real, outside the material Real.

If a practice is "entirely in thought," this practice is separated from what is not thinking. Althusser is very cautious. Naturally, he is conscious of the difficulty and refuses an idealist interpretation which is a possibility. He writes that "thinking is a real system articulated on the real world of a precise historical society." So, you see, after "theory," we have "theoretical practice"; after "theoretical practice," we have "production of knowledge"; after "production of knowledge," we have the "element of production of knowledge is thinking" . . . and we are very close to the simple return of the opposition between "thinking" and "Real," and finally the return of the opposition between theory and practice . . . And so, it is a necessity to say "no, it is really inside a practice; thinking itself, even the most abstract concept, is a real system articulated in the real world in a precise historical sense." And Althusser is also cautious in his use of different metaphors drawn from material technologies; to describe a production of knowledge within thinking, he uses phrases like "thinking is the *system*, historically defined, of a thinking's *apparatus*" (RCC 41, trans. modified). So we have metaphors of a technological nature as a guarantee that, with that sort of thinking, we are not confronted by the return of the classical opposition between "thinking" and the Real.

In fact, in footnote 8 of the text, Althusser introduces a very strong doubt concerning that sort of procedure, the metaphorical technological description of the construction of knowledge: "*Why* does a certain form of scientific discourse necessarily need the use of metaphors borrowed from non-scientific disciplines?" (RCC 529). So, as a very cautious philosopher, when Althusser finally returns to the relationship between "practices" and "thinking," he adopts metaphors of a technological and materialist nature to prevent thinking from exceeding its materialist determination. And, in some sense, theory, here, is also subject to a metaphoric use. Theory here finds its materialist guarantee in the metaphoric use of words like "production," "mechanism," "apparatus," and so on. We will return to this very interesting point.

There is an evident risk, at this point: thinking can be an idealist price paid to the vanishing of theory in two senses. First, it is the return of the ghost. The disparition of theory into practice, its adjectivization via its redefinition as "*theoretical* practice," "theoretical practice as the production of knowledge" and the passage from production to knowledge—all that is completely inside thinking—remains exposed to the threat of idealism. This is necessarily so because if the production of knowledge occurs completely inside thinking, the question becomes: What is the difference between "thinking" and something else? If you determine the topological site of the process of theoretical practices as thinking, if then there is a closure of thinking—and there is a closure of thinking if you can say that the process of the production of knowledge is *completely* inside thinking—the question becomes: To what is this closure opposed? We thus confront the possible return of the opposition between theory and practice (in fact). That is: the return to what, at the beginning, it was necessary to destroy, in the form of a more radical ontological opposition: thinking and the Real.

Althusser affirms that the ultimate problem of his new materialism can be formulated as a question: "By what mechanism does the process of knowledge, which takes place entirely in thought, produce the cognitive appropriation of the real object, which exists outside thought in the real world?" (RCC 57). This sentence is undoubtedly the most difficult in the whole text and the most problematic. It is a question: the radical and *final* question, in some sense: "By what sort of mechanism [we have here the mechanical metaphor] does the process of knowledge [the process of knowledge is the process of the production knowledge; and the process of the production of knowledge is the definition of theoretical practice], which occurs completely in thinking, *produce* the cognitive appropriation of its *real* object, which exists outside thinking in the real world?" We can grasp here, from a philosophical point of view, how the adjectivisation of theory into the *theoretical* finally produces the return of the classical opposition between thinking and the Real (world). And we can also understand that the materialist guarantee of this idealist return is produced by the words *process, production, system, apparatus,* and *mechanism,* against the idealist function of an external guarantee.

So, at the end of this first movement, we understand that the disparition of the dialectical vision of the relationship between theory and practice, clearly produces a sort of materialist unity, but we also understand that finally to determine, inside this materialist unity, the particularity of theoretical practice by its difference from other forms of practice, we must introduce the very real risk of a return to the ontological opposition between thinking and the Real, or thinking and the external world.

There is another use of the passage from theory to the theoretical, which is of a more philosophical nature than the idealist risk. This is the reflexive point introduced by Althusser, when he wants to define what he named a "correct theory of theories." At this point, Althusser is no longer pursuing a line of thinking that would provide a definition of "theoretical practices" but one that would provide a definition of a "theory of theories." This provides him an alternative way to return to the question of "theory" or, more precisely, the "theory of theoretical practices." Althusser is not concerned with the difference between "theoretical practices" and "practices that are not theoretical," but with another opposition: to define theoretical practices from an immanent point of view, and *not* by differences from practices that are not theoretical. And that is why we must define a theory of theoretical practices; that is, a theory of theory, *n'est-ce pas*: that is why the definition is reflexive.

More precisely, Althusser says, "that which we seek is the history of the theoretical value of theoretical practices." The repetition of the word is very important, increasingly important, in Althusser's text: it signifies its reflexive determination ("The history [the scientific history] of the theoretical value of theoretical practices"). Perhaps the most important text, among all of the texts in *Reading Capital*, is a very compact one: "I propose to call this history [the history of the theoretical value of theoretical practices that is, in the end, the history of theories] the history of the *theoretical* as such, or the history of the production (and transformation) of what at a given moment in the history of knowledge constitutes the *theoretical problematic* to which are related all the existing validating criteria, and hence the *forms* required to give the order of theoretical discourse the *force and value of a proof*" (RCC 50). So the idea is clear in this very complex expression. The idea is to discover, by scientific means, the possibility of a history not of particular theoretical practices, such as the history of mathematics, the history of history, the history of physics, and so on; but a history of the theoretical value of all theoretical practices. What then gives to theoretical practice its value in the sense of theoretical value? Why is theoretical practice in fact something like the production of a knowledge that has validity? If we adopt a philosophical vocabulary for a moment, it is the question of finding the scientific history of the mechanism by which theoretical practices contribute to knowledge, a knowledge that is really an appropriation of the real object. So this constitutes something like the possibility of a scientific or theoretical history of truths, truths being the internal, immanent value of theoretical practices.

This much seems clear. The point is the singular signification of the "theoretical" itself. The passage from theory to the theoretical was a materialist passage, designed to reduce theory to practices. But after that, we have here the use of "theoretical" as a differential indicator, occurring at different levels. In total, we find four different uses of the adjective "theoretical" in this text, which is probably Althusser's most important epistemological project as he seeks to develop a scientific history of the theoretical as such. This is a new, materialist epistemology that sought to create the knowledge, the reason, the mechanism by which theoretical practice is useful to the real. In this project, theory and practice as well disappear; there is no theory, there is no practice in the text. We find only different variations on the "theoretical."

First, we have "theoretical problematics." "Problematics" has been introduced before in the text of Althusser as, I quote, "a definite theoretical structure," that is, the forms which determine the orientation of a problem (26). So, it is a very important part of theoretical practice to always have a problematic, that is, a specific form of the problems that are posed in the theoretical practice itself. These Althusser defines as: "The forms which determine the position of a problem [naturally, at a precise moment the history of the theoretical practice in question]." And so, we know what a "problematic" is, a sort of philosophical metaphor, a sort of transcendental of theoretical practice, because a problematic is the rule by which there exist problems within a theoretical practice. "Problematics" is the general conception of what is a problem for any theoretical practice, precisely defined. And so, the theoretical structure, which is a theoretical structure of the problem within a theoretical practice, defines a problematic. But in this manner we are faced with the return of the adjective "theoretical," given that here we encounter "theoretical problematics."

And so a problematic is defined by the theoretical, but the theoretical is simultaneously a definition of problematics. And so we have a circular use of "problematics." This as well is the price paid for the disappearance of theory; that is, the theoretical must be the definition of theoretical practice, but also, within theoretical practice, the definition of the problematic of this specific theoretical practice occurs in the form of "theoretical problematics."

This constitutes a general lesson: when we substitute an adjective for a noun, we are forced to constantly use the adjective, which is not the case for the noun. So, to summarize: of all the nouns which stand in relationship to theoretical practice, and which are of a theoretical nature, we find "problematics," "theoretical problematics"—as well as, in the same passage, "theoretical validity" and "theoretical discourse." So the point is that the theoretical is the general characteristic of all that happens in theoretical practice. So the adjective, in this case, circulates inside the definition, at all the levels of the definite object. And this is why we have the various uses of the "theoretical": theoretical problematics, theoretical validity, theoretical discourse.

After theory, science, knowledge, and thinking, then, we note that the theoretical becomes a sort of circulating nomination. But the most remarkable aspect of the text is the presentation of the history of the theoretical as such. This is the point of departure for Althusser, and it is explicit in the text: there is no theory as such that can be opposed to practice as such. We cannot accept the abstract contradiction between theory and practice. In this sense, there is no opposition between an abstract theory as such and an abstract practice as such. But we have here the "theoretical as such"; "the theoretical as such" not as opposed to something else—for example, "the practical as such"—but omnipresent in all the levels of theoretical practice. And perhaps this can be stated as a law: when you destroy the dialectical relationship, you produce the liberation of a word that is, finally, everywhere. And this is the case of the "theoretical." "Theoretical" in Althusser's text is finally a word that has been liberated by the destruction of the dialectical couple. The term then comes to circulate, however, such that we have: "theoretical validity," "theoretical discourse," "theoretical problematics," as well as the theoretical as such.

We can perform the same exercise in reference to another passage that I will discuss quickly. This is a passage that concerns an object much more common than the history of the theoretical as such, that is, what Althusser names the "concept of the history of knowledge." We are now much closer to epistemological considerations of a classic nature. Here is Althusser: "To go beyond the merely *formal concept of the structure of theoretical practice*, i.e., of the production of knowledges, we must work out the *concept* of the history of knowledge, the concepts of the different modes of theoretical production (most important the concepts of the modes of production of ideology and science), and the peculiar concepts of the different *branches* of theoretical production and of their relations" (RCC 44). Once again, we encounter the invasion of the "theoretical." I will quickly summarize this process in the passage:

1. "theoretical practice," that is, theory, in fact
2. After that, we have "theoretical production"
3. And finally, "theoretical relationships"

So, here again, we find that Althusser's project to substitute a unified materialist vision of knowledge is paid for by a sort of adjectivization without limit.

At the beginning of Althusser's text, the word theory seems essential. It is in fact the name of the Maspero collection in which the book appears: the "Theory Collection." And so, theory is a sort of emblem, a sort of fetish of the radical movement that Althusser proposes, a proposal to completely transform the dominant conception of Marxism and, finally, the dominant conception of revolutionary politics itself. But immediately after, theory is subtracted from its classical opposition to practice. And this is a materialist gesture made against the dialectical. Next, theory is replaced by "the theoretical" in a process of adjectivization. And this is done under the law of difference: because this act of adjectivization opposes the dialectical pair of theory/practice, to create the possibility of defining theory as "theoretical practice." This adjectivization provokes the apparition of a new conceptual context, but also, finally, the opposition between thinking and the real world, which is elaborated as an opposition between a knowledge-object and a real-object. The possibility Althusser pursues, in this point, is to say something like the following: within a Spinozist vision—and Althusser, in some sense, proposes this sort of vision—we have the real, but the general real must be understood as the Spinozist Substance, that is, the totality of what exists. But our relationship to this totality always occurs via some attribute of the totality. And there exist two attributes within the totality: thinking and what is not thinking. In Spinoza, the two attributes are thought and extension, thinking and space; but we can modify all that and say: the substantial totality is the totality of practices, and there exist two different attributes of this totality, which express the same totality either in the form of thinking, of real thinking, or else in the form of objectivity, of the object. So, we have the difference between the knowledge-object, completely inside thinking, and the real-object, completely inside the Real in the external sense of the term. And this is not the reproduction of a metaphysical dualism, but simply two attributes of the same generality, which states that all that exists, exists in the form of practices . . . At least this is a possibility.

In the end, the question of the interpretation of the whole text would be: we have the theoretical as an attributive or predicative determination of the Real; and we have external objectivity, which is what is not completely within thinking, as a realization of the real, which is, in some sense, the same real. But the difficulty here is that, for Althusser, there is no relationship, point by point, between the two.

For Spinoza, the solution is an expressive one: the two attributes, thinking and extension, are the expression of same order: *Ordo et connectio idearum idem est ac ordo et connectio rerum*. Ideas, thinking, and things fall under the same law, under the same order. So, there is no problem of their difference, because there is no difference, in some sense; they belong to the same order, but the same order is expressed, is symbolized in two different forms. So there is no real problem of the relationship between the idea and the thing: the idea and the thing are in the same general order. Althusser, however, explicitly refuses that sort of solution.

What we find in the Althusserian attempt to find a new materialism is first of all a rigorous objectivism concerning practices. Practices are the only form of the Real. We have, after that, the transversality, the disposition, if you wish, via two attributes, in the Spinozist sense, *thinking and the real* . . . but thinking as thinking and real as real. Or thinking as immanent real, real as external real, but, for Althusser, there is no isomorphism, no parallelism, no relationship point by point between the two. It is false to say that they express the same order. I quote him on this point, as it is explicit: "The production process of the object of knowledge takes place entirely in knowledge [and so completely within thinking] and is carried out according to a *different order* . . . which is different from the real order of *real* genesis [. . . that organizes] the process of production of a given real object" (RCC 41). Here we have a categorical refusal of the Spinozist solution in which the two attributes are attributes of the same order. The orders are different. So there is a mystery, a final mystery, which is the final appropriation of the real object by the knowledge object that is a characteristic of scientific practice. Scientific practice is the practice in which there is in fact an appropriation of the real object by the knowledge object. We can name that "truth," we can name it as we wish, but the fact is that we have a real appropriation and this is precisely the difference between a scientific practice and an ideological practice, where we have instead images, false images of the real and not an appropriation of the real. That is the question, the mystery of the mechanism which is the world of Althusser, the mechanism by which is realized the function of cognitive appropriation of the real object by the means of its sought-after object or its knowledge object. What we can say is that this mystery is in fact the mystery of a relationship in which the formal existence of the knowledge object lies completely within thinking and the external existence of the real object stands as the real object of the knowledge object. I insist that, for Spinoza, this problem does not exist . . . because there is in fact no relationship between the two, because they are of the same substance. But, for Althusser, the order is not the same, so there is in fact a real difficulty. And this difficulty, I am convinced, is in fact a Kantian difficulty. It is a difficulty, the solution of which is for Kant "schematism." Schematism, in Kant, is precisely the mechanism by which the formal organization of the categories of knowledge are related to the external existence, which we cannot know, of the world.

In Althusser, "theory," theoretical nature, and so on, must be understood as a mixture of the immanent Spinozist vision of two attributes of the same real with this Kantian schematism. There is only one real: it is not an ontological dualism, but instead we find two attributes of the same substance but without parallelism, without identity of the order. This existence of two attributes, thinking object and real object, must be completed by a sort of materialist mechanism, a materialist schematism, in the sense of Kant. A mechanism, after all, which is absolutely enigmatic, and which is formulated by Althusser, as a question. Furthermore, we know that schematism is described by Kant himself as something enigmatic, something obscure. And so, we find in Althusser a mixture of something that stands in relation to the transcendental of Kant, alongside something clearly on the side of the materialism of Spinoza.

In 1967 I wrote an essay on Althusser, *Reading Capital*, and Karl Marx. At the end of this essay, I said that the difficulty with *Reading Capital* was that, in some sense, Althusser proposes a philosophical disposition, which can be summarized as an aspect of Kant in Spinoza.[4] And now, I discover that I have been saying the same thing, forty-six years later. Thus my melancholic conclusion: in the end, a philosopher always says the same thing. The world changes but not the philosopher. It is why, perhaps, we are eternal.

Notes

1. Louis Althusser, Étienne Balibar, Roger Establet, Pierre Macherey, and Jacques Rancière, *Reading Capital: The Complete Edition*, trans. Ben Brewster and David Fernbach (London: Verso, 2016). Further page references will be cited parenthetically in the text.

2. Alain Badiou, *The Communist Hypothesis* (New York: Verso, 2010).

3. Alain Badiou, *Le concept de modèle: Introduction à une épistémologie materialiste des mathématiques* (Paris: Maspero, 1970).

4. Alain Badiou, "The (Re)commencement of Dialectical Materialism," in *The Adventure of French Philosophy*, trans. Bruno Bosteels (New York: Verso, 2012).

CHAPTER 2

Rereading the Symptomatic Reading

ROBERT J. C. YOUNG

If we read its opening page in the original French, our first understanding of the meaning of the title *Lire le Capital* is that it takes the form of an injunction. Althusser is telling us that instead of understanding Marx through the prism of secondary accounts of his work, we should return to the original text and read Marx in his own words, unmediated by the many political and academic commentaries, paraphrases, and interpretations of his work that have proliferated since *Capital* was first published in 1867—a move that corresponds in a recognizable way to the general "return to" of the 1960s, the rereading of original texts initiated by Jacques Lacan a decade earlier with respect to Freud.[1] The problem is that in some sense we already "read" *Capital* all around us, says Althusser, that is, to the degree that the book is visible in the disputes, conflicts, defeats, and victories of everyday history. So too, we read *Capital* in the writings of the dead and the living, in Engels, Lenin, Trotsky, Gramsci, and so on, in the many fragments from *Capital* that are quoted and selected for us, as well as in the many popular paraphrases and introductions to Marx that have always proliferated and which continue to "introduce" or explain *Capital* to us right up to today: the book is at once overread and yet remains unread. "But some day," Althusser famously adds at this point, "it is essential to read *Capital* to the letter. To read the text complete, all four volumes, line by line."[2]

What might it mean, though, to read *Capital* "to the letter"? Or to read "the text complete"? A literal reading, painfully scrupulous, word by word; a slow, plodding, complete, exact reading that omits nothing. A vast undertaking. Althusser has already given us this message in the epigraph to the book, the prominently displayed letter from Marx to Maurice Lachâtre, his French publisher, of March 18, 1872, where Marx endorses the idea of making *Capital* more accessible to the workers by publishing it in serial form, warning that the reading of the first chapters is "rather arduous," but strictly necessary, because "there is no royal road to science . . . only those who do not dread the fatiguing climb of its steep paths have a chance of gaining its luminous summits" (RCC 9).[3] Reading *Capital* must be like an exhausting climb up a mountain, and only that laborious, almost Sisyphean method will deliver the sublimity of its enlightenment. We must read it to the letter, read the precise words that were written by Marx and which he left for us.

What though, in Althusser's case, can it mean to insist on reading *Capital* to the letter when he is reading a translation? The continued use of Roy's translation as the standard popular text of *Capital* for French readers (despite the publication in 1983 of Jean-Pierre Lefebvre's translation of the fourth German edition)[4] means that in general the French used to read, and in fact generally still read, what is quite literally a different book from the one that everyone else reads—which raises the interesting question, does it make a difference? In Althusser's case, does he only read Marx, as it were, to the French letter? How can we read a translation to the letter given the absence, precisely, of the letters, the signifiers, of the original? Not entirely, Althusser himself admits: "And it is essential to read *Capital* not only in its French translation (even Volume One in Roy's translation, which Marx revised, or rather, rewrote), but also in the German original, at least for the fundamental theoretical chapters and all the passages where Marx's key concepts come to the surface [*affleurent*]" (RCC 11).

We must not only read *Capital* to the letter in translation in French therefore but also "the German original"—though only selectively, that is, just the "fundamental theoretical chapters and all the passages where Marx's key concepts come to the surface." We must read across to the German original only where the key concepts become visible like rocks, outcrops on the surface of the soil, emerging from the depths of the text, a metaphor that seems to contradict the initial emphasis on surface. But then what exactly is this "original" when, as Althusser himself remarks, Marx himself not only supervised the French translation but also "revised, or rather rewrote" the original in doing so—effectively layering even the surface of the text?

The French translation of *Capital* by Joseph Roy, which appeared in serial form from 1872–75, was based on a copy of the first 1867 edition, corrected in manuscript by Marx up to page 280, and was the last printed version that Marx himself supervised.[5] The second German edition, of 1873, contained fewer revisions than the French; the third German edition, edited by Engels, which appeared in 1883 was based on the 1873 edition, with some changes from the French text. Finally the fourth, supposedly definitive edition, of 1890 was issued by Engels and more fully, but not totally, incorporated some of the changes of the French edition. This complex textual history only covers volume 1. Since the publication of the full German MEGA edition of Marx's works from 1972 onward, the textual complexity of *Capital* has become far more serious.[6] The "Capital and Preparatory Manuscripts" section in the MEGA edition amount to twenty-three separate volumes. From this scrupulous editorial work, it has become clear that, as Michael Heinrich puts it, Engels "combined manuscripts, which were taken out of different drafts, written at different times; furthermore Engels altered considerably the original manuscripts of Marx."[7] The editors of the MEGA edition destroyed any remaining idea of *Capital* as a complete, single work, while arguing decisively that the so-called book 4 was in fact always an entirely separate book. It showed that in terms of planning, there were two distinct projects that make up the manuscripts now associated with *Capital*, and that these two projects exist in at least two and three drafts respectively.[8]

Capital exists in an almost undecipherable palimpsest of different books and drafts of different versions in two languages, all of which are in different ways "the original(s)."[9] This means that reading *Capital* to the letter becomes a very different operation than it would be for a straightforward single text. We can read the originals, but if we are to speak of them then the long-standing impulse toward commentary on *Capital* can hardly be avoided, commentary that, as Foucault puts it, paradoxically in order to say what the author said, must say what the author never actually said—in order to say what is there, you must see what is not there.[10]

Althusser of course knew something of this textual complexity—aside from the different published editions, the *Grundrisse*, as well as the manuscript on surplus value (the so-called *Capital* book 4), were already published by 1965—even if he necessarily remained unaware of the vast depths of the forest of manuscripts that have more recently been made available. But even if the text of *Capital* can now be seen to be a good deal more complex than Althusser ever envisaged, he was nevertheless already responding to something of the labyrinthine multilingual condition of *Capital* in suggesting that it must be read in two languages ("also in the German original, at least for the fundamental theoretical chapters"). Even before the baggy monster of the various published versions and thousands of pages of manuscript were published, it was already obvious that there was no single version of the book, let alone an authoritative one in which it could be claimed that there Marx achieved a clean-cut epistemological break between the humanist and scientific. Rather, it was precisely because of the unfinished nature of *Capital* that Althusser sought to identify the break through his particular reading of the text. That textual complexity provides the basis, in fact, for the major claim that Althusser proceeds to make, namely that if we read *Capital* literally, to the letter, we discover that it contains its own, "new theory of reading. When we read Marx, we immediately find a reader who reads to us, and out loud" (RCC 16).

In order to try to reconstruct the complexity of Althusser's theoretical intervention here, I shall here follow his own method, namely not attempt an overview of the subsequent reception of, and commentaries on, the work (beginning with his own collaborators, Balibar, Macherey, and Rancière), nor even of his contributions to this particular book, nor even (on this occasion) consider the specific historical conjuncture in which this intervention was made, but return to the letter of the original in order to reread his own contributions so as to reconstruct and establish the force of his theoretical, translational intervention. In short, I shall be reading Althusser's contribution to *Reading Capital* to the letter.

We generally use the phrase, to the letter, less for reading than for following instructions—"but I followed your instructions to the letter!"—or for fastidiously obeying rules—"his orders were carried out to the letter." And this in fact is how Althusser does read Marx, for it turns out that for Althusser to read Marx "to the letter" is to follow a rule, in this case a rule of reading. In its own day, *Lire le capital* became famous as much for its account of a new methodology of reading as for its reinterpretation of Marx's *Capital*. For many in the humanities and social sciences, reading was (and is) an innocent activity, simply something that you learn how to do, like riding a bike, after which you do not have to think about. Althusser's idea was startling: not just that we should read the text of *Capital* itself, rather than its summaries, paraphrases, and commentaries, but that we should also recognize that it provides a method of reading—a method through which Marx dictates his philosophy to Althusser from beyond the grave.

Reading Marx to the letter produces the discovery of a second kind of reading practiced by Marx himself, a method which Althusser will call *symptomale*, "symptomatic." Althusser discovers this in Marx's own reading of the classical economists, in a passage from *Capital* which he cites at length, from the Roy translation (presented here, in turn, in Brewster's English translation):

In this way, classical political economy believed it had ascended from the accidental prices of labour to the real value of labour. It then determined this value by the value of the subsistence good necessary for the maintenance and reproduction of the labourer. It thus unwittingly changed terrain [*A son insu, elle changeait ainsi de terrain* (italics in original)] by substituting for the value of labour, up to this point, the apparent object of its investigations, the value of labour power, a power which only exists in the personality of the labourer, and is as different from the function, labour, as a machine is from its performance ... The result the analysis led to, therefore, was *not a resolution of the problem as it emerged at the beginning, but a complete change in the terms of that problem.*

Classical economy never arrived at an awareness of this substitution [*L'économie classique ne parvint jamais à s'apercevoir de ce quidproquo* (italics in original)].[11]

There is an interesting difference here between the French translation which Althusser cites, and the later German "original" of the fourth edition. As we shall see, without mentioning it explicitly, Althusser seems to draw on both versions. Here *a son insu* means "unknown to them, without their knowledge" here nicely translated in English as "unwittingly," while the French "quid pro quo"—here translated as "substitution"—has a meaning slightly different from its English usage, where it carries the idea of giving something in return, as compensation—scratch my back and I'll scratch yours. The French usage is closer to the original Latin meaning, referring to a misunderstanding or a mistake, taking one thing for another. But in Althusser's French there is not just "awareness" of this but direct perception: *s'apercevoir:* "to perceive something," "to become aware or conscious of something." From this Althusser therefore defines Marx's insight as that of the classical political economists *not seeing* something, not being aware of it; and what they don't see, paradoxically, is what they see:

I take this astonishing text for what it is: a protocol of Marx's *reading* of classical economics ... What classical political economy does not see, is not what it does not see, it is *what it sees;* it is not what it lacks, on the contrary, it is *what it does not lack*; it is not what it misses, on the contrary, it is *what it does not miss.* [Ce que l'économie politique classique ne voit pas, ce n'est pas ce qu'elle ne voit pas, c'este *qu'elle voit:* ce n'est pas ce qui lui manque, c'est au contraire *ce qui ne lui manque pas:* ce n'est pas ce qu'elle rate, c'est au contraire *ce qu'elle ne rate pas.*] (RCC 19)

Rereading the text, Althusser argues that classical political economy has "produced" a correct answer. But what catches Marx's eye is a remarkable property of this answer, namely that "*it is the correct answer to a question that has just one failing: it was never posed*" (20). It is rather Marx who produces the original question from the answer, which effects "a complete change in the terms of the problem." What Althusser will first call the symptomatic reading, therefore, involves identifying "the paradox of *an answer which does not correspond to any question posed.*"[12]

What political economy does not see is what it *does*: its production of a new answer without its question, and simultaneously the production of a new latent question resting invisible in the gap between the unasked question and the new answer. Through the lacunary terms of its answer political economy has produced a new question, but "*unwittingly.*" It made "'*a complete change in the terms of the*' original '*problem,*'" and thereby produced a new problem, without knowing it. It remained convinced that it was still on the terrain of the old problem, whereas "*it had unwittingly changed terrain.*" Its blindness and its "oversight" [*bévue*, blunder, mistake, slip] lie in this misunderstanding [*quidproquo*], between what it produces and what it sees, in this "'*substitution,*' which Marx elsewhere calls a '*play on words*' (*Wortspiel*) that is necessarily impenetrable for its author." (23)

The symptomatic reading that Althusser finds in Marx, that seeks the unstated question for the offered answer, therefore involves not interpretation but the production of new knowledge from a reading that identifies an invisible gap in the text. This is the version of the symptomatic reading that Étienne Balibar pursues in his own essay in *Reading Capital*. "In reality," says Balibar, "this Preface to *A Contribution,* if it is read attentively, does not present us with the form of a hypothesis, but explicitly that of an answer, an answer to a question we must try to reconstitute" (RCC 360). To read to the letter is to find that the letter appears to be missing, not in place.

Startling though this idea is, the symptomatic reading also draws on other, more Freudian resonances that shift it from Althusser's initial question/answer formulation. The insight of Marx's "astonishing" reading that Althusser emphasizes is to spot the blindness of the slip, which Marx at other times calls a play on words or pun (*Wortspiel*), but here a "quid pro quo" which, literally in fact describes a slip of the pen, for quid pro quo originally designated a scribal mistake of substituting the nominative *qui* for an ablative, *quo* (qui pro quo). At one level, Althusser here seems to be moving Marx's reading toward an anticipation of a deconstructive reading—of blindness and insight—while at another, the obvious resonance is that of Freud's wordplays, puns, slips of the tongue. The Freudian echo, despite the removal of one paragraph in the second edition, noted by Warren Montag,[13] remains strong with the topographic imagery of surfaces and depths, of puns and wordplay, of doing things "unwittingly." Althusser did not make this connection unknowingly either: as he would have noticed, the Freudian resonance is even stronger in the original, later, German, where in the fourth edition Marx explicitly uses the word *bewußtlos*—unconscious—and *die Bewußtlosigkeit*—unconsciousness. In Ben Fowkes's 1976 English translation:

> The political economists unconsciously [*bewußtlos*] substituted this question for the original one, for the search after the cost of production of labour as such turned in a circle, and did not allow them to get any further at all . . .
>
> Classical political economy's unconsciousness [*Die Bewußtlosigkeit*] of this result of its own analysis and its uncritical acceptance of the categories "value of labour" [etc.] led it into inextricable confusions and contradictions, as will be seen later [note "a reference forward to the projected Volume 4, known now as *Theories of Surplus-Value*"].[14]

In making this connection with Freud at the invitation of Marx's own text, Althusser himself at times moves toward what one might call a more recognizably Lacanian account of the symptomatic reading, where the reader looks for gaps, fissures, unconscious moments of the unsaid in the text: "At the same time, I suggested that we had to submit Marx's text not to an immediate reading, but to a '*symptomatic*' *reading*, in order to discern in the apparent continuity of the discourse the lacunae, blanks and failures of rigour, the places where Marx's discourse is merely the unsaid of his silence" (RCC 294).

Arguably this formulation, of the kind subsequently developed by Pierre Macherey, is rather less radical than Althusser's original observation that "it is not what it lacks, it is what it does not lack." The letter is not missing, it is rather in place but cannot be seen. It is not that it is not there (lacking) but that it is not not there. This symptomatic reading, which Althusser points to as a sign or symptom of the degree to which the epistemological break was never clean, has led to descriptions of the kind we find in Jacques Rancière, where Althusser's project is equated with Freud's and Lacan's as "a search for those unsuccessful (i.e. inadequate) modes of expression that exemplify such symptomatic procedures of misrecognition."[15] There is clearly a Lacanian component at work here, for what is distinctive about Lacan, says Althusser, is that he takes Freud's "words literally."[16] For Lacan the unconscious, like the purloined letter, is always there, visible, but not seen, like the large letters of names for mountain ranges that spread in a different scale from everything else across the map. So Althusser emphasizes that the classical political economists rather see something without knowing it: "What classical political economy does not see, is not what it does not see, it is *what it sees*." That is why the letter, as Lacan puts it, "insists."

However, this paradoxical statement—"what classical political economy does not see . . . *is what it sees*"—suggests something more complex. At its most radical, Althusser's model conforms neither to the Freudian/Lacanian model of identifying what is repressed or visibly invisible to provide an interpretation of such a symptom that explains its meaning, nor to the Derridean model in which a text's mistakes (*bévues*) enable its deconstruction into mutually incompatible contradictory arguments or narratives, a maneuver that is satisfying to perform but ends typically at a state of impasse. Althusser's model is more challenging, since for him reading involves the production of new knowledge from the text, something that is there but not there, defined, visible, but excluded. The heart of the symptomatic reading is the idea that reading is always a double reading, what, following Rancière, we might call a poetics, a making, or a remaking. When reading moves from single to double, and becomes "symptomatic," it moves from innocence (they do not see what they see) to experience and guilt. It is, we might say, *traduisible* in the sense of *traduisible en justice*, liable to prosecution, to be sued. Just as the symptom implies a fall (Latin *symptōma*, from Greek σύμπτωμα: chance, accident, mischance, disease; συμπίπτειν: to fall together, fall upon), so in order to move from the readings of economists, historians, or logicians, which Althusser characterizes as "innocent," the philosophical reading must become "guilty." "Hence a philosophical reading of *Capital* is quite the opposite of an innocent reading. It is a guilty reading, but not one that absolves its crime on confessing it. On the contrary, it takes the responsibility for its crime as a 'justified' crime and defends it by proving its necessity. It is therefore a special reading which exculpates itself as a reading by posing every guilty reading the very question that unmasks its innocence, the mere question of its innocence: *what is it to read?*" (RCC 13).

The philosophical reading that distinguishes *Capital*'s place in the "history of knowledge" is guilty (*coupable*), guilty perhaps insofar as its epistemological question repeats *Capital*'s own "crime" of undoing the ideology of capitalism and detecting the real object through which it is constituted. But why crime, exactly, or guilt? Because it is not innocent, and produces knowledge.

The new knowledge of "our age," Althusser claims, will be marked by the "most difficult trial of all," that is, "the discovery of and training in the meaning of the 'simplest' acts of existence—seeing, listening, speaking, reading" (RCC 13). Althusser ascribes this constitutive knowledge to the interventions of "Marx, Nietzsche and Freud"; tantalizingly but characteristically, he says nothing about Nietzsche, and goes straight to Freud: "Only since Freud have we begun to suspect what listening, and hence what speaking (and keeping silent) means (veut dire); that this meaning (vouloir dire) of speaking and listening reveals beneath the innocence of speech and hearing the culpable depth of a second, quite different discourse, the discourse of the unconscious" (RCC 14).

Althusser reads Freud too in terms of innocence and guilt: the Freudian reading is the guilty reading because it exposes what should have remained hidden—in Marx, for example, to whom Althusser immediately returns after this single sentence. It is at this point that we see that the philosophical reading is indeed still being modeled to some degree on a Freudian depth/surface model, of the innocent surface and the "culpable depth," and recall Althusser's claim that for his philosophical reading it is necessary to read "the German original, at least for the fundamental theoretical chapters and all the passages where Marx's key concepts come to the surface" (11).

In distancing himself from an innocent, or as he also puts it a "transparent" reading, Althusser moves not just back to Freud but more predictably to Spinoza, the man who "linked together the essence of reading and the essence of history in a theory of the difference between the imaginary and the true" (RCC 14), a distinction which is identified both with those of the innocent and the guilty, and the "historical distinction between ideology and science" (15). Spinoza, Althusser argues, undid the religious myth of reading, of the prefallen world in which the world is read as the language of God. As Walter Benjamin puts it in his essay "On Language as Such and on the Language of Man" (1916): "The whole of nature, too, is imbued with a nameless, unspoken language, the residue of the creative word of God."[17] Marx's Capital by contrast, Althusser argues, recognizes "an internal dislocation" (décalage) in the real, inscribed in its structure, which allows him to break with reading God's word in nature. Marx interrupts the innocent "religious myth of reading" (15), in which each part expresses the whole, to pursue the Promethean quest of understanding that "the truth of history cannot be read in its manifest discourse . . . but [in] the inaudible and illegible notation of the effects of a structure of structures."

The truth of history is not there on the surface ("manifest discourse") but remains hidden by its inaudibility and illegibility. Until Marx it could not be heard or read.

Marx's new method of reading therefore is not just another form of reading, an alternative hermeneutic, it is a new kind of reading that breaks with the history of reading for the Logos in order to read the text of history in all its precariousness and rupture, to read history in terms of its disjunctive delays, to read a text by recognizing its "internal dislocation," *décalage*. For Althusser, following the method of Marx himself which allows us to recognize the "fantastically *innovative character*" of texts that are theoretically in advance of the concepts that were then available (73), reading must become double, a form of dislocation, hence duplicitous, enforcing delay, inserting temporality, historicity into the transparent immediacy of conventional reading—recall his opening remark "we have been able to read [*Capital*] every day, transparently" (11)—articulating the synchronic with diachrony, the visibility of space with the process of time. This kind of reading as rereading, repetition, produces a mutation, a translation and transformation of the text. At this point, consequently, we encounter a spectacular reversal, the literal reading is rejected: "A merely literal reading of Marx's text, even an attentive one, will leave us unsatisfied or even make us *miss the question altogether*" (RCC 219). Reading must become differential, doubled up, and take the form of *décalage,* unwedging, staggering, shifting, of displacement, slippage, difference of phase, become out of step, enforce a time-lag, all of which must necessarily prompt a form of "double reading" (220).

Although Althusser does not acknowledge this, his method of reading is rather different from another that he highlights as an illustration of his own: the account by Engels of Marx's theoretical innovation with respect to the concept of surplus value. Engels describes this as transformative of the whole basis of knowledge in the subject in the same way as the scientific discoveries of Galileo or Lavoisier, a theoretical revolution that achieves "a mutation of the problematic," a changing of the theoretical base, by "posing as a problem what had been seen as a solution" (RCC 305), a *"labour of theoretical transformation which necessarily affects the object of knowledge"* (308). For his part, Althusser asserts himself in a footnote by comparing Marx to Freud instead, an analogy much more problematic than Engel's comparison of Marx to Galileo. But while Engels recognizes the importance of the production of a new concept that transforms the object of knowledge, what Althusser does not emphasize here is that Marx himself did not fully achieve this in *Capital* in the form(s) in which he left it, and that it was precisely through the continuous production of new editions, involving editing and rewriting, that Engels himself sought to produce the definitive new concepts from Marx's text. What Althusser recognizes is that in doing so, Engels was applying the same reading method to *Capital* as Marx himself had applied to the classical political economists: the double reading that generated a rewriting through which the original text was mutated or transformed to bring out the underlying transformative new concept anachronistically concealed within it. The new concepts could only be produced through a continuous process of the rewriting and translation of the original text.

The most powerful example of this method is not, however, discussed explicitly in *Lire le Capital*, but itself appears symptomatically for future readers of the text, flagged shamelessly at the beginning of the volume. *Le cadavre dans le placard* is entirely visible: just as Lachâtre himself put Marx's letter to him at the front of the first French edition, so, as I have already mentioned, Althusser places as epigraph to the book Marx's same letter to Lachâtre. This letter about the Roy/Marx translation, that as we have seen Althusser himself uses as the explicit metaphorical structure of his book—the laborious journey in the search for truth—also provides the visible, invisible model of reading for *Reading Capital*—it's there, but you don't see it. As we saw earlier, Althusser mentions parenthetically that we must read Marx in "Roy's translation, which Marx revised, or rather, rewrote." This revision/rewriting by Marx himself of the original German first edition constitutes the basis of the special authority of the French text. Paradoxically, however, the reason that Marx felt impelled to revise and rewrite the translation was because the translator Roy had made the mistake of reading *Capital* to the letter, the very procedure that Althusser himself advocates at the beginning of *Reading Capital*. In 1872 Marx wrote to Nicolai Danielson, who had just published the first translation of *Capital*, into Russian: "Even though the French edition . . . may be the work of someone quite knowledgeable in the two languages, he (the translator) often translated too literally. I was therefore compelled to edit anew, in French, whole passages which I wanted to make readable. Later it will be all the easier to translate the whole from French into English and the romance languages."[18]

We now know, thanks to the researches of Jean-Pierre Lefebvre, that the story was in certain ways more complicated, but Marx's own summary here is that he rewrote the French because the problem of the French translation was that the translator read *Capital* too much to the letter, as a result of which he felt impelled to rewrite it. Marx's response to his translator's "too literal" reading was to take things out, and to refashion the book in a less philosophical manner for French readers who are "always impatient to come to a conclusion," as Marx puts it. The popularization of *Capital* for French readers, as Ben Fowkes the translator of the English Penguin edition suggests, involved making it more accessible and smoothing over or omitting more complex philosophical passages which Roy had complained French was ill-suited to reproduce—which makes Althusser's use of the French edition in order to "read *Capital* as philosophers" (RCC 12) somewhat paradoxical. On the other hand, if Marx took things out, he also put new things in: it was precisely rereading and then rewriting *Capital* in translation that enabled Marx to produce some of the most productive concepts of the book from his own original text—in particular, the sections on accumulation and the fetishism of commodities that have become absolutely pivotal for generations of Marxist theorists: both these were the products of Marx's reading and rewriting of the French translation of his own German original.

So, despite his famous opening announcement about reading to the letter, the result of that is that Althusser comes to reject "a merely literal reading of Marx's text" in favor of a double reading in which the literal reading is only the first stage (RCC 219). Hidden behind this idea of double reading is a concept of translation: Marx's insight begins with his translation of the political economists answering an unasked question, in translation's literal meaning in English of translation as "carrying across": they "thus unwittingly changed terrain." The reading that Althusser then performs, however, is more akin to the French form of translation, *traduire*, from *traducere*, to lead across, induct, draw out, where the reader reads the text across time to draw out and produce a new, but already implicit, reading—the afterlife of its translatability as it were. Although Althusser's own concept of language is faithfully Stalinist—"Science can no more be ranged within the category 'superstructure' than can language, which as Stalin showed escapes it" (RCC 283)—his concept of translation is less literal than Marx's. Althusser himself uses the term translation to designate a conceptual elaboration and rewriting similar to that which Marx felt obliged to perform: "Every terminology is linked to a definite circle of ideas, and we can translate this [*ce que nous pouvons traduire*] by saying: every terminology is a function of the theoretical system that provides its bases, every terminology brings with it a determinate and limited theoretical system" (RCC 299).

The symptomatic reading therefore involves a double process of reading the text to the letter, performing a literal translation, and then, as a result of that reading of the visible, and hinged on the *décalage* of the time lag between readings, articulating the invisible through a rewriting. Just as Marx rewrote the classical economists, and then rewrote his own text, and then Engels rewrote Marx, so Althusser too reads Marx in order to rewrite him, to produce the visible invisible concepts in Marx in his text, anachronistic concepts that were ahead of the theoretical vocabulary of their time. The symptomatic reading, therefore, is not at all a Freudian reading in which symptoms are traced back to their explanatory cause, but a translation of the text forward into the terms of the new concepts toward which it was working.

Althusser in *Reading Capital* seeks to retrieve another method of reading that is Marx's own. Just as he would deliberately leave *Lire le capital* unfinished, as Marx left *Capital* unfinished, just as he would revise *Lire le capital* and publish different editions, with added material and some omitted, as Marx did with *Capital*, so too he will read Marx carefully enough, to the letter, in order to detect and repeat his method of reading and rewrite his text in order to produce, draw out, Marx's own philosophical concepts from the visible invisible in his texts. The symptomatic reading becomes not so much the analyst producing the solution from a reading of the text as in Freud, but reading as a form of stenographic dictatorship, where the remote, disembodied Marx is discovered to be instructing the reader and prescribing—(prescribe: to write in advance, "to lay down a rule, to dictate")[19]—a second, more fundamental text that shall be written on his behalf: "In this we are absolutely committed to a theoretical destiny: we cannot *read* Marx's scientific discourse without at the same time *writing at his dictation* (*sous sa proper dictée*) [my italics] the text of another discourse, inseparable from the first one but distinct from it: the discourse of Marx's *philosophy*" (RCC 297).

Notes

1. Althusser himself discusses this phenomenon with respect to Lacan and Husserl. See Louis Althusser, "Freud and Lacan," in *Lenin and Philosophy, and Other Essays*, trans. Ben Brewster (London: New Left Books, 1971), 185.

2. Louis Althusser, Étienne Balibar, Roger Establet, Pierre Macherey, and Jacques Rancière, *Reading Capital: The Complete Edition*, trans. Ben Brewster and David Fernbach (London: Verso, 2016), 11. Further page references will be cited in the text (RCC).

3. Althusser, et al., *Reading Capital*.

4. Karl Marx, *Le Capital: Critique de l'économie politique*, 4th ed., trans. Jean-Pierre Lefebvre (Paris: Éditions sociales, 1983).

5. Karl Marx, *Le Capital*, trans. M. J. Roy (Paris: Éditeurs Maurice Lachatre, 1872–75); Kevin Anderson, "The 'Unknown' Marx's *Capital* Volume 1: The French Edition of 1872–75, 100 Years Later," *Review of Radical Political Economics* 15, no. 4 (1983).

6. Karl Marx and Friedrich Engels, *Gesamtausgabe* (MEGA)/*herausgegeben vom Institut für Marxismus-Leninismus beim Zentralkomitee der Kommunistischen Partei der Sowjetunion und vom Institut für Marxismus-Leninismus beim Zentralkomitee der Sozialistischen Einheitspartei Deutschlands* (Berlin: Dietz, 1972).

7. Michael Heinrich, "Deconstructing *Capital*: New Insights from Marx's Economic Manuscripts in 'MEGA,'" summary of the Historical Materialism Annual Conference, 2006, "New Directions in Marxian Theory," 2.

8. Michael Heinrich, *An Introduction to the Three Volumes of Karl Marx's Capital* (New York: Monthly Review Press, 2012).

9. See, among others, Jacques Bidet, *Exploring Marx's Capital: Philosophical, Economic and Political Dimensions*, trans. David Fernbach (Leiden: Brill, 2007), and Regina Roth, "Karl Marx's Original Manuscripts in the Marx-Engels-Gesamtausgabe (MEGA): Another View on *Capital*," in *Re-Reading Marx: New Perspectives after the Critical Edition*, ed. Riccardo Bellofiore and Roberto Fineschi (Basingstoke, UK: Palgrave Macmillan, 2009).

10. Michel Foucault, *L'ordre du discours* (Paris: Gallimard, 1971).

11. RCC, 21–22. Roy's text can be found in Marx and Engels, *Gesamtausgabe* (MEGA), II.7.464.

12. The production of a new question differentiates Althusser's symptomatic reading from Freud's, which according to Althusser produced a new object (the unconscious) ("Freud and Lacan," 184).

13. Warren Montag, *Louis Althusser* (London: Palgrave, 2003), 82–83.

14. Karl Marx, *Capital*, 3 vols., trans. Ben Fowkes and David Fernbach (Harmondsworth, UK: Penguin Books, 1976–81), 1:678–79.

15. Jacques Rancière, "Dissenting Words: A Conversation with Jacques Rancière" (interview by Davide Panagia), *Diacritics* 30, no. 2 (2000): 114. See also Rancière's early critique of Althusser, *La leçon d'Althusser* (Paris: Gallimard, 1974).

16. Althusser, "Freud and Lacan," 185; cf. 199, "even if they were compared with the letter of Freud's analysis." Althusser's emphasis on "reading to the letter" was obviously inspired by Lacan's famous essays of 1957, "L'instance de la lettre dans l'inconscient ou la raison depuis Freud," and "La séminaire sur la lettre volée" (*Le Séminaire de Jacques Lacan*, livre 16: *D'un Autre à l'autre, 1968–1969*, ed. Jacques-Alain Miller [Paris: Éditions du Seuil, 2006], 412–43, 6–50).

17. Walter Benjamin, "On Language as Such and on the Language of Man" (1916), in *Selected Works,* 4 vols., ed. Marcus Bullock and Michael W. Jennings (Cambridge, MA: Harvard University Press, 1996), 1:74. According to Althusser this Promethean reading is projected onto nature "so as not to perish in the daring project of knowing it" (17).

18. Cited by Anderson, "The 'Unknown' Marx's *Capital* Volume 1," 73.

19. S.v. prescribe, "2. To lay down . . . dictate" (*Merriam-Webster*, 1980).

CHAPTER 3

Translation and Event

Rereading *Reading Capital*

EMILY APTER

Reading Capital (*Lire le Capital*), a radical reworking of Marx collectively undertaken by Louis Althusser, Étienne Balibar, Roger Establet, Pierre Macherey,
and Jacques Rancière, was and remains a significant event in the history of
philosophical translation.[1] Its project was to think in and through translation,
as both *cursus* and praxis, the new language of French Marxism and scientific
socialism Althusser had called for in *For Marx* (*Pour Marx*, FM) to be built up
from the messy editorial object of Marx's *Das Kapital* in the original German.
Reading Capital from this perspective amounted to nothing short of actual-
izing the momentous passage of critique into existence, and of new philoso-
phemes into language.

Though Althusser was always suspicious of philosophy (Warren Montag
convincingly asserts that for him "there can be no philosophy that would itself
embody the very conflicts in which it seeks to intervene"), his practice of philosophical translation yielded a marked lexicon—a Marxist metalanguage—
that appeared in its most distilled guise as a glossary of terms, commented on
by Althusser himself, compiled by the work's English translator Ben Brewster,
initially as an appendix to his English translation of *Pour Marx*, later reprised
and slightly expanded in the English translation of *Reading Capital*).[2] Viewed
in hindsight, which is to say, from the vantage of a much later work on which
Balibar collaborated—Barbara Cassin's *Vocabulaire européen des philosophies:
Dictionnaire des intraduisibles* (*Dictionary of Untranslatables: A Philosophical
Lexicon*, which appeared in French in 2004)—the glossary should itself be
seen as an important evental form; a practice of philosophical translation and
concept-labor with the theoretical force of an *après-coup* in Marxist theory.
As the philosopher who bridges *Reading Capital* and the *Vocabulaire,* Balibar

emerges as a pivotal figure in a larger story about "how to do things with Untranslatables," which is to say, with terms that defy translation, are subject to mistranslation, which require constant retranslation, and which make of translation as such a politics, a praxis, an event. Balibar, between Althusser and Cassin, I will argue, gives us translation as a possible hinge between the translation considered as an evental form and a politics of translation *of* and *contra* "theory," *with* and *resistant to* political concepts.

Rereading *Reading Capital* as a philosophical translation carries the risk of dehistoricizing it; distancing it from the politics of party, the dynamics of antihumanist Marxism, and the language of psychoanalysis and structuralism that makes of the text a distinct chronotope. But my aim would be rather to rehistoricize it in the context of theory now, using it to critique an often monolingually Anglophone Marxism that, in its most recent efforts to critique finance capital, frequently forgets the actual languages of *Das Kapital*; most pointedly its original German and extended philosophical vocabulary of German idealism and classical economics. While I won't be taking up the task of rereading Marx in German or in any other language into which his work was translated, I do want to retrieve a renewed *politics of translation* from *Reading Capital*, or at the very least frame the import of its theoretico-political afterlife as a text in and of translation.

Much has been said and written about the complex genetics of *Reading Capital* as a manuscript: its testimony to live interactions of a seminar held at the École Normale Supérieure, its status as a reactive record of the party politics of Euro-Communism in the lead-up to and aftermath of May '68, and its authorial purges. This last point includes Rancière's denunciation, in *Althusser's Lesson*, of his teacher's endorsement of how the French Communist Party (PCF; Parti Communiste Français) described on May '68. For Rancière, the PCF's wrongheaded dismissal of the event as a mere student rebellion prevented it from recognizing its significance as a spontaneous popular insurrection; an expression of collective action minus the imposing directives of a master or intellectual class. Rancière rejected the PCF's efforts—via the teachings and intellectual pedigree of Althusser—to promote an image of itself as *the* party capable of peacefully transitioning socialism to "true democracy."[3]

On the occasion of the fiftieth anniversary of *Reading Capital*'s publication it is interesting to attend to the materialism of the published text in its different guises, formats, authorial history, interventions, and translations (Nick Nesbitt's introduction to this set of essays on *Reading Capital* offers an illuminating review of the text's complex publication history). The text's mul-

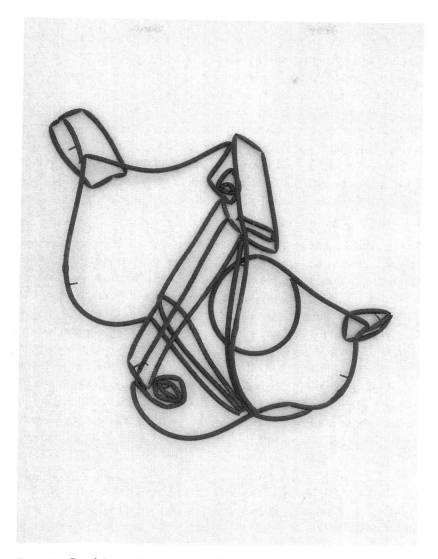

Figure 3.1 Gareth James, *Money stands for limitlessness. Art will too if it lasts too long.* Whitney Museum of American Art, 2009.

tiple iterations archive a history of theoretical praxis. By all accounts, *Reading Capital* was "palimpsestic" (the word is Robert Young's) in a similar way to *Das Kapital*, both in the original German and in Joseph Roy's 1872–75 French translation. Marx revised some of the French translation himself, adding material that was not in the original German. And as Young reminds us, the German edition itself was a complex object, volumes 2–3 largely stitched together from different manuscripts by Engels, while volume 4, *Theories of Surplus Value*, was only assembled by Karl Kautsky after Engels's death, in 1905–10. There was and remains a looming and vexed question around the identity of *Kapital* as a textual object, which in turn yields the problem of where, and in what, "the event" of translation occurs or in what material it actually inheres. For Young such issues are of signal importance:

> Just as Marx rewrote the classical economists, and then rewrote his own text, and then Engels rewrote Marx, so Althusser too reads Marx to rewrite him, to produce the visible invisible concepts in Marx in his text, anachronistic concepts that were ahead of the theoretical vocabulary of their time . . .
>
> Althusser then in *Reading Capital* seeks to retrieve another method of reading that is Marx's own. Just as he would deliberately leave *Lire le capital* unfinished, as Marx left *Capital* unfinished, just as he would revise *Lire le Capital* and publish different editions, with added material and some omitted, as Marx did with *Capital*, so too he will read Marx carefully enough, to the letter, in order to detect and repeat his method of reading and rewrite his text in order to produce, draw out, Marx's own philosophical concepts from the visible invisible in his texts. The symptomatic reading becomes not so much the analyst producing the solution from a reading of the text as in Freud, but reading as a form of dictatorship not of the proletariat but of the dead that instructs and prescribes us to write their words on their behalf.[4]

Keeping Young's new kind of symptomatic textual reading in mind, along with the retrospect of recent historicist and object-oriented critical tendencies that privilege the focus on print culture and the modes of existence of textual objects, we are struck anew by the profusion of auxiliary materials to the English editions of *Reading Capital*: prefaces, notes, glossaries, and addenda. Ben Brewster's English translation, brought out by New Left Books in 1970, came equipped with an apparatus that included a "Translator's Note," a translation of Althusser's "Foreword to the Italian Edition" (which ended with the immodest line "In a forthcoming series of studies, we shall have the opportunity of rectifying the terminology and correcting the definition of philosophy"), an epigraph taken from Marx's letter to Maurice La Châtre, a glossary compiled as mentioned by Brewster, and a "Letter to the Translator" from Althusser to Brewster.

The material history of *Reading Capital* in translation, which extends to a looser notion of translating Marxism into a French Marxism of the 1960s worthy of diffusion in the context of global colonial struggles, general strikes, and radical mobilizations, also sits in an expanded field of social relations inclusive of the persons and linguistic competencies of translators. Franca Madonia, the Italian translator of *For Marx*, warrants acknowledgment in this context because her relationship to Althusser introduced determinative affective residues and symptoms into a Marxist-Althusserian lexicon born of its international translations. In the passionate correspondence between Althusser and Madonia between 1961 and 1973, translation—especially the language used to describe its difficulty—becomes an amorous cipher impossible to disentangle from the terms and expressions translated.[5] Althusser teasingly chides Franca for her "péchés mignons" de traductrice, "ton besoin d'expliquer ce que tu traduis, ton souci de remplacer un mot trop dur par un mot plus courant etc. [her adorable little sins as a translator, her need to overexplain what she translates by substituting a more commonly used term for a more difficult one]." He cajoles her into humoring his compulsion to add phrases and corrections that were not in the original up to the last minute before going to press (*Lettres à Franca* 668). In a letter of April 22, 1966, he claims to respect her "national idiocies," by which he means her fidelity to forms of expression that make sense in the *habitus* of the national tongue, all the while insisting that the language of philosophy translates untranslatably, which is to say, it surmounts obstacles of idiom as it transitions through the national languages of philosophy.[6]

Languages carry an erotic charge for Althusser. He sends poetry to Madonia written in a mixture of Polish, Italian, and French. And in the epistolary record of their temporary rupture, which ends with him entreating her to send the translations of his texts even if she won't respond to his letter, his recourse to geometric and juridical metaphors is coded as a kind of untranslatability. Franca's silence, her telegram consisting of the single word "Impossible," is compared by Althusser to a Euclidian point where infinite lines ("les droites") converge and are effaced. Althusser was engaged at this time in the study of non-Euclidean geometry (Riemann, Frege, Hilbert). The idea of sufficient geometric axioms independent of reality and relative to a particular model of space would be mined for a theory of the relative autonomy of the philosophical concept and of theory as a mode of production.

In the letter to Franca, geometry is introduced there where the gulf of non-translation separates the lovers. The point and the lines are drawn together to make an X, a diagram of the cross: "one puts a cross," one makes a sign of the cross over ("on *fait une croix sur*") the expression, Althusser writes, "this expression, like all others, even the most untranslatable, says well what it means: one makes a cross to erase, to destroy, to say no . . . A cross over the face: a way of saying, *it's you* who will suffer [l'expression, comme toutes les expressions, même intraduisibles, dit bien ce qu'elle *veut* dire: on fait une croix pour rayer, détruire, dire non . . . Une croix sur un visage: manière de dire: c'est toi qui souffriras]." This cross over the untranslatable, and over the face of the lover, sets off another of Althusser's epistolary *tours de force* in the form of an associative chain. In the play among *croix*, *droite*, and *droit* a through-line may be traced from the barred translator, to the Derridean trace (Being under erasure), to the letter's relation to the Imaginary, to the question of the *right* to the imaginary ("une question de *droit* à l'imaginaire") and from thence, to the rights (*les droits*) of the juridical subject in excess of real power (*Lettres à Franca* 672–73). The references to geometry indicate a convergence (as well as a tension) between formal modeling and translational symptom that can be tracked throughout Althusser's writing and thinking in the early and mid-1960s, especially in his attempt to define "overdetermination" in relation to the historical event. The model can be read as the form assumed by the untranslatable, where language fails or where the aporia of linguistic difference (the not-translated) exerts pressure on the translation, articulating the very problem of translation in theoretical work.

Here I am advancing the thesis that *Reading Capital* is itself an event in the history of translation because Althusserian theoretical practice: (1) establishes a critical dialectics between abstract formal model and linguistic sign; (2) translates heuristically between psychoanalysis and Marxism; (3) practices symptomatic translation within the practice of symptomatic reading; and (4) gives us a way to think of the translative event as coextensive with the theory of the event.

A crucial text for substantiating these propositions is found in the appendix to "Contradiction and Overdetermination" (published in 1965 in *For Marx*, three years after the original essay appeared in the journal *La Pensée*). An effort to pry loose the event from economic necessitarianism and the welter of accidents and self-canceling competitive wills that confound historical determination, the appendix consists of a close reading (and translation) of an 1890 letter from Engels to Joseph Bloch. Contesting Engels's default to the teleology of economic determination "in the last instance," Althusser homes in on a passage in which Engels describes the historical event in terms of multiple, intersecting parallelograms of forces:[7]

> Il y a donc là d'innombrables forces qui se contrecarrent mutuellement, un groupe infini de parallélogrammes de forces, d'où ressort une résultante— l'événement historique—qui peut être regardée en elle-même à son tour, comme le produit d'une force agissant comme un tout, de façon inconsciente et aveugle. Car ce que veut chaque individu est empêché par chaque autre, et ce qui s'en dégage est quelque chose que personne n'a voulu.[8]

> Es sind also unzählige einander durchkreuzende Kräfte, eine unendliche Gruppe von Kräfteparallelogrammen, daraus eine Resultante—das geschichtliche Ergebnis—hervorgeht, die selbst wieder als das Produkt einer, als Ganzes, bewusstlos und willenlos wirkenden Macht angesehen werden kann. Denn was jeder einzelne will, wird von jedem andern verhindert, und was herauskommt, ist etwas, das keiner gewollt hat.[9]

> There are innumerable intersecting forces, an infinite series of parallelograms of forces which give rise to one resultant—the historical event. This may again itself be viewed as the product of a power which works as a whole, unconsciously and without volition. For what each individual wills is obstructed by everyone else, and what emerges is something that no one willed. (For Marx, 120)

Engels dissolves individual wills into a micropolitical field of infinite and indefinite determinations that aggregate into an unintelligible, volitional unconscious, a "force without a subject," or "nobody's force" (FM 121). And as Althusser reflects further: "the effect of this infinitesimal dispersion is to *dissipate* the effectivity granted the superstructures in their *macroscopic* existence *into a microscopic non-existence*" (FM 118, italics in original). How to recover effectivity or an evental noncausality without falling back on a paradigm of explanation in which the economy has its "sovereign way" (FM 118)?[10] One answer lies in faulting Engels on his understanding of superstructure as an infinity of microscopic effects. Althusser characterizes this bad reading as a "'monnayage' de l'efficace des formes de la *superstructure*"; an interesting turn of phrase translated by Brewster as "cashing the effectivity of the forms of the superstructure" (*FM* 119).[11] The phrase could be taken to suggest that Engels "cashed out" superstructural effectivity, trading on its cancelation in order to underwrite an economy of "free wills" that was totally alien to Marx's idea of ideological superstructure. It may thus be swept aside like counterfeit currency or a bad credit default swap.

A second strategy for rescuing effectivity lies in the performance of a symptomatic reading that repurposes Engel's use of the classic physical model of the "parallelogram of forces." Engels's *Kräfteparallelogrammen*—forces that produce a third force (referred to by Althusser as a transcendent or global resultant) when they confront each other by twos different in size from each force by itself—are, according to Althusser, taken by Engels as a representation of how "the infinite diversity of microscopic causes" are organized into "discrete and visible unities." Althusser will change out the sublatory organizing principle or "internal essence of accidents" (the third force of the parallelogram), for an actant; an evental incision into preexisting historical forms that will *disturb* their environment (he favors the verb *ébranler* for disturbance, with its connotations of shake-off, dismantling, sexual excitation) (*FM* 121). "What makes *such and such* an event *historical* is not the fact that it is an *event*, but precisely its *insertion into forms which are themselves historical . . .* an event, which has the wherewithal to fall within one of these forms, *which is a possible content for one of these forms*, which affects them, concerns them, reinforces or disturbs them, which provokes them or which they provoke, or even choose or select, that is a *historical event*" (*FM* 126).

In what perhaps might be considered a leap in my argument, I would suggest that the "event" of translation takes place as an action on forms of language, becoming manifest in myriad symptomal effects: mistranslations, compulsive retranslations, and aporias of translatability. Translation is both indeterminate and overdetermining insofar as "*it is the very form of the interiority of the structure, as a structure, in its effects*," to borrow from Althusser and Balibar's subsequent formula in *Reading Capital* (*RCC* 344, emphasis in the original).

The translational parallelogram of forces is also a parallax, a mediating relation between Freud and Marx. Here, something subjective—the Freudian definition of psychical intensity arising from the effects of condensation and displacement in the dream work—is "translated" (in the sense of imported into, transposed, deposed) to the discourse of historical determination; specifically, the contradictions that make the structural conditions of the social body inseparable from the conditions of its real existence. While later critics would revert to the use of overdetermination as a general designation for the infinite factoring of causality (to wit, Ernest Mandel's "parametric determinism"), Althusser remains faithful to Freud.[12] "This transfer of an analytical concept to Marxist theory," he wrote in *Reading Capital*, was "not an arbitrary borrowing but a necessary one, *for the same theoretical problem is at stake in both cases: with what concept are we to think the determination of either an element or a structure by a structure?*" (RCC 343, italicized in original). In his glossary entry on "Overdetermination" Brewster will foreground the Freudian uses of *Überdeterminierung* as the primary semantic platform:

> Freud used this term to describe (among other things) the representation of dream thoughts in images privileged by their condensation of a number of thoughts in a single image (condensation/*Verdichtung*), or by the transference of psychic energy from a particularly potent thought to apparently trivial images (displacement/*Verschiebung-Verstellung*). Althusser uses the same term to describe the effects of the contradictions in each practice, constituting the social formation on the social formation as a whole, and hence back on each practice and each contradiction, defining the pattern of dominance and subordination, antagonism and non-antagonism of the contradictions in the structure in dominance at any given historical moment. (RCC 539)

Embedded in this digest of how determinant contradictions can have displaced evental effects, there lies an evental translational displacement: a keyword of psychoanalysis has been subject to transvaluation; rendered applicable to the uneven development of dominant structures, to contradictory conditions within the social body that allow for the opening up of superstructures to instances of non-pregivenness.

Translation—conceptual, disciplinary—is happening here on many levels. And yet, the most ostensive aspect of the translational event is occluded when Brewster writes of "Althusser using the same term as Freud." For it is not the same term. Freud's *Überdeterminierung* has been replaced by the French *surdétermination*. *Surdétermination* (resonating with the common French translation of Nietzsche's *Übermensch* as *surhomme*) overtranslates *Überdeterminierung* insofar as it turns the term to specific uses in the theory of historical and dialectical materialism and suppresses a nexus of German conceptual cognates associated by Freud with *Überdeterminierung: Verdichtung, Verschiebung-Verstellung*. Though it adds connections to Marx's *Darstellung* (representation), a central term of his theory of value, as well as the function of "metonymic causality" (courtesy Lacan) to the structural effects of displacement and condensation, *surdétermination* reduces the surfeit of effects triggered by the neighboring vocabulary ascribed by Freud to *Überdeterminierung*: notions of compaction, densification, concentration, concretion, and "coming-togetherness [*zusammendrücken*]" inhering in *Verdichtung*; notions of shift, move, deferment, alteration, the transference of something important to something trivial or infinitesimally small in scale inhering in *Verschiebung*; and notions of opposition (*Gegenständen*) adjustment, blockage, obstruction (*Versperrung*), inhering in *Verstellung*. The latter is identified as a crux for Paul Ricoeur where the discourse of meaning (Husserlian *Erfüllung* [fulfillment]) fuses with the discourse of force [*Verdrängung* (repression)], producing a "violence done to meaning."[13] "Violence done to meaning" is of course another way of saying translation; so the (circular) argument becomes something like this: Freud's *Überdeterminierung* translates as "translation"; or more precisely, as a translative site and structure of *forçage* that reproduces the evental effectivity of overdetermination.

There are many other kinds of translative event in *Reading Capital*. Althusser's open letter to Ben Brewster alerts the Anglophone reader to the fact that he has turned Brewster's glossary (which, in addition to the entry on overdetermination, contains a host of notable entries on alienation, epistemological break, conjuncture, consciousness, contradiction, humanism, ideology, dialectical materialism, practice, problematic, theory), into the site of a theoretical "intervention": "Thank you for your glossary; what you have done is *extremely* important from a political, educational and theoretical point of view . . . I return your text with a whole series of corrections and interpolations (some of which are fairly long and important, you will see why)" (RCC 548). After noting the genealogy of "break" and "problematic," from Gaston Bachelard's early coinage of "epistemological break," to Georges Canguilhem's unsystematic usage, to Michel Foucault's Althusserian appropriation, he underscored the importance of "correction":

> Much more important are the corrections I have suggested for some of your rubrics. In most cases they are merely *corrections* (*précisions*) which do not affect the state of the theoretical concepts that figure in the book . . . But in other cases they are corrections of a different kind [Lenin's concept of spontaneity]. You will understand why I am so *insistent* on all these cor-

rections and interpolations. I urge you to give them a place in your glossary, and add that (1) I have myself gone over the text of the glossary line by line, and (2) I have made changes in matters of detail (which need not be indicated) and a few *important interpolations* . . . The procedure I have suggested has the advantage that it removes any misunderstanding of this kind *in advance* [i.e. discrepancies of positions], since, *on the one hand*, I leave the system of concepts of 1960 to 1965 as it was, while *on the other*, I indicate the *essential point* in which I have developed in the intervening years—since, *finally*, I give references to the new writings that contain the new definition of philosophy that I now hold, and I summarize the new conception which I have arrived at (provisionally—what is not provisional?). (RCC 548–49)

There are a number of points to be made here, some obvious, others perhaps less so. First, as has been much commented, there is the immense weight assigned to the action of "correction" which at first blush smacks of party discipline and doctrinaire ideological alignment. But this is no simple matter of party line, or of finding a just translation, or of ramping up the accuracy of a concept definition. When we see the initials *L. A.* in a glossary entry, we know that the generic form of the glossary itself has been changed; turned into a *dispositif* for a materialist dialectics of the theoretical object.

The labor of lexical agency is especially apparent in the entry on theory, where Althusser "intervenes" in order to stress that he *now* considers "false" his former conception of Theory (big T) as theoretical practice. The "now" of his intervention gives on to the "new"; in philosophy, corrected to represent "the class struggle in the realm of *theory*," "a theoretical practice in the realm of politics," and "an original 'instance' . . . that represents the one instance alongside (*auprès de*) the other, in the form of a specific *intervention* (political-theoretical)." Leaving aside for the moment the opaque contents of these formulations, what comes to the fore is a procedure that involves baffling the terminus of the term.[14] Althusser's "concept" one might say, performs as a copula, a temporal term between terms that keeps the name of the concept from being pinioned by philosophical nominalism, conceptualism, or intentionalism.

Terminology interminable; a good-enough definition of translation as a theoretical practice of conceptual incompletion and recall. Warren Montag underscores Althusser's desire to recall his books as soon as they were published and this is of a piece with his effort to inject *Jeztzeit* into writing, reading and translating such that the text in real time is dialectically posed against the actuality and tempo of its historic conditions of articulation. In the famous opening of *Reading Capital* this process *is* the set-up:

> The following papers were delivered in the course of a seminar on *Capital* held at the ENS early in 1965. They bear the mark of these circumstances: not only in their construction, their rhythm, their didactic or oral style, but also and above all in their discrepancies, the repetitions, hesitations and uncertain steps in their investigations. We could, of course, have gone over them at our leisure, corrected them one against the other, reduced the margin of variation between them, unified their terminology, their hypotheses and their conclusions to the best of our ability, and set out their contents in the systematic framework of a single discourse—in other words, we could have tried to make a *finished* work out of them. But rather than pretending they are what they should have been, we prefer to present them for what they are: precisely, incomplete texts, the mere beginnings of *a reading*. (RCC 11)

Balibar would run with this program of philosophical incompletion. In a 1995 essay titled "The Infinite Contradiction" he referred to

> the type of *incompleteness* [*inachèvement*] proper to philosophical texts—an incompleteness that my readings constantly illustrate, and that has led me to use the verb *to incomplete* [*inachever*] in the active form: Marx *incompleted Capital* (and toiled all his life to incomplete it); Heidegger *incompleted Being and Time*. At the risk of superstition, I have even proposed that there would be a certain logical benefit in reading the interruption of Spinoza's *Political Treatise as if* it were an active incompletion, comparable to that of the *Regulae* or *De intellectus emendatione*. One might go even further and assert that the nature of a great philosophy is not only to incomplete itself, but to *incomplete others*, by introducing itself or by being introduced in their writing: thus, from the "Manuscripts of 1843" up to *Capital*, Marx prodigiously incompleted Hegel's *Philosophy of Right*. And if it is true that the regulating idea of "system" is fundamentally a modern version of the old *imago mundi*, the meaning of all these aporetic undertakings is, if not to 'transform," probably to *incomplete the world*, or the representation of the world as "a world."[15]

In "Lockean Concepts: A Philosophical and Philological Glossary," included in the 1998 book *Identité et différence: L'Invention de la conscience,* and updated in the recent Verso English translation, Balibar effects a return to the concept restituted not as a unit of reified nominalism, but as a philosophical Untranslatable. In his preface to the English edition of *Identité et différence* (itself an exercise in comparative translation starting with Pierre Coste's 1700 French translation of Locke's *An Essay concerning Human Understanding*), *untranslatability* emerges as the site of a conceptual conjuncture. The translational aporia between English "person" and French *sujet* generates something on the order of a *hapax legemenon*, the singular occurrence of *self/consciousness/conscience*:

> My argumentation takes up the question of the idea of the "person" (the Lockean *name for the subject*), linked together above all by what I call an "anti-linguistic turn" or an "isolation of the mental" (whose relevance to current debates about cognitivism is not simply archeological). But this always proceeds on the basis, and as a function, of problems of translation . . . I am effectively convinced—as was the group that produced the *Vocabulaire européen des philosophies*—not only that the difficulties of translation (and in particular the case of untranslatability, which leads to terminological inventions and to strategies of paraphrase and of periphrasis) constitute privileged indicators of the meaning of concepts, but that they form an important part of the conditions of possibility of philosophical thought (as important as logic or rhetoric) in that philosophers *think by means of writing* in a determinate conjuncture, and most often at the intersection of several languages.[16]

Balibar's Untranslatable is arguably nothing short of a heresy of the concept; the concept traduced by quanta of the "inessential," that makes of it a "structure" or structuring force harking back to chapter 9 of *Reading Capital* ("Marx's Immense Theoretical Revolution"). There, in taking up the task bequeathed by Marx of defining the object of political economy, Althusser posed "structure" against "concept," only to recognize that to be "graspable" structure reverts to *Begriff*. Marx's use of *Begriff* and *Darstellung* are the translational conjunctures that spawn Althusser's endeavor to produce "an indispensable philosophical concept *which does not exist in the form of a concept*" (RCC 340). What, one is compelled to ask, is the form of a concept that does not take conceptual form?

Althusser's "concept" gives way to the *unthought* theoretical object inter-pellated by different names: the Spinozist void/*vide*, Machiavelli's *insaisissable* (referred by Montag to "Machiavelli's theory of the non-accomplishment of Italy, the 'atomized country, every atom of which was descending in free fall without encountering its neighbor,'"[17] the Incomplete text, Absence, Silence, the Unknown, the Authorless Theater, the absent cause in the structure's "met-onymic causality" (a form of interiority of the structure, as a structure, in its effects, that will become the core of Žižekian Lacano-Marxism).[18] The concept not in the form of the concept is accessed on the oblique through a symp-tomatic reading. Althusser will zero in on Marx's "weaknesses, his lacunae, his omissions: they concur with his greatness, for in returning to them we are only returning to the beginnings of a discourse interrupted by death. The reader will know how volume 3 ends. A title: *Classes*. Forty lines, then silence" (*RCC 349*; "Un titre: *les classes sociales*. Vingt lignes, puis le silence" [*LC* 71]).[19] Marx's silence anticipates what late Althusser dubs Machiavelli's "solitude." In the 1977 essay "Solitude de Machiavel" he alights on the "enigma" of Machiavelli's thought, its ungraspability, political indeterminacy, formal in-terruptions, digressions, suspended contradictions, and anomalousness in the history of philosophy ("le caractère *insolite* de sa pensée").[20] These theoreti-cal inexistents are clearly variants of what Althusser had, in *Reading Capital*, credited Marx with producing; a proposal "to think the determination of the elements of a whole by the structure of the whole [which] posed an abso-lutely new problem in the most theoretically embarrassing circumstances, for there were no philosophical concepts available for its resolution [Se proposer de penser la détermination des éléments d'un tout par la structure du tout, c'était se poser un problème absolument nouveau dans le plus grand embarras théorique car on ne disposait d'aucun concept philosophique élaboré pour le résoudre]" (*RCC 342*; *LC* 2:63). Marx, Althusser continues, "'*produced*' this problem, he did not pose it as a problem,* but set out to solve it practically in the absence of its concept, with extraordinary ingenuity, but without completely avoiding a relapse into earlier schemata which were necessarily inadequate to pose and solve this problem [Marx, qui a '*produit*' ce problème, ne l'a pas posé en tant que problème*, mais s'est employé à le résoudre pratiquement, sans disposer de son concept, avec une extraordinaire ingéniosité, mais sans pou-voir tout à fait éviter de retomber dans les schémas antérieurs, nécessairement inadéquats à la position et à la solution de ce problème]" (*RCC 343*; *LC* 2:63). "Structure," "Problem," "Concept," "Determination": each of these terms is thrown off its hinges and placed in suspended, yet dynamic relation, giving rise to a set-up or *dispositif* for the unnamed theoretical object to come. What comes to the fore, albeit hypothetically, as Bruno Bosteels tracks it in the later Althusser, is a "politics of theory," a new practice of philosophy, grounded in Marxist philosophy (dialectical materialism).[21]

The politics of translation, an unfulfilled project in *Reading Capital* despite its evident program to reread Marx's German original in order to retheorize its basic terms and arguments, would only come to fruition in Balibar's work long after the collaborative writing ventures with Althusser were over. In and through the politics of translation, Balibar, it could be said, develops an explicit "politics of theory," affirmed specifically in a practice of philosophical translation that activates untranslatability in political concepts, not as an essence, but as a relational remainder among terms and languages. The Untranslatable as a subtractive force—manifest as failure or reversal of fortune—would become consistently operative in Balibar's theoretical practice, with a good example furnished by his essay on C. B. Macpherson titled "'Possessive Individualism' Reversed: From Locke to Derrida." Setting the terms "power," "property," and "proprietorship" in conflictive apposition, Balibar mobilizes the negative form of Lockean self-ownership and property in the person ("one cannot be expropriated from oneself"), drawing on a Lacanian formula—"In a deep sense—as Lacanians might say—legitimate property not only *excludes others* from what is my own, it basically *excludes myself from something (some 'Thing') that I can never 'own'*"—for a model of what might be thought of as dispossessive collectivism. Dispossessive collectivism, catalyzed by Balibar's citizen-subject, itself defined by self-de-ownership, goes against the grain of the propertied, fully capitalized "individual" who self-owns by destituting others; a figure all too familiar at the present conjuncture where "corporations" are "people" in the eyes of the American legal system. "Working off the reversal," doubling down on concepts of "self," "own," and "appropriation" for a retranslated political ontology, Balibar effectively "incompletes" Lockean categories:

> We have seen the emergence of categories which were apparently absent from the Lockean conception of "self-ownership" as the pivotal element in the articulation of individual and community, but perhaps not completely out of it. Rather, they postpone self-ownership in the direction of an impossible unity with oneself. We can thus wonder if we are really out

of the field of variations virtually enclosed in the axiomatics of possessive individualism. I should rather say: possessive individuality has stamped itself with negativity; it took the figure of a splitting whose symptoms are visible not only in the fundamental dissatisfaction of the individual qua citizen, but in the incompleteness of the "body politick" itself. And I would dare to add: in the incompleteness of the very theoretical writings in which they are exposed.[22]

Translational practice or praxis (it is not clear which term is the right one), emerges as a theoretical mode of production that engenders new forms of being; such that not only different economic and political determinations become thinkable, but also that differently abled bodies, intellects, identities, subjects, subjectivities, and forms of the social come to be. In regard to the latter point, it might be interesting to work out how translational praxis relates to Catherine Malabou's notion of a "new materialism" of ontic "plasticity"; with plasticity a term drafted from Hegel and applied to subjects characterized as "the new wounded [*les nouveaux blessés*]."[23] "The new wounded"—treated as untranslatable by psychoanalysis—include those whose mental impairments, sexual disorders, and physical disabilities become the reconstructive material—the difference changers—of normatively bodied persons and subjectivized somas.[24]

Malabou's plasticity is strikingly *practical* in its application to the critique of theories of the subject and in this regard it would be compatible with Althusserian usage. Althusser shunned *praxis* for being too philosophical, too freighted with Sartreanism. He warned Franca in a letter of March 23, 1966, to pay special attention to "*pratique*," expressing his hope that the word *pratica* in Italian would prevail. "I never say praxis, despite its currency in philosophy (cf. Sartre); for the very reason that I don't want to fall into using this overly 'philosophical' word. I prefer 'practice.' Since the word is used often in the following chapter, I hope the word *practica* will be used in the Italian [Je ne dis jamais praxis, pourtant courant en philosophie, cf. Sartre, justement pour ne pas tomber dans l'usage de ce mot trop 'philosophique.' Je préfère dire 'pratique.' Comme le mot revient souvent dans le chapitre qui suit, j'espère que l'italien comporte le mot de *pratica*]" (*Lettres à Franca* 665). For Althusser, "practical" was what characterized Marx's approach to producing a determination that was neither a concept nor a problem.

In his coauthored entry "Praxis" for the *Dictionary of Untranslatables*, Balibar would show that from its earliest uses on, the Greek *praxis* stands in dialectical if not contradictory relation to "practice," from Aristotle's philosophy of action (untranslatable in Latin), to the Kantian nominalization and moralization of *"praktisch* in the form of *das Praktische*, 'the practical' or 'the practical element.'" (For Kant, says Balibar, it is a matter of showing that this element does not reside in prudence or skill [*Klugheit, phronêsis*], because the latter concerns the intelligent arrangement of means and ends, or a "technique" and the conditions of its effectiveness, whereas *das Praktische* resides solely in morality. It thus determines the "concept of freedom," and emerges as a "supra-sensible" principle inseparable from the categorical imperative.") Balibar's strong philosophical translation of praxis continues with a nuanced analysis of "reversed Idealism" in Marx, and a genealogy of Gramsci's *filosofia della prassi*, that arrives at a newly potentialized theory of "actualism" via Antonio Labriola's Vicoan situation of praxis as "a historicist variant of the Second International's Marxism." Here, in the vocabulary of untranslatability opened up in the differences among practice, praxis, *das Praktische*, and *prassi*, we can now discern a "plastics" of concept-form and actualism that works to renew the connection between *Reading Capital*'s "Marxist philosophy" (of dialectical materialism) and the "event"—marked by thinkers as divergent as Balibar, Badiou, Derrida, and Žižek—of contemporary political ontology. On the occasion of the fiftieth anniversary of *Reading Capital*, coinciding with the publication in multiple translations of Cassin's philosophical *Dictionary of Untranslatables*, there is arguably an "event" discernible in renewed practices of political translation that involve rereading *Reading Capital* and reworking political concepts.

Notes

1. Louis Althusser, Étienne Balibar, Roger Establet, Pierre Macherey, and Jacques Rancière, *Reading Capital: The Complete Edition*, trans. Ben Brewster and David Fernbach (London: Verso, 2016), 480. All further references will be given in the text.

2. Warren Montag, *Althusser and His Contemporaries: Philosophy's Perpetual War* (Durham, NC: Duke University Press, 2013), 7.

3. Paraphrasing Jacques Rancière's *Althusser's Lesson* as cited in Todd May's review of the English translation, *Notre Dame Philosophical Reviews*, January 14, 2012. Accessed May 2, 2014. ndpr.nd.edu/news/28304-althusser-s-lesson/.

4. Robert J. C. Young, "Rereading the Symptomatic Reading," paper at the conference "Reading Capital 1965–2013," Princeton University, December 6, 2013.

5. Louis Althusser, *Lettres à Franca: 1961–1973* (Paris: Stock, 1998).

6. "Je respecte tes idiotismes nationaux (idiotisme = expression, forme d'expression propre à une langue et intraduisible *directement* dans une autre), mais je suis convaincu, connaissant de l'intérieur les 'péchés mignons' des philosophes et leurs arts de servir, en la déformant philosophiquement, de leur propre langue, que tu peux tranquillement traduire réfléchir par *riflettere*, qui a sûrement, dans la langue philosophique italienne le double sens qu'il a en français" (*Lettres à Franca*, 668).

7. The figure of the parallelogram of forces has been the subject of deep and protracted debate in the reception of Althusser's thought. Chris Burford, in "Rethinking Overdetermination," traces it to Newtonian mechanics and touches on whether it should be read as a model of a closed or open system: "The parallelogram of forces comes straight out of Newtonian, closed, mechanically deterministic, physics. It is a small step—but were Marx and Engels revolutionary in making it?—to apply this to an open system of innumerable individuals. What is described here is something much better understood now in terms of complexity theory: how the interaction of large numbers of component parts produce 'emergent patterns' that are larger than the sum of the individual parts. This is central to Marxian political economy: how the exchange of a commodity, over billions of cases, and over centuries, produces powerful patterns independent of the will of individual human beings." Chris Burford, "Rethinking Overdetermination," at "The Critical-Realism List," run by EHRBAR at economics.utah.edu. Accessed November 28, 2016. http://lists.csbs.utah.edu/pipermail/critical-realism/1996-August/000348.html.

Katja Kolsek, working off of Žižek, affirms that "the paradox of overdetermination can . . . only be understood from the point of view of the parallax object. It is the point from which the concept of overdetermination can be considered scientific and simultaneously thoroughly political . . . Althusser criticizes Engels's elaboration of the problem of considering the unity of overdetermination as the 'relative effectiveness of superstructures' in history as a kind of tautology on two different levels. When Engels does not find an answer to the first problem—of how the relative autonomy of the superstructures goes hand in hand with the thesis of 'the determination in the last instance by the economy,' due to the impossibility of evaluating the impact of all the endless host of accidents (that is, of things and events) whose inner connection is so remote or so impossible of proof that we can regard it as non-existent, as negligible, such that economic movement ultimately asserts itself as necessary—he passes to another model, the parallelogram of the forces of individual wills. Althusser disapproves of Engels's use of the metaphor . . . based on the elements of the 'individual wills' and dismisses Engels's argument as not meeting the critical standards of Marxist science, which is based on the always-already existing and necessary relations and not on the bourgeois ideological notion of free will." See Katja Kolsek, "The Parallax Object of Althusser's Materialist Philosophy," in *Encountering Althusser: Politics and Materialism in Contemporary Radical Thought*, ed. Katjia Diefenbach et al. (London: Bloomsbury, 2012), 80.

8. Louis Althusser, *Pour Marx* (Paris: La Découverte, 1996), 120.

9. Friedrich Engels, *Brief an Joseph Bloch*, September 21–22, 1890, in Marx and Engels, *Werke* (Berlin: Dietz, 1983), 37:462.

10. Thomas Carmichael, along with others, will affirm that for Althusser, "the non-arrival of the last instance should not be read as projecting the economic as that which is external to the accidents amid which it asserts itself, but rather that the economy 'is the *internal essence* of these accidents.'" Thomas Carmichael, "Structure and Conjuncture: Literary Study and the Return to Althusser," *Revue électronique d'études sur le monde* 3, no. 1 (2005), http://erea.revues.org/618.

11. Louis Althusser, *Pour Marx* (Paris: François Maspero, 1967), 119 (italics in the original).

12. David Macey, a distinguished translator of psychoanalysis and Marxist theory, writes not of translation per se, but of conceptual borrowings and an "import process" (which is and is not a way of talking about translation) in reference to Althusser's applications of Freudian and Lacanian terms. "When allied with Mao's essay *On Contradiction* (1973), psychoanalysis supplies the concept of overdetermination, originally elaborated in *The Interpretation of Dreams* to describe the manner in which every element of the dream-content is expressed many times in the dream-thoughts. It provides the protocols for the practice of symptomatic reading, modeled on the manner in which Marx read the texts of classical political economy, exposing the second text which exists in their slips and silences, and reproduced in the reading that allows Althusser to detect the epistemological break divorcing the mature Marx from the young humanist of the *1844 Manuscripts*. The model is the suspended or evenly poised attention with which the analyst listens to his or her analysand, refusing to reject or privilege any verbalization, just as the analysand follows the fundamental rule of saying all and omitting nothing. Having had years of personal experience of analysis, Althusser was well aware of just what the analytic situation involved and, as if to forestall the obvious objection that analysts listen rather than read, he argues again in terms of tacit analogies: since Freud, we have begun to understand what is meant by speaking; since Marx, we have begun to suspect what reading means. In a slightly more mysterious way, psychoanalysis provides the raw materials for the construction of the idea of metonymic or structural causality, which describes the effects of a structure on its component elements. Here, the import process is less clear than it might be; the reader tends to be referred by Althusser to Jacques-Alain Miller, and thence to Lacan." David Macey, "Thinking with Borrowed Concepts: Althusser and Lacan," in *Althusser: A Critical Reader*, ed. Gregory Elliott (Oxford: Blackwell, 1994), 145.

13. Paul Ricoeur, *Freud and Philosophy: An Essay on Interpretation*, trans. Denis Savage (New Haven, CT: Yale University Press, 1970), 92.

14. That said, Althusser's autocritique is straightforward, consisting in the observation that *Lire le Capital* presents Marx's theoretical production in *Capital* in the form of an Idealism, i.e., as Marx's isolated, voluntarist invention ex nihilo, rather than being determined by what Althusser in his 1967 "Notes sur la philosophie" calls

the "condition" of class struggle and proletarian imperatives to which Marx became subject after 1845 (Louis Althusser, *Écrits philosophiques et politiques, Tome II* [Paris: Stock, 1995]), 319.

15. Étienne Balibar, "The Infinite Contradiction," *Yale French Studies* 88 (1995): 146.

16. Étienne Balibar, *Identity and Difference: John Locke and the Invention of Consciousness*, trans. Warren Montag (London: Verso, 2013), ix.

17. Montag, "The Late Althusser: Materialism of the Encounter or Philosophy of Nothing?," in *Althusser and His Contemporaries*, 178. On this and related topics, see Clare Monagle and Dimitris Vardoulakis, eds., *The Politics of Nothing: On Sovereignty* (New York: Routledge, 2013).

18. Žižek on Sohn-Rethel's criticism of Althusser: "Sohn-Rethel is . . . quite justified in his criticism of Althusser, who conceives abstraction as a process taking place entirely in the domain of knowledge and refuses for that reason the category of 'real abstraction' as the expression of an 'epistemological confusion.' The 'real abstraction' is unthinkable in the frame of the fundamental Althusserian epistemological distinction between the 'real object' and the 'object of knowledge' insofar as it introduces a third element which subverts the very field of this distinction: the form of the thought previous and external to the thought—in short: the symbolic order." Slavoj Žižek, *Mapping Ideology* (London: Verso, 2012), 304.

19. Balibar will similarly frame "class" as aporia in the chapter of *Reading Capital* titled "The Basic Concepts of Historical Materialism." On what conditions (he asks with reference to Marx's Preface to *A Contribution [to the Critique of Political Economy]*) can the claim that history is the history of class struggles be a scientific utterance? In other words what classes are these? what are classes? what is their struggle? (RCC 361).

20. Croce, à la fin de sa vie, disait: la question de Machiavel *ne sera jamais réglée*. Cette énigme peut prendre différentes formes, par exemple la forme bien connue: Machiavel est-il monarchiste ou républicain? Elle peut prendre des formes plus subtiles: comment se fait-il que sa pensée soit à la fois catégorique et se dérobe? Pourquoi procède-t-elle, comme l'a remarquablement montré Claude Lefort dans sa thèse, par interruptions, digressions, contradictions laissées en suspens? Comment se fait-il qu'une pensée apparemment si maîtrisée soit en fait aussi présente et fuyante, achevée et inachevée dans son expression même? Autant d'arguments déconcertants pour soutenir l'idée que la *solitude* de Machiavel tient au caractère *insolite* de sa pensée." Louis Althusser, *Solitude de Machiavel*, ed. Yves Sintomer (Paris: PUF, 1998), 313.

21. Bruno Bosteels, "Alain Badiou's Theory of the Subject: Part I. The Recommencement of Dialectical Materialism?," *Pli* 12 (2001): 201. www.plijournal.com/files /12_12_Bosteels.pdf.

22. Balibar, "'Possessive Individualism' Reversed: From Locke to Derrida," in *Equaliberty* (Durham, NC: Duke University Press, 2014), 307.

23. Catherine Malabou, *Les nouveaux blessés: De Freud à la neurologie, penser les traumatismes contemporains* (Paris: Bayard, 2007). Of particular relevance to the hypothetical link between between praxis and plasticity would be Malabou's notions

of a "new materialism" or of the event that includes brain trauma, psychic accidents, physical and mental disabilities that are "untranslatable" or classed as off-limits to both psychoanalysis and philosophy (see 342, 34, 36). Malabou makes the case for a redefinition of cerebral, sexual, or physical disability as a "neuro-psychoanalytic event" (38–45), as well as for rethinking plasticity as a term that describes giving form to, accepting form into, and exploding the very idea of form as such (48–53).

24. Here my expression "difference changers" is a free translation of the title of another book by Malabou: *Changer de différence: Le féminin et la question philosophique* (Paris: Galilée, 2009).

CHAPTER 4

To Have Done with Alienation

or, How to Orient Oneself in Ideology

KNOX PEDEN

The Young Marx of the *1844 Manuscripts* read the human essence at sight, immediately, in the transparency of its alienation. *Capital*, on the contrary, exactly measures a distance and an internal dislocation (*décalage*) in the real, inscribed in its
structure, a distance and a dislocation such as to make their own effects themselves
illegible, and the illusion of an immediate reading of them the ultimate apex of their
effects: *fetishism*.

—LOUIS ALTHUSSER, "From *Capital* to Marx's Philosophy"

In a recent indictment of "neoliberal aesthetics," Walter Benn Michaels suggests that any aesthetic or interpretative effort that promotes vision over
form—that is, the primacy of the beholder over the unity of the artwork—is
complicit with a politics in which "the structural difference between capital
and labor (a difference that no degree of identification can alter) is imagined
out of existence."[1] Michaels's argument takes the form of an extended reflection on the fate of absorption and theatricality in a neoliberal age, using the
originator of these aesthetic concepts, Michael Fried, as its guide, alongside
critical discussions of Roland Barthes and Jacques Rancière. For something
to be endowed with form requires it to be imbued with intention; it is to be
the result of an action that is purposive at a minimum. In Michaels's vision,
any interpretive account of the artwork that privileges the beholder's experience
of the art, which is to say the art object's status as an object that, qua object, cannot but cause effects in a physical space irrespective of the intention
that produced it, serves ultimately to render art and objecthood indistinct
(to deploy a second set of canonical terms from Fried).[2] The worry is that if
you render these concepts indistinct, you are unable to provide an account of

how purposive actions produce specific results, in art, or in fact in any other domain—results that are consequences in the strong sense of the term. And if you can't relate specific actions to specific results, then you can't provide a well-motivated criticism of the specific actions that yield such results.

Michaels has been challenging the denigration of aesthetic intentionality for decades, but in recent years he has become more explicit about the ways in which the contested nature of such interpretation provides an analogue for the eclipse of inequality as a structural concern in favor of a vision of class as one identity among others.[3] For Michaels the distinction between what an artwork materially is and what it is about is absolutely crucial, and not unrelated to the distinction between a culturally conceived notion of class differences as sets of behaviors and experiences that have a kind of material primacy and class difference as an objective phenomenon that must ultimately be inferred. What an artwork *is* is how you see it or experience it; what it is *about* depends on the artist, knowledge of which can only be procured inferentially. In other words, there must be a kind of ontological discrepancy in the work to make the object into a "work." Without aboutness, there is no way to contest, criticize, or appreciate the actions that have yielded a certain state of affairs—there's just an experience that is what it is, and though it may be ultimately amenable to epistemic elucidation it is in principle immune to normative justification.

In August 1962, Louis Althusser momentarily ceased writing articles skeptical of the return to the young Marx to offer an extended reflection on Carlo Bertolazzi's melodrama *El Nost Milan*, which had been performed at the *Piccolo Teatro* in Milan in June of that same year. Central to Althusser's positive appraisal of an otherwise panned production was a discussion of Brecht and the various ways critics have construed his "alienation-effect" as a theatrical principle. In Althusser's view, far too much attention has been paid to "the technical elements of alienation" in Brechtian theater: al fresco acting, the austerity of the set, and so on.[4] This should give us pause. Isn't Althusser the model of a materialist philosopher? Indeed, the subtitle of Althusser's article is "Notes on a Materialist Theatre." We would expect a materialist to focus on all those material aspects of Brecht's theory and the *Piccolo Teatro's* production, those sites where objects are imbued with objective force, producing unavoidable effects. But Althusser's analysis proceeds otherwise. The power of Brechtian aesthetics lies precisely in the difference it helps us see between the work itself and its extrinsic conditions, all those things that the play is about.[5] This difference finds its correlate in the difference between the play and the spectator, although "difference" is not really the right word here. Rather, Althusser writes, "if a distance can be established between the spectator and the play, it is essential that in some way this distance should be produced within the play itself, and not only in its (technical) treatment, or in the psychological modality of the characters." In spite of any frustrated identifications with the play's personages, it is nevertheless "within the play itself, in the dynamic of its internal structure, that this distance is produced and represented, at once criticizing the illusions of consciousness and unraveling its real conditions."[6]

For Althusser, the difference between art and experience is not that between form and vision; rather, art provides a way to see form, that is, to see that which is not otherwise visible or capable of being figured in an imaginary identification, the unity that comprises the "dynamic of an internal structure." This is what Althusser means when he writes in a letter to André Daspre: "What art makes us *see*, and therefore gives to us in the form of '*seeing*,' '*perceiving*,' and '*feeling*' (which is not the form of *knowing*), is the *ideology* from which it is born, in which it bathes, from which it detaches itself as art, and to which it *alludes*."[7] Ideology is, as we know, one of the most contested concepts in the Althusserian corpus. But if we take it here in the sense that Althusser used the term in 1966, when the letter to Daspre was written, then we understand that Althusser does not mean ideology in a pejorative sense.[8] Whatever it is, it is certainly not false consciousness. Several years before ideology was coined as "the imaginary relationship of individuals to their real conditions of existence," Althusser had come to recognize that ideology was the exclusive domain of all kinds of subjectivity, or what I'm tempted to redescribe as subjecthood.[9] This is not subjectivity in the denigrated sense one finds in poststructuralism, but in the more Lacanian sense of subjectivity as the site of action—the *cause qui cloche*.[10] The subject is what makes things happen, what acts purposively (which is why the ego often wants to know very little about it). So when Althusser says art alludes to ideology, he surely means that art figures—without precisely making visible—various aspects of social relations and real conditions. But he also means that art alludes to a space in which the subject holds sway, in which things are inscribed with a purposiveness that the spectator may be indifferent to but that he cannot will away.

When Althusser criticizes approaches to Brechtian aesthetics that focus on its material apparatuses or thwarted identifications, his aim is to focus our attention squarely on the formal discrepancy that constitutes the artwork itself. This difference, or distance, inherent in the artwork is not to be overcome because to overcome it would be to obliterate the artwork as such and its allusive capacity, or what Michaels would call its "aboutness." Here Althusser exploits a homonymy where no doubt many are quick to assume a synonymy. When Brecht seeks an alienation effect, this has little relation to the alienation that is the existential condition of labor under capital. To be sure, Althusser suggests that the Brechtian play is one that the spectator completes in life.[11] But it's not that Brecht wants to alienate us in the theater so as to help us realize that we're alienated in real life, thereby desiring to end alienation and reconcile ourselves to ourselves. Rather, the aim is to maintain this discrepancy. For overcoming the alienation effect would mean a return to pure specularity; it would mean overcoming the difference between the artwork and itself and thereby its capacity to allude to ideology, that set of actions and beliefs that produces specific, determinant, and ultimately intelligible consequences.

Reading Capital Today

Though it's probably never been described this way, the desire to render exploitative actions intelligible and hence contestable was at the core of Althusser's rereading of Marx in the early 1960s, which culminated in the *Capital* seminar he hosted at the École Normale Supérieure (ENS) throughout 1965. The collective volume *Lire le Capital* published by Maspero in January 1965 is the central monument of Althusser's effort, and the fiftieth anniversary of its publication is a salutary reminder of that fact in a moment when Althusser's posthumous publications now outnumber those that appeared in his lifetime. Verso's decision to bring out the full edition of *Reading Capital*, with the contributions of Roger Establet, Pierre Macherey, and Jacques Rancière restored to their place alongside Althusser's and Étienne Balibar's, is also to be welcomed. This complete volume gives a stronger sense of the document as a massive work-in-progress staggering in its fecundity and intellectual power. Readers will now have a better grasp of the genealogies of many contemporary projects, not least Rancière's, and will also have the benefit of encountering a work composed before the May events of 1968, which is to say, a work composed at a moment when the reign of capital in the global North (then known as "the West") faced no viable political challenges and its opponents were under no illusions about the kinds of challenges that would be up to the task.[12] The inspiration Althusser and his students found in Chinese developments was more than offset by a sober realism, at least on his part, about the state of political affairs in Europe and the need for a complete rethinking of Marxism as a theoretical and political mode of contestation. In a word,

Althusser returned to Marx in order to develop an interpretation that would make the structures of capitalism visible in a moment when their effects were positively blinding. The confidence Althusser showed in this basically epistemological project might seem strange in the current conjuncture. In its own time it was largely responsible for the charges of Leninism and vanguardism that attended its uneasy reception into the canon of "Western Marxism."

There are many ways that one might revisit *Reading Capital* today. One could pursue its genealogical significance, or attempt to restore its centrality to any plausible interpretation of Althusser's thought. Yet I hope the reason I've begun this chapter with an account of Walter Benn Michaels's contemporary challenge to neoliberal aesthetics is clear enough. Prima facie, Althusser and Michaels have little in common, apart from a weakness for polemic and a tendency toward associative modes of argument. And it would certainly seem unpromising to suggest common ground between the progenitor of "theoretical practice" and the coauthor of "Against Theory." But the fact is that Michaels's current work, along with that of many of his collaborators at the online journal nonsite.org, is conceptually, not to say wittingly, reconvening the set of concerns that motivated Althusser and his collaborators in the 1960s.[13] Such is not so much an argument as a presupposition of this chapter. My point is certainly not to persuade Michaels or anyone else that he's an Althusserian manqué. For one, there are massive historical and contextual discrepancies here. Althusser was laboring after the catastrophe of Stalinism, which was the primary condition for his rereading of Marx. His broadsides against humanism were part and parcel of his rejection of Stalinism. The central provocation of *For Marx* was the idea that Stalinist economism and so-called Marxist humanism were cut from the same cloth insofar as they figured human history as a matter of "essence" to be expressed in time. Any obstacles to this expression were to be eradicated in the Stalinist case, or "overcome," in the more dulcet tones of the humanist vernacular.[14] Yet even here there's an analogy with Michaels's effort insofar as Althusser's challenges to the concept of alienation as a barrier to full self-presence resonate with Michaels's hostility to the unencumbered expression of identity as a goal of political practice in a neoliberal age.

The substance of what follows will focus on the details of Althusser's critique of alienation in his contributions to *Reading Capital* and related writings in order to clarify the rationalism on offer in his work of this period. Much has been written attempting to untangle the skein of "structural causality" at the heart of Althusser's understanding of the mode of production as the preeminent category of historical and political analysis.[15] In particular, attention has focused on how the same set of structural relations that determine our cognitive and experiential capacities can be transformed by acts grounded in those capacities. This discussion naturally opens on to the problem of Spinozist metaphysics in general and its peculiar conception of freedom as a kind of intellectual reconciliation with necessity. The dilemma for Althusser, as for Spinoza, is that the critique of apparent purposiveness at the level of lived experience, the domain of the imaginary, works not to eliminate intentionality but to displace it into so many antecedent "structures." But where Spinoza's structures were unapologetically metaphysical, Althusser's were ostensibly physical—the array of phenomena grouped under the concept of the "mode of production."

The wager here is that a better or at any rate different understanding of Althusser's project is possible if we suspend efforts to seek metaphysical coherence or justification and focus instead on his account of how actions are at once visible as spontaneous, lived phenomena and interpretable as intelligible consequences of specific intersubjective (i.e., social) actions. In Michaels's efforts to rehabilitate the concept of ideology as a name for political conviction he has been explicit about its distinction from the Marxist notion.[16] But there is a connection with the Althusserian framework here insofar as ideology is coded as the site of motivation and of action. Michaels's conception of political ideology works by an appeal to facts that are explicable in terms of the reasons for them; when those reasons are located in human action they become politically contestable. Likewise, the history of the concept of ideology in Althusser's work is in effect understandable as a growing awareness that ideology is the site of political contestation and that any political challenge to capitalism will need to be articulated, promoted, and developed in ideological terms.

In the end, however, there is a significant divergence between these projects that goes beyond historical distance and contextual setting. Michaels describes the discrepancy between capital and labor as structural, which has an Althusserian if not generically Marxist ring to it. Yet his account of intention more or less requires it to be a discrete event located in a discrete individual, which is usually typified by the artist. But, once he departs from the artwork as exemplar, Michaels has no way to link structure and intention conceptually because he has no operative concept of collective action and the idea of collective intention such a concept presupposes. Like Althusser, Michaels rejects the concept of society as a totalizing entity that obscures the discrepancies of inequality.[17] But unlike Althusser, he's uninterested in developing an alternative concept of the "social formation" that would afford a firmer cognitive grasp of such discrepancies. So if there's an analogue between the artist's intention as a condition for the formal unity of the work, on the one hand, and capital's intentions and the formal relation that is economic inequality, on the other, the argument turns on the phenomenon of intention irrespective of the units the term relates. But then it's unclear how capital—a collective action if ever there was one—is intentional. Althusser's project provides resources for how one might regard capital as intentional and hence contestable via equally collective oppositional means. The form of the project turns initially on a rejection of theoretical figures that would serve to obscure capital's strange ontological feature of being at once purely structural and exhaustively intentional. Chief among these figures is that of "alienation."

Against Alienation

It seems any assessment of *Reading Capital*'s method ought to begin with the most notorious apothegm to emerge from it: the *symptomatic reading*. Using Freudian notions filtered through Lacan, Althusser described a symptomatic reading as one that "divulges the undivulged event in the text it reads, and in the same movement relates it to a *different text*, present as a necessary absence in the first" (RCC 27). Subjecting *Capital* to a symptomatic reading was appropriate in Althusser's view because of certain analogies he saw between Marx's "immense theoretical revolution" and Freud's. In both instances, ostensible meaning and action were rendered intelligible in light of a more foundational, structural, and relational set of actions that generated such meaning even as it obscured it.[18] It would be left to Althusser's students to explore these resonances further in the *Cahiers pour l'Analyse*.[19] But for Althusser's purposes in *Reading Capital* the conceptual symmetry between the two frameworks, the psychoanalytic and the historical materialist, was enough to justify the symptomatic reading as a methodological directive.

Yet it must be admitted that the mélange with psychoanalysis creates no small amount of confusion in Althusser's effort. For instance, it's hard to establish any genuine analogy because history is not an appropriate correlate for an individual's life, which is the site of psychoanalytic intervention and explication. In fact, Althusser is committed to a conception of history that would not be understood in developmental or progressive terms. And even if Lacanian psychoanalysis indulges sometimes in a pathos of the event—subjective shatterings that work like so many epistemological breaks in life—its basic schema is teleological and narratological. The psychoanalytic element in Althusser's work was as innovative as it was institutionally contingent, stimulated by Lacan's arrival at the ENS in the year of the *Capital* seminar. But the deeper roots of Althusser's method were located in philosophical rationalism, and a specifically Spinozist rationalism at that. Near the beginning of his introduction to *Reading Capital*, Althusser writes:

> The first man ever to have posed the problem of *reading*, and in consequence, of *writing*, was Spinoza, and he was also the first man in the world to have proposed both a theory of history and a philosophy of the opacity of the immediate. With him, for the first time ever, a man linked together in this way the essence of reading and the essence of history in a theory of the difference between the imaginary and the true. (RCC 15)

The precise meaning of this passage, and in particular the phrase "the opacity of the immediate," is puzzling. Its meaning becomes clearer if we consider it in terms of the broader argument regarding the difference between the work and the object that inheres in every entity that is marked by specific consequences. When Althusser writes that the essence of history and the essence of reading are linked "in a theory of the difference between the imaginary and the true," he is pointing toward the difference—or rather the distance or discrepancy—between the Brechtian play and its conditions, between our experience of it, and what there is in it that makes our knowledge of the conditions it alludes to true. Recall that for Althusser art alludes; the form in this case is not a form of knowledge but allusion or intimation. By contrast, science knows. But the significant point is that art's referent and science's referent are the same referent, approached or limned in different ways.

Althusser's commitment to rationalism involves the possibility that our beliefs can be true or false, which entails the possibility that we can know some things truly. This rationalism is what makes Althusser's project foreign to any poststructuralist pragmatism or deconstructive skepticism. This commitment on Althusser's part is at the heart of the theory of the difference between the imaginary and the true—it is the difference between the domain of experience, which is shaped if not exhausted by your perspective and its position, and what we can know about the conditions that make that experience what it is. The conditions in question here are not those that make experience possible (in a Kantian sense), but that make it what it is in a determinant sense, causes conceived as actions, and vice versa. To know those conditions is to know a set of structural relations, and one can be right or wrong about what one purports to know about them. This kind of knowledge is nothing less than historical knowledge in Althusser's view.[20] Furthermore, this insistence on knowledge in the strong sense is what's at stake in the much maligned distinction between science and ideology, and the effort to effectively develop a science of ideology that would be integral to the science of historical materialism.

The rebus-like relation between history and ideology, where the latter alludes to the former, is already figured in *For Marx*. Here Althusser writes: "The only history possible is that of reality, which may dimly arouse in the sleeper incoherent dreams, but these dreams, whose only continuity is derived from their anchorage in these depths, can never make up a continent of history in their own right."[21] The history is only experienced as dream; but the continent of history discovered by Marxist science, by analogy with the continent of physics discovered by Galileo, is the only reality. The significant point is that this history as reality and history as dream are the same history; there is no way to distinguish them materially. In this, the distinction is not unlike that between the artwork as object and the artwork as artwork. In both cases, the material is the same, as is the physical experience; what matters is whether or not your interpretation or understanding of the material will treat it as given in itself or as consequentially dependent upon a set of determinations. Error occurs when one mistakes this fundamental material sameness for an absence of difference, or distance.

This evaluative difference between material sameness and differential determination is in play in Althusser's effort to distinguish the mature from the young Marx. It is worth parsing a particularly dense passage in order to see how this differentiation works. In "From *Capital* to Marx's Philosophy," Althusser writes:

> The Young Marx of the *1844 Manuscripts* read the human essence at sight, immediately, in the transparency of its alienation. *Capital*, on the contrary, exactly measures a distance and an internal dislocation (*décalage*) in the real, inscribed in its *structure*, a distance and a dislocation such as to make their own effects themselves illegible, and the illusion of an immediate reading of them the ultimate apex of their effects: *fetishism*. (RCC 15)

To say that the young Marx "read the human essence at sight, immediately, in the transparency of its alienation," is to suggest that Marx believed himself to have glimpsed the ultimate reality of the human situation as a site devoid of discrepancy. To be sure Marx materializes Hegel's dialectic, rendering it "concrete" through the mediations of alienated labor. But Althusser's point is to suggest that the way the early Marx framed alienation was as a false problem. To identify alienation as a problem, or indeed as *the* problem, is to believe oneself to be already in possession of the solution to it—hence "the transparency of its alienation." Overcoming alienation means reconciling oneself to oneself, establishing one's self-identity and developing it to its fullest potential. The goal of a political practice aiming to overcome alienation is thereby one focused on removing obstacles to this self-fulfillment. That this is an endless task is in a way beside the point. More troubling is that its achievement would result in a kind of ontological flattening that may resemble science but that would make impossible any space of argument, disagreement, or judgment, precisely in the elimination of discrepancy that makes this space possible, or, more to the point, is this space itself.

Marxist scholarship concerned with Althusser has seen no small amount of handwringing over the fact that he is plainly antiutopian. The lonely hour of the last instance never comes. How to square such a set of commitments with anything recognizable as Marxism? This is the project of *Reading Capital* laid out in the second half of this passage: "*Capital*, on the contrary, exactly measures a distance and an internal dislocation (*décalage*) in the real, inscribed in its *structure*, a distance and a dislocation such as to make their own effects themselves illegible, and the illusion of an immediate reading of them the ultimate apex of their effects: *fetishism*." What does it mean to say that *Capital* measures a distance and dislocation in the real? It is to say that *Capital* works like a Brechtian play, except in an epistemic register rather than an aesthetic one. It takes a set of empirical facts and arranges them so as to make clear the conditions, the structural relations, that make these facts hang together, one after the other. Against ideas associated with Engels and various other materialists who like to play up the analogies with natural science, the entire significance of the claim that *Capital* harbors a new kind of science is bound to its focus on human action, which precisely cannot be explained by the same tools that describe natural phenomena. *That's* why it's a new science; not a new application of science, conceived univocally, but a *new* science. The point is to provide an account of human behavior that doesn't translate it into a species of naturalist causality and nevertheless retains explicative force by focusing on the reasons why people do what they do. And those reasons are to be found in ideology. More precisely those reasons *are* ideology, which means that the science of history entails the science of ideology. Internally differentiated, ideology is a set of material practices and hence purely physical; but it is also why we do what do, and hence essentially motivated.

This explains why Althusser chose a passage from Marx's notebooks on Wagner for the epigraph to "Marxism and Humanism." It reads: "My analytic method does not start from man but from the economically given social period."[22] There is no science of man; of this we can be assured by any number of sources, French or otherwise. But to start with an "economically given social period" is still not to start with a natural phenomenon, much less a metaphysical once. It is to start with facts and structural relations. The dilemma of Marxism and any dialectical project is the relationship between such facts and their relations; which illuminates which? Which has priority? Again, the aim of Althusser's reading is to eliminate the question of dialectical priority and reconciliation in this relation and refigure it as one of ineliminable discrepancy. This is the sense of "inscribed in its *structure*" in the passage cited.[23]

Continuing on, he says it is in the nature of this discrepancy to make its effects illegible. What does this mean? If we take the case of economic inequality we can see all the ways in which it is obscured, and that it succeeds precisely by making its effect illegible. Neoliberal capitalism loves civil rights victories and identity politics because they eliminate barriers to labor flexibility. If you can't discriminate in whom you can exploit, this gives you a lot more people to exploit. To be sure, social justice victories are describable as victories in overcoming alienation; they are victories insofar as they allow selves to express themselves as selves without fear of recrimination. This is all well and good, but it has very little to do with the structure of capital or the fact of inequality. To paraphrase Michaels: although the structural difference between capital and labor cannot be eliminated by any process of "identification," it *can* be imagined out of existence, in which its absence is precisely an imaginary absence. And this imagining out of existence takes the form of an overcoming of alienation. Such is Althusser's meaning when he describes the "illusion of an immediate reading" as "the ultimate apex of their effects: *fetishism.*"

Fetishism involves treating the part as the whole. Put differently, it is to mistake the part for a whole, to think of it as all that is. The fetishist regards the fetish as a unity without any sense of whence the unity is bestowed. But objects don't have unity in themselves, form in themselves. Natural things result from natural processes; others result from actions, actions that function as causes, and are intelligible as causes. In nature, form is ephemeral; in action, form is the goal. A fetishist doesn't appreciate that although actions function as causes, indeed might be objectively indistinguishable from causes in a naturalist vision, they are not "just" causes to the extent that they are endowed with purpose and hence might be explicated with reference to reasons that are contestable as reasons.[24] The "illusion of an immediate reading" results from the loss of a mediate reading that sees the work as two things—an object and a work. And when you lose that distinction you lose the capacity to contest all those things that go into making an object not merely an object but also a work.

Or a use value, rather than simply an exchange value. Capital converts works back into objects; it deprives them of unity, purposes, specificity, in order to reduce them to fungible units of measure. Irreducibility is here belied by the reducibility capital undertakes every day. Such are the theological niceties of the commodity—that it can be both one single thing and two things at once. But the whole point of Marx's effort was to prise this distinction, so as to create a space in which to contest capital, theoretically and politically, to get us to see a difference that must be, indeed can only be, transformed by political action alone. To return to Michaels's line again on the idea that the structural difference between capital and labor cannot be imagined out of existence, we can see the significance of the structural blocking against the imaginary. Racism can, in a way, be imagined out of existence to the extent that people can stop imagining others to be different and recognize their sameness; or instead and more accurately it dissipates when people begin to celebrate such imaginary differences rather than despise them. Such is not an option for the impoverished, or those "damaged" by capital.[25] And yet, the point is that these people are in fact the same insofar as they are people (that is, the same kinds of objects). Whatever the difference is between them is the result of specific actions that can be known, analyzed, and interpreted, with an eye toward eliminating them.

How we *know* this structure is Althusser's primary concern in *Reading Capital* and central to his Spinozist epistemology, which insists that knowledge of the "real" involves no phenomenological transgression of the borders of mind and body or mind and world which might obscure such formal differences. Rather, knowledge is completely internal to thought. He writes: "No doubt there is a relation between *thought*-about-the-real and this *real*, but it is a relation of *knowledge*, a relation of adequacy or inadequacy of knowledge, not a real relation, meaning by this a relation inscribed in *that real* of which the thought is the (adequate or inadequate) knowledge." He then goes on: "The distinction between a relation of knowledge and a relation of the real is a fundamental one: if we did not respect it we should fall irreversibly into either speculative or empiricist idealism" (RCC 233). If one loses this distinction, one loses the distinction between work and object. Objective relations are physical relations. These relations are causal, to be sure, but a physical science seeks to eliminate causal explanations in order to establish lawlike regularity. As a materialist, Althusser has to insist that in some way the world is exhausted by such relations. But as a Marxist, he is committed to the idea that such relations can be transformed by purposive action, which commits him to the idea that reasons are what remain as causes—that is, vectors of determination—once a materialist science converts physical causes into laws. And when we're dealing with the capitalist mode of production we're dealing with a state of affairs in which reasons as causes are integral. And the only way to combat them is with better reasons as causes. A relation of knowledge cannot simply be a relation of the real because only knowledge can discern form as unity—can come to know if not precisely see the invisible form that accounts for the "dynamic unity of internal structure." Such is a condition of intelligibility for Marxist analysis.

For Ideology

One of the confusions of Michaels's recent work, or at any rate an underdeveloped point in it, is the equivocal sense of intention and its relationship to discrete subjects or agents in the case of aesthetics on the one hand and economic inequality on the other. In other words, if we understand the significance of his analysis of the artist's relationship to the artwork, it's hard to see who plays the analogue of the artist in capitalism—the capitalist? The foreman? Hedge fund manager? None of these is quite right. Michaels's point is that seeing action as endowed with purpose is not a matter of knowing those purposes but of recognizing actions as actions rather than mere events. Knowing that they can be known is one thing; knowing them is an altogether different, more arduous affair. In this regard, a serious objection to my comparison between his work and Althusser's is that the purposiveness in structure in the latter case is decidedly that of the capitalist mode of production, and not agents or—perish the thought—the individual, who is more often than not a *Träger* or bearer of suprahistorical forces.[26] For Michaels, it would seem, intention must be indexed to a specific agent or individual. For Althusser, it is the mode of production that orders the whole, however riven or discrepant. Such is the importance of the economic structure as "determinant in the last instance." And in *Reading Capital* he develops this point as follows:

This "determination in the last instance" [by the economic structure] is an absolute precondition for the necessity and intelligibility of the displacements of the structures in the hierarchy of effectivity, or of the displacement of "dominance" between structured levels of the whole; . . . only this "determination in the last instance" makes it possible to escape the arbitrary relativism of observable displacements by giving these displacements the necessity of a function. (RCC 246)

When Althusser writes of "the displacements of the structures in the hierarchy of effectivity," I take him to be saying something along the lines of "what happens." So, what happened in 1917 in Russia? In the first place, there was certainly a displacement of the structures of the hierarchy of effectivity as the army first sided with the peasants when the Tsar ordered them to fire on the bread queues in St. Petersburg in February. This collapse of one repressive state apparatus then led to a more general weakening of the Tsar as a political unit and made clear the fraudulence of the Duma, and on down the hierarchy of effectivity—which I'm tempted to render as the "order of action"—until total collapse, seizure, and transformation in October with the Bolshevik putsch. But how do we avoid an "arbitrary relativism" in our assessment of these observable displacements? In other words, what makes them "intelligible"?

The answer is the economic structure, which is to say the contradictions that arise within the capitalist mode of production and its tenuous relation to other modes of production that compete or obtain alongside it.[27] In light of this, I think we can ultimately split the difference between Althusser and Michaels by recognizing that capitalism, or rather the capitalist mode of production, is supervenient on the actions of capitalists and laborers and the *trans*actions of everyone else (if there is anyone else).[28] No actions, no capitalism. Such a relation is not causal in a mechanical sense, with the base "causing" superstructure. But there is arguably a kind of immanent causality at work, which unites the whole and renders the distribution of parts intelligible. Spinozist metaphysics may be unavoidable after all.

Yet once you take this kind of view, you can reconcile the competing visions of ideology in Althusser's work. To be sure, ideology is ubiquitous—our imaginary state. But since it is unavoidable and inescapable, it is also fated to be the mechanism or milieu in which all motivated action takes place. So ideology produces the subject; but the subject works in ideology. In "Three Notes on the Theory of Discourses," Althusser makes the subject constitutive of ideology, not the other way around. Unless you want to run a very difficult line about the mind's being divided into faculties, the mechanism whereby we imagine differences out of existence is the very same mechanism whereby we articulate our reasons for combatting inequality and demand reasons from others who seek to maintain it. This is why it's so significant that our vision of capital never become naturalized (and why, respectful words notwithstanding, Engels is in many respects one of Althusser's prime targets). Because if capitalist exploitation is a natural state of affairs then we are in no position to ask for reasons—in the sense of justifications—for why it takes place. This view is central to Michaels's own rehabilitation of ideology and its crucial relationship to the possibility of disagreement. In *The Shape of the Signifier,* he writes:

> We do not disagree about what we want—we just want different things; we disagree about what is true, regardless of what we want. Indeed, it is only the idea that something that is true must be true for everyone that makes disagreement between anyone make sense . . . The reason that we cannot appeal to universal truths as grounds for adjudicating our disagreements is just because the idea of truth's universality is nothing but a consequence of our disagreement. The universal does not compel our agreement; it is implied by our disagreement; and we invoke the universal not to resolve our disagreement but to explain the fact that we disagree.[29]

In a footnote, Michaels is even more explicit. He rejects the idea that his position has anything to do with the Habermasian notion of giving "good reasons," opting instead for a Davidsonian position. "Our reasons always seem good to us; that's what makes them our reasons. My commitment is, rather, to the difference between those things (beliefs, interpretations) that seem to us true or false and for which we can give some reasons and those things that require no justification."[30]

It is something like this idea that is in play in Althusser's insistence on the need to take a synchronic view that counters a diachronic, dialectical vision in which all distinction is lost in a necessitarian sequence. A materialist has to be a necessitarian to some degree, but the question is how we conceive this necessity. Althusser's authority is again Spinoza. Referencing Spinoza's injunction to see things *sub specie aeternitatis,* Althusser writes: "*The synchronic is eternity in Spinoza's sense,* or the adequate knowledge of a complex object by the adequate knowledge of its complexity." What does this mean? What is the difference between the adequate knowledges in play here? When Althusser suggests that we only acquire adequate knowledge of a complex object by the adequate knowledge of its complexity he is rejecting all manner of empiricism. A compositional account of the complex object will never elucidate for us the object's complexity. It will just accumulate facts and properties; this is the naturalist mandate. But to know the object's complexity is to know *what makes it complex*, what bestows the unity that is its complexity. Complexity is relative, but relative to what? Other unities, other agglomerates worthy of attention and explication. This complexity goes all the way down. What is inadmissible is for the unity to be explained by a single expressive core or animus; such accounts have the structure of theology in the secularized, Hegelian sense that Althusser is keen to avoid.

Spinoza famously argued that the mind is nothing more than the idea of the body. In this sense, the mind is the complexity of the complex object that is the body. Analogously we might say God is nature's complexity in Spinoza's heretical theology. And exploiting the theology/ideology analogy further, ideology is humanity's complexity, which makes it the terrain on which political contestation must take place. And to orient ourselves in this terrain requires thinking about the nature of our truth claims as essentially disputable yet possibly true. We must consider, that is, how our "science" informs our "ideology." Where Michaels's work is allusive in its gestures toward inequality, Althusser's work, and especially the *Reading Capital* project, gives us a wealth of resources that might help us to *know* something more about the structures that are inscribed in and condition the art that is Michaels's concern and much else besides. Althusser agrees with Michaels avant la lettre on the essential aboutness of art, its allusive capacity that is lost when it is no longer regarded as an artwork endowed with unity. But Althusser thinks that such a structure is at work as well in our cognitive claims about economic inequality. His aim is to make such claims as strong as they can be, hence the scandalous brief for Marxist science as the science of historical materialism and Marxist philosophy as the theory of theoretical practice.

A final question remains concerning the place of *Reading Capital* in Marxism, and in particular Althusser's understanding or "reading" of Marx. With various ebbs and flows, for fifty years Althusser's grasp of Marx has been challenged, starting with Althusser himself whose *Essays in Self-Criticism* made pathetic apologies for his wayward theoreticism. In particular, the idea of an epistemological break between the young and the mature Marx has been recused on a variety of grounds. But as *Reading Capital* becomes a historical document, rather than a "living" one, it opens itself to a new reading, one less concerned with scoring points in a sectarian enterprise. Given its status as a historical document that repays reading, we can forgive it its infelicities, or its philological dubiousness. Above all we can concern ourselves less with the possibility that Althusser might be wrong about Marx. Of course such contestation is still possible, just like my understanding of Althusser in this chapter is contestable (in fact, that's partly my point). But it's worth considering to what extent Althusser, in challenging the place of alienation in Marxist thought, and thereby quite possibly getting something about Marx wrong, may have gotten something else right. And if the reason we spend so much time talking about inequality these days is because we recognize it as a problem that demands a political solution, questions of what properly counts as Althusserian or indeed Marxist start to seem not simply sectarian, but petty. At its heart, Althusser's effort in *Reading Capital* sought to separate the wheat from the chaff in a specific inheritance and committed itself so thoroughly to getting a better understanding of the truth of inequality and how we come to know it that, despite itself, it became indifferent to the authority of its sources. There are worse lessons for those seeking an end to exploitation today.

Notes

1. The epigraph is from Louis Althusser and Étienne Balibar, *Reading Capital*, trans. Ben Brewster (1968; reprint, London: Verso, 1997), 171. First published at nonsite.org in 2011 as "Neoliberal Aesthetics: Fried, Rancière and the Form of the Photograph," the article reappears with minimal revisions as the second chapter in Walter Benn Michaels, *The Beauty of a Social Problem: Photography, Autonomy, Economy* (Chicago: University of Chicago Press, 2015), 43–70, 67. References will be to this version.

2. In 1967, Michael Fried published "Art and Objecthood," which challenged the emergent "literalism" in art in the name of a modernism that insisted on art's ontological distinction from mere objects capable of causing experiences in a more or less physical or at any rate unmediated sense. Fried's later historical work on absorption and theatricality reconfigured this dyad in multiple ways, discussion of which is beyond the purview of this chapter. But the denigration of theatricality as an artistic comportment aiming to achieve unavoidable effects was consistent with the anathema ascribed to objecthood in his early work. See Michael Fried, *Art and Objecthood* (Chicago: University of Chicago Press, 1998), and *Absorption and Theatricality: Painting and Beholder in the Age of Diderot* (Chicago: University of Chicago Press, 1980).

3. See W. J. T. Mitchell, ed., *Against Theory: Literary Studies and the New Pragmatism* (Chicago: University of Chicago Press, 1985), which anthologizes Steven Knapp and Walter Benn Michaels's "Against Theory" (1982) and various responses

to it. More recently, see Walter Benn Michaels, *The Shape of the Signifier: 1967 to The End of History* (Princeton, NJ: Princeton University Press, 2004), and *The Trouble with Diversity: How We Learned to Love Identity and Ignore Inequality* (New York: Metropolitan Books, 2006).

4. Louis Althusser, *For Marx* (1965), trans. Ben Brewster (London: Verso, 2005), 146.

5. Cf. Jennifer Ashton, "Poetry and the Price of Milk," nonsite.org, Issue 10, "Affect, Effect, Bertolt Brecht," September 2013, http://nonsite.org/article/poetry-and-the-price-of-milk.

6. Althusser, *For Marx*, 146–47.

7. Louis Althusser, *On Ideology* (London: Verso, 2008), 174.

8. The key text here is "Three Notes on the Theory of Discourses," an unpublished working document that Althusser circulated among his students and collaborators in 1966, reprinted in Louis Althusser, *The Humanist Controversy and Other Writings*, ed. François Matheron, trans. G. M. Goshgarian (London: Verso, 2003), 33–84.

9. Althusser, *The Humanist Controversy*. The first two notes witness Althusser trying to integrate Lacan's project with his own nascent rereading of Marx around a theory of the difference between regional and general theories. Here the interpellative nature of ideology as producing "subject-effects" is emphasized, as is the need to think of how other discourses, e.g., the scientific, produce their own kinds of "subject-effect." In the third note, however, Althusser writes: "I have come around to thinking that *the notion of subject cannot be employed unequivocally*, not even as an index for each of the discourses. Increasingly, the notion of subject seems to me to pertain to *ideological* discourse alone, of which it is constitutive" (77). This remarkable reversal has been insufficiently remarked. Here Althusser makes clear that political action is a wholly ideological affair, for which the subject is constitutive. The challenge is how to integrate this idea with Althusser's equally strong conviction that a scientific discourse produces genuine knowledge about its object, in this case the capitalist mode of production.

10. See Jacques Lacan, *Seminar XI: The Four Fundamental Concepts of Psychoanalysis*, ed. Jacques-Alain Miller, trans. Alan Sheridan (New York: W. W. Norton, 1977), 20–22. Here Lacan distinguishes "cause" from "law," as something that produced effects and invites and confounds explanation at the same time. Lawlike regularity invites no interpretative effort, since "il n'y a de cause que de ce qui cloche" (or, as the English translation has it, "there is cause only in something that doesn't work").

11. Althusser, *For Marx*, 151.

12. Louis Althusser, Étienne Balibar, Roger Establet, Pierre Macherey, and Jacques Rancière, *Reading Capital: The Complete Edition*, trans. Ben Brewster and David Fernbach (London: Verso, 2016), 480. All further references will be given in the text.

13. In addition to Michaels, regular contributors include Jennifer Ashton, Todd Cronan, Ruth Leys, Adolph Reed, and many others. The website's "about" page tells us "nonsite.org emerges in part out of interest in a set of theoretical topics—the ontology of the work of art, the question of intentionality, the ongoing appeal of

different and sometimes competing materialisms—and in part out of opposition to the dominant accounts of those topics." Avant-garde in aspiration, the journal pursues a strong ideological line largely oriented around Michaels's and Fried's interventions, past and present. For a related and brilliantly executed critique of affect theory, see Ruth Leys, "The Turn to Affect: A Critique," *Critical Inquiry* 37 (spring 2011): 434–72.

14. I pursue this argument in Knox Peden, *Spinoza contra Phenomenology: French Rationalism from Cavaillès to Deleuze* (Stanford, CA: Stanford University Press, 2014), 134ff.

15. Gregory Elliott, *Althusser: The Detour of Theory* (1987; reprint, Leiden: Brill, 2006), is the classic account, but it has recently been supplemented by Warren Montag, *Althusser and His Contemporaries: Philosophy's Perpetual War* (Durham, NC: Duke University Press, 2013). See Montag, *Althusser and His Contemporaries*, 73–100, for an illuminating analysis of the differences between the 1965 and 1968 editions of *Reading Capital*, which turned on Macherey's challenges to Althusser's conception of structural causality.

16. Michaels, *The Shape of the Signifier*, 186n16.

17. See Michaels, *The Beauty of a Social Problem*, 105–52, in particular the discussion of August Sander's photography of the "social order" at 129ff.

18. Michaels noted in his first monograph that the ingenuity of psychoanalysis was not to undermine intention with irrationality but to relocate intention in psychic domains previously thought to be unintelligible. See "Action and Accident: Photography and Writing," in Walter Benn Michaels, *The Gold Standard and the Logic of Naturalism: American Literature at the Turn of the Century* (Berkeley: University of California Press, 1987), 217–44.

19. See Peter Hallward and Knox Peden, eds., *Concept and Form, I: Key Texts from the* Cahiers pour l'Analyse (London: Verso, 2012).

20. As Althusser famously remarked: "The knowledge of history is no more historical than the knowledge of sugar is sweet" (RCC 253). For a recent assessment of Althusser's contribution to historical thought, which emphasizes its antigeneticism, see Joshua Kates, "Against the Period," *differences* 23, no. 2 (2012).

21. Althusser, *For Marx*, 30.

22. Althusser, *For Marx*, 219.

23. It remains the case that in the distinction between the "means of production" and the "relations of production," Althusser regarded the latter as primary. Such was not the least of the contrasts with G. A. Cohen's analytic Marxism, which reversed this priority and which otherwise shared with Althusser's project the principle that class is not a matter of experience or identity but of structure and relation. See G. A. Cohen, *Karl Marx's Theory of History: A Defence* (Princeton, NJ: Princeton University Press, 1978), 73–77. Cf. Grahame Lock, "Louis Althusser and G. A. Cohen: A Confrontation," *Economy and Society* 17, no. 4 (1988): 499–517.

24. The locus classicus for the argument that reasons can be construed as causes and hence human behavior can be construed in ways commensurable with, if not

assimilable to, the natural sciences, is Donald Davidson's "Actions, Reasons, and Causes" (1962), in Donald Davidson, *Essays on Actions and Events*, 2nd ed. (Oxford: Oxford University Press, 2001), 3–19. Aligning aspects of Davidson's rationalism alongside Althusser's might seem implausible, until one considers the affiliation for Spinoza in both cases. The resonance between these rationalisms has gone largely unremarked but for a footnote Žižek penned in 1991 that suggested Davidson's semantic concept of truth is "strictly homologous to that of Louis Althusser." Slavoj Žižek, *For They Know Not What They Do: Enjoyment as a Political Factor*, 2nd ed. (London: Verso, 2008), 226n24. In "Against the Period," Kates cites Davidson in a note, but positions his "analytic holism" alongside Heidegger's. By and large Davidson's rationalism is what accounts for the trouble otherwise sympathetic scholars have had incorporating his work into a broadly hermeneutic enterprise. Cf. Jeff Malpas, ed., *Dialogues with Davidson: Acting, Interpreting, Understanding* (Cambridge, MA: MIT Press, 2011).

25. James Agee and Walker Evans's classic *Let Us Now Praise Famous Men* (1941; reprint, London: Penguin Books, 2006) is a crucial document for Michaels, not least for the way it treats the difference in aesthetic capacity between the Alabama sharecroppers that are the subject of Agee and Evans's work and the producers and consumers of the work as one that is not really a difference at all in a significant cultural sense, but rather a consequence of the sharecroppers' being "an appallingly damaged group of beings," damaged, that is, by the exploitative relations and conditions of capitalism. See Agee and Evans, *Let Us Now Praise Famous Men*, 5, and Michaels, *The Beauty of a Social Problem*, 60–62, 109–48.

26. There are exceptions. In his 1976 memoir, "The Facts," Althusser remarks on the inspiration he drew from his friend Jacques Martin's description of communism as a situation "in which there are no longer human beings, but individuals." Louis Althusser, *The Future Lasts Forever* (New York: New Press, 1993), 328.

27. See "Contradiction and Overdetermination," in Althusser, *For Marx*, 94ff.

28. The concept of supervenience is a prevalent and increasingly debated one in philosophy of mind and analytic metaphysics. Coined by Davidson, but borrowed from G. E. Moore, it figures centrally in the work of David Lewis, David Chalmers, and other analytic luminaries. See, inter alia, David J. Chalmers, *The Conscious Mind: In Search of a Fundamental Theory* (Oxford: Oxford University Press, 1996). The key idea is that a relation of supervenience between A and B obtains—that is, A supervenes on B—when there cannot be a change in the properties of A without a corresponding change in the properties of B, but not necessarily vice versa. This is often used to describe the relation between mind and brain; mind supervenes on brain in the sense that any change of property of the former must rely on one in the latter. A familiar example to illustrate the phenomenon is newsprint. Any image in a newspaper supervenes on the dots it comprises, which means you cannot change the image without changing the arrangement of the dots.

29. Michaels, *The Shape of the Signifier*, 31.

30. Michaels, *The Shape of the Signifier*, 188n16.

PART II

Reading Capital in Context

CHAPTER 5

A Point of Heresy in Western Marxism

Althusser's and Tronti's Antithetic Readings

of *Capital* in the Early 1960s

ÉTIENNE BALIBAR

To reread *Lire le Capital* today takes us back to a time long passed—the beginning of my intellectual life, in fact—with which I would have difficulties now to communicate, if it were not for two reasons, which perhaps are not independent.[1] The first is a current renewed interest in the work and thinking of Althusser, which is partly fostered by the publication of many posthumous texts, offering a very different image from the one that had been registered by historians of ideas in the aftermath of his death. The second is that Marxism as a philosophical and political discourse, but particularly Marx, author of *Das Kapital*, the "critic" of political economy, enjoys a new popularity in the context of one of the most brutal crises of capitalism in the last decades, affecting the whole world, albeit not everywhere in the same forms and to the same degree. At an intersection of these phenomena, there is, understandably, a curiosity for the kind of "revision" or "reconstruction" of Marxism that was attempted by Althusser and a group of young scholars around him, earning them at the time an enormous reputation, raising considerable hopes and provoking equally virulent objections and rejections. Perhaps to return to all this today with a critical eye could be a fruitful way to once again assess the powers and limitations of Marxism in a different conjuncture, to learn how to use it and not to use it, to measure which openings are worth reviving, and which interpretations are closed. If done in that spirit it would not be only a piece of antiquarian history.

Certainly I claim no "coauthor's" privilege in assessing the contemporary relevance of these texts from half a century ago, but I cannot really abstract from the fact that I was directly associated to the framing and the realization of the seminar out of which the book *Reading Capital* emerged, and it is true that until today I have kept ruminating many of the questions and formulations proposed in the seminar and the book.[2] All this makes it less simple (or more challenging) for me to speak here than simply saying: here is what it was, and here is where I stand today. A first difficulty comes from the fact that I am not really a contemporary of the formulations and ideas expressed by Althusser himself in *Reading Capital*. Although Althusser had an extraordinary capacity to share ideas with others, neutralizing as it were the hierarchies of age and erudition, and a real need to transform a personal project into a collective endeavor, against the background of shared commitments and interests, I, like other participants in the group, had an extremely partial perception of what his intentions exactly were, where they came from, and how they had reached a certain point of problematization. On the contrary, I took many assumptions for granted, and I embarked on illustrating what I thought was the right track. Of course Althusser did not discourage me, because in a sense he was carrying an experiment *in vivo* on the young generation which he thought could regenerate "theory" and as a consequence also "politics." It took me years before I could really consider these assumptions, and then we were already in a different conjuncture, where many axioms had been displaced or even reversed. On the other hand, as is well-known, Althusser himself soon declared that much of *Reading Capital* was to be rejected, or radically reformulated, for reasons which were partially good (having to do with the fact that, in theory as in any practice, *on s'avance et puis on voit*—meaning that you need to say and write something which you think in order to really understand its meaning and adjust or correct it). But other reasons were extremely bad, since they were associated with violent pressure from institutions and people from which he could not even think of dissociating himself, amounting to a kind of blackmail before which, clearly, he sometimes bowed, or which in any case barred the road toward developing some of his initial intuitions. This gave rise to different layers of self-criticism.[3] They had destructive dimensions with respect to the more original of his first claims in the field of theory, but also, interestingly, contained stubborn reiterations of these claims in a somewhat different perspective. The situation is rendered more complex by the fact that, in the posthumous publications, there has now emerged a whole layer of repressed thoughts, which probably were not entirely constituted at the time of *Reading Capital*, but are not alien to its preoccupations, forming a latent counterpoint to the published text without which its intentions in fact could only become misinterpreted. Acute readers like Emilio de Ípola call this in Straussian manner the opposition between the esoteric and the exoteric Althusser.[4] Warren Montag in what is arguably the best book published on Althusser recently calls it his internal war. So if we want to try and assess the meaning and interest of the ideas expressed in *Reading Capital*, whose influence still looms large in the history of ideas, we can neither completely ignore the self-criticisms and the posthumous revelations, nor embark on a teleological reading whose implicit assumptions would be that the posterior developments (or developments revealed a posteriori) represent the truth after which *Reading Capital* must be measured. We must look for a more polyphonic method of reading.

It is in part to handle these difficulties, but also to address the articulation between Althusser's text in *Reading Capital* and its conjuncture in a more objective form, that I have chosen a specific form of historicization of Althusser's "intervention," consisting of a parallel reading of his discourse and that of Mario Tronti, the leading figure of the Operaista school in Italy, during exactly the same period. I believe that the sharp contrast but also some symmetry and affinity will reveal the choices that a "critical" Marxist philosophical project was facing in the years 1960 to 1965–66, therefore also the presuppositions they may have had in common.[5] This is what I call *à la Foucault* a "point of heresy," which as always I take to be the core of any intellectual work. Althusser's two books: *For Marx*, collecting essays from 1961 to 1965, and *Reading Capital*, cowritten with some of his students, were published in the fall of 1965. Tronti's major work, *Operai e capitale* (still incompletely translated into English), was published in 1966: it contained essays from 1962 to 1964 followed by a central unpublished piece from '65 (a later edition in 1971 added a new series of texts).[6] So the two works belong to the period of the "thaw" which follows "destalinization" in the communist parties (of which Althusser and Tronti were both members, each in his country), and precede the '68 upheaval (at least for the main texts, in Tronti's case).[7] In this way I hope to be able to propose at the same time a situation and a decentering of Althusser's discourse.

My thesis will be that we are presented here with two antithetic ways of understanding the necessity of a "Leninist" reading of Marx himself, which was also a transformation of Marx, or rather a *countertransformation*, since it aimed at undoing the transformations that Marx's theory had undergone as a party ideology in the Second and Third Internationals (with all their differences). But one of them, as we know, leads to emphasizing the (relative) *autonomy of theory*, notwithstanding the "revolutionary" character conferred upon it, whereas the other leads to emphasizing the *autonomy of politics*, or working-class politics, even if it is not to be confused with what the same Tronti will propose under this name a few years later.[8] The fact is, nevertheless, that the two "choices" partially rely on the same identification of adversaries, what we may call generically *historicism*, and localize the critical developments of Marx in much the same places of the exposition of *Capital*.

Before I come to this comparison, in a partial manner of course, I need to propose some historical considerations, because the world in which we are now thinking and discussing is a completely different world. Sometimes I have the feeling that a curtain of oblivion and denial has been pulled down toward the end of the "short twentieth century," hiding from our view a whole history as well as a language. The age to which the Marxist elaborations of Tronti and Althusser belonged was the "Age of Extremes," as Eric Hobsbawm has called it.[9] But more precisely it was the age of "communism," as a form of political activity centered on the construction and vicissitudes of the *"professional" revolutionary party*, in the form created by Lenin and the Bolsheviks during and just after the October Revolution in 1917, which was then expanded to the whole world, particularly Europe, in the early 1920s, then split along the dividing lines of the socialist-capitalist confrontation and the Cold War, between the radically different functions of exercising power in the "East" or challenging capitalism from the inside in the "West" (and the "South"), but always unified by a certain doctrine (that of the "dictatorship of the proletariat," despite its many "heresies") and a certain principle of organization (that of so-called democratic centralism, despite its many "crises"). This age lasted until the late 1970s or early 1980s, even if officially it was brought to an end only in the early 1990s. Althusser and Tronti both were and remained members of the Communist Party, with more or less decided marks of independence with respect to the official line. Moreover, they belonged to the only two countries of Western Europe where communism was organized as a mass ideology and could be seen as an explicit challenge to the power of the bourgeoisie. What they dreamed of with more or less lucidity was a renovation of the existing organizations with the help of external and internal elements, for which they wanted to gather forces, essentially recruited among students and intellectuals in the case of Althusser, among a new generation of working-class militants joined by radical Marxist intellectuals in the case of Tronti. Their thinking is certainly *not reducible* to the circle of ideas gathered around the idea of the Communist Party as the revolutionary force of history, if only because (as for many other intellectuals in the twentieth century), they combined the Marxist and Leninist legacy with a philosophical, aesthetic, and political culture which had also quite different sources. But it would not be *understandable*, and in fact it would make no sense outside of that tradition, to which also belong Lukács, Mao, or Gramsci (I name those who, for different reasons, seem most important to understand Althusser or Tronti). What I submit is that Althusser's and Tronti's theoretical productions in the early 1960s express the last moment in which communist discourse, combining "theory" and "politics," was produced *as such* in a creative manner by party intellectuals, provided they gained or imposed some distance with respect to the official elaborations, while remaining attached to the organization. I do not say that they were the only ones, not even in their own countries (with wide differences from that viewpoint between France and Italy). But in order to better understand this situation, a quick supplement to the former periodization is needed.

Clearly, the history of communism in the twentieth century can be divided along two major lines: geopolitically, between the two "camps" of socialism in one or several countries, where a Communist Party is in power, exercising the "dictatorship of the proletariat," and capitalism, with its own internal divides (which indeed from our current perspective appear no less radical); and chronologically, between the prewar and the postwar period, the first being marked (especially in Europe) by the "triangular" confrontation between communism, fascism, and liberalism, and the second by the Cold War and its aftermath, the progressive globalization of capitalism (which leads to the defeat of communist internationalism), and the achievement of decolonization (whose orientation toward one camp or the other, after a series of violent confrontations, was perhaps the decisive historical factor). It is in the first phase (the prewar period) that *the two typical "tactics"* of communist revolution in the twentieth century were successively tried by the Komintern, and theoretically elaborated: namely the "class against class" tactics, and the "popular front" tactics.[10] But it is in the second period, after the death of Stalin, or more precisely after 1956,[11] when the political perversion of the regime of state socialism was revealed by the Khrushchev report, but also the Hungarian uprising and its violent suppression, *and* a new wave of working-class and anti-imperialist struggles had begun, that the question for the communist militants and intellectuals really became that of "revolution within the revolution" (to borrow and expand Regis Debray's felicitous formula). This means at the same time a capacity to restore a revolutionary agenda, for the transformation of capitalism, out of the political stalemate and the "equilibrium of terror" imposed by the Cold War after 1945, and a capacity to propose an internal critique of the dogmatism and political opportunism that dominated the communist parties before and after destalinization. "Revolution in the revolution" was sought for by Marxists—both within and outside the official communist organizations—in many different ways, involving a more or less radical revision of the Marxist, and especially the Leninist heritage, a critique of the party form itself and its mimetic relationship to the state, a reworking of the distinction between reformism and revolution, and so on. To be sure, Althusser and Tronti are only a small part of that moment, and I am claiming no privilege for them. Rather, what I suggest is that they illustrated a relatively special case, being both Leninists (although not referring to the same aspects of Lenin's doctrine, therefore also highlighting in retrospect its internal complexity), and both drawing on the potentialities of those "tactics" defined in the previous period by the Komintern, albeit *not the same* (therefore testifying for the fact that these two tactics retained a transhistorical capacity to become revived in different conjunctures). Essentially, what I want to argue is that Tronti's *operaismo* can be considered a rebirth of the "class against class" tactics, which had dramatically collapsed in its confrontation with European (and non-European) fascism, but would seem relevant again now that fascism had been defeated and replaced (particularly in Italy) by advanced forms of "planned" capitalism. Symmetrically, I will argue that Althusser's *structural Marxism* (a name that he quickly disowned, but for which his admission of *theoreticism*, whether "deviant" or not, can be considered as a code name), was embedded in the tradition of the "Popular Front" tactics, not only in its French, but in its European and extra-European varieties (for which the question of "complexity" of the class structures and class conflicts is especially relevant). This point, I believe, is important if we want to trace back and assess the *intellectual genealogies* within Marxism, which help understanding the constitution of Althusser's and Tronti's conceptual apparatus. Apart from Lenin and also indeed Stalin (whose very strong but ambiguous influence on Althusser can be retrieved not only in the form of explicit references, but above all in his continuous insistence on the duality of "historical materialism" and "dialectical materialism" as the two "disciplines" or "sciences" forming Marxism, until the latter was eventually blown up in his proclamation of "aleatory materialism," which of course cannot leave the former unchanged), the two important names are indeed Lukács and Gramsci. Throughout his career, Althusser is a consistent anti-Lukácsian, focusing his critique on the ultra-Hegelian notion of the Proletariat as the "subject-object of history," whereas Tronti, albeit certainly not an "orthodox" Lukácsian (if this formula makes sense), remains consistently attached to ideas and questions which clearly originate in *History and Class-Consciousness*, whether it is the idea that "capital" as a totality is an inverted or alienated expression of the productivity of social labor, or the idea that the revolutionary party is identical with the negativity of the class itself.[12] As for Gramsci, even with the proviso that what is mainly attacked by Tronti is an official version of his thought calibrated and institutionalized by Togliatti, he is clearly understood by the *operaisti* as the main source in Marxism of a historicist and "populist" deviation, therefore also a form of idealism, whereby the revolutionary function of the working class becomes transferred to the "people" or the "historical bloc" of the popular classes, and the revolution against capital becomes understood as a repetition, a continuation, or a radicalization of the "bourgeois revolution"—which may also involve that in certain conditions (marked by backward and uneven development of the modern state and the national unity), the working class undertakes to realize what the bourgeoisie was unable to achieve. For Althusser the situation is more complicated, and more ambivalent, because a trajectory in his thought that leads from the essays in *For Marx* to the posthumous volume *Machiavelli and Us* and other texts from the 1970s, through the well-known essay on "ideological state apparatuses," clearly shows how deeply concerned he had been throughout his life with rethinking, improving, displacing the Gramscian articulation of structure and superstructure, the respective "hegemonies" of the bourgeois class and the proletariat, or the necessity of a "politics of ideology."[13] But on the other hand the central essay in *Reading Capital*, to which I will return, includes a virulent critique of Gramsci's "historicism" (which is also Tronti's main target), presented as a mere transposition in Marxist terms of a Hegelian philosophy of history as a "becoming subject of substance," or a reading of the dialectics of consciousness as realization of social *praxis*. Perhaps the best interpretation—apart from tactical considerations linked to the controversies between the French and Italian Communist Parties, where the "reception" and use of the work of Gramsci played a non-negligible role—would be to acknowledge that Althusser's sharp criticism of Gramsci does not result from absolute incompatibility, but on the contrary, from the fact that he sees him as the only Marxist (with the possible exception of Mao) with whom he shares a problem of the "overdetermination" of historical contradictions and conflicts, although he wants to propose a different philosophical (and perhaps also political) solution of the problem.[14] All this, it seems to me, makes sense if we admit, at least as a working hypothesis, that Lukács's early work (which he was forced to immediately disavow, as we know) provided the most rigorous and ambitious philosophical foundation for a "class against class" vision of history (before it became implemented by the Komintern in the catastrophic form of a "friend/enemy" dichotomy, whereby the social-democratic organizations were deemed to be as dangerous as fascism itself for the labor movement); whereas, on the other side, Gramsci's *Prison Notebooks*, written in the desperate hope of rallying the Komintern to a strategy of antifascist unity before it was eventually adopted in a controlled manner, were also aiming at providing the idea of "Popular Front" with a Marxist foundation in order to make it, not a simple tactical move in the conjuncture of resistance against fascism, but a genuine political and cultural form of the "transition" toward communism from within capitalism itself.[15] In this sense, if my suggestion is correct, Tronti's post-Lukácsian transposition of the idea of class negativity into the conditions of Keynesian neocapitalism, and Althusser's critical engagement with Gramsci's notion of a "historical bloc" that is constructed in the interplay of structure and superstructure, illustrate symmetric returns to the previous history of twentieth-century communism with the hope of "leaping" beyond their historical and theoretical limitations.

I shall now select some specific elements in Althusser's and Tronti's quasi-simultaneous readings of *Capital*, in order to illustrate my idea of the "point of heresy." It is interesting that they almost never refer to one another. But the fact is that they had identified exactly the same development in Marx as a place where a *critique* of political economy becomes independent of its conditions of possibility in the "bourgeois" discourse (or in the "self-consciousness" of capitalism). This is the section in Marx's *Capital* that concerns "wages" (*Capital*, vol. 1, part 6), a development seldom discussed in commentaries of the book because it seems either simply empirical or an anticipation of more complete developments on the distribution of revenues and the constitution of classes which "logically" would belong to a later moment of the theory.[16] Here, as in other passages of the book where Marx discusses the importance of a terminological shift from the idea of a contractual relationship between capitalists and wage laborers, which takes the form of "selling" and "buying" labor at a "just" or "normal" price, to the idea that this form is a juridical coverage for an incorporation of the *labor power* of the workers into the production process of capital, what is at stake is the relationship between the *appearance* (or "phenomenon") of capitalist relations (in German *Erscheinung*) and the *illusion* or *mystification* that it produces for its own agents (in German *Schein*—note the explicit reminiscence of the Kantian critique of dialectical categories). Both Althusser and Tronti share the idea that this is the turning point in the analysis of *Das Kapital*. They indeed agree that it is through a metamorphosis of the economic problematic of wages as a price of labor into a problematic of the appropriation of the labor power of the workers that the "secret" of the extraction of surplus value—therefore the "secret" of the capitalist form of exploitation and accumulation—can be revealed. For Althusser, this is the moment which best illustrates the practice of "symptomatic reading" that he attributes to Marx as a critical method of reversing the ideological presuppositions of classical political economy and producing a new scientific "object" out of the deconstruction of the old one—perhaps also it is the moment where Marx's epistemological break appears unfinished, or needs to be permanently reasserted, since Marx himself is not consistent in the recognition of the two discourses as incompatible.[17] For Tronti, this is the place where the idea of the "double character of labor," which is the root of the Marxian deduction of the forms of exchange and value, in fact reverses its meaning: instead of abstractly referring antithetic aspects of the commodity (use value and exchange value) to hypothetic characters of labor which respectively "produce" them (concrete labor and abstract or social labor), it shows that *abstract labor is concretely incorporated into capital* in the form of a class of interchangeable, homogeneous workers or labor powers, therefore it is surplus value that commands the production of value, not the reverse, although this social process is concealed under the appearance of a contractual relationship that binds individual workers to individual capitalists. To redress this appearance also has the meaning of highlighting a difference between two types of conflict: one simply relative, which regards the negotiation of wages, their fluctuations with respect to a distribution of revenues in society, another one which can be said absolute, because it regards the violence forever inherent in the transformation of labor into a "productive factor" in the accumulation of capital.[18]

From this point we can move in different directions which illustrate the increasing gap that separates the consequences derived from the *same* strategic choice of the point of application of the critique of political economy. Allow me to briefly comment on two of them, which we may call methodological and substantial. The methodological consequence has to do with the use of the category *ideology*. Since it is well-known that Althusser's discussion of this category has evolved over time, I limit myself to the doctrine that was presented in *Reading Capital*. We must pay attention not only to formal definitions, but also to the examples that are invoked, or the applications that are made of the category. For both authors it is essentially a negative category (although we know that, for Althusser, there is also a *primary process* of ideological recognition and misrecognition, which we might call anthropological, accounting for the fact that there can be no such thing in history as a society "without ideology"). And it is also deeply critical with respect of the existing labor movement. In fact, for both authors, the dominant form of ideology against which the Marxian critique of the wage labor form must be reasserted is a combination of economic calculation (or, in the case of Tronti, planning) and "humanist" discourse of justice that blurs or differs the class structure of the production process. This is the core of the dominant bourgeois ideology that has become reiterated from within the labor movement (including Stalin's anticipations of today's discourse of "human capital": "Man, the most valuable capital"). It is also interesting to notice that, for Althusser, the most disturbing aspect of this ideological domination seems to refer to the fact that, increasingly, the capitalist and the socialist societies speak the same discourse of competition and efficiency—which seems to justify the idea of a "convergence" of politically heterogeneous systems, based on economic and technological necessities, that was very fashionables in the years of the "peaceful coexistence" between East and West.[19] Whereas for Tronti the strategic aspect lies in the fact that the labor movement has become tendentially the main "organizer" of capitalist production itself, or the conscious "agent" of the "plan of capital," that is, a development of capitalist production where the conflicts over redistribution, however acute they can become, are essentially instrumental to implement a "common" project of economic growth and the increased productivity of labor, and become the cornerstone of a new development of the state as a "social state"—which is basically the function of Keynesian economics and Fordist "compromise" elaborated after the American New Deal and the European victory of democratic forces over fascism.[20]

From this we may derive the great divergence between two "critiques of ideology," which arise from a confrontation between the theory of *Capital* as a "critique of political economy" and the conjuncture of the development of reformism within Marxist organizations themselves. One which sees "ideology" essentially as the other of a *scientific analysis* of capitalist exploitation, or which confers to "science" in the last instance the function of revealing the roots of ideological mystifications, and one which sees "ideology" essentially as the other of *political realism*, a political and intellectual attitude which is able to identify the core of irreducible antagonism in the relations of production, however mediated it can appear in circumstances of class compromise, by referring to a destruction of the illusions of a "common interest" that the class struggle itself is bound to produce. This leads us to understand that, where Althusser believes that the "appearances" of capitalist circulation and the fetishism of commodities essentially conceal a *structure* of which they are the inevitable effects (without which the structure could not work), Tronti believes that the same appearances essentially conceal an *antagonism* which they serve to differ and postpone, but which is bound to cyclically return and explode in the open, because it is necessary for production itself. The structure is the essential object of Althusserian theory—or, better said, it is the essential *problem*, which calls for an infinite analysis in the field of theory. Whereas antagonism is the essential situation in which a political practice can become revolutionary: accordingly for Tronti the question that commands the very possibility of a revolutionary practice is to identify a place, or a "site," where social conflicts become antagonistic. Of course, since they are both Marxists, Althusser's structure is a structure of antagonism, or class conflict, just as Tronti's antagonism is "structural" or continuously reproduced with the capitalist domination itself, but the different ordering of categories, as I suggested, opens a gap that becomes wider and wider.

This is the "substantial" element which corresponds to the methodological divergence. Indeed both Althusser and Tronti are led to highlight the importance of another crucial passage in *Capital* (in the chapter on "simple reproduction" in volume 1), where Marx concludes his phenomenology of the modalities of class struggles associated with different methods of extracting surplus value, and opens his discussion of the "laws" (or tendencies) of capitalist accumulation by asserting that capitalist production not only produces commodities or surplus value, but also continuously reproduces the *social relations of production themselves*.[21] "Structure" and "antagonism" are in a sense the two sides of the very notion of the "relations of production," which is the central notion of Marx's *Capital* (defining its "object," in Althusser's terms). But the fact of reading them in reverse order leads to completely divergent identifications of the point where an apparent stability (or "eternity") of the capitalist social form can become challenged or destabilized: in Althusser's case, it is essentially in the *superstructural conditions* of the "reproduction" of the relations of production, whereas in Tronti it is essentially in the possibility that the antagonism rises to an extreme "life or death" confrontation (as Marx himself had written with a different purpose in his chapter on *machinery*) within the production process itself, more precisely within the factory, which forms its material site.[22]

On this basis, I would like to indicate a second point of heresy, where, again, the theoretical dimensions are permeated with political implications. This is the question of *totality*, as a philosophical category but also as a scheme for the articulation of history and political action, or agency. Simply formulated, as we probably all know, the antithesis arises from the fact that, for Tronti, there is a totality (or, perhaps better, there can be a *totalization* of the political struggles whose subject is the working class) because there is a *center*, objectively determined as a "central place" in society where the tendencies of transformation are decided, and subjectively reinforced when a *partial point of view* imposes its hegemony in a decisive civil war.[23] Whereas, for Althusser, developing his famous formula (in *For Marx*): "the lonely hour of the last instance never tolls," not only every totality is structurally "decentered," but in fact there is no such thing as a "center" that is not an ideological construct (such as, in particular, the centrality of the state, or the state power). I believe that this was (and remains) one of the most interesting dilemmas in contemporary critical theory, for which Marxism has provided not only a contingent field of application, but a fundamental terrain of elaboration.

Allow me to put it in a somewhat brutal manner: what I take to be perhaps the most enduring philosophical achievement in *Reading Capital* is the chapter on "historical time."[24] Interestingly, it is presented by Althusser as a "digression" within his quest of an identification of "Marx's object." But quite often digressions are in fact more important than what they are supposed to lead to. And disturbingly, this remarkable piece of speculative philosophy, which is centered on the critique of Hegel's concept of the historical "present" as recapitulation of the successive moments of its past development (a critique not deprived of secret references to the Heideggerian critique of Hegel's dialectics as an idealized version of the "vulgar idea of time"), is coupled in the following chapter ("Marxism is not a Historicism") with an extremely dogmatic reiteration of Dialectical Materialism against the alleged Gramscian reduction of philosophy to history, and history to ideology, or a development of culture. I see this as an intellectual contradiction, which itself calls for "symptomatic reading." But what I find more interesting is the fact that Althusser's major philosophical statement, the "noncontemporaneity" of time, or the intrinsic heterogeneity of the historical present (which is the site of political action), can be read in fact in two opposite manners. The most obvious, which derives from a simple antithesis with Hegel, explains that, because the Hegelian totality, although made of multiple moments or "masses," is always reducible to the expression of a single spiritual principle, its own temporality (or temporalization) must reconcile continuity and discontinuity in the primacy of the "essential present," where the present is nothing other than the *self-reflection* of its own historical conditions. Conversely, a different notion of totality, attributed to Marx by Althusser on the basis of his reading of the 1857 introduction to the *Critique of Political Economy* (part of the *Grundrisse*), where there is no internal principle generating the multiplicity of the whole, but only the multiplicity itself of uneven processes, articulating practices or instances and subjecting them to a relationship of domination, will produce in the realm of "existence" (*Dasein*) a *noncontemporaneous time,* or a time which permanently differs from itself, displaces its own developments with respect to one another, desperately running after an impossible synchronization as it were. This is, if I may, the exoteric reading of the text. It is clearly not false. But another one, more radical, is also possible, which surfaces again and again, particularly in the uses of the Freudian terminology of "instances" (or "agencies") and not only "levels" or "parts" of the social whole.[25] In this second reading, the heterogeneity of historical times is not just a phenomenological dimension of the processes taking place within a complex, or structured, totality: it is in fact the only reality of the "totality" itself, or it is the "society effect" as such, to borrow a formula that Althusser proposed after the event, in the introductory essay to the whole volume ("From *Capital* to Marx's Philosophy").[26] To put it brutally, the consequence of such a reading is no longer to understand a social or historical totality as a *given* structure, as an *invariant of* subsequent *variations,* in order to make it possible to articulate and differentiate the complexity of political conjunctures where historical mutations may or may not take place: it is to suggest that the only "objects" for theory are the *conjunctures themselves,* that there is no other use of the category "structure" than forming a concept of the intrinsic complexity of a conjuncture, a historical "actual moment" where some tendencies are prevalent over others, and some forces are dominant in a relationship that could become reversed. Thus the quasi-transcendental notion of "overdetermination" (now explicitly coupled with "underdetermination," its symmetric term), is not one that "descends" or goes down from the structure to the conjuncture, or from totality (*Ganzheit*) to existence (*Dasein*), it is one which expresses the conjunctural character and "mutability" of every existing structure. At the cost of a "forcing"—or perhaps a rectification—of Marx's own understanding of the "laws (tendencies) of historical development," no doubt, this thesis which was already central in *For Marx,* where it was founded on a spectacular interpretation of the unpredictability of the Russian Revolution, becomes here asserted again and pushed one step further, not only describing a configuration of forces, or the displacements of their conflicts from one social realm to another (the economy, the political institutions, the ideological battlefield), but interpreting these displacements and the temporary "condensations" of a multiplicity of antagonisms in situations of historical crisis as the essence of historicity itself. In historicity there is nothing other than time, but time is intrinsically "material," because it is intrinsically heterogeneous.

We may now turn to Tronti's description of the phenomenology of class struggles in capitalism: it relies on a remarkable circulation of the types of conflicts between Marx's analyses (e.g., on the "civil war" in England around the regulation of the working day, or the violence of the "automatic" and "autocratic" system of the factory produced by the Industrial Revolution) and the description of contemporary forms of antagonism in the advanced capitalist division of labor, where the working class is not simply made of a juxtaposition of individual workers hired on a contractual basis, but is an organized working class, with its endogenous institutions (the union, but also the party) establishing a *social antagonism* at the level of the collective labor power and the collective capitalist class (the *Gesamtkapital,* whose interest and strategy are not reducible to those of individual capitalists).[27] What interests Tronti is the fact that the *negativity* of the working class at the same time provokes the technological and industrial development of capitalism, and threatens it with an interruption of its accumulation or, in fact, a potential destruction. Thus it is not only the resistance of workers to the violent abuses of exploitation that are characteristic of the class struggle; it is also the transformation of such resistances into a *refusal* of the very form of alienated labor, which can be compared to a "rising to the extremes" of antagonism.[28] When the negativity or destructivity of the social relation of production is consciously enacted by the workers themselves, there occurs a *moment of truth,* with or without continuation over time (but never without consequences, because it forces capital to "socially" or "globally" reorganize its strategies of exploitation, invent new technologies, apply new forms of the "division of labor" and "scientific management," etc.). Ironically this moment of truth could be well described in the terms that Althusser attributed to the Hegelian concept of history (and its Marxist reiterations), namely the idea of the "essential cut" within the continuity of time. And we know that it is with this representation of the "essential cut" in a metaphysical present that Althusser associated his proclamation that there could be no such thing as a "Hegelian politics."

But we can see here that things are more complicated than an "Althusserian" might think, because in Tronti's "decisionist" representation of the crystallization of antagonism in a moment of full expression of the negativity of the class with respect to its conditions of existence, or its reproduction as a "labor power" really subsumed under capital, there are some aspects that are not purely Hegelian, nor even simply Lukácsian. One of them has to do with the interpretation of the crucial thesis of the *centrality of the factory*: this is a double centrality, in fact. There is the idea that, in contemporary capitalism (the capitalism of the "Fordist" era), the whole society becomes an extension of the capital-labor relations established within the factory, particularly the use of the professional hierarchy and the bargaining of wages as a way to regulate social conflicts in general. And this is combined with the idea that the factory is a *political arena*, where "abstract social labor" is realized in the form of a rebellious working class, and capitalists must function as representatives of the interests of their whole class, and are forced to submit their particular interests to a general strategy of exploitation, that of *Gesamtkapital*. This would explain why, for Tronti and other *operaisti*, the factory is not only—as Marx would say—a material place for the development of productive forces and their exploitation, but also the ultimate place where the political actors and strategies are confronting each other, in fact it is the place where the *State* qua "monopoly of power" is constituted, where the *Leviathan* is created. But this leads to an even more interesting suggestion: a political confrontation is taking place at two interrelated levels. On the one hand, political struggles oppose forces which are like camps or armies—and Tronti, undoubtedly, is very fond of the Marxian analogy, in the *Communist Manifesto* and in *Capital*, between the class struggle and a "protracted civil war": since it is the civil war which reveals the ultimate political character of the "economic" struggle, making it impossible to "govern" or to "police" the class struggle in the manner in which other social conflicts can become handled by a ruling class or an elite.[29] But the civil war is certainly not just a "life or death" confrontation between already constituted adversaries. More profoundly, it is about the possibility for each class to *organize itself through the disorganization* of the antithetic class—an idea that undoubtedly has affinities with the way in which Carl Schmitt had described in Sorelian terms a conflict *of the second order*, not only between "enemies," but between strategies, or two different ways of mobilizing the masses of contemporary politics, the nationalist way pursued by fascism and the socialist way pursued by communism as a class ideology.[30] For capital to "organize" production is to dismantle permanently the class organizations of the working class, and for the working class to build its own revolutionary organization is to make the "plan of capital" unworkable.[31]

This is also, it seems to me, a form of *overdetermination*, although not the same as in Althusser, of course, because it is not produced by the irreducible *exteriority* of all the factors, or the singular "histories," which are combined in the class struggles (including, according to Althusser, a different and heterogeneous history of the bourgeois class and the proletariat), but it is produced by the *dissimilation* of the "enemies" that internally emerge out of the same relationship of production, or the alienation of labor. Not exactly the same overdetermination, but in a sense addressing an identical question: the production of the revolutionary moment as a moment of "exception," in which the reproduction of domination is interrupted. From this point of view it is probably symptomatic that the only place where, to my knowledge, Tronti has referred to Althusser, long after the event, was a passage in his political autobiography, *Noi operaisti*, where he approvingly refers to the idea (expressed in Althusser's posthumous essay, *Machiavelli and Us*) that every political thinking is not only *about* the conjuncture, but *under the conjuncture*, in other terms subjecting the "objectivity" and the "partiality" of its analyses to the very relationship of forces and instances of which it is itself a part. And the only place where Althusser had referred to Tronti was a footnote in *Reading Capital* where he quoted from a 1959 essay commenting on the now famous article written by Gramsci in 1917 to greet "a Revolution against *Das Kapital*."[32] These are symptoms of the insistence of the aporia of the revolution as a present, or a *Jetztzeit*, which is not yet there, because it is no longer there.

What to conclude? The affinities are plain: antihistoricism, antihumanism, antieconomicism. The incompatibilities are no less clear: a primacy of "theory" as a way to transform the concept of science into an apparatus for the analysis of the unpredictable conjunctures, at the cost perhaps of a disproportionate epistemological and speculative detour, or a primacy of "the political" which transfers it from one "part" to another in the antagonistic relationship of power established by capital, at the cost perhaps of a reduction of agency to decision, and the identification of the site of politics with a single place promoted by industrial history. Returning to our starting point, what they illustrate are the antinomies of the project of organization, or the "party form," in the Marxist tradition of the twentieth century (or perhaps the *Euro-*

pean Marxist tradition). These ideas of the "revolution" are impossible to retrieve today in identical form, but they remain strangely active in every attempt that we make at bringing together politics and theory at the level of "grand" thinking. Another indication that time is not reducible to "vulgar" linearity.

Notes

1. I understand this essay, which was delivered as a paper at the Princeton Conference in December 2013 in anticipation of the fiftieth anniversary of the publication of *Reading Capital* by Louis Althusser and his students, as a work in progress and certainly not as a final word. As indicated in the footnotes, there are several other inquiries into this "virtual encounter" (or, as I call it, "point of heresy") and its relevance for the understanding of twentieth-century Marxism that are simultaneously undertaken. Some of them are yielding results already fit for publication (and there might be others that I am not aware of). This is also, most certainly, what prompted (anonymous) reviewers of my preliminary draft to ask for clarifications and additions. While I did my best to address the first, I mainly left the second pending, because I expect a better judgment to arise from a confrontation between several contributions, each of which remains incomplete, rather than a single effort. I am very grateful to those remarks all the same.

2. Throughout this article, I refer generically to *Reading Capital* to indicate the collective book first published in France as *Lire le Capital* in 1965, with contributions from Althusser, Balibar, Establet, Macherey, and Rancière, arising from a seminar held at École Normale Supérieure in Paris, under the supervision of Althusser. In 1968 a second, paperback edition was published, which contained only the (revised) contributions of Althusser and the (revised and enlarged) contribution by Balibar, while the others were left aside. It was on the basis of this second truncated and modified version that foreign translations were made, including the standard English translation by Ben Brewster, published in 1970 in England by New Left Books, and in America by Pantheon Books. In 1996, I published a "critical" new edition of *Lire le Capital*, complete and indicating the modifications, with the help of Yves Duroux and Pierre Bravo-Gala. Verso has now published a revised and complete translation of the original book in 2016 as *Reading Capital: The Complete Edition*, trans. by Ben Brewster and David Fernbach (London: Verso, 2016).

3. See, for instance, Louis Althusser, *Essays in Self-Criticism*, trans. Grahame Lock (London: New Left Books, 1976), and the standard commentaries by Gregory Elliott in the introduction to *Althusser: The Detour of Theory* (Chicago: Haymarket Books, 2009), and Montag (*Althusser and His Contemporaries* [Durham, NC: Duke University Press, 2013]).

4. See Emilio de Ípola, *Althusser: L'adieu infini*, preface by E. Balibar (Paris: Presses Universitaires de France, 2012).

5. I am not the only one in elaborating this comparison these days. I will refer to an excellent essay by Sara Farris: "Althusser and Tronti: The Primacy of Politics versus the Autonomy of the Political," in *Encountering Althusser: Politics and Materialism in Contemporary Radical Thought* (New York: Bloomsbury Academic, 2013), and also to recent contributions by Andrea Cavazzini and the whole group of Italian and French young Marxists working in the Groupe de Recherches Matérialistes (http://revueperiode.net/althusser-et-loperaisme-notes-pour-letude-dune-rencontre-manquee/). The latter directly intersects with my argument in this paper and, on several points, will help qualifying, rectifying, and broadening it. As for Farris, her interest is mainly in confronting Althusser with the "later" Tronti (that of the "autonomy of the political"), therefore not immediately intersecting with my argument here. It would be worthwhile, of course, bridging the theoretical and historical gap between the two "moments." I hope that this could be done in the near future in a dialogical manner.

6. See references to available editions in Italian, French, and English in the bibliography.

7. It is quite remarkable that Tronti's "Poscritto di problemi," dated December 1970, essentially consisting in a long essay on "class struggles in America" that discusses the meaning and consequences of the "Keynesian revolution," contains no explicit allusions to the '68 and post-'68 developments (in Italian, that was called *l'autunno caldo*, the "hot autumn" of 1968–69).

8. See Farris, "Althusser and Tronti," and Alberto Toscano, "Chronicles of Insurrection: Tronti, Negri and the Subject of Antagonism," *Monthly Review*, October 2010, http://mrzine.monthlyreview.org/2010/toscano271010.html.

9. Eric Hobsbawm, *Age of Extremes: The Short Twentieth Century 1914–1991* (London: Michael Joseph, 1994).

10. A clarification is needed here: I do not take the notions of "class against class" and Popular Front lines in the narrow senses referring to successive congresses of the Komintern, which adopted them respectively in 1927 and 1935, but in the broad sense in which the two strategic orientations permanently oppose each other (and sometimes also intersect) during the postrevolutionary period: see in particular Fernando Claudin, *The Communist Movement: From Comintern to Cominform*, trans. Brian Pearce and Francis MacDonagh (New York: Monthly Review Press, 1975).

11. Mario Tronti is absolutely right to insist on this point in his recent—and beautiful—retrospective assessment, *Noi operaisti* (Rome: Derive approdi, 2009); an abridged version is published as "Our Operaismo" in *New Left Review* 73 (January–February 2012).

12. See Andrea Cavazzini, *Enquête ouvrière et théorie critique* (Liège: Presses Universitaires de Liège, 2013). I consider that Lukács in his book gave in anticipation the best possible philosophical interpretation of a "class against class" tactics—but of course when it was officially adopted it had been degraded to a way of having the communists' struggle target the social-democrats (seen as traitors) rather than the common fascist enemy.

13. See Louis Althusser, *Machiavelli and Us*, 2nd ed., trans. and intro. Gregory Elliott (New York: Verso, 2011), and *On the Reproduction of Capitalism: Ideology and Ideological State Apparatuses*, trans. G. M. Goshgarian (London: Verso, 2014). The famous essay from 1970 on "Ideology and Ideological State Apparatuses" was an extract from a longer book *On Reproduction*, remained unfinished, now published posthumously.

14. This also calls for a clarification and perhaps a rectification, which would require a long development, however. A recent conversation with Lucien Sève (a French communist philosopher, student, and early friend, later adversary of Althusser's orientation in the Communist Party) has convinced me that he had read Mao's philosophical essay "On Contradiction" from 1937 as soon as it was translated into French in 1951, and immediately considered it a crucial starting point for a "dialectical materialism" liberated from the pseudo-Hegelian "laws" that had been sacralized and imposed by Stalin.

15. Gramsci's relations to the successive lines of the Komintern (and the form in which it was mediated by Togliatti) are again a matter of intense controversy. See Giuseppe Vacca, *Vita e pensieri di Antonio Gramsci (1926–1937)* (Torino: Einaudi Editore, 2012), and Fabio Frosini, "I *Quaderni* tra Mussolini e Croce," *Critica Marxista*, no. 4 (July–August 2012): 60–68.

16. Marx, *Capital*, vol. 1, chap. 19: "The Transformation of the Value (and respectively the Price) of Labour-Power into Wages," in Marx, *Karl Marx: Selected Writings*, ed. David McLellan (Oxford: Oxford University Press, 1977), 675–82.

17. See Louis Althusser and Étienne Balibar, *Reading Capital*, trans. Ben Brewster (London: New Left Books, 1970), 28–30, 145–57.

18. See Mario Tronti, *Operai e capitale*, new ed. (Rome: Deriveapprodi, 2006), "Prime tesi," 121–57.

19. This was illustrated by a whole group of "theorists" working with the notion of the "industrial society" as a more general category encompassing the socialist and capitalist systems, including in France the well-known "liberal" sociologist Raymond Aron (*Dix-huit leçons sur la société industrielle* [1962] in Raymond Aron, *Penser la liberté, penser la démocratie* [Paris: Gallimard Quarto, 2005]).

20. It is to be regretted that the section on "Marx in Detroit" was apparently lost or omitted when posting on the Internet the chapter from *Workers and Capital*, "Postscript of Problems," dealing with "class struggles in America" (see Tronti, *Workers and Capital*, English translation of *Operai e capitale*).

21. See Marx, *Capital*, vol. 1, chap. 23: "Simple Reproduction," in Marx, *Karl Marx: Selected Writings*, 711–24.

22. See Marx, *Capital*, vol. 1, chap. 15: "Machinery and Large Scale Industry," in Marx, *Karl Marx: Selected Writings*, 618–19.

23. See Tronti, *Operai e capitale*, "La fabbrica e la società" ("The Factory and Society").

24. Althusser and Balibar, *Reading Capital* (1970), 91–118.

25. See my entry "Agency/instance" in Barbara Cassin, ed., *Dictionary of Untranslatables* (Princeton, NJ: Princeton University Press, 2014), 22–24.

26. See Althusser and Balibar, *Reading Capital* (1970), 66.

27. See Tronti, *Operai e capitale* (2006), Prime ipotesi, "Il piano del capitale," 56–83.

28. See Tronti, *Operai e capitale* (2006), Prime tesi, "La strategia del rifiuto," 236–53.

29. See my essay "Marxism and War," *Radical Philosophy* 160 (March–April 2010).

30. See Carl Schmitt, *Crisis of Parliamentary Democracy*, trans. Ellen Kennedy, Studies in Contemporary German Social Thought (Cambridge, MA: MIT Press, 1985).

31. See Tronti, *Operai e capitale* (2006), Prime tesi, "Tattica=organizzazione," 254–61.

32. Althusser and Balibar, *Reading Capital* (1970), 120.

CHAPTER 6

Reading *Capital* from the Margins

Notes on the Logic of Uneven Development

BRUNO BOSTEELS

Nothing in this world develops absolutely evenly.
—MAO ZEDONG, *On Contradiction*

Between a Rock and a Hard Place

The questions I want to raise in the following pages concern an issue that lies in wait for us as if wedged in between two apparently unrelated statements. The first statement is from the hand of Louis Althusser himself and appears in "On the Materialist Dialectic (On the Unevenness of Origins)," an article first published in the communist journal *La Pensée* in 1963, before being included in the 1965 collection *For Marx*, and in many ways still the most systematic companion piece, together with "Contradiction and Overdetermination," first published in *La Pensée* in 1962 and likewise taken up in *For Marx*, to the collective project of *Reading Capital*. In the statement in question, speaking of the "great law of uneven development," Althusser explains why we are in fact dealing with a law and not just an exception. "This unevenness suffers no exceptions because it is not itself an exception: not a derivatory law, produced by peculiar conditions (imperialism, for example) or intervening in the interference between the developments of distinct social formations (the unevenness of economic development, for example, between 'advanced' and 'backward' countries, between colonizers and colonized, etc.)," Althusser states with his customary aplomb. "Quite the contrary, it is a primitive law, with priority over these peculiar cases and able to account for them precisely in so far as it does not derive from their existence."[1] The second statement, by contrast, is from Althusser's most loyal disciple and collaborator, Étienne Balibar, and appears as the closing lines for an obituary titled "Althusser and the rue d'Ulm." Originally meant for the exclusive eyes of alumni of that branch of the École Normale Supérieure (ENS), this obituary ends with an enigmatic contrast between, on one hand, the enclosure of the school grounds within the walls of 45, rue d'Ulm that would have been familiar to this in-group only, and, on the other hand, a possible broadening of the horizon, both spatially and conceptually, beyond the narrow confines in which Althusser produced his classical works. This contrast—perhaps another confirmation of the law of uneven development—is only heightened by the fact that the times have changed considerably since the decade of the 1960s when these works were produced. Balibar concludes: "No one could any longer feel 'at home' between the Pot, the infirmary, and the Cour du Ruffin, no one could imagine that the fate of the world was at stake in the salle Cavaillès. Hence there is more freedom, to be sure, and less power. The question of 'theoretical practice,' subjectively and objectively, will be raised in other places, perhaps; and certainly in other styles."[2]

How—I want to ask—does the first statement impact the chances for the broadening of our horizon promised in the second to become a reality? If indeed we take uneven development to be a primitive law rather than an exception that would be due to secondary, historical or geographical circumstances, can we still raise the question of theoretical practice "in other places," for example, from the margins of Latin America—rather than from the limited vantage point of a prestigious school in one of the most enlightened capitals of Western Europe? And, furthermore, can we do so "in other styles," for example, not just in terms of Marx's philosophy (dialectical materialism, or the materialist dialectic) or of the science of history (historical materialism) but also in terms of politics, art, and literature—rather than of "theoretical practice" alone? Indeed, we should not forget that the concluding statement in Balibar's obituary echoes his final words from two decades earlier in his original contribution to *Reading Capital*: "In the problems of theoretical practice, all that is ever at issue, beneath their peculiar form as theoretical problems, i.e., beneath the form of the production of concepts which can give their knowledge are the tasks and problems of the other practices."[3] So then, let us put the question the other way around: if we want to take into account some of these other places, other styles, and other practices, can we still affirm the universal and primitive nature of the law of uneven development?

In asking these questions I should immediately clarify what I am certainly not trying to do:

1. I am not interested in "provincializing Althusser" (along the lines of Dipesh Chakrabarty's *Provincializing Europe*), by pretending to write an intellectual ethnography of the ENS or of the French pedagogical system in general, which no doubt thanks to its unabashed elitism has been capable of producing a series of master thinkers like no other.
2. I am also not concerned with showcasing the vital interest of "Althusser at the margins" (this time along the lines of Kevin Anderson's *Marx at the Margins*), either by documenting the French thinker's continued relevance for the peripheries or by bringing the peripheries themselves into the center.

To be sure, regardless of whether the intention of such studies might be denigrating or celebratory, there would be no shortage of materials should we want to pursue either of these two options. Balibar, for one, also offers some fascinating clues in his obituary about the unique role Althusser played for more than thirty years as a resident teacher and public intellectual who engaged with the École not only as a revered institution of higher education but also as a political arena riven by antagonisms, as well as about the enormous impact the ENS in turn had on Althusser's mode of practicing theory and philosophy—an influence perhaps as great as that of the Communist Party, insofar as "it would not be wrong to say that, for Althusser, the Party was, like the École, a place where the material necessity of an institution, in which one constantly had to work toward its transformation, made itself felt in general and in particular, through the contradictory demands of teaching and tactics, analyses and relations of force, collective action for national stakes and personal influence."[4] On the other hand, even though the only person he mentions by name when it comes to Althusser's influence abroad is that of the Mexican philosopher Fernanda Navarro, Balibar also begins to indicate the extent to which, by the 1970s, the author of *For Marx* had in fact reached true stardom, to the point where, "now that he had won international renown—certain Latin American militants considering him almost a new Marx—the pressures of political immediacy weighed on him ever more heavily."[5] Although on Balibar's account Althusser was reluctant to shoulder this weight of becoming a militant political leader, especially on a global scale, the fact of the matter remains that perhaps in no region in the world did he reach greater status as a potentially revolutionary thinker than in Latin America.

Raising the stakes well beyond the tiresome First World problems encapsulated in the terms "structuralism" and "theoreticism," Althusserianism in

Latin America could become a matter of life and death. Under the military dictatorships in the Southern Cone, for instance, being caught with a copy of *La revolución teórica de Marx* in one's library could lead to imprisonment, torture, or forced disappearance on the grounds of subversive behavior against national interests. For this reason, as the Argentine photographer Marcelo Brodsky documents in his installation *The Wretched of the Earth*, many militants in the 1970s moved preemptively to bury their copies of Althusser's work together with books by Fanon, Lenin, or Mao, only to dig them up in the 1990s with the return to democracy, if indeed they had the good fortune of surviving or being able to come back from exile. The books that they would unearth had been eaten by the elements, often to the point of becoming unreadable and blurring the boundaries between paper and earth as if to mock the idealist-humanistic presupposition of a sharp boundary between culture and nature.

This is not to suggest that the truth about Althusser lies in wait for us buried somewhere in the earthy ground of the periphery, ready to be dug up in its pristine authenticity. For the effects of deformation, misprision, and unreadability are perhaps no less strong in those cases where Althusser's books have been safely kept—perhaps without being opened for years—on the shelves of some personal library in France or Belgium. But it does invite us to at least try to tell the story of the fate of these books in other places such as Latin America.

Althusser in Latin America

The evidence of Althusser's stellar rise to fame in Latin America, from the tumultuous years of the late 1960s all the way to the 2000s, is overwhelming and in recent years has attracted renewed attention from young scholars who have begun documenting and expanding upon the impact of his writings. Without pretending to be exhaustive, let us revisit a few key moments in this—at once militant and scholarly—reception of Althusser in Latin America.[6]

As early as in December 1965, as part of his formation as an autodidact who kept a series of *Cuadernos filosóficos* that have recently been published in a single volume as if to suggest a parallelism with the famous *Philosophical Notebooks* that make up volume 38 of Lenin's *Complete Works*, Ernesto "Che" Guevara had read, underlined, and marginally annotated the first Cuban translations of *Pour Marx* as well as "Contradiction and Overdetermination" and "On the Materialist Dialectic," which already in 1964 had been published as separate booklets in Cuba.[7]

Guevara thus read Althusser well before the Chilean-born Marta Harnecker, who went to study with Althusser in rue d'Ulm, would come to dominate the reception of Althusserianism in Latin America with her canonical translations of *La revolución teórica de Marx* (as *Pour Marx* is rendered in Spanish) and *Para leer el Capital* (the abridged version of *Lire le Capital* limited, as in the 1968 French edition, to Althusser and Balibar's contributions), both with the publishing house Siglo XXI. Anecdotally, I perhaps might add, this work of dissemination also found its way back from Latin America to Europe: in my parents' personal library in Belgium, to go no further, I still remember coming across a Dutch translation of one of Marta Harnecker's *Cuadernos de estudio* (Study Guides), in which—together with her enormously popular *Los conceptos elementales del materialismo histórico* (1968), which went through more than sixty editions as well as numerous translations into French, English, Portuguese, and Greek—she intended to provide her readership with a socialist training of profoundly Althusserian inspiration.[8]

Perhaps the most important early publication in the Latin American region came in the form of a booklet combining Althusser's well-nigh orthodox-Stalinist article "Dialectical Materialism and Historical Materialism" with Alain Badiou's review of this article and of the canonical works *Pour Marx* and *Lire le Capital*, in "The (Re)commencement of Dialectical Materialism."[9] This early publication was crucial not only because of its many reprints but also because the booklet set the tone for the reception of Althusser in Latin America as a whole, by adding a discussion with Galvano Della Volpe and other Italian thinkers about the thought of Antonio Gramsci. Thus, whereas the occasionally vicious polemic against Gramsci's historicism was pivotal to the development of Althusser's own thought, in Latin America many Althusserians were at the same time Gramscians, just as those thinkers known as "the Argentine Gramscians" (allegedly a coinage from the hand of Ernesto Laclau) around the journal and book series *Pasado y Presente* that José Aricó animated between Argentina and Mexico were frequently portrayed, if not maligned, as Althusserians.[10]

For all the early enthusiasm, criticisms of Althusser's influence also did not take long to appear in Latin America. Jacques Rancière's harsh take in "On the Theory of Ideology: The Politics of Althusser" (originally written in 1969 as a response to the events of 1968 in France that according to Rancière blew canonical Althusserianism to pieces), for example, was first published in Argentina in 1970 (that is, even before appearing in French, first in 1973 in the journal *L'Homme et la Société* and then as an appendix in *La leçon d'Althusser*, which did not come out until 1974), as part of the collective volume *Lectura de Althusser* edited by Saúl Karsz.[11] But in places like Mexico, too, aside from numerous positive appreciations of Althusser's thought in journals such as *Dialéctica*, around the time of E. P. Thompson's *The Poverty of Theory* there also appeared several polemics, for instance, from the Spanish exile Adolfo Sánchez Vázquez, with a book-length response coming from the hand of another of Althusser's translators, Enrique González Rojo, who previously had published an introductory *Para leer a Althusser*.[12]

It would not be long, however, before the momentous ups and downs of Althusser's fate in Latin America in turn impacted the development of his thought. By the mid-1980s, as Balibar mentions, the Mexican philosopher Fernanda Navarro became instrumental in presenting to the world the next stage in Althusser's thought, that is, the move toward an aleatory materialism of the encounter as an underground current running through the history of philosophy, from Lucretius to Machiavelli and beyond. Indeed, Navarro's long interview with Althusser, taped in the winter of 1983–84 and first published in 1988 in Spanish under the title *Filosofía y marxismo*, for a long time—until the admittedly still select publication of the "posthumous" writings—offered the only road of access to this significant part of Althusser's oeuvre.[13]

Another surprising turn of events came in the long wake of the Zapatista uprising in 1994 in Chiapas, which eventually would lead the government of President Ernest Zedillo to lash back by publicizing the real identity of Subcomandante Marcos as that of Rafael Sebastián Guillén Vicente. Now everyone was able to find out in retrospect what only a select few of his teachers, such as the longtime Althusserians Alberto Híjar and Cesáreo Morales, had known all along, namely, that Marcos had finished his undergraduate thesis in 1980 at the National Autonomous University of Mexico (UNAM) on the topic "philosophy and education," a thesis which, after two epigraphs borrowed from Michel Foucault, began with the following words:

> A specter is haunting the history of philosophy: the specter of the inexistent "Althusserianism." All the powers of the old and the new philosophy have entered into a holy alliance to exorcise this specter: neopositivists and metaphysicians, Marxologists and existentialists, specialists of all things Latin American and neo-philosophers.

From this fact results a double lesson:

1. The inexistent "Althusserianism" is already acknowledged by all the powers of philosophy to be itself a power.
2. It is high time that the inexistent "Althusserians" (with the exception of Althusser himself) should openly, in the face of the whole world, publish their concepts, their aims, their tendencies, and meet this nursery tale of the specter of the inexistent "Althusserianism" with a manifesto of their own philosophical undertaking: a new practice of philosophy: PHILOSOPHY AS ARM OF THE REVOLUTION.[14]

If Subcomandante Marcos started out as an Althusserian student of the ideological state apparatus of the Mexican school system through an analysis of its official textbooks, we should not be surprised to see how conversely the Althusserian Fernanda Navarro after her trip to Paris has become a fervent and loyal supporter of the Zapatistas in Chiapas.

However, between the moment when a young Rafael Sebastián Guillén finished his *tesis de licenciatura*, in October 1980, and the emergence of his better-known alias on the stage of history, in January 1994, Althusser's place in Latin America suffered the same declining fate as that of Marxism in general. For a while, even more so than Antonio Gramsci, Raymond Williams may well have served as a temporary antidote to Althusserianism, for example, in the turn to the new paradigm of cultural studies that became all the rage in lieu of the old ideology critique among thinkers such as the Argentinean critic Beatriz Sarlo, who between 1969 and 1976 had been a coeditor together with Héctor Schmucler and Ricardo Piglia of the deeply Althusserian-Maoist journal *Los Libros* before founding its social-democratic successor *Punto de Vista*. About this turnabout, Sarlo writes in retrospect:

> Williams was doubly anti-Althusserian (if I may be allowed to sum up with the adjective "Althusserian" a structuralist version of Marxism, which had had an enormous influence imposing an idea of the social subject as effect produced by ideological apparatuses). It is probably unfair to attribute to Althusser everything against which we reacted. There still remains a reading to be offered that would separate Althusser from the Althusserians and, above all, from a manual of Althusserianism such as Marta Harnecker's. However that may be, Williams restored the weight of actions of subjects who could not be thought of only as simple bearers of dominant ideologies, and he recuperated the temporal density of historical processes.[15]

But no structure of feeling was able to stem the crisis of Marxism. "At last the crisis of Marxism!" Althusser exclaimed in 1977 in the pages of *Il Manifesto*; and for nearly two decades, from the 1980s to the early 2000s, it is no exaggeration to say that in Latin America we also witnessed a progressive waning of interest in Marxist thought.[16]

Interestingly, though, if in general the shift toward a post-Marxist if not openly anti-Marxist framework could not be stopped in Latin America anymore than in the rest of the world, this course change still seemed to require a prior settling of accounts with Althusser. This can be seen in the exemplary story of the late Ernesto Laclau's trajectory in the United Kingdom, where he went to study upon his exile from Argentina, between the Althusserian overtones of his 1977 study *Politics and Ideology in Marxist Theory* and the resolutely post-Marxist and post-Althusserian trend initiated in his 1985 *Hegemony and Socialist Strategy*, coauthored with the Belgian political theorist Chantal Mouffe. Crucial in this regard was "the disarticulation of Althusser's rationalism," which the authors believed they could perform "by radicalizing *some* of its themes in a way that will explode its basic concepts."[17] In particular, they propose radicalizing the deconstructive potential inherent in the category of overdetermination, which Althusser borrowed from psychoanalysis and linguistics as a shorthand notation for something he otherwise would have had to describe in the awkward terms of an always-already-unevenly-developed totality: "Laclau and Mouffe's criticism and appropriation of Althusser is the backbone of their argument. In one stroke, this move allows them to expose the fatal flaw of all previous Marxist theory (including Althusser's) and to appropriate his theoretical concept of overdetermination as the cornerstone and explanatory principle of their own system."[18] The authors of *Hegemony and Socialist Strategy* thus in a sense sign the intellectual death certificate of Althusserianism, five years after it already had been condemned to silence in the wake of Althusser's unfortunate strangling of his wife, Hélène Rytman, on November 16, 1980, in their residence at the École in rue d'Ulm.[19]

And yet, announcing what currently amounts to a veritable Althusser renaissance in Latin America, another Argentine thinker from the same generation as Laclau, Emilio de Ípola, recently produced a refreshingly original and poignantly autobiographical study of all Althusser's work—including the classical as well as the late or posthumous writings—under the title *Althusser, el infinito adiós*. In this study, already translated into French with a preface by Balibar and soon to appear as well in English, the author tries to show the profound unity of Althusser's thought by focusing on an esoteric undercurrent that runs through it from beginning to end, provoking conceptual slippages, marginal asides, and half-developed suggestions in the early works that anticipate many of the explicit statements with which the later Althusser—in the name of the contingency of the aleatory encounter or event—would eventually come to unravel and destroy the assumptions of classical Althusserianism: "First expressed in fleeting and intermittent formulae, what we have called the 'esoteric thought' of Althusser slowly took form while at the same time disorganizing his exoteric thought. Finally, at the cost of grave difficulties, of steps forward and backward, of contradictions, self-criticisms and theoretical blockages, this thought was able to carve out a path for itself until it reached the outline of what Althusser called the *materialism of the encounter*."[20] The "infinite goodbye" in the subtitle of de Ípola's study, in other words, was as much Althusser's own cross to bear as it is now our never-ending task with regard to the specter of Althusserianism. Mixed in with the systematic exposé about the presence of two systems of thought bouncing off one another rather than succeeding each other as separate stages, namely, the exoteric (structuralist, rigid, dogmatically Marxist) and the esoteric (contingent, aleatory, and open to a whole range of non-Marxist sources from Machiavelli to Derrida to Heidegger), the pages of *Althusser, el infinito adiós* also offer us a seductive portrait of the author's own trajectory as an intellectual, the theoretical and philosophical scene in Paris and the rue d'Ulm where he had gone to study in the 1960s, as well as a heartfelt rumination about his own surprised discovery, during a trip in 2005, of the many still unpublished Althusser manuscripts kept at the Institut Mémoires de l'Édition Contemporaine in France.

In the Margins of Althusser

We thus would seem to have come full circle. From the vast expanses of Althusser's influence in Latin America, we have returned to the narrow confines of the French educational system and its supporting apparatuses for the maintenance of a few master-thinkers in Paris, visited or revisited by the occasional wide-eyed scholar from the periphery. As I said in the beginning, however, the point is neither to celebrate the unsuspected relevance of Althusser's thought for "the extremities of the capitalist body," as Marx might have said, nor to denigrate him or his disciples for paying but scant attention to the realities and theories on this side of the Atlantic, due to a persistent strain of what is then often denounced with the facile term of Eurocentrism. Rather, the issue is at once more systematic and internal to the very logic of Althusser's thought. The real question, I repeat, is as follows: To what extent does the logic of uneven development enable or disable the concrete analysis of other styles and other practices in those other places? Put differently, if we are in fact dealing with a tension, perhaps even a contradiction, it concerns not an external contrast between the wealth of empirical data in the periphery and the scarcity of conceptual frameworks coming from the center, but a tension within the conceptual frameworks themselves—regardless of their geopolitical origin or particular site of enunciation.

Nothing—not even the unenviable epistemological privilege of the wretched of the earth—guarantees that the thinkers from Latin America listed above would be any better equipped to avoid the pitfalls that Althusser occasionally incurs. Based on his own readings of the texts by Mao Zedong that likewise guide Althusser in "On the Materialist Dialectic," Che Guevara—to give but one example—after all reaches the same conclusion about the primitive and universal law of uneven development as the *maître à penser* from rue d'Ulm: "Finally, the law of uneven development belongs to nature and not to the dominant social system; therefore, even in socialist countries there exists an uneven development that transforms itself through commerce into an unequal exchange, or, what amounts to the same thing, into the exploitation of some socialist countries by others."[21] But elsewhere, while reading and highlighting Althusser's *For Marx* for his own personal use, Guevara seems to question the universal applicability of some of the conclusions that Althusser draws from the Marxist or Maoist theories of practice and contradiction. Thus, about the passage in "On the Materialist Dialectic" in which Althusser quotes Lenin's analysis of the October Revolution to illustrate the "fusion" or condensation of contradictions into what Mao will call an "antagonistic" one, Guevara writes in the margins of his copy of *Por Marx*: "Does this mean that the non-antagonistic contradiction is an antecedent of the antagonistic one? If this is the case, must its development be considered fatal or not?"[22]

And, about Althusser's well-known arguments, based on Marx's 1857 introduction to the *Grundrisse*, regarding the impossibility of ever finding a simple category such as labor or production in general ("The simplest economic category ... can only ever exist as the unilateral and abstract relation of a pre-given, living concrete whole," Marx had posited, which leads Althusser to conclude: "The *Introduction* is no more than a long demonstration of the following thesis: the simple only ever exists within a complex structure; the universal existence of a simple category is never original, it only appears as the end-result of a long historical process, as the product of a highly differentiated social structure; so, where reality is concerned, we are never dealing with the pure existence of simplicity, be it essence or category, but with the existence of 'concretes' of complex and structured beings and processes"),[23] Guevara asks: "But is this a unique simplicity or are there others? And if it is a simplicity that is historically conditioned, should we not limit the framework to society without involving ourselves with nature as a whole?"[24] Other than a curt "very important" penciled in the margins of another passage from "On the Materialist Dialectic," these are the only annotations Che Guevara made in his copy of *Por Marx* in October 1966, apparently while traveling between Tanzania, Prague, and Cuba. By contrast, we can only speculate what he would have thought of *Reading Capital*, which was not available in Spanish until after Che met his untimely death in October 1967 in Bolivia.

Guevara's marginal annotations highlight a tension that is already at work in Althusser's conceptual framework surrounding the use of the category of uneven development: the tension between, on one hand, its consideration as a primitive and universal law that suffers no exceptions but instead belongs to the nature of things as such and, on the other, its consideration as a particular result of historical and societal conditions that apply only to certain exceptional situations. To anticipate, then, my argument will be that whereas these two ways of treating the principle of unevenness remain as much in conflict in the key texts of Althusser's *For Marx* that deal with the specificity of the materialist dialectic as they are doubtful in the eyes of Guevara, by contrast in *Reading Capital* the first treatment will become completely dominant to the detriment of the second, as all developmental notions of unevenness or inequality (*inégalité* in French, significantly, can mean both) will be relayed and replaced by a new transcendental principle of discrepancy or dislocation (*décalage* in French). Rather than an external contextualization of Althusser's canonical works from the perspective of places such as Latin America, what follows therefore amounts to an immanent critique—including the possible effects thereof on the concept of immanent critique itself, insofar as this concept, closely tied as it is to the need for a symptomatic rather than a naive or immediate reading, presupposes that of a certain unevenness or dislocation in order to become critical and break with immanence in the first place.

The Logic of Uneven Development

If what we must grasp is the becoming-transcendental of the historical principle of unevenness, a first observation concerns the very choice of the category of uneven development over other terms such as under- and overdevelopment, which by the mid-1960s were coming in vogue among social scientists in the Third World. Althusser himself has recourse to the latter terms in his 1961 essay "On the Young Marx," one of the earliest essays collected in *For Marx*, to explain the peculiar drama of Hegel within the larger context described by Marx and Engels in *The German Ideology*. "The counterpart to Germany's *historical underdevelopment* was an *ideological and theoretical 'over-development'* incomparable with anything offered by other European nations," Althusser paraphrases. "But the crucial point is that this theoretical development was an alienated ideological development, without concrete relation to the real problems and the real objects which were *reflected in it*. From the viewpoint we have adopted, that is Hegel's drama."[25] Other than to describe this dramatic impasse in the German ideology, however, Althusser shies away completely from the terms under- and overdevelopment. What is more, whenever he turns to the category of uneven development as a substitute, he makes sure to avoid any confusion with the then-popular debates about dependency and the development of underdevelopment. Notwithstanding the repeated calls to mobilize his recasting of Marxism for the concrete analysis of concrete situations, for example, in Cuba or Vietnam, there is thus an undeniable effect of censorship at work, both politically and conceptually, in the way the logic of uneven development is unfolded in *For Marx*, as if to render impossible any quick and easy appropriation from the margins of the Second or Third Worlds.

A similar effect of censorship also befalls someone who could have provided a second major source for Althusser's elaboration of the logic of uneven development, that is, Leon Trotsky, whose name is however conspicuously absent from *For Marx*. In fact, I would venture to say that if Althusser prefers Mao's "On Contradiction" and "On Practice" as his main sources for proving the law of the unevenness of all contradictions, it is not just to take sides in the Sino-Soviet split but also and perhaps above all to avoid any confusion with the theory of what Trotsky had described in terms of "uneven and combined development" and which starting in the 1960s and 1970s once again proved helpful to Trotskyists such as the Argentine-Mexican Adolfo Gilly or the French-Brazilian Michael Löwy in order to account for the historical realities of Latin America. Gilly, for example, begins his book *The Mexican Revolution* (written between 1966 and 1971 from the Lecumberri Prison and first published in Spanish under the title *La revolución interrumpida*) with the following quote from Trotsky's famous opening chapter, "Peculiarities of Russia's Development," in *The History of the Russian Revolution*:

> Unevenness, the most general law of the historic process, reveals itself most sharply and complexly in the destiny of the backward countries. Under the whip of external necessity their backward culture is compelled to make leaps. From the universal law of unevenness thus derives another law, which, for the lack of a better name, we may call the law of *combined development*—by which we mean a drawing together of the different stages of the journey, a combining of separate steps, an amalgam of archaic with more contemporary forms.[26]

Almost word for word, this definition of combined and uneven development will be rebutted in Althusser's most systematic account of uneven development that is to be found in "On the Materialist Dialectic (On the Unevenness of Origins)," the subtitle of which obviously represents a clever inversion of Jean-Jacques Rousseau's *Essay on the Origins of Inequality* (in French, *Discours sur l'origine et les fondements de l'inégalité parmi les hommes*). Unfortunately, the English translation of *For Marx* loses sight of the fact that the notion of *inégalité* in "Sur la dialectique matérialiste (De l'inégalité des origines)," especially in light of the allusion to Rousseau, should evoke both "unevenness" and "inequality," just as Marx himself, for the examples of "uneven development" he gives in the 1857 *Einleitung* to the *Grundrisse*, uses both the German expression *ungleiche Entwicklung* and the Gallicism *unegale*.[27] For Althusser, in any case, unevenness is neither exceptional nor external to the very nature of contradictions that on his account defines the specificity of the object of the materialist dialectic, from Marx to Mao. Unevenness is not restricted to backward countries as opposed to more mature or advanced ones; it is also not secondary or derived, compared to an original state of affairs that otherwise might have been able to function as the absolutely prior standard of even development. Instead, all origins are marked by unevenness as the result of processes that are themselves complex, without ever leading back to a simple term. In sum, uneven development is an originary and universal characteristic of all social and historical phenomena. It belongs, as it were, to the very nature of things insofar as nothing whatsoever in this world develops evenly.

Without mentioning any contemporaneous theorists of dependency or uneven and combined development by name, Althusser restates this conclusion right after the statement announcing the "primitive law" of uneven development with which we began our investigation, in a long passage from "On the Materialist Dialectic" that is now hard not to read as an indirect rebuttal of Trotsky:

> Only because every social formation is affected by unevenness, are the relations of such a social formation with other formations of different economic, political and ideological maturity affected by it, and it enables us to understand how these relations are possible. So it is not external unevenness whose intervention is the basis for an internal unevenness (for example, the so-called meeting of civilizations), but, on the contrary, the internal unevenness has priority and is the basis for the role of the external unevenness, up to and including the effects this second unevenness has within social formations in confrontation. Every interpretation that reduces the phenomena of internal unevenness (for example, explaining the "exceptional" conjuncture in Russia in 1917 solely by its relation of external unevenness: international relations, the uneven economic development of Russia as compared with the West, etc.) slides into mechanism, or into what is frequently an alibi for it: a theory of the reciprocal interaction of the inside and the outside. So it is essential to get down to the primitive internal unevenness to grasp the essence of the external unevenness.[28]

With this conceptual elaboration of the law of the "primitive internal unevenness" of any contradiction, we are supposed to have reached the famous specific difference of the Marxist dialectic: "The specific difference of Marxist contradiction is its 'unevenness' or 'overdetermination,' which reflects in it its conditions of existence, that is, the specific structure of unevenness (in dominance) of the ever-pre-given complex whole which is its existence," Althusser concludes. Finally, he adds: "If, as Lenin said, the dialectic is the conception of the contradiction in the very essence of things, the principle of their development and disappearance, then with this definition of the specificity of Marxist contradiction we should have reached *the Marxist dialectic* itself."[29] In reality, I believe it is no exaggeration to say that Althusser's definition of uneven development in *For Marx* pushes the Marxist dialectic to the limit of a threshold from where the same category could equally easily be mobilized *against* the entire tradition of dialectical thinking, including this time both Hegel *and* Marx. Unevenness and overdetermination indeed are part and parcel of an intellectual genealogy of so-called French theory in which from the mid-1960s onward we will witness a radical paradigm shift away from the dialectic and toward various philosophies of difference.

We need not wait for Laclau and Mouffe in the 1980s to see this paradigm shift become a reality in the name of an unapologetic plea for post-Marxism. In fact, already in his very first seminar at the ENS in rue d'Ulm, a seminar devoted to *Heidegger: The Question of Being and History* during the same academic year, 1964–1965, in which Althusser taught his seminar that would lead to the collective publication of *Reading Capital*, a young Jacques Derrida similarly defined unequal development as a universal and originary law that suffers no exceptions but belongs to the very structure of historicity. During the very last session of his seminar, on March 29, 1965, Derrida eloquently recapitulates this view by telling the students in his audience, none of whom— apparently much to his surprise and chagrin, as Balibar was later told—had come over from the inner circle of Althusser's favorite disciples: "The historicity of tools, of technology, the historicity of institutions, the historicity of works of art, and within the historicity of art, the historicity of different types of art, etc. All these historicities have their own meaning, their own type of concatenation, their own rhythm, their fundamental unevenness [*inégalité*] of development," which as Heidegger purportedly teaches us much more radically than Marx is without a common end goal. Derrida adds in a long parenthesis:

> Here we should not even say *inequality* [*inégalité*] but *anequality* [*anégalité*], insofar as inequality supposes a flaw or an insufficiency with regard to a measure or telos, a common *entelechy*, a measure for all things. The concept of anequality alone is capable of respecting the originality and radicality of that difference which Heidegger always sought to recall for us first of all, an originary difference, that is to say not thinkable within the horizon of a simple first or last unity.[30]

The uneven development of all levels and kinds of historicity, in other words, is not a defect with regard to the norm of a first or last simplicity that might serve as the teleological principle for an even development. For Derrida as much as for Althusser, the effect of unevenness is irreducible. We might even say that the principle of the irreducible unevenness at the heart of the question of history should make us suspicious not just of the terms unevenness or inequality themselves but also and above all of the term development. No wonder that Althusser in *For Marx* mentions underdevelopment only when accompanied by quotation marks or parenthetical dismissals or that in the collective volume *Reading Capital*, published in October 1965 as the outcome of his own seminar at the École Normale in rue d'Ulm, he will forgo the logic of uneven development altogether.

Here we find ourselves at a veritable crossroads in the intellectual history of French theory and philosophy, the place where two paths meet and at the same time begin to bifurcate:

1. A dialectical path that seeks rigorously to identify and elaborate the philosophy present in a practical state in the mature critical-historical works of Marx.
2. A nondialectical but deconstructive path that seeks radically to define and elaborate the question of history on the prior grounds of the question of being as opened up by Heidegger.

Incidentally, Derrida in the passage quoted above also introduces the new magical keyword into this whole debate: difference—that strange and uncanny concept which is not one, with the result that most proponents take great delight in hailing its aporetic status as a nonconcept for which all kinds of neologisms and typographic innovations are then said to be unavoidable, Derrida's *différance* of course being the most famous among them, and from which in some sense the whole adventure of what became known as French theory first took off.

Without wishing to decide the philological issue of the direction in which the influence runs between these two figureheads of the ENS in rue d'Ulm, Althusser certainly participates in the general trend of placing a principle of irreducible internal differentiation at the heart of all structures of historicity, except that he does so in the name of a conceptual reaffirmation of the Marxist dialectic, while at the very same time the dialectic is already turning into the first and perhaps most important target of deconstruction for Derrida. This shift from dialectics to difference—or, if we may use proper names here as shorthand notations rather than as registered trademarks, from Hegel and Marx to Deleuze and Derrida by way of Nietzsche and Heidegger—is not just the telltale sign of changed intellectual fashions or of a simple taste for novelty as a must-have attribute according to the logic of the commodity that certainly leaves no domain whatsoever untainted, not even the sphere of thought. It is also an internal response and implies a kind of immanent critique of its own, insofar as the emphasis placed on the notion of difference seeks to be a critical answer to some of the perceived shortcomings, delusions, and failures associated with the dialectical tradition, all the while providing in turn what is supposed to be a corrective remedy.

Between the mid-1960s and mid-1970s, Hegel and, to a lesser extent, Marx (certainly the "young" Marx from before 1845, the one who yet had to "settle accounts" in *The German Ideology* with the entire legacy of the Young Hegelians), after having been uncontested heroes from the late 1930s to the early 1960s to figures such as Alexandre Kojève and Jean-Paul Sartre, became the villains in a fairly simple story told over and over again about the dialectic as an intellectual tradition hell-bent on erasing, masking, or subsuming all difference in the name of a higher unity—whether of Reason or of History. What is more, the failure if not the actual defeat of radical political movements that were marked by the thought of Hegel and Marx, including those that were breathing in the air of the heterodox theories of Western Marxism (as opposed to the Marxist-Leninist orthodoxy of Soviet Marxism or Stalinism) so dear to the 1960s New Left, could then be blamed on the persistence of hard-to-die remnants of precisely such dialectical thinking, said to be too ensnared in a centuries-old metaphysical and essentialist tradition to enable a truly emancipatory transformation of our ways of being, thinking, and acting. If the dialectic itself came to be seen as metaphysical, in other words, this was due to the supposition that even a logic of contradictions—based on the famous unity of opposites as the fundamental law of the dialectic—was insufficiently attuned to the contingent play of differences. Far from being open to a radical force of otherness or alterity, the dialectical movement of contradictions, according to this line of reasoning, ultimately remains subordinate to an essential identity, which implicitly was to have been posited from the outset and would come to be appropriately resumed in the end. And so, in a major turnabout that often wreaked havoc on the work of certain thinkers—including, I would argue, Althusser—who previously had been vocal adherents of the dialectic, the philosophical gigantomachy could be reframed as a confrontation, no longer between identity and contradiction, or even between contradiction and overdetermination, but between identity and difference, as in the title of Heidegger's eponymous little book, subsequently echoed in numerous titles by Deleuze and Derrida, among others.

Unlike critics such as William S. Lewis who believe that this is a matter of complete misappropriation, I do not think that Laclau and Mouffe were simply wrong to locate in the Althusserian logic of unevenness and overdetermination an important stepping-stone on the path toward the deconstruction of the Marxist dialectic in favor of a resolute post-Marxism. Rather, I locate the crux of the problem already in Althusser's own work, at the point where unevenness—even more so than the notion of overdetermination for which it serves as a conceptual antechamber—is defined as a primitive and invariant law, itself the transcendental structural cause rather than the secondary or exceptional effect of the concrete historical variants and particular circumstances that give it its existence:

> So unevenness is internal to a social formation because the structuration in dominance of the complex whole, this structural invariant, *is itself the condition for the concrete variation of the contradictions* that constitute it, and therefore for their displacements, condensations and mutations, etc., and inversely because *this variation is the existence of that invariant.* So uneven development (that is, these same phenomena of displacement and condensation observable in the development process of a complex whole) is not external to contradiction, but constitutes its most intimate essence. So the unevenness that exists in the "development" of contradictions, that is, in the process itself, exists in the essence of contradiction itself. If it were not that the concept of *unevenness* [*inégalité*] has been associated with an external comparison of a quantitative character, I should gladly describe Marxist contradiction as "*unevenly determined*" granted recognition of the internal essence designated by this unevenness: *overdetermination.*[31]

Here we begin to see the extent to which unevenness leads to a radical questioning of the quantitative and teleological logic associated with the term "development," which therefore requires the distance of skeptical quotation marks. But we also begin to see the extent to which the principled affirmation of unevenness as a primitive law or structural invariant, which is supposed to define the core philosophical innovation of the Marxist dialectic (or dialectical materialism), makes it exceedingly difficult to take on the study (in what would be the task of historical materialism) of the variations for which that law or invariant is supposed to serve as a condition, if not a precondition. As soon as one would begin studying this, as in Trotsky's analysis of the peculiarities of 1917 Russia that account for the possibility of the October Revolution, one immediately runs the risk of becoming the target of Althusser's mocking criticisms for having fallen prey to economism or mechanism, just as Michel Foucault's attempt in *History of Madness* to try to date the event of the "great lockup" around the time of Descartes, to give just one example, invited harsh criticisms from Derrida for failing to grasp that more radical and originary struggle between reason and madness without which supposedly we would not be able to think through the ontological possibility of history or historicality as such.

In sum, the radicalism of Althusser's position in *For Marx* depends on the principled affirmation of the law of primitive and universal unevenness as a structural invariant. This affirmation is key to Althusser's attempt to breathe new life into Marx's materialist dialectic, also sometimes called by its orthodox name of dialectical materialism, but erects enormous obstacles on the path of anyone interested in engaging with Marx's historical materialism—obstacles that become nearly insurmountable for militant investigations in the developing or underdeveloped margins of capital. Finally, the affirmation of unevenness as the originary difference that in good Heideggerian fashion is the absolutely prior condition for thinking the question of historicity at the level of being, in Derrida's seminar for 1964–65 that is strictly contemporaneous with Althusser's *Reading Capital*, announces a further fork in the road, the one that separates not just the philosophical from the scientific Marx (the materialist dialectic from the science of history), but the entire dialectical tradition (now including Hegel as well as Marx) from its deconstruction in the wake of Heidegger.

Guevara clearly had an inkling of these issues when he asked himself if the rebuttal of *all* simplicity, whether initial or final, does not in fact ignore the historically developed nature of *certain* forms of simplicity. Althusser, in other words, in affirming the unevenly-complexly-structurally-determined essence of all contradictions merely pushes the problem of these exceptional circumstances further down the road ahead of him: "So simplicity is not original; on the contrary, it is the structured whole which gives its meaning to the simple category, or which may produce the economic existence of certain simple categories as the result of a long process and under exceptional conditions."[32] But this only begs the question of those exceptional conditions under which certain categories such as labor do in fact present themselves as simple. In his zeal to postpone or, worse, deny the interest of even asking this question, which supposedly risks leading us back to a form of mechanism, Althusser at the same time fosters the perception that the true problem is a matter not of factual ignorance about empirical data but of conceptual principle. What he writes about Marx in this sense holds all the more true for his own treatment of the logic of uneven development in connection with the underdeveloped or unevenly developed peripheries: "Marx does not only deny us the ability to delve down beneath this complex whole (and this denial is a denial on principle: it is not ignorance which prevents us, but the very essence of production itself, its concept). Marx does not only show that every 'simple category' presupposes the existence of the structured whole of society, but also, what is almost certainly more important, he demonstrates that far from being original, in determinate conditions, simplicity is merely the product of the complex process."[33] Again, the question is asked or at least suggested but not answered: what exactly are these determinate conditions? And how could a Marxist analysis actually contribute to their elucidation?

Finally, similar questions can be asked about Althusser's rebuttal of the simplicity of Hegel's concept of contradiction: "Those yearning after the simplicity of the Hegelian 'womb' might consider the fact that in 'certain determinate conditions' (really, exceptional conditions) the materialist dialectic can represent in a very limited sector, a 'Hegelian' form, but, precisely because it is an exception, it is not this form itself, that is, the exception, but its conditions that must be generalized. To think these conditions is to think the possibility of its own 'exceptions.' The Marxist dialectic thus enables us to think what constituted the 'crux' of the Hegelian dialectic: for example, the *non-development*, the stagnation of the 'societies without history' be they primitive or otherwise; for example the phenomenon of real 'survivals,' etc."[34] If simplicity is not merely the result of a conceptual mistake or lack of rigor, we still have to explain why sometimes the simple or Hegelian contradiction can actually appear to be historically or practically true! What Guevara in my eyes sensed, however, is that among the effects of Althusser's constant reminders of the need first to take account of the already-given complex whole as the invariant condition of the concrete variations, there is also a blockage or foreclosure of the concrete analysis of concrete situations that otherwise might have shed new light on such historical truths.

Climbing the Fool's Bridge: From Uneven Development to Discrepancy

The "unevenness" or "inequality" of the development of contradictions in *For Marx* thus turns out to function as a limit-concept, which pushes dialectical materialism to the outer edges and up to the threshold of historical materialism but at the same time is constantly pulled back into the strictly philosophical realm of the materialist dialectic, with multiple and in my eyes nefarious effects for historical analysis. Perhaps as a result of this double movement or this tug of war between, on one hand, Marx's science of history and, on the other, the philosophy of Marx as the theory of the forms and concepts needed to treat history scientifically, uneven development will give way in *Reading Capital* to another of Althusser's key concepts which, once the teleological and developmental logic is dropped, can be said to have relayed that older concept from *For Marx*, namely, the concept alternatively translated as "discrepancy," "discordance," or "dislocation"—that is, *décalage* in French. This is the same concept that Althusser will pick up again after *Reading Capital* to name the necessarily uneven character of the development of any given structure, for example, in his famous later essay on Rousseau's *The Social Contract* first published in 1967 in the journal *Cahiers pour l'analyse* and subsequently included in the volume *Politics and History*, where *décalages* is translated as "discrepancies."[35]

Perhaps I may be allowed to anticipate the main point of this further argument with an anecdote from my work as a translator. A friend once gently mocked me for having used the expression "climb the fool's bridge" in the translation of Alain Badiou's *Theory of the Subject*: one does not "climb" but "cross" a bridge, so the argument went; and unless this could be explained as a simple translator's mistake, it supposedly showed that Badiou did not have the first idea of what a bridge is. In French, however, Badiou on two occasions uses the expression *pont-aux-ânes*, which I translated as "fool's bridge" and which comes from the Latin *pons asinorum*, that is, literally, a donkey or ass's bridge: once to refer to the relation between Marx and Hegel and the second time to refer to the relation between Marx and Freud. This is no coincidence: already in the French university system of the Middle Ages the Latin *pons asinorum* referred to a false problem or stumbling block whose scholastic difficulty stems from the fact that a given student is too dumb or stubborn to realize that the problem actually contains the solution. For this reason, such students were often ridiculed and forced to wear a pair of donkey's ears, as in numerous engravings later used to illustrate Erasmus's *In Praise of Folly*. In a long story that could not be more painfully relevant to many of Althusser's Maoist ex-students, this practice continues well into the twentieth century with the public shaming of intellectuals forced to wear dunce caps during the Cultural Revolution. In fact, the association between fool's bridges and wild asses is doubly motivated: not only is there an analogy with the stubbornness or lack of intelligence of the animals that are supposed to cross them, but also the bridges in question are said to take the form of the curved back of a donkey with its heavy load. Numerous examples of such bridges survive in the Roman architecture of southern France, all tending to arch steeply toward the middle so that a donkey would refuse to go across because it could not see the other side. What appears to be an insurmountable obstacle is due to the optical illusion of facing an uphill battle with no end in sight, while in actual fact the obstacle is the solution that could carry us across the river or gorge and to the other side.

If this prolonged analogy is taken into account, there is good reason in translating the French expression *arpenter le pont-aux-ânes* as "climb the fool's bridge" in *Theory of the Subject*. On this one occasion, as a matter of fact, Badiou is arguing that Marxism—contrary to both vulgar-materialist or mechanicist and Althusserian-antihumanist orthodoxies—is in dire need of developing a theory of the subject. He proposes to begin doing so himself by way of a passage through Jacques Lacan, since "Lacan is ahead of the current state of Marxism and we must take advantage of this advance so as to improve our Marxist affairs." Badiou concludes:

> The truth is that there is only one theory of the subject. Lacan is ahead of the current state of Marxism and we must take advantage of this advance so as to improve our Marxist affairs. Why do we draw this undivided and masked theory of the subject from Marx-Lenin-Mao and from Freud-Lacan? Should we climb the fool's bridge—the horror!—of Freudo-Marxism? No, because not even for a second is it a matter of reconciling doctrines. Everything depends on the real, but the real that is ours, in turn, depends only on the following:
> —there are two sexes;
> —there are two classes.
> Make do with that, you subjects of all experience![36]

In other words, there are not two theories of the subject but a single unified theory based on an identical and originary division of the one into two.

However, the point of telling this anecdote is not just in retrospect to defend a solution to an awkward translation issue with a self-indulgent plea *pro domo mea*. There are also good conceptual reasons to keep in mind the steep climb up and down the two slopes of what perhaps in a preemptive answer to my friend's gentle mockery I should have translated as a dumb ass's bridge. By using this metaphor to refer to the tradition of Freudo-Marxism, Badiou also suggests that the combination of these two discursive fields presents us with a false stumbling block—or the pseudo-problem of a search for unification that is actually its own solution. Freud and Marx's respective discourses, in other words, are not in need of being bridged or reconciled. It is not the case that Marxism would need to be supplemented with a theory of the individual psyche, nor should psychoanalysis be supplemented with a materialist analysis of its historical preconditions in bourgeois society. The real difficulty consists not so much in bridging these two separate discourses, focused respectively on structure and subjectivity, as in staying on the arched midpoint of the donkey bridge, without sliding down the slope toward either side.

If it is truly a question of "climbing" or *arpenter*, this is because for Badiou the Marxist dialectic itself presents us with two "sides" or "slopes," *versants* or *pentes* in French, one structural and the other historical. In fact, the same passage in which Badiou concisely defines these two sides also contains the second mention of the *pont-aux-ânes* in *Théorie du sujet*, this time no longer referring to Marx/Freud but to the relation Marx/Hegel that presented such a stumbling block to the canonical Althusser:

> We confirmed that there exists no neutral dialectic that could be inserted into the eternal struggle between idealism and materialism. It is the dialectic itself that must be divided, according to the edge of its dialecticity, into its structural side and its historical side: logic of places and logic of forces.
>
> In the pedagogy of this project—which disassembles and reassembles in its entirety the old fool's bridge of the relation Marx/Hegel—we propose that the formulation "idealist dialectic," which one usually reels off to bad-mouth Hegel, be replaced by "structural dialectic."[37]

Now, in a final twist of the argument that should prove we are dealing with more than an anecdote, I want to suggest that through Badiou's diagnosis of the "structural dialectic" it is not Hegel who perversely is being badmouthed so much as his old teacher Althusser whose name is barely even mentioned but whose spectral presence is no less ubiquitous for all that throughout *Theory of the Subject*. "The structural dialectic, by its choice of the prevailing terms, in the long run works only on one side of the concept of contradiction and, in my opinion, it is not the correct one," Badiou writes. "The structural dialectic privileges the weak difference over the strong difference. It tends to reduce any difference to a pure distance of position. This is its spatializing ambition, which works to the detriment of qualitative heterogeneity, for the latter, being as it is unschematizable, can be registered only in its temporal effect."[38]

Even though Badiou does not follow this route, I propose that we use the image of the two slopes of the materialist dialectic in order to also evaluate the slight but crucial change of perspective in Althusser's trajectory between *For Marx* and *Reading Capital*. Thus, if in the first volume "uneven development" was still a limit-concept oscillating on the cusp between historical and dialectical materialism (themselves articulated through a relation of unevenness or inequality) but already sliding down the slippery slope toward the structural hypostasis of the latter, then in the second volume "discrepancy" or "dislocation" (which we can also think of in terms of out-of-jointness, dehiscence, or disjuncture so as to bring out the nascent deconstructive tendency) is a concept that firmly keeps us—as so many stubborn donkeys—on the side of dialectical materialism, which in actuality is only the side of the structural dialectic, with a steep climb separating us from the possibility of ever crossing over to the side of historical analysis.

The Logic of Discrepancy

Aside from serving in the plural as the name of the international journal of Althusserian studies animated by Warren Montag, the concept of *décalage(s)* operates at three different levels in *Reading Capital*, each of which presupposes a new theoretical development of a special kind:

1. At the *methodological* level, presupposing a new *theory of reading*, the principle of discrepancy or dislocation is precisely what enables a symptomatic as opposed to an immediate or naive reading. In the famous example in Althusser's "From *Capital* to Marx's Philosophy," it describes not only the effects of a necessary gap or distance between the oversights in Adam Smith's classical political economy and the insights offered in Marx's critique thereof, but also the relation between Marx's new scientific practice in *Capital* and Althusser's own elaboration of the new philosophy contained therein in a practical state.

2. At the *structural* level, presupposing a new *theory of absent causality*, the principle of discrepancy is key to understanding the action of a structure on its elements. In this sense, it is closely related to the definition of the structurality of the structure that Althusser, thanks to the role of *décalage* in the first sense, is able to reconstruct in a symptomatic reading as being "The Object of *Capital*," in his contribution of the same title. This second use, as I mentioned before, is the closest we come in *Reading Capital* to the previous understanding of unevenness in *For Marx* as a primitive law of the development of any structure, without exception.

3. At the *historical* level, the principle of discrepancy or dislocation is crucial for answering the question of the historicity of the structure and thus opens up the path toward a possible (re)commencement of historical ma-

terialism that would no longer have to rely on the logics of either uneven and combined development or over- and underdevelopment. This third use presupposes both an unspoken *theory of the event* opened up within a given structure, already present as we will see in Althusser's "From *Capital* to Marx's Philosophy," and an explicit *theory of the transition* between modes of production, as part of what Balibar in his contribution to *Reading Capital* describes under the title "The Fundamental Concepts of Historical Materialism."

These three uses of discrepancy or dislocation clearly stand to one another in a systematic relation of reciprocal presupposition and hierarchical combination. The point of the theory of reading, exemplified in Marx's critique of Smith or Ricardo that Althusser then seeks to mobilize as a method for his own reading of the philosophy that Marx practiced in *Capital*, is not just to draw up a balance sheet of sightings and oversights found in classical political economy, for doing so "reduces to nothing the historical distance and theoretical dislocation (*décalage*) in which Marx thinks the theoretical difference that nevertheless separates him from Smith for ever" (RCC 17). In addition to a grid of hits and misses, therefore, a symptomatic reading must also produce the law of the necessary and immanent relationship between such absences and presences, or between the visible and the invisible. Such a law then puts us on the right track to locate the place in any given structure where what is said or seen necessarily carries with it that which is unsaid or unseen. Althusser describes this location as the "other place" of the structure, present within it as its "shadowy obverse," or as "the inner darkness of exclusion," but we might also speak of this in terms of his disciple Badiou's *Theory of the Subject*, as the "outplace" of a qualitatively heterogeneous force that does not fit and yet must necessarily belong by a relation of internal exclusion to the "splace" as the structured space of assigned places: "This other space is also in the first space which contains it as its own denegation; this other space is the first space in person, which is only defined by the denegation of what it excludes from its own limits" (RCC 25).[39] Thus, from the protocols of symptomatic reading we might conclude that according to Althusser those "other spaces" we have been looking for all along, far from constituting forgotten zones of empirical knowledge on the margins or peripheries of capital, are always already included but only as the necessary exclusion of any field or structure.

With this, however, the methodological use of the principle of discrepancy in the theory of reading, as if by its own inner logic, passes over and extends into its second use so as to define the dislocated structurality of any structure in general, as opposed to what Althusser calls the religious—Heidegger and Derrida would have said metaphysical—complicity between Logos and Being. For example: "The Young Marx of the *1844 Manuscripts* read the human essence at sight, immediately, in the transparency of its alienation. *Capital*, on the contrary, exactly measures a distance and an internal dislocation (*décalage*) in the real, inscribed in its *structure*, a distance and a dislocation such as to make their own effects themselves illegible, and the illusion of an immediate reading of them the ultimate apex of their effects: *fetishism*."[40] This dislocation is what the lasting influence of Hegelianism or historicism on the reading of Marx does not allow us to see, insofar as their view of the social totality immediately seeks to tie together the different levels of the latter as so many contemporary sections or expressions of an ideally posited essence: "Thus re-organized, their relationship will exclude the effects of distortion and dislocation [*décalage*], which, in the authentic Marxist conception, contradict this ideological reading of a contemporaneity."[41] Conversely, the new theory of structural causality, which is the object of Marx's great theoretical revolution according to Althusser, among the many effects of a lacking or absent cause allows us to reconsider the presence of Hegelian references in *Capital*, "but this time *from within*, i.e., not as a relic of a past, a survival, a raffish 'flirtation' (the famous '*kokettieren*'), or a trap for fools (the advantage of my dialectic is that I say things little by little—and when they think I have finished, and rush to refute me, they merely make an untimely manifestation of their asininity!—Letter to Engels, 27 June 1867)," Althusser adds as if to avoid being found out as the dumb ass of the story who will be forced to stand in front of the class wearing donkey ears. Now, without our having to resort to the role of *décalage* in the definition of structural causality in his principal contribution to *Reading Capital*, Althusser's reading of this real presence of certain Hegelianisms from within *Capital*, which previously in *For Marx* he had related to an uneven combination of over- and underdevelopment, mobilizes the principle of discrepancy or dislocation on multiple fronts at once:

> From within, as the exact measurement of a disconcerting but inevitable absence, the absence of the concept (and of all the sub-concepts) of *the effectivity of a structure on its elements* which is the visible/invisible, absent/present keystone of his whole work. Perhaps therefore it is not impermissible to think that if Marx does "play" so much with Hegelian formulae in certain passages, the game is not just raffishness or sarcasm,

but *the action of a real drama*, in which old concepts desperately play the part of something absent *which is nameless*, in order to call it onto the stage in person—whereas they only "produce" its presence in their failures [*ratés*], in the dislocation [*décalage*] between the characters and their roles. (RCC 28)

Aside from confirming the importance of Althusser's minor-seeming interest in theater, as in the text on Brecht and Bertolazzi that is literally pivotal in *For Marx*, this passage also highlights the multiple effects of dislocation as part of the logic of structural causality. This, too, can be read in terms of the work of some of Althusser's disciples, in spite of the official animosity against their former teacher. In this case I am thinking above all of the work of Jacques Rancière, whose entire understanding of politics can be summed up in the notion that there exists no necessary or natural connection between a character or agent such as the working class and its role in history. This is why the people, for example, can only ever be staged. "The people's theater, like the peoples revolution, has always had several peoples, equally irreducible to the simplicity of the Marxist proletarian, the trade unionist or the plebs that intellectual fashion formerly celebrated," Rancière affirms in *Staging the People: The Proletarian and His Double*. "To insist on the overly broad words of people, worker and proletarian is to insist on their inherent difference, on the space of dissenting invention that this difference offers."[42]

The point where this whole machinery supporting the multilayered logic of discrepancy, dislocation, and inherent difference risks running aground is in the hierarchized relation between the structural and the historical uses of *décalage* in *Reading Capital*. To be sure, in "From *Capital* to Marx's Philosophy" Althusser promises that by divulging the philosophical omissions and symptomatic silences in Marx's scientific work, that is, by identifying and refining the logic of structural causality implied in this work, "we can hope for other gains from it in the theory of history itself" (RCC 28).[43] However, the fact of the matter remains that in "The Object of *Capital*," which is his main contribution to *Reading Capital*, Althusser constantly subordinates the tasks of historical analysis to the *theory* of history and, even more radically, to the need for a preliminary *philosophical* definition of the materialist dialectic based on the symptomatic reading of Marx's scientific work: "In other words, to return to classical terminology, the theoretical future of historical materialism depends today on deepening dialectical materialism, which itself depends on a rigorous critical study of *Capital*" (RCC 222).

Only in Balibar's often neglected contribution to *Reading Capital* is the concept of *décalage* in its third sense mobilized for the purposes of historical materialism as the privileged space from where to grasp the synchronic tendencies within and the diachronic transition between different modes of production. "The principal analytic principle in the delineation of transition within *Reading Capital* is the lag (*décalage*) between different components of a social formation (e.g., the lag between the social relations of appropriation and production, on the one hand, and the legal forms of property, on the other)," Alberto Toscano has recently argued in a remarkable study of Balibar's theory of transition, starting from its earliest formulation in 1965 at the height of the Althusserian moment. "Balibar's thesis at this juncture is that *décalage* is a feature of periods of transition, conceived of as times of unevenness and conflict."[44] However, if in Toscano's words "the question of transition, the classical hinge between the theories of capital and revolution," still remains "the blind spot of contemporary radicalism," I would argue that this is in part due to the fact that even an Althusserian reformulation of historical materialism for reasons of principle will always experience grave difficulties to account for "the planetary record of revolutions, communes, and uprisings" that "throws up a complex inventory of systematic attempts to undo and transform social relations of production that do not fit the impoverished terms of a homogenizing conception of transition, which continues to be fetishized by certain strains of the revolutionary left."[45] For all the insistence on discrepant temporalities as opposed to both the empty homogeneous time of bourgeois historiographies and the linear, teleological or developmentalist time of what are then called ideological forms of Marxism, the affirmation of a radical principle of lag, dislocation, or discrepancy, to be studied from within the dynamics of a given social formation as the conceptual pivot in the theory of transition, does not seem to be any better equipped to address the complex time of history than Althusser's hierarchical subordination of Marx's science of history to a philosophical theory of structural causality.

Once again, in the case of Balibar as much as in Althusser, these difficulties scream out to us in parenthetical dismissals of theories of underdevelopment or in the symptomatic harshness of attacks against any developmental—as opposed to an immanently and structurally differentiated—use of the category of unevenness, even if this means postponing the conceptual elaboration of a radical alternative. If, as Balibar asserts, only in the "time" of the dynamics—which, as I have said, is not immediately the time of history—is it possible to determine and assess *the forwardnesses or backwardnesses of development*; indeed, only in this internal orientated time can historical unevennesses of development be thought simply as temporal dislocations," it may well seem as though the time of history—like the hour of the finally determining instance of the economy—will never come. "The consequences of this differential determination of time, and of the distinction between the time of the dynamics and the time of history in general for the contemporary problem of 'under-development' (which is a favourite haunt for every theoretical confusion) cannot be expounded here; at least what we have said gives us a foretaste of its critical importance," Balibar further remarks (RCC 472). And, in a final footnote for his contribution to *Reading Capital*, he adds the following suggestion about the time of the economy: "According to the closeness of the analysis, it will be a matter of an average organic composition or of a differentiated analysis of the organic composition of capital from branch of production to branch of production: this is the beginning of a study of the effects of domination and uneven development implied by the unevenness of the organic composition between competing capitals. Obviously, this is not our object here. I am only suggesting it as a possibility" (RCC 530).

The Althusserian formulation of dialectical materialism, summed up in the theory of structural causality, stubbornly remains stuck in its tracks and only occasionally stumbles forward but ultimately is not able to cross over into the time of historical materialism. At best, the theory of history becomes one of the slopes of the materialist dialectic, that is, the historical or diachronic after the structural or synchronic side. At worst, the tasks of historical materialism are seen as necessarily subordinate and premised on the prior settling of scores with regard to the philosophical detour through dialectical materialism. This does not mean that history is some kind of cauldron of boiling empirical complexity that by definition would be recalcitrant to the cold analytical rigor of theory. Given Althusser's lucid critique of historicism and empiricism alike, there would be no point in rehashing such reproaches. Rather, the problem as I have tried to argue throughout this paper must be understood as a constant temptation to interrupt the double movement hither and thither between history and theory, as the two shores of a river spanned by an impressive donkey bridge rising up before our very own eyes.

The Undivulged Event

This is not to say that we cannot also find conceptual elements for overcoming some of these same obstacles in Althusser's own work from the time of *Reading Capital*. Here I will limit myself to elaborating just two of these elements, which taken together with the better-known analysis of the structure of discrepancy can be seen as laying the ground for what today constitutes a fairly broad post-Althusserian consensus.

In the introductory text "From *Capital* to Marx's Philosophy," as I mentioned earlier, we can first of all see an inchoate and unspoken *theory of the event* at work, which soon thereafter will come to dominate the entire field of French theory or philosophy. This is beautifully anticipated in Ben Brewster's bold and prescient decision to translate *déceler l'indécelé* into English as "divulging the undivulged event," in a passage in which Althusser describes Marx's second reading of classical political economists such as Adam Smith. This reading no longer limits itself to listing the gaps and oversights of his predecessors but, through the methodical use of the principle of discrepancy, articulates itself onto an understanding of the immanent necessity of such symptomatic absences:

> Such is Marx's second reading: a reading which might well be called *symptomatic* (*symptomale*), insofar as it divulges the undivulged event in the text it reads, and in the same movement relates it to *a different text*, present as a necessary absence in the first. Like his first reading, Marx's second reading presupposes the existence of *two texts*, and the measurement of the first against the second. But what distinguishes this new reading from the old one is the fact that in the new one the *second text* is articulated with the lapses in the first text.[46]

The larger philosophical problem at issue in this passage will be familiar to all students of Althusser. I am referring to the question of how we can think of a change or mutation in those same structures of which notions such as uneven development, discrepancy, and over- or underdetermination would mark the essential finitude, that is, the lack or excess that is constitutive of the structurality of the structure. This possibility of change, the irruption of the new within an existing structure or state of affairs, is referred to here under the heading of the theoretical event, signaled by Marx's critique, within the field of classical political economy.

Why is it that Marx could see what was invisible for Smith and Ricardo? On what grounds could his theoretical intervention cause the whole problematic of classical political economy to show its necessary absences and shift terrain by changing the terms of the problem at the same time? How can we think of such events more generally, not just in the field of science or philosophy but also in art or politics? What concepts must be produced to think the eventality of an event? These are just some of the questions that indirectly impose themselves as a result of Marx's breakthrough in the critique of political economy that is *Capital*.

For Althusser, in other words, Marx himself would have been a thinker of the event *avant la lettre*. Not only does his critique of political economy mark a double innovation with regard to science and philosophy, respectively. But in his historical analysis of the nature of capital, its origins, its internal functioning, and the promise of its revolutionary overthrow, Marx also would have provided us with the necessary elements for a theory of what constitutes an event in history as such. In fact, already in *For Marx*, as I discussed elsewhere, Althusser had concluded from this double—scientific and philosophical—innovation that the materialist dialectic, far from being limited to a mechanical repetition of the iron "laws" of development, amounts to nothing less than a theory of the historical event, capable of producing the concepts needed to define the historical forms under which an event constitutes an event in the first place: "An event falling within one of these forms, which has the wherewithal to fall within one of these forms, which is a possible content for one of these forms, which affects them, concerns them, reinforces or disturbs them, which provokes them or which they provoke, or even choose or select, that is a historical event."[47] Thus, the detour from historical materialism to the prior elaboration of the materialist dialectic is necessary, because it is not enough merely to register the occurrence of an event at the empirical level; one must also make sure the concepts in which this event thinks itself are adequate to the task: "The theoretical claims of the concepts must be tested to ensure that they really do provide us with a truly scientific knowledge of the event."[48]

In "The Object of *Capital*," Althusser raises the same question again in the context of his interrogation of the philosophical import of Marx's work. If Marx intervenes practically in philosophy, it is not only because he produced a new conception of structural causality that is already implied by his historical analysis, but also because, even more indirectly, he presupposes an unspoken theory of time and history in which we might be able to situate and grasp the occurrence of any event at all. History develops unevenly, according to the different rhythms, times, and turnovers of politics, ideology, science, art, philosophy, and so on. But the aim of studying such unevennesses of historicity is not to confirm a structural law so much as it is to investigate the possibility of a mutation at the level of the structure itself. Using the history of philosophy as a case in point, Althusser insists on the need to give a rigorous definition of the event or historical fact as such. Both concepts of *fact* and *event*, contrary to what will happen in Badiou's *Logics of Worlds*, for example, are here used interchangeably but only in the strong sense of a break or mutation in the way of posing the problem, and not just the addition of new insights to an already existing problematic:

> Without anticipating this investigation, I should like to point out that, in its generality, the *historical* fact, as opposed to all the other phenomena that occur in historical existence, can be defined as *a fact which causes a mutation in the existing structural relations*. In the history of philosophy it is also essential, if we are to be able to discuss it as a history, to admit that *philosophical facts, philosophical events of historical scope*, occur in it, i.e., precisely *philosophical facts* which cause real mutations in the *existing philosophical structural relations*, in this case the *existing theoretical problematic*. Obviously, these facts are not always *visible*, rather, they are sometimes the object of a real repression, a real and more or less lasting historical denegation.[49]

By way of illustration, Althusser discusses the examples of Locke's empiricism and its revolutionary though mostly unacknowledged influence on German idealism, as well as Spinoza's influence on Marx's philosophy. But it is the latter's novelty, above all, which interests him—together with the upheaval that the discovery of concepts such as surplus value or labor power produced in the theoretico-systematic matrix of its time. And, once again, the point of Althusser's investigation is to understand the nature of this mutation as a theoretical event:

> An understanding of Marx, of the mechanism of his discovery and of the nature of the epistemological break which inaugurated his scientific foundation, leads us therefore to the concepts of a general theory of the history of the sciences, a theory capable of thinking the essence of these *theoretical events*. It is one thing whether this general theory as yet only exists as a project or whether it has already partially materialized; it is another that it

is *absolutely indispensable to a study of Marx*. The path Engels designates for us in what he has done is a path we must take at all costs: it is none other than the path of the philosophy founded by Marx in the act of founding the science of history.[50]

Perhaps more so than as a thinker of the primitive law of unevenness which, in the manner of deconstruction, opens up the structurality of the structure to the dislocating effects of its "articulated decentricity" (*décentration articulée*), that is, "the type of 'dislocation' (*décalage*) and torsion of the different temporalities produced by the different levels of the structure," Marx according to Althusser can and should be seen primarily as a thinker of the event:

> With Marx we are at the site of a historical break of the first importance, not only in the history of the science of history, but also in the history of philosophy, to be precise, in the history of the *Theoretical*; this break (which enables us to resolve a periodization problem in the history of science) coincides with a *theoretical event*, the revolution in the science of history and in philosophy constituted by the problematic introduced by Marx. It does not matter that this event went wholly or partly unperceived, that *time* is needed before this theoretical revolution can make all its effects felt, that it has suffered an incredible repression in the visible history of ideas; the event took place, the break took place, and the history which was born with it is grubbing its subterranean way beneath official history: "well grubbed, old mole!" One day the official history of ideas will fall behind it, and when it realizes this it will be too late for it unless it is prepared to recognize this event and draw the consequences.[51]

Regardless of whether this passageway created by the "old mole" can be identified as an esoteric anticipation or a faint shimmering of the equally "subterranean" current of aleatory materialism to be developed much later in the posthumous works, the fact is that already in *Reading Capital* Althusser provides us with the beginnings of a whole new conceptual framework necessary to develop a general theory of the event.

Theory of the Subject: Toward a Post-Althusserian Consensus

A second largely unspoken contribution of *Reading Capital* to the conceptual framework that in more recent years has produced something like a post-Althusserian consensus can be found in the treatment of the question of the subjective element at play in the historical event of Marx's breakthrough. Given Althusser's relentless commitment to theoretical antihumanism, he obviously cannot tackle this question head on. Instead, he skirts the issue by stating that he will simply assume the break of Marx's scientific discovery as a fact, without enquiring into its reasons or motivations along the lines of conventional explanations for his individual genius (in the liberal-bourgeois tradition) or the spirit of his time (in the Hegelian-historicist tradition). Thus, to the question of knowing why Marx was able to see what remained constitutively invisible in classical political economy, Althusser at first seems to answer with a gesture of avoidance. The change of terrain, which allowed Marx to identify the lacunae in the fullness of his predecessors' discourse—this transformation in the whole theoretico-systematic matrix of classical political economy is taken for granted:

> Here I take this transformation for a fact, without any claim to analyse the mechanism that unleashed it and completed it. The fact that this *"change of terrain"* which produces as its effect this metamorphosis in the gaze, was itself only produced in very specific, complex and often dramatic conditions; that it is absolutely irreducible to the idealist myth of a mental decision to change "view-points"; that it brings into play a whole process that the subject's sighting, far from producing, merely reflects in its own place; that in this process of real transformation of the means of production of knowledge, the claims of a "constitutive subject" are as vain as are the claims of the subject of vision in the production of the visible; that the whole process takes place in the dialectical crisis of the mutation of a theoretical structure in which the "subject" plays, not the part it believes it is playing, but the part which is assigned to it by the mechanism of the process—all these are questions that cannot be studied here.[52]

And yet, even as he continues to refuse to assign a constitutive or transcendental role to the type of subjectivity implied in the theoretical or philosophical event of Marx's *Capital*, Althusser at the same time cannot avoid assuming that some subjective element must already have been in place for this philosopher to be able to gain the informed gaze as he did:

> It is enough to remember that the subject must have occupied its new place in the new terrain, in other words that the subject must already, even partly unwittingly, have been installed in this new terrain, for it to be possible to apply to the old invisible the informed gaze that will make that invisible

visible. Marx can see what escaped Smith's gaze because he has already occupied this new terrain which, in what new answers it had produced, had nevertheless been produced though unwittingly, by the old problematic.[53]

Based on oblique statements such as these, I believe that Althusser's canonical works can be read as laying the ground for a minimal *theory of the subject*, which since then has become the single most surprising premise shared by most if not all post-Althusserian thinkers. Marked with elements of both "subjection" (*assujettissement*) and "subjectivization" (*subjectivation*), this theory of the subject has come to define a veritable consensus in contemporary theory and philosophy, well beyond the direct influence of the old schoolmaster from rue d'Ulm. This new consensus, then, is capable of articulating what we might describe as a general deconstruction of the structurality of the structure, based on its constitutive absences, lapses, or lacunae, with an insistence on the need for some subjective element or other to be already in place in order for there to be a true historical event. Put differently, the dislocation or discrepancy at the heart of any structure not only depends on the rare event of a structural mutation; such symptomatic appearances of the impasse within a given structure also do not become visible unless there is already a subject at work in doing the impossible, which is to pass through the impasse.

If we limit ourselves to so-called French theory, aside from the Heideggerian tradition in the deconstruction of metaphysics among disciples of Derrida, we find a number of Althusser's ex-students—among them Badiou, Rancière, and Balibar—who all paradoxically maintain some notion of subjectivization as essential to the sheer possibility of an emancipatory event to take place. This is paradoxical because for Althusser, no less than for Heidegger, the category of the subject is inherently suspect: not just metaphysical so much as ideological, the subject for the author of *For Marx* is never on the side of truth, be it scientific, political, artistic, or otherwise. Contrary to this rejection of the humanist subject found in Althusser's canonical texts, the difficult task faced by his students in the midst of the crisis of Marxism—a crisis often referred to as the moment of the emergence of post-Marxism—consists in having to articulate a theory of the subject that nevertheless would be compatible with the deconstruction of metaphysics. This means that deconstruction does not go all the way down or, to be more precise, that the deconstruction of the structurality of the structure is impossible without at least some element of the intervening subject already being in place. Between the two intellectual traditions marked in France by the names of Heidegger and Althusser, then, there exists both and at the same time an essential compatibility (which we can sum up as the need for the deconstruction of the structure of being qua substance) as well as an essential incompatibility (which we can sum up in terms of the abandonment or maintenance of a minimal theory of the subject).

Even beyond national boundaries, the shift between structuralism and so-called poststructuralism in this sense marks a pivotal turning point in the broader problematic of the production of subjectivity. As I suggested earlier, we can distinguish two dominant trends in this context: one still connected to both Marxism and the dialectic for which, in spite of Althusser's official dogma, the dislocation of a given structure and therefore the possibility of an event will become inseparable from a process of subjection and subjectivization; and the other, very much aimed against the whole Hegelo-Marxist dialectic in the name of difference, for which the subject remains irreparably metaphysical.

Today, in any case, I would argue that on the basis of the nexus structure-event-subject a new consensus has emerged in dialogue with the Althusserian school, in which we may inscribe not only the obvious cases of Rancière, Balibar, and Badiou, but also a series of younger thinkers whom one would not immediately associate with Althusser, such as Slavoj Žižek, Judith Butler, and Sandro Mezzadra. Though for these last thinkers, figures such as Jacques Lacan, Michel Foucault, and Toni Negri respectively may have been more influential references than Althusser, the shared premise behind the new consensus holds that subject and structure can be articulated, like the two texts in Marx's symptomatic reading, onto the essential lapses of the latter, while at the same time these lapses would not be visible without an intervention of the former, on the rare occasion of a contingent event. This is why, in the words of Balibar, all good structuralism is already a form of poststructuralism: "But my hypothesis is precisely that there is, in fact, no such thing as poststructuralism, or rather that poststructuralism (which acquired this name in the course of its international 'exportation,' 'reception,' or 'translation') is always still structuralism, and structuralism in its strongest sense is already poststructuralism."[54] Not only is every structure always already decentered or dislocated from within, marked as it is by a necessary gap or discrepancy that keeps it from constituting a self-contained totality, which is after all the main lesson to be learned from the canonical Althusser, who on this topic is in perfect agreement with post-Heideggerian thinkers such as Derrida. But this gap or discrepancy does not appear unless there is an intervening subject at work on this very site, the site of an event where the historicity of the situation is symptomatically concentrated. Such is, I would say, the major theoretical innovation introduced in common by a number of thinkers working in the aftermath of Althusser's Marxism, Derridean deconstruction, Lacanian psychoanalysis, and Italian *operaismo*. To use the summary offered by Ernesto Laclau in his preface to one of Žižek's first major books, *The Sublime Object of Ideology*: "There is a subject because the substance—objectivity—does not succeed in constituting itself completely."[55]

Only a Clinamen Can Save Us?

The problem with this new consensus as I see it, however, is that the resulting theory of the subject, articulated onto the constitutive gap, discrepancy, or incompleteness of the structure, has once again become ontologized as a new law. Just as Althusser, in his canonical writings from *For Marx*, turned the law of uneven development into a "primitive law," applicable to any structure whatsoever, regardless of historical circumstances such as the clash of civilizations or the peripheral nature of certain countries such as Russia, so too in countless formulations flowing from the pen of Žižek, Butler, or Mezzadra, we now are told that the subject always exceeds its own determination by the power structures that nonetheless bring it into existence in the first place. "Agency exceeds the power by which it is enabled," Butler postulates in *The Psychic Life of Power: Theories in Subjection*, as though this postulate were always and everywhere an irrevocable law of subjectivity as such. "If the subject is neither fully determined by power nor fully determining of power (but significantly and partially both), the subject exceeds the logic of noncontradiction, is an excrescence of logic, as it were."[56] In the words of Mezzadra's *Border as Method, or, the Multiplication of Labor*, coauthored with Brett Neilson: "Constituted by power relations such as those that operate in processes of dispossession and exploitation, the subject is always constitutively characterized by a moment of excess that can never be fully expropriated. To locate our investigation within this battleground means to take into account the material determinations of the emergence of political subjectivity. It also means to take seriously the two senses of the genitive in the phrase 'production of subjectivity,'" namely, to quote Justin Read's influential book *The Micro-Politics of Capital*, "the constitution of subjectivity, of a particular subjective comportment and in turn the productive power of subjectivity, its capacity to produce wealth."[57] Finally, in the name of this constitutive excess or excedence, which opens up the structure to its contingency all while inscribing the subject in the space of this radical opening, contemporary theory also frequently follows in the footsteps of Althusser, when in his posthumous writings he goes in search of an eclectic form of "aleatory materialism," supposedly capable of bypassing the determinism of his own earlier materialist dialectic, in whose name he had at least esoterically begun to articulate some of the same principles in his canonical writings.

If today, in the words of Yoshihiko Ichida, there exists something like a new fundamental ontology, or a revitalized political anthropology, then it is this consensus about the articulation of structure, event, and subject, which gives a new twist to Hegel's dictum that truth must be thought "not only as substance but also as subject."[58] Žižek, of course, is the philosopher who has gone the farthest in affirming the Hegelian credentials behind this new consensus, which in his eyes breaks definitively with the textbook versions of deconstruction that in the name of difference claim to have overcome the totalizing drive of the dialectic toward the Absolute. But, even when the presence of Hegel is less obvious than in the case of the Slovenian, we can find similar assumptions about the articulation of substance and subject among a great many other authors in contemporary theory and philosophy. In this sense, our current situation is still overwhelmingly controlled by the persistent paradigm of German idealism—even or especially when the role of vanishing mediator in this context belongs to a rabid anti-Hegelian such as Althusser.

Any attempt to break with the paradigm of the theory of the subject inherited—after the necessary deconstruction of its metaphysical underpinnings in terms of the principle of a transparent totality—from German idealism, for this very reason, sees itself confronted with the same alternative voiced by another of Althusser's disciples, Pierre Macherey, in the title of his book, *Hegel or Spinoza*.[59] In fact, continuing in the footsteps of the posthumous Althusser, many authors find unsuspected allies for this effort in other, pre-Hegelian or even pre-Kantian thinkers, aside from Spinoza: thinkers such as Machiavelli, if not much earlier, ancient materialists such as Lucretius and Democritus. Finally, like the radical outcome of the Heideggerian path of thinking, such efforts also frequently end up sacrificing the theory of the subject altogether, but now they do so in the name of an ontological affirmation of radical immanence, contingency, and the objective—rather than subjective—freedom of the aleatory.

Contrary to a widespread agreement among readers of Althusser's posthumous and in many cases still unpublished writings, however, I do not believe that the supposed determinism of the materialist dialectic can be avoided simply by flipping the coin in favor of an affirmation of absolute contingency. Nor do I think, as also has become customary and can be seen in Emilio de Ípola's work, that salvation lies in retrieving those elements of the aleatory that Althusser already would have announced, albeit only in occasional slippages or underdeveloped asides, in *For Marx* and *Reading Capital*. Rather, even for the late Althusser, the real problem to be investigated lies in the retroactive becoming-necessary of historical contingency. In Althusser's own words, it is not the contingency of the *rencontre* in and of itself that matters, but the moment when *ça prend* and things by falling into place produce the illusion of historical necessity.

More so than a mere flipping of the coin or a simple reshuffling of the familiar deck of philosophical cards between freedom and necessity, therefore, the current impasse in the general theory of structure, event, and subjectivity in my eyes requires a twofold historicization. Not only should we expand on the notion (originally proposed by one of Badiou's friends and fellow militants, Sylvain Lazarus) of "historical modes of politics," including the Jacobin, Bolshevik, Stalinist, and democratic-parliamentary modes, which would at least begin to account for the fact that certain modes of doing politics, such as the class-based politics of communist or socialist parties and unions, may have been appropriate in the past, even if they have become saturated or obsolete today.[60] But, in addition, we should also historicize different "theories of the subject," this time in the plural, from which the new consensus has been able to emerge uncontested by consolidating itself as if it were the only theory of the subject that ever existed.

In terms of the first historicization, we might want to consider the fact that long before the multiple events of Tahrir Square, the Puerta del Sol in Spain, or Occupy Wall Street in the USA, the current sequence of riots and uprisings may be said to have taken off in 2006 in Mexico with the so-called Oaxaca Commune, which in turn inspired activists in California to call themselves the Oakland Commune, rather than Occupy Oakland. This name should not too quickly be interpreted only as a reference to the heroic example of the 1871 Paris Commune. As even Marx knew all too well, even though he momentarily seems to forget this in his analysis in *The Civil War in France*, there exists a longstanding tradition of *comunero* revolts in the Hispanic world that reaches back at least to the sixteenth century, with the rebellion of the *comunidades* of Castile, through various eighteenth-century indigenous uprisings in the Andes and New Granada, all the way to what Adolfo Gilly describes as the Commune of Morelos of 1914-15 in Mexico, in a yearlong experiment in radical land reform and self-government among the original Zapatistas.[61] The commune thus intermittently appears as a historical mode of political action and organization that seems particularly apt in moments of quasi-anarchist autonomy from the centralized state, with the fusion of peasants and proletarians in particular being a key mobilizing element in the context of Latin America. But this also brings back the question of the community in a way that can no longer be reduced to the ontological register and instead calls for an investigation into the historical fate of so-called primitive or originary communities in the buildup of various political forms of the commune.

Similar questions must come to frame the second task of historicization, in terms of various theories of the subject, aside from the dominant version inherited from German idealism. If, today, the new consensus has established the version in which the subject appears split by the incompleteness of the structure, then we must still come to an understanding of how this version became re-ontologized as the only theory of the subject valid for all times. For all the emphasis on contingency and aleatoriness, this event-based theory nevertheless to this day remains for the most part ahistorical and transcendental. There is, then, always only one theory of how any subject whatsoever intervenes in fidelity to an event in politics, for example, but there are no events—such as the advent of Christianity or the arrival of global capital with the conquest of the Americas—that would come to mark different types or figures of the subject. By contrast, such types or figures call for a theory of the subject that would no longer be structural or transcendental but rather historical or genealogical.[62]

Marx's thought certainly can still be helpful in this context. Even in the *Grundrisse*, whose subject-oriented approach inspired Negri's intervention in Althusser's seminar that was published as *Marx Beyond Marx*, we do well to focus not just on the 1857 *Einleitung* or on the so-called "fragment on the machine" from which all Italian autonomists and post-autonomists took their inspiration, but also on the central section on "Economic Forms that Precede Capitalism," which was edited in English as a separate booklet by Eric Hobsbawm and, particularly in peripheral or postcolonial contexts such as in Latin America, went through numerous reprints in Spanish, published in Aricó's Biblioteca de Pensamiento Socialista, as one of the most fundamental texts in the entire Marxist corpus.[63] What this section highlights is the need to raise anew the question of the historical emergence of capitalism out of the fortuitous encounter of factors that are themselves not capitalist but that subsequently come to be transcoded and reinscribed into the impossible loop of capital, as though they had been the result of capital itself. It is in large part due to such an impossible looping mechanism that the so-called primitive, agrarian, or peasant communes or communities that precede the movement of originary accumulation appear as being lost forever, so that the various uprisings and revolts, which for this reason often call themselves communes, claim to operate in the name of their utopian return. Such a utopian dream is not just the result of a retrospective illusion, to be dispelled through the adoption of an ontological sense of the community that would be always already lost; it is also an inevitable aspect of any political initiative that seems to mobilize a collective subject, there where previously only atomistic individualities seemed to be available on the marketplace of civil-bourgeois society.

There nonetheless exists a strange analogy between the circular loop of capital, as described in these central sections of the *Grundrisse*, and the very structure of revolutionary praxis, which is defined in the third of Marx's "Theses on Feuerbach" as the "coincidence" or, literally, the "falling together" of the changing of one's circumstances and self-change, that is to say, the simultaneous transformation of the structure and of the subject: "The coincidence of the changing of circumstances and of human activity or self-change can be conceived and rationally understood only as *revolutionary praxis*."[64] Even, or especially, when this thesis is translated in terms of the dominant consensus for the articulation of substance ("circumstances") and subject ("human activity"), the fact remains that the notion according to which a subject, though *determined* by circumstances that are not of its own making, can simultaneously *transform* both itself and its own circumstances, offers an uncanny replica of the loop whereby capital seems to posit the effective presuppositions of its own becoming, as though they were the products of its own doing. In fact, in the words of Rancière's original contribution to *Lire le Capital*, this mystification very much defines the structure of the capitalist subject as such: "The capitalist subject, qua perceiving subject, acquires consciousness of certain relations presented by the apparent movement. When it turns these into the motivating causes of its action, it comes to take itself as a constituent subject. It believes it can relocate in the *Erscheinungen* the results of its own constituent activity. In this way that the subject has of posing itself as constituent, we see the culmination of that mystification which we said is constitutive of its being."[65] A sustained engagement with Marx's theories of the subject, which obviously I cannot offer in these concluding reflections, should be able to contribute in a fundamental way to what must be described as a second-order historicization of this process, that is, the historicization of the becoming-transcendental or ahistorical of the political anthropology inherited from Kant and Hegel. Such an undertaking might be able to shed new light on the fact that even the most radical calls for the revolutionary overthrow of capitalism seem to continue to rely on a peculiar theory of the subject, which only in the modern era has been able to present itself as universally and eternally valid. This is not to say that we suffer only from the philosophical influence of German idealism or, in France, from the specter of Althusserianism. Rather, the rise of these specters is part of a broader historical process in which our understanding of subjectivity seems to have been modeled upon the self-change or activity of capitalism, or vice-versa.

The so-called modern subject is not an invention of the philosophers, be they Descartes or Hegel, in the eyes of some preceded along this path by Saint Augustine. A thorough materialist historicization of the becoming-ahistorical of the newly dominant—event-based but still transcendental—theory of the subject cannot afford to obliterate the historical markers that might separate, for instance, a Christian from a pre-Christian understanding of the self, or a capitalist from a pre-capitalist understanding of human speech and thought. This does not mean that we should opt for a position of historical relativism, according to which every culture from every epoch would have a theory of the subject of its own. If we wish to argue that the subject has always existed, we might want to add that it did not always exist in the same subjective form. If the subject is quintessentially modern, to the point where any theory of the subject involves an implicit theory of modernity, then we must come to an understanding of how such a modern subject was able to project itself on the basis of pre-modern circumstances that it did not create but rather found before it as so many effective or historical presuppositions.[66]

In other words, the break between the subject and that which is not the subject (the materials on which the subject operates, whatever they are called: nature, desire, will to power, life, or purely and simply certain quanta of force) must be interrogated in tandem with the break between the modern and the pre-modern, or between capitalist and pre-capitalist economic but also subjective (psychic, libidinal, cognitive, and affective) formations. Only then will it be possible to escape the conundrum in which any call for the transformation of the world, no matter how rabidly anticapitalist in tone, continues to replicate the impossible loop whereby capital, like an eternal Münchhausen pulling himself up from his own hair, sustains the illusion that it is capable of producing everything, even the historical presuppositions of its own emergence. Put differently, only then will we be able to stop thinking and acting like capitalist subjects.

As for the task of theory and philosophy in this context, I can only agree with Balibar that "theoretical practice," both subjectively and objectively, will happen in other styles and in other places. Precisely, these will be *other* styles, in that they will be more historical than logical, more political or artistic than purely theoretical; and *other* places, not necessarily only in those marginal, underdeveloped, or peripheral regions from the Third World that are occasionally referred to in *Reading Capital* but also no longer limited to the necessary absences of the structure discovered at Althusser's venerable old institution in rue d'Ulm.

Notes

1. Louis Althusser, "Sur la dialectique matérialiste (De l'inégalité des origines)," in *Pour Marx*, with an avant-propos by Étienne Balibar (Paris: La Découverte, 1996), 218; in English, "On the Materialist Dialectic (On the Unevenness of Origins)," *For Marx*, trans. Ben Brewster (London: Verso, 2005), 212. I owe a word of thanks to Nick Nesbitt, first, for inviting me to the conference on *Reading Capital* at Princeton University; and, then, for his patience with the written version.

2. Étienne Balibar, "Althusser and the rue d'Ulm," trans. David Fernbach, *New Left Review* 58 (July–August 2009): 107.

3. Étienne Balibar, "Sur les concepts fondamentaux du matérialisme historique," in Louis Althusser, Étienne Balibar, Roger Establet, Pierre Macherey, and Jacques Rancière, *Lire le Capital*, new rev. ed. (Paris: Quadrige/PUF, 1996), 567; in English, "The Basic Concepts of Historical Materialism," in Louis Althusser, Étienne Balibar, Roger Establet, Pierre Macherey, and Jacques Rancière, *Reading Capital: The Complete Edition*, translated by Ben Brewster and David Fernbach (London: Verso, 2016), 480. All further references will be given in the text. These words, in turn, echo the conclusion in Althusser's essay "On the Materialist Dialectic" in *For Marx*: "To justify its general scope, to verify that this definition of the dialectic really does go beyond the domain *vis-à-vis* which it was expressed and can therefore claim a theoretically tempered and tested universality, it remains to put it to the test of other concrete contents, *other practices*," in *Pour Marx*, 224; *For Marx*, 218.

4. Balibar, "Althusser and the rue d'Ulm," 104.

5. Balibar, "Althusser and the rue d'Ulm," 100.

6. See also the investigations of young scholars such as Marcelo Starcenbaum and Anna Popovitch into Althusser's influence in Argentina, Luiz Eduardo Motta in Brazil, Marcelo Rodríguez in Chile, or Jaime Ortega and Víctor Hugo Pacheco

in Mexico. Many of these scholars gathered in 2012 in Morelia, Mexico, for an international conference on the theme of "Althusser in Latin America." Not without sarcasm, one of the Mexican Althusserians of the first hour commented on this event by contrasting the purely academic reception with the militant political legacy Althusser left in Mexico. See Alberto Híjar Serrano, "Althusser en Morelia," published online in the blog *El calambre cultural: Educación y formación ideológica*. Finally, the recent revival of interest in Althusser in Latin America can also be appreciated in the collective volumes published in Chile and Argentina, *Louis Althusser: Filiación y (re) comienzo*, ed. Zeto Bórquez and Marcelo Rodríguez (Santiago de Chile: Programa de Magíster en Teoría e Historia del Arte, 2010); *Lecturas de Althusser: Proyecciones de un campo problemático*, ed. Sergio Caletti, Natalia Romé, and Martina Sosa (Buenos Aires: Imago Mundi, 2011); *La intervención de Althusser: Revisiones y debates*, ed. Sergio Caletti and Natalia Romé (Buenos Aires: Prometeo, 2011); and *Sujeto, política, psicoanálisis: Discusiones althusserianas con Lacan, Foucault, Laclau, Butler y Žižek* (Buenos Aires: Prometeo, 2011).

7. See Ernesto Che Guevara, *Apuntes filosóficos*, ed. María del Carmen Ariet García (n.p.: Ocean Sur, 2012), 306–41. Guevara uses the Cuban editions in book form of Althusser's *Contradicción y superdeterminación (Notas para una investigación)* (Havana: Venceremos, 1964) and *Sobre la dialéctica materialista (de la desigualdad de los orígenes)* (Havana: Venceremos, 1964); as well as *Por Marx* (Havana: Edición Revolucionaria, 1966). *Leer el Capital* was also published, in two volumes, in a Cuban translation (Havana: Edición Revolucionaria, 1967) but too late anyhow for Guevara to take up the book's study. For a reminiscence about Althusser's influence in revolutionary Cuba, particularly through the journal *Pensamiento crítico*, see the critical reflections of the journal's founding editor Fernando Martínez, "Althusser y el marxismo," *Pensamiento crítico* 37 (1970): 210–18. Several of Althusser's essays were also translated into Spanish in the same journal, among them: "Materialismo dialéctico y materialismo histórico," *Pensamiento crítico* 5 (1967): 3–25; "Dos cartas sobre el conocimiento del arte," *Pensamiento crítico* 10 (1967): 111–21; and "Lenin y la filosofía," *Pensamiento crítico* 34–35 (1970).

8. Marta Harnecker, *Imperialisme en afhankelijkheid*, trans. Marleen Huybregts (Odijk: Sjaloom, 1974). See also Marta Harnecker, *Los conceptos elementales del materialismo histórico* (Buenos Aires: Siglo XXI, 1968). Althusser wrote a preface for the 1970 edition of Harnecker's book, which was subsequently included as an afterword in further reeditions of *Pour Marx* in France.

9. Louis Althusser and Alain Badiou, *Materialismo dialéctico y materialismo histórico*, trans. Nora Rosenfeld de Pasternac, José Aricó, and Santiago Funes (Mexico City: Siglo XXI/Pasado y Presente, 1969). Althusser's original text was first published in *Cahiers marxistes-léninistes* 11 (1966): 88–122. For a fairly exhaustive bibliography of Althusser's work in Spanish translation, see Natalia Romé and Carolina Duer, "Acervo bibliográfico parcial de Louis Althusser en castellano," in *Lecturas de Althusser*, 179–245.

10. See Raúl Burgos, *Los gramscianos argentinos: Cultura y política en la experiencia de Pasado y Presente* (Buenos Aires: Siglo Veintiuno, 2004). As José Aricó writes: "Althusser's dissemination had a paradoxical effect: he made Gramsci fashionable and prepared a readership for coming to know him," in *La cola del diablo: Itinerario de Gramsci en América Latina* (Caracas: Nueva Sociedad, 1988), 102. Aricó believes that the label "Argentine Gramscians" may have been the invention of Ernesto Laclau in an article from 1963 for the journal *Izquierda Nacional*, "Gramsci y los gramscianos," signed with the pseudonym of Ricardo Videla. See Aricó, *La cola del diablo*, 67.

11. Jacques Rancière, "Sobre la teoría de la ideología (La política de Althusser)," in *Lectura de Althusser*, ed. Saúl Karsz (Buenos Aires: Galerna, 1970), 319–57. For further background, see Rancière's "Introductory Note," included in the recent English translation of *Althusser's Lesson*, trans. Emiliano Battista (London: Continuum, 2011), 127–28. The same volume *Lectura de Althusser* also contains another Spanish edition of Alain Badiou's review, "El (re)comienzo del materialismo dialéctico," which originally had appeared in *Critique* 240 (May 1967): 438–67.

12. Enrique González Rojo, *Para leer a Althusser* (Mexico City: Diógenes, 1974); Adolfo Sánchez Vázquez, "El teoricismo de Althusser (Notas críticas sobre una autocrítica)," *Cuadernos políticos* 3 (1975): 82–99; Sánchez Vázquez, *Ciencia y revolución (El marxismo de Althusser)* (Madrid: Alianza, 1978; new ed., Mexico City: Grijalbo, 1983); Sánchez Vázquez, "Sobre la teoría althusseriana de la ideología," in *Ideología y ciencias sociales*, ed. Mario H. Otero (Mexico City: UNAM, 1979), 63–76; and the response by Enrique González Rojo, *Epistemología y socialismo: La crítica de Sánchez Vázquez a Louis Althusser* (Mexico City: Diógenes, 1985). See also the comparable polemic published in Cuba by Pablo Guadarrama González, "¿Ciencia o ideología? Estructuralismo y marxismo en Louis Althusser," *Marx ahora* 23 (2007): 61–77. For a good sampling of Althusser's positive reception in Mexico, with added input from Argentine exiles such as Óscar del Barco, see several issues of the journal *Dialéctica: Revista de la Escuela de Filosofía y Letras de la Universidad Autónoma de Puebla* 3 (July 1977); 8 (June 1980).

13. Louis Althusser, *Filosofía y marxismo: Entrevista por Fernanda Navarro* (Mexico City: Siglo XXI, 1988). See also Fernanda Navarro, "La actualidad de las últimas reflexiones sobre la política de Louis Althusser," *Youkali: Revista crítica de las artes y el pensamiento* 3 (2007): 5–13. The translation of Navarro's interview, "Philosophy and Marxism," unfortunately is still incomplete, as the third chapter of the Mexican edition is omitted from both the French and the English editions. But this absence is amply compensated for by the inclusion of the detailed correspondence between Navarro and Althusser. See Louis Althusser, "Correspondence about 'Philosophy and Marxism'" and "Philosophy and Marxism," in *Philosophy of the Encounter: Later Writings, 1978–87*, ed. François Matheron and Oliver Corpet, trans. G. M. Goshgarian (London: Verso, 2006), 208–89; in French, *Sur la philosophie* (Paris: Gallimard, 1994). A new Mexican edition now also includes this same correspondence. See

Louis Althusser, *Filosofía y marxismo: Entrevista y correspondencia con Fernanda Navarro* (Mexico City: Siglo XXI, 2015).

14. Rafael Sebastián Guillén Vicente, *Filosofía y educación (prácticas discursivas y prácticas ideológicas) (sujeto y cambio históricos en libros de texto oficiales para la educación primaria en México)* (Mexico City: UNAM, 1980). For a commentary, see Hugo Enrique Sáez Arreceygor Fuente, "La tesis de filosofía del sub Marcos: Una lectura de Althusser," *Pacarina del Sur: Revista de Pensamiento Crítico Latinoamericano* 12 (July–September 2012). *La filosofía como arma de la revolución*, of course, is also the title of an extremely popular collection of writings by Althusser, including "Ideology and Ideological State Apparatuses," meant to accompany the Spanish translations of *Pour Marx* and *Lire le Capital* and published in the same series of the Library of Socialist Thought (Biblioteca del pensamiento socialista), edited by José Aricó (Mexico City: Siglo XXI, 1968).

15. Beatriz Sarlo, "Raymond Williams: Una relectura," in *Nuevas perspectivas desde/sobre América Latina: El desafío de los estudios culturales*, ed. Mabel Moraña (Santiago de Chile: Cuarto Propio/Instituto Internacional de Literatura Iberoamericana, 2000), 310. For Althusser's influence on Sarlo's earlier journal *Los Libros*, see the dissertation of my ex-student Anna Popovitch, "In the Shadow of Althusser: Culture and Politics in Late Twentieth-Century Argentina" (Ann Arbor: UMI Dissertation Publishing, 2011).

16. Louis Althusser, "Finalmente qualcosa di vitale si libera dalla crisi e nella crisi del marxismo," *Il Manifesto*, November 16, 1977; in English, "The Crisis of Marxism," trans. Grahame Lock, *Marxism Today* (July 1978): 215–20, 227.

17. Ernesto Laclau and Chantal Mouffe, *Hegemony and Socialist Strategy: Towards a Radical Democratic Politics* (London: Verso, 1985; 2nd ed., 2001), 97, 99. Compare with Ernesto Laclau, *Politics and Ideology in Marxist Theory: Capitalism-Fascism-Populism* (London: New Left Books, 1977); in Spanish, *Política e ideología en la teoría marxista: Capitalismo, fascismo, populismo* (Mexico City: Siglo XXI, 1978).

18. William S. Lewis, "The Under-theorization of Overdetermination in *Hegemony and Socialist Strategy*," in *Althusser and Us*, ed. David McInerney, special issue of *borderlands e-journal* 4, no. 2 (2005). http://www.borderlands.net.au/issues/vol4no2.html. The author goes on to show in what way Laclau and Mouffe misunderstand and misappropriate Althusser's concept of overdetermination.

19. An early anti-Althusserian, the Argentine philosopher León Rozitchner devoted a polemical article to what this fatal incident and its author's autobiographical account thereof reveal about the theoretical shortcomings of Althusserianism, in "La tragedia del althusserismo teórico," *El Ojo Mocho* 17 (2003): 43–50.

20. Emilio de Ípola, *Althusser, el infinito adiós* (Buenos Aires: Siglo XXI, 2007), 215; in French, *Althusser, l'adieu infini*, trans. Marie Bardet, preface by Étienne Balibar (Paris: PUF, 2012), 118.

21. Guevara, *Apuntes filosóficos*, 290. This statement is part of Guevara's marginal annotations in the Cuban edition of Mao Zedong, *Acerca de la práctica* (Havana: Editora Política, 1963).

22. Guevara, *Apuntes filosóficos*, 338. This is one of just three of Guevara's marginal annotations in the Cuban edition of *Por Marx*.

23. Althusser, "Sur la dialectique matérialiste," *Pour Marx*, 200–201; "On the Materialist Dialectic," *For Marx*, 196–97.

24. Guevara, *Apuntes filosóficos*, 333.

25. Althusser, "Sur le jeune Marx," in *Pour Marx*, 73; "On the Young Marx," in *For Marx*, 75–76 (translation modified, as I see no reason why *le drame de Hegel* should necessarily be made into a "tragedy," as Ben Brewster suggests with his rendering).

26. Leon Trotsky, *The History of the Russian Revolution*, trans. Max Eastman (Atlanta: Pathfinder, 2010), 32; and Adolfo Gilly, *The Mexican Revolution*, trans. Patrice Camiller (New York: New Press, 2006), 38. For a genealogy of the concept that goes back to Marx and Engels, see also Michael Löwy, *The Politics of Combined and Uneven Development: The Theory of Permanent Revolution* (Chicago: Haymarket Books, 2010). This recent reedition unfortunately omits the case studies that included Cuba in the first edition (London: Verso, 1981).

27. "Das unegale Verhältnis der Entwicklung der materiellen Produktion z.B. zur künstlerischen," Marx writes in the same section of notes "in regard to points to be mentioned here and not to be forgotten" from the *Grundrisse* also quoted by Althusser. "Der eigentlich schwierige Punkt, hier zu erörtern, ist aber der, wie die Produktionsverhältnisse als Rechtsverhältnisse in ungleiche Entwicklung treten. Also z.B das Verhältnis des römischen Privatrechts (im Kriminalrecht und öffentlichen das weniger der Fall) zur modernen Produktion." See Karl Marx, "Einleitung," in *Grundrisse der Kritik der politischen Ökonomie*, in Karl Marx and Friedrich Engels, *Werke* (Berlin: Dietz, 1983), 42:43. In English: "*The uneven development of material production relative to e.g. artistic development* . . . But the really difficult point to discuss here is how relations of production develop unevenly as legal relations. Thus, e.g., the relation of Roman private law (this less the case with criminal and public law) to modern production." See Karl Marx, *Grundrisse: Foundations of the Critique of Political Economy*, trans. Martin Nicolaus (London: Penguin, 1973), 109. When Althusser quotes this passage as an epigraph to a section from "On the Materialist Dialectic," he uses *rapport inégal* and *développement inégal* as respective translations for Marx's *unegale Verhaltnis* and *ungleiche Entwicklung*. See Althusser, *Pour Marx*, 206; *For Marx*, 200. For discussions about the etymology of *ungleich* and *unegal* in German, I am grateful to Paul Fleming and Geoff Waite.

28. Althusser, "Sur la dialectique matérialiste," 218; "On the Materialist Dialectic," 212.

29. Althusser, "Sur la dialectique matérialiste," 223; "On the Materialist Dialectic," 217. Regardless of whether we are dealing with a strategic silence, a genuine ignorance, or a mutually reinforcing combination of the two, Althusser's failure to mention Trotsky by name in *For Marx* does not take away the fact that his *negative* description of uneven development, in terms of what the concept should *not* be understood as meaning, cannot fail to remind the reader of the opening chapter in *The History of the Russian Revolution*. When asked about the presence or absence

of Trotskyist references in his discussions with Althusser around 1965, Balibar answered the following in a personal message:

> Perhaps my memory is failing a bit, but I do not have the slightest recollection of conversations with Althusser about Trotsky or having heard him evoke Trotsky when we spoke of the theoretical legacy of Marxism. The reference points were Lenin, Stalin (whose "lucidity" Althusser evoked with regard to the text on linguistics against the "leftism" of Marx), Mao, Gramsci, and to a certain extent Lukács (as privileged "philosophical adversary"). Also Brecht, considered "great" by Althusser. And, at least in the beginning, Della Volpe and his school. Later on, one notices numerous absences, either contemporary or older, in particular of Rosa Luxemburg, of Bukharin, and, of course, of Trotsky. In fact I believe that Althusser was not very interested in the detail of the internal history of Marxism, and he worked with a nucleus of authors (cited above) as well as external references (in philosophy and in politics).

Perry Anderson deplores the fact that Althusser chose Lenin over Trotsky as his main point of reference in his account of the causes of the Russian Revolution:

> The failure here was political as much as intellectual. For historical materialism actually possessed an account of October of incomparably greater depth and relevance—Trotsky's *History of the Russian Revolution*, which precisely advances an overall Marxist theory of it, worked through a detailed narrative reconstruction of the events themselves. Althusser's organizational allegiances at the time of *For Marx* foreclosed even the possibility of an allusion to it. The consequence is a drastic weakening of the force of his exposition of over-determination itself, which remains more a sobriquet for the multiform surface of the revolutionary process in Russia than an explanation of its inner unity and intelligibility.

See Perry Anderson, *Arguments within English Marxism* (London: Verso, 1980), 77–78. I owe this reference to Harrison Fluss. Others before Anderson had made much the same point ("Trotsky: symptomatic Althusserian silence"). See Norman Geras, "Althusser's Marxism: An Account and Assessment," *New Left Review* 71 (1972): 78. For personal exchanges about the Marxist history of the concept of uneven development, I am grateful to Stathis Kouvelakis and Panagiotis Sotiris.

30. Jacques Derrida, *Heidegger: La question de l'Être et l'Histoire. Cours de l'ENS-Ulm 1964–1965*, ed. Thomas Dutoit with the help of Marguerite Derrida (Paris: Galilée, 2013), 303–4; in English, *Heidegger: The Question of Being and History*, trans. Geoffrey Bennington (Chicago: University of Chicago Press, 2016), 208 (translation modified). Compare with an almost identical passage in Althusser, "L'objet du Capital," in *Lire le Capital*, 284; "The Object of Capital," in *Reading Capital*, 99–100. In a private conversation prompted by the recent publication of Derrida's course, Balibar recently told me how he wondered why he had no recollection and no notes of this seminar, until Yves Duroux reminded him that this should not be surprising at all, since none of the Althusserians attended Derrida's seminar, too busy as they

were with the 1964–65 seminar in preparation for *Reading Capital*! At the time, there seemed to be no immediate connection between the recommencement of dialectical materialism with Marx and the deconstruction of metaphysics with Heidegger. Since then, there have been more than a few attempts to connect Derrida and Althusser, including most notably Jason Smith, "Jacques Derrida, Crypto-Communist?," in *Critical Companion to Contemporary Marxism*, ed. Jacques Bidet and Stathis Kouvelakis (Chicago: Haymarket, 2006), 625–45; and Balibar himself, in "Eschatology versus Teleology: The Suspended Dialogue between Derrida and Althusser," in *Derrida and the Time of the Political*, ed. Pheng Cheah and Suzanne Guerlac (Durham, NC: Duke University Press, 2000), 57–73. Rather than praising both, either by finding canonical or late Althusserian motifs in Derrida and thus making Derrida out to be a "crypto-communist" or by showing how Althusser's materialism of the "encounter" would have been anticipated by Derrida, I try to locate a crossroads in 1964–65 where *both* the dialectic *and* deconstruction, no doubt due to the reciprocal influence between Althusser and Derrida, become equally derailed. For more biographical information about the intimate relation between the two, see the chapter "In the Shadow of Althusser 1963–1966," in Benoît Peeters, *Derrida: A Biography*, trans. Andrew Brown (Cambridge: Polity, 2013), 144–54.

31. Althusser, "Sur la dialectique matérialiste," 219; "On the Materialist Dialectic," 212 (translation modified to render *condition* in the first sentence simply as "condition" and not as "precondition," since any predetermined teleological relation between condition and conditioned, or between structural invariant and historical variations, is here being questioned).

32. Althusser, "Sur la dialectique matérialiste," 201; "On the Materialist Dialectic," 196.

33. Althusser, "Sur la dialectique matérialiste," 200–201; "On the Materialist Dialectic," 196. See also Althusser's comparable point in *Reading Capital* that today history does in fact present simple abstractions that are practically true: "In some sense, history has reached the point and produced the exceptional, specific present in which scientific abstractions exist in the state of empirical realities, in which science and scientific concepts exist in the form of the visible part of experience as so many directly accessible truths." As Marx writes in *Capital* about the stage of development reached in the United States of America: "There the abstraction of the categories 'labour,' 'labour in general,' labour sans phrase, modern economics' starting-point, is for the first time true in practice (*wird praktisch wahr*). Hence the simplest abstraction, which modern economics puts before all else and which expresses an ancient relation and one valid for all forms of society, nevertheless only appears in this abstraction as true in practice (*praktisch wahr*) as a category of the most modern society," quoted in Althusser, "L'objet du Capital," *Lire le Capital*, 317–18; "The Object of Capital," *Reading Capital*, 124–25.

34. Althusser, "Sur la dialectique matérialiste," 224; "On the Materialist Dialectic," 217.

35. Louis Althusser, "Sur le *Contrat Social* (Les décalages)," *Cahiers pour l'analyse* 8 (1967): 5–42; in English, "Rousseau: *The Social Contract* (Discrepancies)," in *Politics and History: Montesquieu, Rousseau, Marx*, trans. Ben Brewster (London: Verso,

2007), 111–60. In a translator's note to this last text, Brewster offers an insightful explanation for his different renderings of *décalage*: "In *Reading Capital* and *Lenin and Philosophy and Other Essays*, I translated this word as 'dislocation.' Its literal meaning is something like the state of being 'staggered' or 'out of step.' I have shifted from a more mechanical to a more mental metaphor in my translation here because it makes the sense of the term in this essay emerge much more clearly, but also because the standard English translations of Lenin use 'discrepancy' to translate the Russian *nesootvetstvie*, where Lenin is clearly using the word for the concept embodied by all Althusser's uses of 'décalage,'" and by way of example Brewster goes on to quote Lenin himself:

> We, the Russian proletariat, are in advance of any Britain or any Germany as regards our political order, as regards the strength of the workers' political power, but we are behind the most backward West-European country in organizing a good state capitalism, as regards our level of culture and the degree of material and productive preparedness for the "introduction" of socialism. . . . It would be a fatal mistake to declare that since there is a discrepancy between our economic "forces" and our political forces, it "follows" that we should not have seized power. Such an argument can be advanced only by "a man in a muffler" who forgets that there will always be such a "discrepancy," and that it always exists in the development of nature as well as in the developments of society.

See Lenin, "'Left-wing' Childishness and Petty-Bourgeois Mentality," in *Collected Works* (London: Progress, 1965), vol. 27, 346–47, quoted by Brewster in Althusser, *Politics and History*, 114n2. More recently Althusser's long paper on Rousseau was also reissued as a separate booklet in France. See Louis Althusser, *Sur le Contrat Social*, with a study by Patrick Hochart (Houilles: Manucius, 2009).

36. Alain Badiou, *Theory of the Subject*, trans. Bruno Bosteels (London: Continuum, 2009), 115.

37. Badiou, *Theory of the Subject*, 53.

38. Badiou, *Theory of the Subject*, 54. For a more detailed account of Badiou's relation to Althusser, see chaps. 1 and 2 in my *Badiou and Politics* (Durham, NC: Duke University Press, 2011). I should add that Badiou's formalization of the structural dialectic as a dialectic of absent causality is not the same as repeating the old reproach against Althusser's structuralism in *For Marx* or *Reading Capital*; and, insofar as the ancient atomism of Lucretius and others for Badiou confirms the dominant terms of the structural dialectic (absent cause of pure chance, metonymical chain effect, and the dead end of foreclosed terms), Althusser's turn in *Philosophy of the Encounter* to an aleatory materialism, based on such notions as the clinamen, is already preemptively diagnosed and subjected to a forceful rebuttal in *Theory of the Subject*. The clinamen will not save us from the canonical Althusser's purported fixity.

39. We should keep in mind that *en personne* or "in person" can also be understood as "in nobody" in French.

40. Compare also with nearly identical definitions of fetishism for Marx as the form in which a specific *décalage* appears or presents itself in the perception of everyday reality, in Jacques Rancière's original contribution, "Le concept de critique et la critique de l'économie politique des *Manuscrits de 1844* au *Capital*," in *Lire le Capital*, 143, 191–92. Rancière, too, insists on the fact that neither Hegel nor the Young Marx are capable of *seeing* this discrepancy as such. See *Lire le Capital*, 91, 107.

41. Althusser, "L'objet du *Capital*," in *Lire le Capital*, 328; "The Object of *Capital*," in *Reading Capital*, 132. Earlier, Althusser had added an important footnote in which he calls for a more substantial theory of the irreducible *décalage*, now translated as "dislocation," which separates Marx's discourse from that of his predecessors: "The fact and necessity of this dislocation are not peculiar to Marx but common to every scientific founding moment and to all scientific production generally: a study of them is part of a theory of the history of the production of knowledges and a history of the theoretical the necessity for which we feel here also," *Lire le Capital*, 313n12; *Reading Capital*, 121n14.

42. Jacques Rancière, "Preface to the English Edition," in *Staging the People: The Proletarian and His Double*, trans. David Fernbach (London: Verso, 2011), 15, 18. The inherently theatrical or dramatic effects of the logic of discrepancy, in which human beings never correspond immediately to the role they are supposed to play as actors who would appear "in person" on the stage of history, are also exploited throughout Althusser's contributions to *Reading Capital*. See, for example, Althusser, "L'objet du Capital," *Lire le Capital*, 338–39; "The Object of Capital," *Reading Capital*, 139–40.

43. The tendency to subordinate the "concrete analysis of concrete situations" to the prior philosophical definition of the concepts needed for such an analysis remains a constant throughout Althusser's work. Even when in his final texts he abandons the nomenclature of dialectical materialism in favor of an underground current of aleatory materialism, this tendency remains unchanged: "This concrete analysis of the political economical and ideological conjuncture, that is, in the last instance *the analysis of the relations and forms of the class struggles* in the current conjuncture and of the contradictory tendencies of these conflicts, can be accomplished only if one has at one's disposal a *scientific theory* . . . capable of providing the abstract-general overall concepts of the evolution, non-evolution or repression of the current conjuncture." See Louis Althusser, "Qu'y faire? Que faire?" (unpublished manuscript from May 1985), cited in William S. Lewis, "Althusser's Scientism and Aleatory Materialism," *Décalages* 2, no. 1 (2016). http://scholar.oxy.edu/decalages/.

44. Alberto Toscano, "Transition Deprogrammed," in "Communist Currents," ed. Bruno Bosteels and Jodi Dean, special issue, *South Atlantic Quarterly* 113, no. 4 (fall 2014): 765.

45. Toscano, "Transition Deprogrammed," 761, 763–64. Toscano goes on to address Balibar's subsequent reformulations and rectifications of the theory of transition. For obvious reasons, however, I am restricting myself here to the historical use of *décalage* in *Reading Capital*.

46. Althusser, "L'objet du *Capital*," *Lire le Capital*, 22–23; "The Object of *Capital*," *Reading Capital*, 28.

47. Althusser, "Contradiction et surdétermination," in *Pour Marx*, 126; "Contradiction and Overdetermination," in *For Marx*, 126. For further discussion, see my *Badiou and Politics*, 60–61.

48. Althusser, "Marxisme et humanisme," in *Pour Marx*, 229; "Marxism and Humanism," in *For Marx*, 223.

49. Althusser, "L'objet du *Capital*," *Lire le Capital*, 286; "The Object of *Capital*," *Reading Capital*, 102.

50. Althusser, "L'objet du *Capital*," 356; "The Object of *Capital*,"153.

51. Althusser, "L'objet du *Capital*," 290, 357–58; "The Object of *Capital*,"104, 154.

52. Althusser, "Du *Capital* à la philosophie de Marx," *Lire le Capital*, 22; "From *Capital* to Marx's Philosophy," *Reading Capital*, 27.

53. "Du *Capital* à la philosophie de Marx," 22; "From *Capital* to Marx's Philosophy," *Reading Capital*, 27–28.

54. Étienne Balibar, "Structuralism: A Destitution of the Subject?" trans. James Swenson, *Differences: A Journal of Feminist Cultural Studies* 14, no. 1 (2003): 11.

55. Ernesto Laclau, "Preface," in Slavoj Žižek, *The Sublime Object of Ideology* (London: Verso, 1989), xv.

56. Judith Butler, *The Psychic Life of Power: Theories in Subjection* (Stanford, CA: Stanford University Press, 1997), 15, 17.

57. Sandro Mezzadra and Brett Neilson, *Border as Method, or, the Multiplication of Labor* (Durham, NC: Duke University Press, 2013), 252. See also Jason Read, *The Micropolitics of Capital: Marx and the Prehistory of the Present* (Albany: SUNY Press, 2003), 102; and compare with numerous references to this moment of "constitutive excess" or "excrescence" of the subject (*il momento dell'eccedenza soggettiva*) over the existing structures of capitalist determination, in Sandro Mezzadra, *Nei cantieri marxiani: Il soggetto e la sua produzione* (Castel San Pietro Romano: Manifestolibri, 2014), 13–32, 45–56, 63, 88, 97. Even Mezzadra concludes, however, with an open question: "In such a situation, we must ask ourselves if it is not necessary to reconsider the very same image of the subjective excess that Marx elaborated, as we saw, in a specular relation to the way in which capital constructs the subjectivity of the 'bearer' of labor power" (*Nei cantieri marxiani*, 132).

58. Yoshihiko Ichida, "Héros (post-)structuraliste, politique de politique," *Zinbun* 46 (2016): 3–20. The most systematic expression of this new philosophical anthropology, without a doubt, can be found in the massive collection of Étienne Balibar's papers on the subject, in *Citizen-Subject: Foundations for Philosophical Anthropology*, trans. Steven Miller, with an introduction by Emily Apter (New York: Fordham University Press, 2016). I want to take advantage of this occasion to express my gratitude to both Yoshihiko Ichida and Kenta Ohji for inviting Balibar and myself to the Institute for Humanities Research at Kyoto University for a joint discussion on the question of politics and subjectivity, from which my concluding remarks here are partly drawn.

For the fuller version, see my "Twenty Theses on Politics and Subjectivity," *Zinbun* 46 (2016): 21–39.

59. Pierre Macherey, *Hegel or Spinoza*, trans. Susan M. Ruddick (Minneapolis: University of Minnesota Press, 2011).

60. See Sylvain Lazarus, *Anthropology of the Name*, trans. Gila Walker (Chicago: Seagull Books, 2015).

61. See Bruno Bosteels, "The Mexican Commune," in *Communism in the 21st Century*, vol. 3, *The Future of Communism: Social Movements, Economic Crisis, and the Re-imagination of Communism*, ed. Shannon K. Brincat (Santa Barbara: Praeger, 2013), 161–89.

62. I am thinking here in particular of the work of the Argentine philosopher León Rozitchner, especially in *La Cosa y la Cruz: Cristianismo y capitalismo (en torno a las* Confesiones *de san Agustín)* (Buenos Aires: Losada, 1996).

63. See Antonio Negri, *Marx Beyond Marx: Lessons on the Grundrisse*, trans. Harry Cleaver, Michael Ryan, and Mauricio Viano (New York: Autonomedia/Pluto, 1991); Karl Marx, *Pre-capitalist Economic Formations*, trans. Jack Cohen, with an introduction by Eric J. Hobsbawm (New York: International Publishers, 1965); and, in Spanish, Karl Marx, *Formaciones económicas precapitalistas*, with an introduction by Eric J. Hobsbawm (Mexico: Siglo XXI, 1971).

64. Karl Marx, "Theses on Feuerbach," *Collected Works* (London: International Publishers, 1975), 5:4.

65. Rancière, "Le concept de critique et la critique de l'économie politique des *Manuscrits de 1844* au *Capital*," in *Lire le Capital*, 143. A more detailed elaboration of this strange analogy between the theory of the subject and the impossible loop of capital would have to engage with the arguments in Pierre Dardot and Christian Lavalle, *Marx, prénom Karl* (Paris: Gallimard, 2012); and Gavin Walker, *The Sublime Perversion of Capital: Marxist Theory and the Politics of History in Modern Japan* (Durham, NC: Duke University Press, 2016).

66. For the argument that every theory of the subject is at the same time a theory of modernity, I owe everything to ongoing discussions with Simone Pinet, who uses this argument as one of the guiding threads for her seminar on the theory of the novel.

CHAPTER 7

"To Shatter All the Classical Theories of Causality"

Immanent and Absent Causes in

Althusser and Lacan (1963–1965)

WARREN MONTAG

If a return to *Reading Capital* is to be more than an exercise in nostalgia or the exhibition of a museum piece whose value would lie precisely in the fact that, as in Kant's idea of the beautiful, it cannot (or, in this instance, any longer) be an object of interest or use to us, we must read the text, not as a completed object, closed upon itself (or even as a case, "*le cas Althusser*," that must be regarded as closed), but as a radically unfinished work. Its incompleteness, however, must be understood neither as the internal determination of an inevitable failure, the intrinsic unfinishability of its project or projects, nor as externally determined by the historically specific complex of forces that suddenly interrupted the work of Althusser and his students and scattered them across the political/theoretical landscape. Instead, I propose that we begin to chart the pattern of fault lines and striations that mark its surface and which increasingly appear in our own conjuncture less like the signs of an ancient upheaval than so many paths to the outermost limit of the present. They are the lines along which the text, moved by opposing forces, separates from itself; not simply traces of the discontinuities that disrupt the coherence of the project, but also the openings that permit something new to be thought within and through it. Although I will refer here primarily to Althusser's contribution to *Reading Capital*, I would argue that these remarks apply perhaps to an even greater extent to the other contributions, not only Balibar's, but also those that, only now have appeared in English (the texts by Macherey, Rancière, and Establet).[1]

To read *Reading Capital* in this way, that is, to read Althusser reading Marx (himself reading Smith who was reading others and so on), is to apply the notion of symptomatic reading to the very text in which Althusser first developed it as a kind of conceptual instrument that allowed him to detect the gaps and silences in Marx's *Capital*. To find and describe the fissures in Althusser's text, however, is not always an easy task. As he himself argued in the opening of *Reading Capital*, "the religious myth of reading" (which even nonreligious and empirically detailed readings tend only to confirm) renders the discrepancies and lacunae produced by the very movement of the text itself illegible as such by instructing us to interpret them as necessary functions of the textual order (RCC 15). Let us recall that Althusser went so far as to insert in (that is, add to) a passage he cites from Marx concerning the value of labor, two ellipses enclosed in brackets to show that when Marx reads a text of classical political economy "it is not Marx who says what the classical text does not say, it is not Marx who intervenes to impose from without on the classical text a discourse which reveals its silence—it is the classical text itself which tells us that it is silent: its silence is its own words" (RCC 20). Althusser's demonstration is transformative: the sentence in its literal existence will no longer require visible markers of "these sites of emptiness" (*les lieux du vide*) to reveal to us that it produces "so many locations of a lack" (*autant de sièges d'un manque*) by means of the very 'fullness' of the utterance itself" (RCC 21). The lack to which Althusser refers here is that of the question which Marx's utterance answers, the unasked question whose absence resounds in "hollowness," as if by its movement the unmarked discourse hollows itself out as it proceeds, subtracting itself from its own increase (RCC 28). This absence is not a trivial matter: "in it, some part of the life of the Marxist theory of history perhaps depends on this precise point where Marx shows us in a thousand ways the presence of a concept essential to his thought, but absent from his discourse" (RCC 29). It is here that the drama of Marx's thought is played out, "the action of a real drama, in which old concepts desperately play the part of something absent, which *has no name*, in order to call it onto the stage (*sur la scène*) in person—whereas they only 'produce' its presence in their failures, in the discrepancy between the characters and their roles" (RCC 28; translation modified).

After having put this protocol of reading into practice both by tracing its itinerary through Marx's *Capital*, and, in doing so, simultaneously reading Marx's reading, that is, applying to Marx the protocol the latter had applied in his reading of the texts of classical political economy, Althusser finally gives this reading a title: it is a reading "we will dare to call symptomatic [*nous ose-rons de dire 'symptomale'*], insofar as in one and the same movement it detects the undetected in the very text that it reads and relates it to *another text* present as a necessary absence in the first" (RCC 27; translation modified). That other text, however, like Freud's other scene, *der anderer Schauplatz,* is not pres-ent behind or before, and thus spatially or temporally, the text afflicted with symptoms; on the contrary, the text suffers from the reminiscences of what it cannot recall except in the form of something other than what is missing. The symptomatic reading is a reading able to detect the otherwise inaudible hollowness or invisible gap in a text crowded with words, the empty place in what is already full and overflowing. In a text written about the same time as Althusser's overture to *Reading Capital* and cited by him in his discussion of symptomatic reading, Pierre Macherey extends Althusser's arguments to the work of theory itself, to the work, the text, of those who read texts symptom-atically: a science, the science whose obstacles and impediments Althusser seeks to remove, "can only progress, that is, live, through an extreme attention to its points of theoretical fragility." According to Macherey, "Theory is there-fore in incessant rupture with itself; not that it speaks to itself in a reflected discourse from which nothing could escape, but on the contrary because, in-stead of admiring the illusion of completeness in a fictional double of itself, it is in perpetual search for what sounds hollow in its discourse, the possible and decisive way out of itself and towards a new form."[2] If we take these words se-riously, we must listen, then, for the hollow spaces in Althusser's discourse on Marx's hollow spaces and ask whether there is not at work in his discussion of the absent, nameless concept or concepts necessary to think adequately what Marx had produced, the absent concept or concepts necessary to think what Althusser himself wants to think but which are missing.

It does not take Althusser long to identify the missing concept whose absence resounds in Marx: it is "the effectivity of the structure on its elements" (RCC 28; translation modified), a phrase he will repeat twice for emphasis within the space of a single page. He will not explain it, however, until his second contribution, "The Object of 'Capital,'" by asking the question whose absence rendered Marx's discourse hollow: "'*By means of what concept, or what set of concepts, is it possible to think the determination of the elements of a structure, and the structural relations between those elements, and all the effects of those relations, by the effectivity of that structure?' His inability to pose the problem in this way, led him almost inevitably to make use of the oppositions*

between appearance and essence, inner and outer to conceptualize 'the effectiv-
ity' (l'efficacité) of a structure on its elements" (RCC 341; emphasis in original).

This little phrase, certainly calculated to offend and provoke his readers by appearing to suggest a very "structuralist" solution to Marx's problem, represents nothing more or less than its continuation or even active preservation by Althusser, who gives this absence a place and title in his own theoretical world only to see it unmasked and revealed as such, above all by his own efforts to consecrate it as presence. Here, we might for a moment turn to "external" history, the history specific to the text of *Reading Capital* itself, its successive editions and translations, specifically the ways in which this history has succeeded in obscuring some of the most significant fractures in Althusser's text. In fact, what may well be the most significant symptomatic sequelae in *Reading Capital*, are produced by a theoretical deficit that marks Althusser's discussion of "Marx's immense theoretical revolution," the empty place that the future of Marxism depends on filling, but only with the true and necessary concept rather than an imposter or placeholder: namely the radical transformation of the very notion of causality, that is, by what is necessary to the argument and marked as such, but which is finally missing, the notion of structural causality. The deficit to which I refer is most visible, paradoxically, in a long note to the first edition which was omitted from the second edition—on which nearly all foreign-language translations were based—which traced the movement from "the effectivity of a structure on its elements" (which occurs two times in his introductory text, "From Capital to Marx's Philosophy" [RCC 28], and three times in "The Object of Capital" [RCC 346, 348]), to "the presence of a structure in its effects" (RCC 344) or "the existence of a structure in its effects" (RCC 344) (each appears once in "Marx's Immense Theoretical Revolution," the concluding section of Althusser's contribution), to "the structure is immanent in its effects, a cause immanent in its effects in the Spinozist sense of the term" (RCC 344), and, finally, concerning structure, "the effectivity of an absence" (which appears only in the first edition, in a note appended to Althusser's statement that the structure is an "absent cause," near the conclusion of his contribution as a whole). Readers of the English translation, were not only deprived of a page-length note that captures in a condensed form the unresolved conflicts that prevented Althusser from developing the concept of structural causality beyond the level of a slogan, but encountered a version from which important aspects of Althusser's reasoning had been erased. Further, some of the most perceptive critiques of Althusser's contribution to

Reading Capital, both privately and publicly communicated, from Pierre Macherey's letters to Althusser in the summer and fall of 1965 to André Glucksmann's "Un structuralisme ventriloque," published in *Les Temps Modernes* in 1967, focused precisely on the content of the note whose subsequent suppression Althusser never explained or even acknowledged. Finally, though, there can be no avoiding of the fact that neither presence nor immanence nor absence are precisely synonymous or theoretically equivalent, and to the extent that Althusser treats them as such by using them interchangeably and without qualification, he is engaged in papering over a hole in his own account of the hole in Marx's notion of causality.

We cannot allow the paradox to escape us: what the omission of the note on the absent cause renders absent is the theory of the effectivity of absence, the very theory, in however preliminary a form, that allows us to assign to absence the status of a cause that produces effects, the very theory that allows us to read the effects of absence in *Reading Capital*'s attempts to deliver a theory of the effectivity of absence. Further, to make things even more serious, we need this absent theory of absence in order to recognize the absence of absence or perhaps the absence of absence dissimulated as presence. Fortunately, as Spinoza said, "we have a true idea" (*habemus enim ideam veram*)[3] and it is this true idea that is the standard both of itself and of the false versions of itself (*verum index sui et falsi*):[4] unless there is first an idea, we cannot have an idea, even a false idea, of the idea. In this case, we have a true idea of absence and perhaps even a true idea of the effectivity of absence thanks to Althusser himself. By rendering absent the postulation of the effectivity of absence, and by doing so in the most ambivalent way possible, that is, allowing two versions of the same text to circulate, the first edition which contains the discussion of absence as cause and the second which does not, by therefore allowing the play of the presence/absence of the theory of absence, and doing so moreover without any attempt to explain or clarify this divergence, Althusser has not so much erased this absence as simply crossed it out, not subtracting it but adding to it in a way that leaves it legible, leaving traces in the act of effacing his traces. He has thus enacted the absent theory of the effectivity of the absent cause, as if the symptomatic residue of his action calls upon or interpellates us to supply the theory present and effective only in the dispersion of its effects.

I want to look at this absent or rather absented theory of absence, of the effectivity of absence, the site of a simultaneous avowal and denial on Althusser's part, because it not only names but effects an absence at the very time and place, that is, the specification of "Marx's Immense Theoretical Revolution," whose interrogation of historical determination "contained within it what was sufficient to shatter all the classical theories of causality," which is to say all that was required "to render itself misperceived, unseen, buried before it was born." It is here, the end of Althusser's discourse which loses itself in the silence that follows the cessation of Marx's *Capital* ("forty lines, then silence"), where the encounter with the practical truth, *la verità effetuale*, of Marx's discovery, that is, the new notion of causality, should take place in Althusser's text but does not. We might again borrow a figure from Althusser himself and say that this notion "is absent by *lieu-tenance*" (placeholding or delegation). It is submitted to "a structure of flight or gap [*béance*]" and disappears into its attributes or properties: structural, metonymic, immanent, and, finally, absent, perhaps reappearing in Althusser's later work in the evocative form of *le vide*, the void or vacuum, emptiness or nothingness, as if he were finally gesturing at questions that could no longer be asked, after having taken to care to commit to posterity the beginning of an answer in an edition replaced and displaced, but in its material existence ineffaceable. One of the deferred effects of this moment in Althusser's work, and indeed a direct allusion to the central question of causality, was the resurgence of interest in Spinoza, certainly one of the great absent causes of Althusser's thought in that he never produced a real study of Spinoza in the manner of his former students Balibar and Macherey, but also in that sense that Spinoza was never more actual and actualized for Althusser than when he talked about anything other than Spinoza, as if the latter was never really present in person but only in the metonymic sequences in which he acted only through a chain of substitutions that did not originate or end in Spinoza's own work. Althusser's Spinoza, a very powerful Spinoza ("the greatest lesson in heresy the world has ever seen"), did not exist prior to or outside of his effects in philosophy. But the very question of cause, or the question of cause as explored by Spinoza and "represented" through a series of displacements led Althusser, in the singularity of the conjuncture that produced *Reading Capital,* to an interlocutor without whom he could not have thought as he did: Lacan.

It might well seem that to identify Lacan as one of Althusser's most important interlocutors is simply to repeat, as if it were a discovery, what a substantial body of commentary has already explored at length. My objective here, however, is somewhat different from the comparison of systems that characterizes much of this commentary. I want to explore the specific moment, the specific moment out of which *Reading Capital* emerged, at which there occurred between Althusser and Lacan, that is, between the movements of their thought, something akin to what Spinoza described as the formation of a composite body or individual. When two or more bodies are brought into close contact though the pressure of other, external bodies or are simply moving "so as to preserve an unvarying relation of movement among themselves, these bodies are said to be united with one another and together compose one body or individual thing, which is distinguished from other things through this union of bodies" (EII, P13, Lemma 3, Axiom 3, Definition). There is nothing essential about this union and nothing guarantees that it will persist; subjected to the pressure of external forces, the composite thing will decompose. I propose to examine the moment of composition that united Althusser and Lacan in a body of thought for a time which, although brief, was of sufficient duration for their union to produce effects. This is not a comparison of theories, or an attempt to establish influences: it is rather the capture of bodies in motion as they communicate their movements, joined long enough to be together the cause of effects, and thus a singular thing.

To do so, however, requires two postulates:

1. It is impossible not to talk about, or think with, Lacan (which is not the same as "applying" his theory) if one wants to think rigorously about the limits of Althusser's philosophical experiments, or more accurately the limit-concepts first put into practice and only retrospectively identified and theorized as such, that mark his most powerful interventions. And of these, none has left a more indelible trace than that carried out under the slogan of structural causality, or "the structure present in its effects," announced in *Reading Capital* only to disappear from view and left to produce its effects clandestinely, anonymously, as it were. While the Ideological State Apparatuses essay is often (although decreasingly) read as if it were an application of Lacanian concepts to the Marxist notion of ideology, it is in *Reading Capital*, far more than in the later text, that something like a genuine dialogue with Lacan took place, a dialogue that has not received the attention it not only deserves, but requires, if we think that the phrase "structural causality" marks a threshold in the movement of theory and practice. To identify the theoretical transaction that took place as a dialogue is to place it outside the realm of already constituted concepts and in a process of theoretical production in which both Althusser and Lacan participated, an attempt to forge a new concept of causality through a return, beyond Marx and Freud, to such figures as Aristotle, Lucretius, and Spinoza. Perhaps it is possible today to read

Reading Capital in conjunction with *The Four Fundamental Concepts of Psychoanalysis*, read them, or certain parts of them, side by side, as if each were a gloss on the other, or perhaps as if each were a translation of the other into its own idiom, thereby also offering a kind of commentary. To do so is to discover not only a common lexicon but even a set of questions and problems whose very intelligibility depends upon reading these texts as if they carried on, or carry on even now, an urgent conversation, a communication of movement or force, once undetectable but which the conceptual instruments provided to us by the present allow us to capture.

2. To hear this dialogue, that is, to amplify but also isolate it so that it will not be drowned out by the sound and fury of "Lacanianism," however, necessitates a setting aside of the grid of interpretation that has so far been imposed on Lacan's texts. We are thus compelled to risk entering into Lacan's work without the map of Lacanianism to guide us, just as we had to identify and then set aside the "Althusserianism" of the 1970s to read Althusser's texts in a new way, as if Lacan's oeuvre were, as Althusser said of Marx's *Capital*, simultaneously the most familiar and, paradoxically, the least explored territory. To adopt this perspective is to renounce any ambition of proposing a new, more accurate, grid of interpretation to replace the old, that is, a different account of Lacan's theory as a coherent set of propositions. The task, instead, is far more modest but perhaps no less difficult: to find a point of entry, a passage through the theoretical fortress that surrounds Lacan's work, both protecting and imprisoning it, to seek within it the new concept of causality.

From the very beginning of his attempts to initiate the development of a theory adequate to "Marx's discovery," Althusser often spoke of theory's preceding itself in a "practical state [*l'état pratique*]," of having been practiced or put to work prior to its being stated in theoretical form. But the phrase also serves to remind us that theory, no matter how rigorous or coherent, necessarily operates in and through the practical existence of apparatuses and institutions that may impose an order (or disorder) of their own, determining what can and cannot be said or thought and by whom. We cannot completely understand the issues at stake in the attempt to recast the notion of cause by Althusser and Lacan without confronting the material circumstances in which they thought and whose imperatives governed them at least in part without their knowledge or consent.

Following his seminar on structuralism in the academic year 1962–63, Althusser organized a seminar devoted to psychoanalysis that took place between November 1963 and March 1964. He himself delivered two long lectures to the seminar: one in late November (posthumously given the title "Psychanalyse et sciences humaines" by Olivier Corpet and François Matheron) and the other, entitled by Althusser himself "Psychanalyse et psychologie," probably in late January 1964 (the exact date remains unknown). His remarks, read from texts that have since been lost, were recorded and the transcripts published nearly two decades ago. Significantly, these texts have been largely overlooked by commentators (and remain untranslated into English) even though they exhibit a lucidity, density, and theoretical breadth that makes them arguably more significant than the essay "Freud and Lacan," which Althusser wrote for a wider audience, an audience specifically in and around the French Communist Party, at the conclusion of the seminar.[5] As in the latter essay, Althusser announces at the beginning of his first lecture that he (and the members of the seminar, which included Michel Tort, Étienne Balibar, Jacques-Alain Miller, Jean Mosconi, Achille Chiesa, and Yves Duroux) will seek to determine the place of psychoanalysis in the constellation of the human sciences and above all the specific difference that characterizes it as a field of knowledge "through Lacan's interpretation."[6] Lacan's reading of Freud, Althusser tells us, is unprecedented: it both identifies the originality of Freud's fundamental discovery, the unconscious, and simultaneously asserts the inadequacy of the concepts, necessarily borrowed from other disciplines, through which Freud attempted to think this discovery. Althusser's second lecture, "Psychanalyse et psychologie," concerns the primary threat facing psychoanalysis posed by the very attempts by analysts themselves to reformulate Freud's discovery in terms adequate to it. Here, the difficulty that Lacan's work presents to the reader is not a matter of appearances, his "baroque" style or the "intimidating witnesses," from Plato to Heidegger, whose testimony he brings to bear in his inquiry into the current conduct of psychoanalysis.[7] It is rather the objective and absolutely unavoidable consequence of the essential problem before him: the inadequacy of every available notion of causality, leaving him to construct out of the materials available to him, if not an adequate notion of cause, at least one that will allow him to continue the work of theorizing the most fundamental concept of psychoanalysis, the unconscious. At this point, Althusser comments that the most powerful and dangerous attempts to negate the Freudian discovery and its rupture with all previous theories of the mind or soul are those, above all emanating from the field of psychology that work to "deny this rupture," not by simply rejecting but by attempting "to digest or assimilate the new discipline" (PSH 80). They work, above all, by denying what is unprecedented in Freud's discovery, in part because it remains unintelligible from the position they occupy, as if, and it is this that confers upon Lacan's enterprise its urgency and difficulty, it could be sighted at all only from a vantage point in the topography of theory that has yet to be discovered. Every attempt to grasp Freud's thought by means of preexisting concepts of causality can have no other effect than that of translating it into a foreign idiom in which what are perhaps its most important notions are rendered unintelligible.

What gives these themes, sufficiently interesting in themselves, an even greater interest, if not a kind of pathos, was the fact that Althusser's seminar on psychoanalysis had barely begun when, on November 19, 1963, Lacan was removed from his position as a training analyst in the Société Française de Psychanalyse and thus denied the role of training analyst and teacher. The International Psychoanalytic Association, dominated by its affiliate in the United States, had expressed concern for some years at Lacan's rejection of a fixed time for the analytic session and his position that the duration of a session should be determined by the specificity of the analysis and by the analyst's responsibility to intervene not simply through appropriately timed interpretations, but also through a punctuation of the discourse of the analysand.[8] This particular concern was in fact simply one expression of the growing divergence between the French in their majority and the Americans, particularly around the argument that psychoanalysis should be reformulated as an "ego-psychology" whose primary therapeutic objective could be summed up as adaptation to a pregiven environment or milieu. Such a notion drew on contemporary theories of "system" in biology, and functionalism in both psychology and sociology. Lacan's increasing sense that adaptation in this sense meant subjection, led him to a lifelong concern with the problem of the institutionalization of psychoanalysis, a problem very similar to Althusser's sense, from the mid-sixties on, that the French Communist Party, in theory committed to the destruction of capitalism, was in danger of becoming what he would later call an Ideological State Apparatus, a necessary element in the homeostasis of the capitalist system.

Lacan's decision, in some sense inevitable, to leave the society in response to what he regarded as his "excommunication" (invoking Spinoza and thus securing Althusser's identification with Lacan's struggle and his fate), deprived him of a place to hold his annual lecture series and thus potentially of the audience whose attention was necessary to the development of his thought. He delivered one final lecture at Saint-Anne's Hospital, the first and last of what was to have been a yearlong study of "*les noms du père* [the names of the father]" in order to announce his departure.[9] Within two days, Lacan wrote to Althusser, whom he had never met, for the first time, ostensibly to thank him for mentioning him favorably in a footnote to the essay "Philosophie et sciences humaines" published in the summer of 1963.[10] There thus began a brief and increasingly one-sided correspondence in which Althusser's attempts to engage Lacan in a theoretical discussion or even to acknowledge a connection between his own attempts to defend the specificity of Marx's thought and Lacan's defense of "the Freudian thing" were deflected. Althusser succeeded in securing Lacan an amphitheater at the École Normale Supérieure, and the seminar began, but on a new theme which in fact replicated in its own way the Althusserian insistence on the epistemological break that makes possible the emergence of a science: "The Four Fundamental Concepts of Psychoanalysis." The first lecture took place on January 15, 1964; its theme: excommunication from Spinoza to Lacan.

The correspondence between Althusser and Lacan might appear to confirm that the conceptual borrowings and references were as unidirectional as the correspondence itself and that the dialogue that could, and indeed should, have taken place did not. A closer examination of the texts that emerged from this encounter, however, reveals that, despite Lacan's elaborate staging of his theoretical solitude (another Althusserian theme), a kind of dialogue or exchange did take place, one fittingly characterized by a process of condensation and displacement that obscured both the stakes and the positions proper to this exchange. It was in the ceaseless activity of this laboratory of theory that some of the most original and difficult attempts to formulate or at least lay the groundwork for formulating a new way of thinking causality, first proposed in the essays that were later collected and published as *For Marx*, were tested and in certain cases modified. It was here that the diverse lines of inquiry that might be summarized under the heading of "structural causality" (the presence/absence of the structure in its effects, the site of an oscillation rather than a dialectical unity) merged to produce the fault that runs across *Reading Capital*, giving it its unevenness and conferring upon it the permanent instability that is the source of its power.

Thus, in the second of Althusser's lectures on psychoanalysis, the center of his critique of psychology is not simply an account of its political or ideological effects, its simultaneous subjectivation/subjection of the individual and its inability to break with the philosophies of consciousness, but just as, if not more, compellingly, the problem of causality posed by the Freudian concept of the unconscious understood in its specificity and originality. Classical psychology rests on the dualism of nature and culture or nature and society, according to which the human individual is above all a subject of (biological) needs (as well as, despite its denials, of body and mind) first developed by the great political philosophers of the seventeenth and eighteenth centuries. Althusser takes Anna Freud's genetic or developmental psychology as a nearly perfect specimen of a defensive mobilization of ideological and philosophical motifs and myths to ward off the destabilizing effects of the Freudian "break." At the center of a psychologized psychoanalysis is an ego understood not simply as a perception-consciousness system, but even more as will in the classical sense, that faculty, whether stronger or weaker, that allows the human individual to command and subjugate the passions (or, later, instincts or drives), and in doing mediates between the inner (natural/ biological) reality of the human organism, "a biological Id, an interior of the subject, ungraspable from within" (PSH 104) and its milieu or environment, the outer social, cultural reality introjected in the form of a more or less punitive superego and lived as self-condemnation of one's more or less inescapable, because biological, drives. The ego, properly strengthened, must forge a synthesis between the otherwise antagonistic demands of primal biological instincts and cultural renunciation that overcomes (sublates or sublimates) their opposition by uniting the energy of the first with the limiting and ordering function of the second. In this sense, Althusser argues, "it may be said that Anna Freud represents, if you will, the old classical psychology, that of the ego as moral subject that rests on a duality between the subject's interiority and the exteriority of the objective world, meaning both the objective world of perception or the objective world of social norms, of the dominant ethical norms in a society, of the moral demands of society" (PSH 98).

Thus, Anna Freud's revision of psychoanalysis results in "a veritable dissolution of Freudian theory in its entirety," in part because it mimics the theory, familiar to readers of Descartes, Locke, and Kant, of a moral subject whose worth (or health) is determined by its ability to master the passions that arise from the, his, body and who is judged, on the basis of the authority imputed to him, both responsible and accountable for "his" actions (PSH 107). But perhaps more important here are the contradictions that animate and finally disrupt the attempt (not limited to Anna Freud) to theorize the id (le ça) in biological terms and to ground it in the process of somatic development, a project that necessarily calls upon precisely "the classical conceptions of causality," above all what Althusser variously labels expressive or emanative causality, to explain the biological determination of the psyche. According to the model she develops, the unconscious is understood as the seat of urges and the sexual drives as arising within the interiority of the subject as the effect of its physical development; the resulting distribution of both knowledge and desire between consciousness and the unconscious takes place entirely within the confines of the interiority in which both are enclosed. Such a model does not even permit us to speak of an intersubjective realm except as a secondary effect of the unending process of the satisfaction of needs that leads individuals in search of others who may serve as the necessary means to the end of their fulfillment. According to such a view, language itself, otherwise inconceivable except from an interindividual perspective, is the instrument of the psychological subject, the subject "defined by his needs and language intervenes simply as a theory of the sign in relation to the thing or to the subject's own needs in relation to the thing" (PSH 89). The model of successive emanations from a primary hypostasis or substance (from the biological arises need which in turn gives rise to language) thus both guarantees a continuity of what follows from the original ground and that it necessarily takes the form of a dualism in which spirit, dependent on its physical substrate, is the means by which this substrate is perpetuated.

According to Althusser's reading of Lacan, whose theory he brings to bear at this point, the biological does not appear in person on the scene of the unconscious; if it appears at all it is in the paradoxical form of a necessary absence, necessary because in the absence of this absence, the unconscious properly speaking could not exist. It is "Lacan's great discovery" that the "passage from the biological to the cultural is in fact the effect of the action of the cultural on the biological" (PSH 91). It is culture in a movement of "pre-cession" that assigns the biological its place as originary cause, a paradox that leads Althusser to speak of "an inversion of determination." But a few lines later, even this paradox must give way to the assertion that "society always precedes itself" (PSH 93) which evacuates every notion of a chronological transition from a natural state to the social, of an original condition that is both temporally and logically prior to (and is thus the condition of) the transition to society. The presocial individual now appears in the face of Lacanian theory to be a kind of primal scene projected retroactively as what Derrida called a prosthetic origin or original prosthesis, the effect above all of language that precedes and makes possible the needs it expresses. Every attempt to postulate a continuity between the biological and the psychic must have recourse to the notions of causality once employed to derive material creation from an immaterial God: derivation, expression, and emanation. But, as Spinoza remarked, how can one substance produce another, different, substance whose nature is foreign to its own? The attempt to trace the psychic back to its origins in the somatic can only discover its absence, as if the somatic has always already been supplanted by the psychic and instinct by drive. Althusser points to Rousseau's critique of Hobbes "and in a general sense all the philosophers of natural right in that they had sought to imagine a being who was purely natural when in reality they simply projected into the state of nature the very structures of the social state. They attempted to represent as non-cultural a being which they had in fact endowed with all the cultural properties necessary to think the social state from which it had been abstracted" (PSH 92–93). Rousseau himself discovered that every attempt to strip away the remnants of culture and society in hopes of reaching an authentically natural nature was doomed to failure: nature itself never appeared in person but only through a sequence of stand-ins. To imagine natural man, without language, thought, or emotions, solitary but without even a consciousness of himself, was to discover an origin that never existed, an original nothingness or absence that could not even be said to have initiated the process from which man emerged.[11] This is, according to Althusser, the philosophical significance of Lacan's notion of the symbolic: "Culture is what always precedes itself, and this precedence, this permanent antecedence of culture in relation to itself is what is represented by this circle" (PSH 94). The notion of the unconscious as the seat of instincts existing prior to culture is thus a reenactment of the philosophical/political myths of the seventeenth and eighteenth centuries and remains as enclosed in the circle of consciousness as they were in the circle of culture, equally devoted to the pursuit of an object whose absence is the effect of the inquiry itself.

In fact, Althusser had formulated this problem in very similar terms, a year earlier in the essay "Contradiction and Overdetermination" (1962), but in relation to the question of the effectivity of the economic base on the political, legal, and cultural superstructure, an effectivity often understood as "expression" or "representation": the superstructure "expresses" both the forms and requirements of the economic base. He examines Engels's famous letter to J. Bloch in which the former argues against the notion "that the economic element is the *only* determining one." In contrast, Engels argues, "according to the materialist conception of history, the production and reproduction of real life is the determining moment in history in the last instance [*in letzter*

Instanz]."[12] The economic situation is the basis but the different moments of the superstructure determine the "form" of class struggles and their results. "There is an interaction of all these elements in which, amid all the endless host of accidents (that is, of things and events whose inner interconnection is so remote or so impossible of proof that we can regard it as nonexistent, as negligible), the economic movement finally asserts itself as necessary [*die ökonomische Bewegung sich durchsetzt*]."[13] Here, Althusser transposes Engels's account of the superstructural mediation of the economic which must lie at the origin of the levels of the superstructure in order to "assert" itself or "break through" at the end, at the last, as if the economic required the middle term of superstructure in order to return to itself and its role as determinant instance. In a surprising turn, Althusser argues that the economic instance never acts "in a pure state," that the "superstructural instances never step aside respect-fully when they have done their work or dissipate as if they were its pure phe-nomenon to allow his majesty the Economy, its Time having come, to advance on the royal road of the dialectic."[14] Althusser evokes the messianic concept of parousia or advent, the coming of the king whose time is surely near, to capture the paradoxes of Engels's formulation: behind "its" phenomena, its expressions, its effects, all of which have arisen on its foundation only now to conceal it, the economic cause will be revealed, the first and the last. But, Althusser adds, if we rigorously follow Engels's argument, "neither at the first instant nor the last, the solitary hour of the 'last instance' never comes."[15] The cause does not precede its effects, nor is it present to them as their basis. But neither is it exactly immanent: it is absent from both beginning and end, or rather is the absence of both beginning and end, the origin that, always already superseded and thus originally absent, was only constituted retroactively, as if the absent cause were only made present in and by its effects.

Lacan began his seminar, *The Four Fundamental Concepts of Psychoanaly-sis,* by invoking Spinoza only in part to define himself as having been subject to an excommunication; he also sought through Spinoza to call attention to the nature of the guarantee of truth that can only be conferred by the pro-cedures of authorization. Lacan, following Spinoza's argument in the *Trea-tise on the Emendation of the Intellect,* raises the question of the nature and function of a truth that, insufficient to itself, requires a guarantee, that of the truth of truth. In this sense, the demand for the *auctoritas* that will establish the credibility of the psychoanalyst is finally a demand for surety or security made necessary by the infinite regression toward the truth of the truth of the truth that the demand itself sets into motion. In such a context, no question could be more provocative or revealing than "what are the foundations, in the broadest sense of the term, of psychoanalysis? Which means: what founds it as a practice?"[16] The answers to these questions will determine whether the psychoanalytic community is functionally identical to a church, its practice in both form and content, a religious practice or in opposition whether "it is a science" (FFC 11).

For Lacan, the question of the scientificity or what might be called the objectivity of psychoanalytic theory, of the knowledge produced by its practice, cannot be addressed by seeking to adapt or assimilate it to an already existing science. On the contrary, such attempts represent a short-circuiting of the work of the specification of the theoretical object proper to psychoanalysis, given that "what defines a science is that it has an object . . . or at least a certain reproducible level of operation that is called experience. But we must be very cautious, because this object changes, and singularly, in the course of the evolution of a science" (FFC 8). Writing at the same moment, January 1964, and in response to the same events, the same crisis, simultaneously institutional and theoretical, Althusser describes the essential task of Lacan's "return to Freud" as that of "situating *the object* of psychoanalysis in order to give it an initial definition in concepts that allow its localization, a preliminary step indispensable to the elucidation of this object. Further, these concepts must be put into operation "as much as possible in their most rigorous form, as does every scientific discipline."[17] Althusser's description of the immediate tasks of psychoanalysis serves quite well as a brief introduction to the objectives of Lacan's seminar. But his analysis perhaps even more importantly allows us to understand not only the choice of the four concepts, but also their order, which is anything but arbitrary. Psychoanalysis does indeed have an object, according to Althusser, and it is the primary stake in the struggle Lacan has waged using every weapon at his disposal against the numerous attempts to annex psychoanalysis to an existing science or philosophical doctrine and thereby neutralize and contain Freud's discovery: this object is the unconscious, the first of the four fundamental concepts. In this way, the unconscious is the foundation of the fundamental concepts and therefore the foundation of the foundation. And to tie this inquiry even more directly to his own, Althusser would write soon after his seminar on *Capital*: "The unconscious is manifested, that is, *exists* in its *effects*." And further, "this manifestation is not that of an essence whose effects are its phenomena,"[18] such that the unconscious as a cause does not exist prior to or outside its effects.

In "The Freudian Unconscious and Ours," the first of the lectures Lacan devoted to the topic of the "Unconscious and Repetition," that is to the object of psychoanalysis itself, all the paradoxes that Althusser noted in both relation to psychological notions of the unconscious and to Engels's letter to Bloch, the paradoxes that haunted and destabilized every notion of foundation and basis, are repeated. Lacan immediately moves to exclude the idea that the unconscious can be grasped as a location, a seat or site of instincts, urges, or even desires (*Wunschen*). Further, even language which offers the material support for the work of the unconscious cannot be understood in its existence as a "presubjective" and therefore unconscious "combinatorial game operating spontaneously" (*FFC* 20) to transmute the potential into the actual as the unconscious in Freud's sense. The Freudian unconscious cannot be understood in the form of a potential existence that has not yet been actualized by means of a process of selection itself determined by a set of rules external or internal to language itself (and whose existence cannot be explained). The "solution" to this problem, the formalist notion of the unconscious, is often found through recourse to a dynamic theory, which simply replaces one mystery with another, that of "force" which "is used to designate a locus of opacity" (*FFC* 21). In opposition to both the formal and dynamic models of the unconscious, Lacan announces that he will instead address the problem they work in their very opposition to obscure: "the function of cause" (*FFC* 21), the very notion that has forever troubled and embarrassed philosophers. It has taken Lacan no more than three pages to join Althusser in problematizing in an intransigent and provocative way the very idea of cause in its current forms and in suggesting that to rethink it in the light of psychoanalysis will likely result in a shattering of the classical notions of causality. Like Althusser, and just as at ease with paradox and contradiction, Lacan recognizes that the very inquiry he pursues demands a theory of causality that does not (yet) exist and which can only emerge from the very inquiry that cannot proceed in its absence.

To find a way out of this vicious circle, Lacan turns to Kant, not for a new theory of causality, but to grasp the precise way that the function of cause in philosophical and scientific discourse poses a problem. In his "Attempt to Introduce the Concept of Negative Magnitudes into Philosophy," Kant openly questions the notion of cause as presence, that is, as what he calls real or positive ground (another foundation or basis), present to its effects, guiding and conferring meaning upon them. In opposition, Kant maintains that we often call cause what is a lack or absence: in this early work, an absence of resistance and thus an absence of force. This lack is not a privation (*Beraubung*) of what was originally present, but an originary absence (*Mangel*) which can be said to produce effects only in absentia. It is in the later work, however, and here Lacan cites the *Prolegomena*, that the problem of cause is posed as such: in response to Hume, Kant shows that the term "cause" is a gap (Lacan uses the word *béance*) in a sequence, an interruption that cannot be understood at the empirical level insofar as it is a hole in perception that must be compensated for at the level of the a priori. But the compensatory function of the Kantian a priori only succeeds in calling attention to the fact that cause understood as *béance* is unanalyzable from the perspective of reason. Lacan insists that "each time we speak of cause, there is always something of the anti-conceptual, of the indefinite or undefined" (FFC 22). In the statement, for example, that "miasmas are the cause of fever," "cause" not only has no meaning, it is rather a "hole" (*trou*) or interval through which something oscillates. In brief, there is no cause except from what does not work, or what stumbles (FFC 22).

Here Lacan uses every means at his disposal to problematize what he identifies as the continuity presupposed by the notions of causality that have governed all previous attempts to think the specificity of the unconscious. On the one hand, the direct contact of what Althusser would call transitive causality, which he associates with Descartes and the theoretical necessity of the pineal gland as the point at which the mind, otherwise without communication with the body, can act directly on the body, touching it, as it were, and thereby determining or causing it to act. On the other, expressive or emanative causality, according to which the effect "flows" from the cause (the verb *mano* signifies "to flow") which emits it, continuous with it, but always inferior to it. In opposition to both models, Lacan locates cause at the moment of disconnection, the point at which "impediment, failure, split [*achoppment, défaillance, fêlure*]" (FFC 25) interrupt the continuity we associate with the causal relation. In fact, it is discontinuity, which Lacan will call "absolute" and "inaugural," that is "the essential form in which the unconscious first appears to us as a phenomenon—the discontinuity in which something is manifested itself as a vacillation" (FFC 25, translation modified). To conceive of an absolute, original, or inaugural discontinuity is to exclude any notion of its disruption of a totality that would precede it and against which it would alone be defined: "is there a *one* anterior to discontinuity?" For Lacan, the only "*one* introduced by the experience of the unconscious is the *one* of the crack [*la fente*], the line [*le trait*], and the rupture [*la rupture*]" (FFC 26, translation modified). If there exists an "*un*" (a one), it is the German prefix "*un*," as in *Unbewusste*, that is, the "un" in unconscious: "let us say that the limit of the *Unbewusste* is the *Unbegriff*— not the non-concept, but the concept of lack" (FFC 26). Here again, Lacan is uncompromising in his opposition to a philosophy of the negative or negation, as well as to a philosophy of the void, resolutely refusing to postulate an original ground: "Where is the foundation [*le fond*]? Is it absence? Not at all. The rupture, the crack, the line of the opening produces [*fait surgir*] absence" (FFC 26, translation modified). It is a syncope, the movement of forgetting and erasure, the line that draws the gap between two points, the mark of absence absenting itself, of that which, neither being nor nonbeing, realizes its own nonrealization in a movement without end.

It is precisely in relation to the imperative to develop a conception of causality adequate to Freud's discovery that Lacan turns to Descartes and the notion of the subject of certainty (and doubt). The notion of the unconscious as gap, fissure, syncope, as that which fails, stumbles, and arrests, in short, as the hole through which the perpetual oscillation captured in the phrase, "*wo Es war, soll Ich werden*" as read by Lacan, renders every recovery of memory or of truth, above all the memory or truth of a dream, the loss and return of what has never been present. For Lacan, Descartes's *Meditations* represents the *mise en abime* of the subject of certainty.

Martial Gueroult, a decade before Lacan's seminar, described in detail the theoretical cost of the certainty with which Descartes endowed the Cogito: in order for me to be certain that I exist, I must think that I think, for even though I cannot *not* think, I cannot always think only of my own thought.[19] The certainty of my existence is then never given or permanently established; it is a certainty that must be perpetually enacted or reenacted. I cannot be sure (and therefore I must doubt) that I exist when I cease thinking of my thought, as I must, to arrive at the knowledge of external things (including my own body) that the certainty of my existence as a thing that thinks is supposed to make possible. There is no certainty in the only expedient I have, that is, memory, because nothing assures me in the absence of the thought I remember thinking that it is not rather a dream I am having now than a reality that existed in the past. Thus, the very attempt to think about the world can only result in the disappearance into doubt of both self and world. What is this if not the oscillation between presence and absence that afflicts every attempt to think, and even more to speak, in the first person? There can be no I without a guarantee of its otherwise precarious certainty, the certainty of certainty. Even what I have taken to be clear and distinct ideas of external things, even a mathematical truth like two added to three make five must not be accepted as true, given that a God might have created me in a such a way that I am deceived in even the simplest things. And the *"praeconcepta"* of God's "supreme power" constrains him to admit that God could easily deceive him, if he so chose (*Med.* III.4). Thus, it is only "through a blind impulse that I believed that there were things that existed outside of me [*ex caeco aliquo impulsu, credidisse res quasdam a me diversas existere*]" (*Med.* III.12). The one exception is the idea of God, infinite, eternal, all-knowing and omnipotent, creator of all things, an idea so foreign and superior to him that it could not have originated in his mind. Such a perfect being could not deceive him, given that the desire to deceive is a defect. It is this fact alone, the fact of the individual's incompleteness, his dependence on another that allows him access to the certainty (and not simply the truth) that his mind requires to know the world outside of himself. As Lacan comments, the truth remains outside for Descartes, placed in the hands of an Other whose very existence he can nevertheless find only within himself, among the ideas that he has and in the thoughts that he thinks, whose foreignness and irreducible alterity alone guarantees or certifies not only the distinction between the true and the false, but the very identity of his person.

It is at this point that Lacan's formula "the real as encounter" (FFC 55) takes on its significance. He attributes the idea of encounter not to Epicurus or Lucretius, the sources of Althusser's materialism of the encounter, but to Aristotle, drawing particularly on the discussion of causes in the *Physics* (II.4–6). Of particular interest to Lacan, is the fact that, following his explanation of the famous "four causes," material, formal, efficient, and final, Aristotle notes "that there are many things that exist or are produced by chance or accident [ἡ τύχη καὶ τὸ αὐτόματον]." While most previous philosophers have rejected the notion that chance and accident can produce effects, and that everything which we ascribe to chance or spontaneity has some definite cause, nearly everyone distinguishes between things that happen by chance and things that do not. But just as Aristotle rejects the notion that nothing happens by accident or chance, he even more vehemently rejects the argument "that everything in the cosmos" is attributable "to an accidental or spontaneous cause [αἰτιῶνται τὸ αὐτόματον]." He finds astonishing the idea that the cosmic order, including the movements of heavenly bodies which never deviate from their fixed course, could arise from chance collisions and conjunctions of atoms moving through space is surely a paradox.

For Aristotle, "chance" applies to things that do not follow necessarily, always or even in most cases from others, but only to sequences that occur outside of necessity or through a kind of para-necessity. Here, Aristotle introduces the distinction between "chance" (τύχη) and accident or fortune (αὐτόματον). The stone that falls on a man's head, if it was determined by natural causes and was not aimed at him, is an example of accident or fortune. In contrast, chance appears only in the case of "a being capable of choice" and of purposive conduct. According to Lacan, the intended act produces in realizing itself a gap or fissure in the necessary sequence of things, producing, as it in a sense reproduces an intention, a hole within necessity itself through which a kind of para-necessity emerges and with it, the possibility of another necessary sequence, contrary to the first. Lacan finds in Aristotle a pluralization of necessity that frees it from determinism and teleology: there will always be the chance of chance events and therefore of the sudden emergence of new necessities and new causal series as if, as Althusser himself would later say, necessity were a modality of chance. In fact, Lacan has produced a Lucretian reading of Aristotle according to which chance is that which "breaks the decree of destiny [foedera fati rumpat]" (DRN II.225), the swerve without which cause would follow cause in an unchanging order; τύχη (tuché) is the "real as encounter," but the missed encounter, that which is beyond the repetition on which the order of things is based. Like the last instance of the economy, the real as Lacan defines it is present only in the form of absence, the missed encounter ("le rencontre manqué" [FFC 55]) that interrupts the chain of causes.

Here, Althusser's reformulation in Reading Capital of the paradox of the last instance that never arrives functions as a kind of commentary on Lacan's meditations on the unconscious as a knot of absent causes:

> The structure is not an essence *outside* the economic phenomena which comes and alters their aspect, forms and relations and which is effective on them as an absent cause, *absent because it is outside them. The absence of the cause in the structure's "metonymic causality" on its effects is not the fault of the exteriority of the structure with respect to the economic phenomena; on the contrary, it is the very form of the interiority of the structure, as a structure, in its effects.* This implies therefore that the effects are not outside the structure, are not a pre-existing object, element or space in which the structure arrives to *imprint its mark:* on the contrary, it implies that the structure is immanent in its effects, a cause immanent in its effects in the Spinozist sense of the term, that *the whole existence*

of the structure consists of its effects, in short that the structure, which is merely a specific combination of its peculiar elements, is nothing outside its effects. (RC 188–89)

"The absence of the cause" which produces what he calls "metonymic causality" must be understood not as its distance or exteriority in relation to what it affects, as if it were an imminent rather than immanent presence, already constituted as an object waiting to impose itself through its effects. On the contrary, its absence is essential and constitutive of the always already displaced forms of a present that takes the form of a metonymic representation of the absence of what is represented. But to conceptualize such a notion of cause, Althusser was compelled to draw a line of demarcation which divided, and in dividing made visible, the distinction between absence and negation, and releasing within the concept of absence itself two incompatible meanings: the external absence that is nothing more than a distant presence, producing effects, but at a remove, and the internal absence of the immanent cause whose immanence is its radical absence from both the outside and the inside, the absolute immanence of a cause utterly absent outside of its effects, unable to take the form even of an "indwelling" that would allow it to be distinguished from the cause with which it coexists. Finally, then, Althusser renders absent absence itself; even absence must not be allowed to stand as such in its "presence." Has Althusser thus returned to Hegel, to the very figure of the negation of the negation necessary to the teleological movement of Spirit? If so, he has returned to the place from which Hegel was present only in his absence, the metonymic cause of a discourse that cannot negate the antagonism that constitutes it to become a unified totality, a discourse whose very existence postpones its end. Rather than negate the negation, Althusser occupies the place of the negative in a way that dismembers it, or in a way that shows that, rather than overcome contradiction, the labor of the negative reveals the gap, the fissure that separates the negative from itself, the lack, the failure, the stumbling of the negative that finally prevents it from returning upon and negating itself.

Althusser and Lacan, for a certain duration conjoined as a singular thing, communicating their movements and producing effects even as they hurtled toward the smash-up. This thing exists now as the absent cause of a new conception of causality, the broken chain, the interrupted sequence where no encounter takes place, the site of the break, the cut, the fracture, the cause that does not exist prior to or outside of its effects. To read Althusser reading

Capital is to see in the figures of gap, break, fracture, absence the paradoxical forms of a real contracted into itself, that is, into a conflictual diversity that, simultaneously cause and effect of itself, remains irreducible, the concepts indispensable to a new conception of materiality and the theory adequate to it.

Notes

1. Louis Althusser, Étienne Balibar, Roger Establet, Pierre Macherey, and Jacques Rancière, *Reading* Capital: *The Complete Edition* (London: Verso, 2015). Further page references will be cited in the text as RCC.

2. Pierre Macherey, "On the Rupture," *Minnesota Review* 26 (1986): 125; original, "Apropos de la rupture," *La Nouvelle Critique* 166 (1965): 133–41.

3. Baruch Spinoza, *Treatise on the Emendation of the Intellect*, trans. Samuel Shirley, ed. Seymour Feldman (Indianapolis: Hackett, 2002), 10.

4. Baruch Spinoza, Letter 76, To Albert Burgh, December 1675, *Selected Letters*, trans. Samuel Shirley, ed. Seymour Feldman (Indianapolis: Hackett, 1992).

5. Louis Althusser, "Freud and Lacan," in *Lenin and Philosophy* (New York: Monthly Review Press, 1971), 189–220.

6. Louis Althusser, *Psychanalyse et sciences humaines: Deux conférences* (Paris: IMEC, 1996), 19. Further page references will be cited in the text as PSH.

7. Althusser, "Freud and Lacan," 203.

8. Elisabeth Roudinesco, *Histoire de la psychanalyse en France*, vol. 2 (Paris: Editions du Seuil, 1986), 328–77.

9. A transcription of Lacan's lecture from November 20, 1963, may be found at www.mathinees-lacaniennes.net/en/articles/111-les-noms-du-pere-seminaire-du -20111963-de-jacques-lacan.html.

10. Louis Althusser, "Philosophie et sciences humaines," in *Revue de l'Enseignement philosophique*, June–July 1963, 7–11.

11. For a later and more *expanded* analysis of Rousseau on these questions, see Louis Althusser, *Cours sur Rousseau* (Paris: Le Temps de Cerises, 2012).

12. Engels, Engels to J. Bloch, London, September 21, 1890.

13. Engels to J. Bloch.

14. Althusser, "Contradiction and Overdetermination," in *For Marx*, trans. Ben Brewster (London: Verso, 1969), 113.

15. Althusser, "Contradiction and Overdetermination," 113 (translation modified).

16. Jacques Lacan, *The Four Fundamental Concepts of Psychoanalysis* (New York: W. W. Norton, 1978), 6. Further page references will be cited in the text as FCC.

17. Althusser, "Freud and Lacan," 15.

18. Althusser, "Three Notes on the Theory of Discourses," in *The Humanist Controversy and Other Writings* (London: Verso, 2003), 47.

19. Martial Gueroult, *Descartes' Philosophy Interpreted according to the Order of Reasons*, 2 vols., trans. Roger Ariew (Minneapolis: University of Minnesota Press, 1984).

CHAPTER 8

Marx's Bones

Breaking with Althusser

ADRIAN JOHNSTON

To commemorate the publication of *Reading Capital* and *For Marx* is, rather obviously, not to celebrate Louis Althusser's oeuvre in its entirety. By the late 1970s, this oeuvre itself becomes less than wholeheartedly celebratory about these two landmark 1965 volumes, developing as regards them a self-critical ambivalence producing a proliferation of caveats, hesitations, qualifications, and reservations.[1] Instead, the commemoration of *Reading Capital* and *For Marx* is that precisely of the thesis for which Althusser is best known, the contention most responsible for his combined fame and infamy: the alleged Bachelardian-style "epistemological break" in Karl Marx's corpus, the purported "rupture" of 1845 (specifically with Feuerbachian humanism) inaugurated that year by Marx with *The German Ideology* and the eleven "Theses on Feuerbach."

Through my brief intervention here, I wish to pay homage to this now-fifty-year-old Althusser by repeating with respect to him the maneuver he sometimes describes *Reading Capital* in particular as performing vis-à-vis Marx. Specifically, Althusser's backward glance subsequently recasts his and his students' labors circa 1965 as attempting to furnish (as attempted by some of Althusser's later struggles too) the mature Marx's historical materialist critique of political economy with an explicit philosophy implicit within but nonetheless conspicuously absent from Marx's post-1845 corpus (and also lacking in Friedrich Engels's and V. I. Lenin's conjunctural, nonsystematic moves to make consciously present this nascent, unconscious philosophy).[2] In what follows, I intend to do the same apropos Althusser's works about Marx's "Works of the Break."[3] That is to say, my goal herein is to sketch the contours of a philosophical position arguably required by but still palpably missing from the strain of Althusserianism being specially remembered in this volume. Whether what results from these gestures of mine is digestible by (and not toxic to) the classic Althusser of *Reading Capital* and *For Marx* will have to be seen.

Notwithstanding both Althusser's tricky relations with (and within) the French Communist Party (PCF) as well as his entirely appropriate disgust with Stalinism generally and Joseph Stalin's *diamat* particularly (with the latter including certain regrettable Engelsian and Leninist props),[4] he recurrently sings the praises of "dialectical materialism." He sometimes even speaks favorably of versions of it tracing back to the Eastern-loved (and, more often than not, Western-despised) Engels of the trilogy, with its *Naturdialektik*, formed by *Anti-Dühring*, *Dialectics of Nature*, and *Ludwig Feuerbach and the Outcome of Classical German Philosophy* (an Engels carried forward most notably by the Lenin of *Materialism and Empirio-Criticism* and the *Philosophical Notebooks*).[5] In this same vein, he also insists upon *Natur an sich* being objectively dialectical.[6] I think it safe to observe that, although Althusser certainly is no proponent of orthodox Soviet *diamat*, there is ample textual evidence that he nevertheless remains steadfastly convinced during much of his career that the phrase "dialectical materialism" is a not unsuitable label for Marx's (non) philosophy[7] (or, at least, Althusser's own creative reconstruction of this philosophy). For instance, 1963's seminal essay "On the Materialist Dialectic: On the Unevenness of Origins" in *For Marx* christens this materialism "Theory" with a capital *T*.[8]

To go into more detail along the preceding lines, Althusser, throughout his writings, tends quite consistently to describe historical materialism as a "science" (i.e., the science of history discovered by Marx starting in 1845, whose scientificity allegedly is equal to that enjoyed by mathematics, physics, chemistry, biology, etc.)[9] and dialectical materialism as the "philosophy" called for by this science as its crucial philosophical accompaniment and foundation.[10] In multiple texts, including many closely tied by date and content to *Reading Capital* and *For Marx* as well as these two 1965 texts themselves, Althusser describes the philosophy of dialectical materialism as lagging behind the science of historical materialism and stresses the theoretical and practical urgency of strenuous efforts aimed at getting dialectical materialism up to speed.[11] However, in the combined lights of Althusser's self-criticisms of the 1970s and 1980s (including his repudiation of the idea that there is or could be a truly scientific "science of history")[12] and, especially, his regrets of the 1980s apropos the topic of dialectical materialism ("that 'yellow logarithm' [*logarithme jaune]"* and "philosophical monstrosity [*monstruosité philosophique]"* with its "unthinkable theses [*thèses impensable],"* "that horror, a *dialectical* materialist [*matérialiste* dialectique, *cette horreur]"*),[13] what, if anything, does Althusser bequeath to posterity specifically in terms of a distinctive philosophical legacy? Across the span of Althusser's works, does he at one or more moments succeed, however consciously or unconsciously, with or against himself, at articulating something on the order of Marx's philosophy, a Marxist philosophy, "a philosophy *for Marxism*,"[14] a materialist dialectic, and/or a dialectical materialism?

My answer to the immediately prior question is affirmative—and, I consider both *Reading Capital* and *For Marx* to be two of multiple textual moments contributing to the articulation of an Althusserian philosophical materialism—albeit with accompanying riders to the effect that, as with Marx for Althusser, so too with Althusser for me. This Althusserian philosophy, which, following most of Althusser himself (prior to the 1980s), I will continue to refer to as "dialectical materialism," is more implicit than explicit in Althusser's writings and teachings. Moreover, in my eyes, Althusserian dialectical materialism subsists latently between the lines of what Althusser manifestly states about it at least as much as it consists in these manifest lines themselves. Additionally, and taking the liberties a psychoanalytically informed and Marxist-materialist[15] interpretive approach affords (liberties indispensably underpinning the exegesis of Marx's *magnum opus* in *Reading Capital* itself),[16] I will allow myself here to (re)assemble an Althusserian dialectical materialism on the basis of an arc of his texts from the early 1960s through the 1980s, including the inconsistencies, lacunae, and shifts within and between these myriad pieces drawn from different periods of Althusser's thinking. In short, I will try to read Althusser as he reads Marx (and as Jacques Lacan reads Sigmund Freud)—to raise a body of theory, whether with it and/or against it, to the dignity of its philosophical Notion. This will be my specific "return to Althusser."

The best manner to begin my (re)assemblage of an Althusserian dialectical materialism (maybe, as Lacan might describe it, extimately in Althusser more than Althusser himself)[17] might be to highlight certain of Althusser's theses apropos both materialism and dialectics. For starters, Althusser, on a number of occasions in both the 1960s and 1970s, sees fit to emphasize that, in a truly materialist dialectical materialism, its "materialism" component is primary and its "dialectical" component is secondary; there is an unevenness of weight or priority, an imbalance favoring the side of materialism.[18] In one of the texts in which this is stressed (1974's essay "Elements of Self-Criticism"), he also equates the "dialectical-materialist" with the "non-speculative and non-positivist."[19] I take this equation to express an insistence that dialectical materialism must strive to navigate carefully between, on one side, the Scylla of nonmaterialist dialectics (i.e., "speculation" qua idealist armchair philosophizing disconnected from the sciences in its hermetically sealed study) and, on another side, the Charybdis of nondialectical materialism (i.e., "positivism" qua non/antiphilosophical adhesion to those aspects of the "spontaneous philosophies of the scientists" involving mechanism, reductionism, and the like).

As I underscored above, Althusser regularly distinguishes between historical and dialectical materialisms as science and philosophy respectively (with, in the case of Marxism, the philosophical arguably being underdeveloped by comparison with the scientific). More generally, a frequent Althusserian refrain has it that epistemological breaks in the sciences—Althusser's preferred examples of Thales, Galileo Galilei, and Marx indicate that, for him, "science" (like the German *Wissenschaft*) includes bodies of knowledge dealing with the formal, the natural, and the sociohistorical—are conditions of possibility for subsequent emergences of corresponding new philosophies.[20] In his renowned 1967 lecture course on "philosophy and the spontaneous philosophy of the scientists," he goes so far as to claim that "the relation between philosophy and the sciences constitutes the *specific* determination of philosophy"[21] and even that "*outside of its relationship to the sciences, philosophy would not exist.*"[22]

Before proceeding further—I still have a ways to go in terms of making the case I want to make on the basis of Althusser's texts—I should put my cards squarely on the table right up front at this relatively early stage in my contribution. For both Marx and Engels, the "Darwin-event" (to misappropriate former Althusser student Alain Badiou's language) provides a key scientific resource, inspiration, and justification for their then-novel materialism.[23] That is to say, Charles Darwin's earth-shattering historicization of nature, his epoch-making subversion of the traditionally rigid distinction between the natural and the historical, promises, in Marx's and Engels's eyes, significantly to buttress and help advance historical and dialectical materialism.[24] This noted, the rest of what unfolds below will be devoted to extracting from Althusser's writings a theoretical apparatus responding to the contention that philosophy as dialectical materialism still lags behind not (only) historical materialism as the science of history à la Marx, but the science of natural history as per Darwin and his scientific descendants. In this vein, I think it is no accident that the later Althusser explicitly situates Darwin as a major figure in the subterranean philosophical tradition of the "underground current" of the "aleatory materialism of the encounter."[25]

Although this just-declared agenda of mine might sound to some like a bit of an implausible stretch in relation to Althusser, such, I would contend, is not in fact the case. First of all, Althusser himself unambiguously identifies the life sciences as genuinely scientific in the strictest of senses.[26] In this, he tacitly takes some distance from the mid-twentieth-century neorationalism of French epistemology and history of science (such as that associated with Alexandre Koyré)[27] in which a Galilean-Cartesian (over)emphasis on formalization privileges mathematics and physics as the epitomes of scientificity (and correlatively tends to downplay or disqualify biology as a science). Elsewhere, Althusser observes, in the context of taking a swipe at Paul Ricoeur's *De l'interprétation: Essai sur Freud* (1965), that recourse to biology is integral to Freud's forging of a distinctively anti-hermeneutical theory of the unconscious (an antihermeneutics brought out by Lacan's "return to Freud" and dovetailing with Althusser's version of a genuinely Marxian approach to ideology).[28] Relatedly, he baptizes Freud a dialectical materialist.[29] Finally, and most importantly for my specific purposes, there is the 1967 essay vigorously defending *Reading Capital* and *For Marx*, "The Humanist Controversy." Not only does this essay identify (contra the late, quasi-Marxist as well as the early, existentialist humanism of Jean-Paul Sartre) Engelsian-style *Naturdialektik* as invaluable and irreplaceable for combatting anthropocentric idealisms of wholly antinatural human subjectivity[30]—in line with this identification, it also foregrounds the (post-)Darwinian life sciences as on the front lines of an ideological war against antimaterialist "spiritualism" and the like.[31] Along the same lines, Althusser, in *Philosophy and the Spontaneous Philosophy of the Scientists* (also of 1967), contrasts the tendencies of post-Newtonian physics to facilitate idealist and spiritualist hijackings of science (something hammered home at length in Lenin's 1908 *Materialism and Empirio-Criticism*)[32] with the absolutely central role of a militantly materialist position for biology and biologists.[33]

Of course, any discussion of science (especially the empirical, experimental natural sciences of modernity) in connection with Althusser cannot pass over in silence Althusser's multiple reflections on the relations between the scientific and the ideological. And, especially in a contemporary theoretical context colored by intense anxieties specifically about the life sciences and their scientistic offshoots—"biopolitics"/"biopower" à la Michel Foucault and Giorgio Agamben as well as "democratic materialism" à la Badiou are the most familiar recent expressions of these philosophical and political worries[34]— I would be particularly remiss not to address these issues in the course of (re) constructing a type of Althusserian *Naturdialektik*. Althusser himself readily admits that the sciences, including Marx's historical materialism as the science of history, constantly are threatened with the prospects of contamination, exploitation, and misdirection by dominant ideologies (with, in Althusser's avowedly Lenin-inspired view, a correctly formulated dialectical materialism being desperately needed as "a *true* guide" steering the sciences clear of these ideological/epistemological obstacles).[35]

As regards Althusser on the science-ideology rapport, I will proceed here from science in general to biology in particular. To begin with, and on the basis of Althusser's justified thesis that all sciences contain within their very bases nonempirical and ideological elements, he maintains that sciences emerge from, albeit then break with, ideologies—with the very distinction between the scientific and the ideological being visible only retroactively, after the fact of the the emergence of the science in question.[36] Moreover, a science's breaking with ideologies is a perpetually, indefinitely repeated gesture/process; any science again and again has to push away ideological (re)encroachments.[37] However, at the same time, Althusser rightly avoids reducing science qua science *in toto* to ideology. Despite the ceaselessly ongoing entanglements of the scientific with the ideological, there is a real difference-in-kind between science and ideology. In this same vein, Althusser proposes that the sciences do not fit, cannot be neatly situated within, the classic Marxist social-topographical distinction between infrastructure and superstructure.[38]

In terms of the life sciences specifically, Althusser, faithful to his anti-Stalinism, has nothing but harshly condemnatory words for the intellectual and political disaster in the USSR centered on the figure of Trofim Denisovich Lysenko, the Ukrainian agronomist favored by Stalin whose "Michurian biology" ideologically condemned Mendelian genetics in the Soviet Union for many years.[39] Althusser categorically rubbishes anything resembling the politically dictated Lysenkoist pseudo-distinction between bourgeois and proletarian science(s). Obviously, his dismissal of Lysenko's Stalinist Michurianism as charlatanism, as a scientistic ideological imposture, is solid evidence to the effect that he does not confuse and conflate biology with biologism.

That said apropos Lysenkoism, Althusser, immediately after insisting on an Engels-inspired dialectics of nature as essential to a materialist position within philosophy (particularly in relation to the contested, ideologically charged field of [post-]Darwinian biology) in "The Humanist Controversy," launches into a detailed discussion of evolutionary theorizations and paleontological findings with reference to Engels's unfinished 1876 essay "The Part Played by Labour in the Transition from Ape to Man" (an important chapter of his *Dialectics of Nature*).[40] Althusser's main concern in this specific context is to warn that these life-scientific "Recent Discoveries" of the mid-twentieth century—a footnote specifying these biological developments is missing from Althusser's manuscript, with François Matheron guessing that the intended reference is to André Leroi-Gourhan[41]—promising to demystify and delineate the natural-historical genesis of human history as distinct from natural history, the immanent emergence of more-than-natural/denaturalized human beings out of pre/nonhuman nature, are double-edged swords to be handled very carefully. On the one hand, Marxism can and should endorse such biological research insofar as it indeed further reinforces and cements in place an anti-anthropocentric, (quasi-)naturalist dialectical materialism in which life is made even more difficult for idealist and spiritualist ideologies hostile to historical materialism.[42] But, on the other hand, certain (pseudo-)Marxist uses (or, rather, abuses) of these same "Recent Discoveries," the very ones that drive additional nails in the coffins of antimaterialist worldviews external and opposed to Marxism, allegedly (re)introduce into Marxism Althusser's much-hated archenemy: humanism.

To be more precise, Althusser charges that evolutionary and paleontological analyses of and data regarding the rise of *Homo sapiens* in all their distinctiveness can and do get pressed into the service of privileging Marx's Feuerbachian humanist characterization of humans qua "social laboring" creatures in the 1844 *Economic and Philosophical Manuscripts* as the purported root notion for the mature historical materialist critique of political economy of the later Marx circa the 1850s and 1860s especially[43] (as is well known, Althusser goes to great lengths to disqualify the pre-1845 Marx as not yet properly Marxist, as a Feuerbachian humanist rather than a historical materialist qua antihumanist avant la lettre).[44] For this Althusser, "social labor" is a dangerous phrase. First, it places emphasis on the noun "labor" qua the transhistorical praxis of humanity's invariant "species-being." This *Gattungswesen* itself tends thereby to be cast in the role of the *Ur*-Subject, the ever-selfsame Prime Mover, inaugurating and forever underlying human history as a necessarily recurring set of patterns involving alienating self-objectification both religious and secular[45] (with Althusser frequently lambasting "alienation" as a speciously

Marxist and really Feuerbachian notion).[46] Second, society is downgraded in this phrase to the secondary status of the adjective "social," with sociality referring here to the historically unspecific notion of collective group life in general (like that of an animal pack) rather than the exact(ing) historical materialist categories and concepts of specific, varying combinatories of infrastructural and superstructural elements in different times and places,[47] combinatories within which labor is always already "*labour-process*, the structure of the social conditions of the labour-process, labour-power (not labour), value of labour-power (not of labour), concrete labour, abstract labour, utilization of labour-power, quantity of labour, and so on."[48]

A number of Althusser's observations and assertions from this section of "The Humanist Controversy" warrant closer examination. Speaking of the "borderline problem" (*problème-frontière*) of the relations between the life sciences and historical materialism, he states:

> it must still be demonstrated that the borderline in question *clearly is* the one that runs between ecological and biological laws on the one hand and, on the other, the social laws of history that make human history properly so called what it is—and that it is not a borderline internal to the prehistorical realm, that is, one which is still subject to bio-ecological rather than social laws. On this point, the question is far from being closed.[49]

Althusser here highlights the uncertain status of the evolutionary and paleontological "Recent Discoveries" latched onto by various Marxists (perhaps too hastily and uncritically) as life-scientific confirmations of the Marx of the 1844 *Manuscripts* and the Engels of the *Dialectics of Nature*. Nonetheless, he both acknowledges that in fact there truly is a "borderline" (*frontière*) between natural and human histories as well as recognizes that pinpointing this genetic juncture is important for Marxist materialisms.

Furthermore, despite Althusser's above-mentioned criticisms of and cautionings about the notion-phrase "social labor," he goes on to remark in "The Humanist Controversy" that "the novelty of Marx's discovery is not *unrelated to* (*pas sans rapport avec*) what an expression like 'social labour' can mean for us, retrospectively [*après coup*], and on condition that it is subjected to a radical critique [*critiquer radicalement*]."[50] My sense is that this retrospection as regards the Marx of 1844 would include and be informed by both, one, Marx's post-1844 historical materialism (as inaugurated in 1845) and its elaboration by the subsequent Marxist tradition as well as, two, an interfacing of dialectical materialism's *Naturdialektik* with ongoing work in the life sciences.

Radically critiquing "social labor" à la the *Manuscripts* hence would involve retroactively modifying the two concept-terms in this compound phrase with the benefit of this specific *après-coup* hindsight. Althusser appears to be suggesting that, thus modified, the idea of humans as socially laboring animals perhaps could serve as a valid link between and further vindication of both dialectical and historical materialisms, a link and vindication furnished by the natural sciences themselves. As I already have professed, my intervention here is an attempt to capitalize on just this kind of suggestion. Moreover, the remaining portions of this piece will seek to outline in greater detail exactly what an Althusser-inspired biomaterialism of human beings might look like.

One final passage from the section of "The Humanist Controversy" here under consideration is important for my present purposes. Althusser declares:

> I do not—I repeat—mean . . . that the problem of the origins of the human species is not a scientific problem, or that it is not of some interest to historical materialism. A materialist, scientific theory of human palaeontology certainly does matter to historical materialism, because it does away with a whole set of alibis for the spiritualist ideologies of history that are constantly being opposed to historical materialism. But historical materialism managed to emerge without benefit of the scientific basis provided by the findings of modern human palaeontology (it was barely ten years ago that . . .) and *Capital* was conceived some time before the *Dialectics of Nature*, that is to say, before Engels's celebrated text on the difference between man and the apes. If historical materialism could manage without the palaeontologists, that is because its object is *autonomous* with respect to the findings of human palaeontology, and, as such, can be treated in perfectly independent form.[51]

These declarations, while conceding the scientificity of biological investigations into human beings and their place in natural, evolutionary history (as well as, maybe inadvertently, conceding that "problems of origin" are not all to be dismissed as idealist qua antimaterialist, as Althusser sometimes recommends),[52] relegate the relevance of these investigations for Marxism to the restricted spheres of anti-idealist ideology critique. Althusser's main argument in favor of this relegation is the chronological fact of the anteriority of the discovery of historical materialism to both Darwin's 1859 *On the Origin of Species* and Engels's 1876 "The Part Played by Labour in the Transition from Ape to Man."

It is here, at this specific point, that I feel compelled to mount an immanent (i.e., Althusserian) critique of Althusser's (mis)handling of the life sciences in the immediately preceding quotation from "The Humanist Controversy." The argument for historical materialism's autonomy vis-à-vis biology based on linear historical time alone is lame because, to put it in language Althusser himself would use (as is entirely fitting in an immanent critique), the synchronic "order of reasons" of theoretically systematized content is not to be mistaken as being the same as the diachronic, historical unfolding of the order of presentation of the theory in question. As I observed earlier, Althusser not only defends dialectical materialism as the appropriate philosophy springing from historical materialism qua science of history—he pleads for the pressing need to cultivate and advance dialectical materialism as a philosophical "guide" essential for ensuring that historical materialism stays on an unerringly materialist course. Althusser's own completely justified criticisms of the young Georg Lukács's idealist deviations circa 1923's *History and Class Consciousness*[53]—this is the Lukács who appeals to certain construals of historical materialism in order to replace the realist naturalism of dialectical materialism with a macro-subjectivism/solipsism in which "nature" and the natural sciences are never anything else but ideologically compromised social constructions[54]—indicate that a historical materialism divorced from *Naturdialektik* (as itself thoroughly made possible and conditioned by the sciences of nature) easily ceases to be genuinely materialist in sinking back into the old spiritualist fogs of antinaturalism and antirealism. All of this is to say that, although the original surfacing of Marxist historical materialism predates the advents of both Darwinian evolutionary theory and the not-unrelated (*pas sans rapport*) Engelsian dialectics of nature, at the logical (rather than chronological) level of philosophy/theory, historical materialism, as materialism, ultimately ("in the last instance") cannot do without the priceless bases supplied exclusively by the two dovetailing sources of natural science and *Naturdialektik*.

However, at the same time, I by no means intend categorically to deny the "autonomy" of historical materialism asserted by Althusser in the preceding 1967 passage. However, whereas he seems on this occasion to consider its autonomous status to be absolute in (non)relation to biology and the dialectics of nature, I instead lean toward the thesis that this status is relative. To be more precise, what I mean by the relativity of this autonomy is that, for historical materialism to entail the irreducibility of socio-structural forces and factors to evolutionary, ecological, anatomical, and physiological determinants in a nonetheless uncompromisingly materialist manner, this materialism necessarily requires the supplement of a science-supported *Naturdialektik*. Such a dialectics of nature would aim to pinpoint, with the indispensable guidance of the natural sciences, the precise material conditions of possibility within natural history for the nature-immanent real geneses of more-than-natural/denaturalized human history. In order for the structures and dynamics of the social histories of concern to historical materialism to be, at least in some ways, independent of the structures and dynamics of nonhuman history (i.e., nature and its perpetually ongoing kinetics), it must be shown that and how the latter allow for the autonomy of the former—at least, if historical materialism is indeed to remain a materialism proper.[55] Additionally, this dialectical materialist supplementary demonstration is crucial so as, in line with the first of Marx's "Theses on Feuerbach," to establish historical materialism as different-in-kind from pre-Marxian "contemplative" materialisms. The contemplative quality of the latter involves, among other things, their inability, from within their own philosophical/theoretical confines, to account for their very surfacings and existences as philosophies/theories in which, as it were, material nature thinks and conceptualizes (as well as acts and labors upon)[56] itself (in which, as a Hegelian would say, "substance becomes subject").[57] Althusser himself denounces any and every contemplative stance as essentially idealist[58] and, parallel with this, insists that Marxist historical materialism must explain from within itself its own possibility and actuality.[59]

Returning to Althusser's previously- quoted admission in "The Humanist Controversy" regarding the potential for a legitimate Marxist recuperation of the early Marx's conception of social labor ("the novelty of Marx's discovery is not *unrelated to* [*pas* sans rapport *avec*] what an expression like 'social labour' can mean for us, retrospectively [*après coup*], and on condition that it is subjected to a radical critique [*critiquer radicalement*]"), I believe that the set-up work performed in the preceding three paragraphs enables me now to propose just such a recuperation. This operation of extracting, as it were, "the rational kernel within the mystical shell"[60] of the 1844 *Manuscripts* is one whose legitimacy is even greater given the past half-century's advances in the life sciences over and above the mid-twentieth-century "Recent Discoveries" to which Althusser refers in 1967. I particularly have in mind here such life-scientific developments as punctuated equilibrium, epigenetics, neuroplasticity, mirror neurons, affective neuroscience, and neuro-psychoanalysis.[61]

So, in exactly what does my version of a (heterodox) Althusserian retroactive recuperation of the early Marx's "social labor" consist? Starting in the works of his youth, Marx, instead of moving toward an eventual wholesale liquidation of the very notion of "human nature," tends to hold to a certain definition of this nature, albeit, crucially, one that is extremely minimal and bare bones. Relatedly, I would suggest, *pace* Althusser,[62] that Marx's post-1845 dropping of the term *Gattungswesen* is an abandonment specifically of a Feuerbachian contemplative materialist conception of human nature (qua ahistorical, timeless, unchanging, and filled with a multitude of fixed features and facets), rather than a rejection of any conception whatsoever resembling that of so-called human nature. *Contra* the hypothesized 1845 epistemological break, Marx, from the 1844 *Manuscripts* through *Capital* and onward, maintains a consistent austere characterization of human beings throughout their history as socially laboring animals.[63] However, despite the evident tensions with the classic Althusser of *Reading Capital* and *For Marx*, I am convinced that Marx's minimalist rendition of human nature as social labor(ing) can and should, following some of Althusser's own post-1965 suggestions, be synthesized with Althusserianism. Such a synthesis promises precisely to fulfill two above-appreciated Althusserian *desiderata*: one, a reinforcement of the scientificity of historical materialism as the science of history; and, two, an advancement of the philosophy of dialectical materialism, with its *Naturdialektik* and conditioning by the natural sciences, in a way that constructs a bridge between dialectical and historical materialisms, a bridge securing the materialist credentials of historical materialism.

To cut a very long story very short, Marx's minimalist rendition of human nature as social laboring entails that this nature is auto-effacing, namely, a self-denaturalizing nature inherently inclined toward the predominance of, so to speak, nurture over nature. The two words constituting the phrase "social labor" refer to two distinct-yet-overlapping fundamental dimensions of relations always already affecting the "nature" of each and every human being: first, relations with other human beings ("social") and, second, relations with nonhuman objects and processes in the material world ("labor"). Both Marxist materialism[64] and Freudian-Lacanian psychoanalysis underscore how humans are inserted even before birth and thrown (*Geworfen*) by birth into sociohistorical matrices of mediation decisive for their very being (a convergence between Marxism and analysis I plan to address more thoroughly in a sequel piece to the current essay).[65] Human nature primordially is open from the very beginning to these two fundamental dimensions of relations (i.e., the social and labor). Therefore, humanity's first nature is a peculiar essenceless essence, a natureless nature as an underdetermined and underdetermining first nature determining its own overwriting and colonization by second natures, the latter as configurations taking shape in and through each and every human creature's unavoidable entanglements with material, intersubjective, and trans-subjective milieus.[66]

Before I proceed to unpack further the implications of Marxian social labor as (re)interpreted within the framework of a dialectical materialism informed by the life sciences (as well as psychoanalysis), a not insignificant consequence of the immediately preceding for the Althusser of *Reading Capital*, *For Marx*, and related texts should be identified and explained (my intervention will conclude later with a second consequence for this Althusser—specifically, for his [in]famous thesis of the 1845 break). My gloss on human nature à la Marx problematizes Althusser's fashions of distinguishing between humanism (with its proposal of a primal "nature" qua an eternal, transhistorical, universal set of contents shared by all individuals in all times and places) and antihumanism (with its proposal of a primal "anti-nature" qua socioeconomic class antagonisms in shifting historical arrangements as irreducible differentiators within and between various and varying populations). From an Althusserian perspective, I could be said to be proposing that Marxism puts forward an antihumanist humanism (signaling an instance of a dialectical-speculative convergence of opposites similarly explored by Badiou through his side-by-side reflections on the humanist Sartre and the antihumanist Foucault).[67] Marxism does so insofar as, on my construal, it humanistically hypothesizes a human first nature that, anti-humanistically, always already spontaneously sublates itself into historical-structural second natures. Additionally, this situates Marx within a strain of the humanist tradition evidently unrecognized by Althusser but to be found in black and white within the founding document of Renaissance humanism, namely, Giovanni Pico della Mirandola's 1486 oration "On the Dignity of Man." Therein, Pico della Mirandola, as foregrounded by Lucio Colletti and Agamben, celebrates the uniqueness of humanity as springing from nothing other than its natural lack of a well-fleshed-out first nature.[68]

Althusser is adamant that the topic of species-being *als Gattungswesen* is the very crux of the divide he identifies as separating Marx from Feuerbach starting in 1845.[69] And, despite Althusser's on balance more negative than positive ambivalence vis-à-vis Hegel, he still maintains that a primary reason for the shortcomings of Feuerbach's (ostensibly) materialist philosophy in the mature Marx's eyes is this philosophy's failure to retain certain cardinal features of Hegelianism, especially Hegelian philosophy's insistence on the centrality of movements of historical mediation[70] (a critical assessment conveyed in *The German Ideology* by the indictment "As far as Feuerbach is a materialist he does not deal with history, and as far as he considers history he is not a materialist").[71] Referring to the well-known Engelsian-Leninist account of Marx's "three sources" (i.e., British liberal economics, French revolutionary politics, and German idealist philosophy),[72] Althusser, implicitly following the line laid down by Marx himself in Thesis One, insists that any authentic materialism must incorporate within itself "German philosophy" (i.e., Kantian and post-Kantian idealisms) in order to achieve a thoroughly materialist standing.

In Althusser's assessment of the Feuerbach-Marx split, this salutary, inoculating dose of, in particular, Hegelian "absolute idealism" is the very thing that vaccinates Marx's historical materialism from anti-materialist idealism itself.[73] Correlatively but conversely, the absence of this vaccine in Feuerbach's system is precisely what makes it contemplative as per the "Theses on Feuerbach." This system, like every other pre-Marxian (mechanistic) materialism as neither historical nor dialectical, surreptitiously relies for the formulation of its theorizations upon a disembodied "view from nowhere" transcending time, space, and all the material objects it speculates regarding (hence, every contemplative materialism, up to and including Feuerbach's, inadvertently regresses back into the crudest idealism, namely, spiritualist dualism as centered upon an immaterial, mental-subjective perspective).[74]

A number of Althusser's overarching propositions about philosophy, ones tightly interwoven with each other so as to compose a single, unified tapestry, are visible in the background of this specific assessment of the Feuerbach-Marx rupture by him. Every idealism contains within itself elements of materialism and vice versa, there being no such philosophical position as either pure idealism or pure materialism.[75] Any philosophical position, whether idealist, materialist, or whatever else, rests on posited theses which, as theses, are what they are in being diametrically opposed to corresponding antitheses, with every thesis also being an antithesis (for another thesis).[76] In order for a philosophical position with its theses successfully to advance and defend itself, it must take over and somehow assimilate within itself the antitheses of its polar-opposite philosophical enemy.[77] In general, philosophy in its entirety is a massive, sprawling *Kampfplatz* (Immanuel Kant's term favored by Althusser) of interminable conflicts between irreconcilable warring factions (with "class struggle in theory" being "determinative in the last instance" for these conflicts).[78]

Taking into consideration the prior three paragraphs here, if, first, Althusser is right (which I believe he is) that the subject matter of species-being is the pivot between Feuerbach and Marx and if, second, I am right about Marx's human nature as social laboring, then what Marx could be said to accomplish starting in 1845 is the forging of a partly Hegel-inspired reconceptualization of humanity's *Gattungswesen* as, so to speak, immediately mediated, naturally (self-)denaturalizing, invariantly varying, and transhistorically historical (a reconceptualization articulated in such key works as *The German Ideology*, the first volume of *Capital*, and "Critique of the Gotha Programme").[79] Althusser himself paraphrases this very Marx in his 1975 *Initiation à la philosophie pour les non-philosophies* (posthumously published only in 2014):

> Is not man himself also a natural product—his force, the force of muscles or brain? So, one can say, in the end, that in the laboring process, a part of nature (man) who, utilizing forces or parts of transformed nature (energy, tools), transforms another part of nature (raw material): which would tend to prove that nature transforms itself.[80]

Moreover, from Althusser's perspective, "nature transforms itself" so radically that its transformations (i.e., second natures, the denaturalized/more-than-natural, etc.) come to be, for human beings as simultaneously both the subjects and objects of these transformations, more foundational than what precedes and generates these same transformations (i.e., first nature, the pre/nonhuman natural, etc.). In 1965's "Theory, Theoretical Practice and Theoretical Formation," Althusser speaks of "all the real practices upon which scientific practice is founded and to which it is related," including "the practice of the transformation of nature, or economic practice."[81] He immediately adds regarding "economic practice" that it "puts man in relation to nature, which is the material condition of his biological and social existence."[82] It is crucial to register that the biological (i.e., human first nature) as well as the social (i.e., human second nature as social structure generally) is here rendered ontologically-materially dependent for its very existence not upon brute, raw material nature alone, but, instead, upon this nature as "metabolized" (Marx) and reworked by "economic practice" (i.e., social laboring) as "the practice of the transformation of nature" (i.e., human second nature as social infrastructure specifically). Human nature is nature's self-transformation in which, through a dialectical reversal, second nature becomes first nature.

Althusser also pointedly emphasizes this reversal while discussing Lacan's thinking in the second part of a two-part seminar, "Psychoanalysis and the Human Sciences," given in the 1963–1964 academic year. Therein, he states:

> What is crucial—Lacan insists on this, and it is his great discovery—is that this human becoming which has hitherto been figured for us by this vector "passage of the biological into the cultural" is in truth the effect of the action of the cultural on the biological. What is represented here by this vector should be in truth represented by another vector: it is the cultural that acts on the biological, as condition of possibility of the insertion of the little human being. In place of having to do with this vector "biology → culture," we have to do with a very different structure where culture produces this movement of procession: we have to do with an inversion of the determination. It is by the action of culture on the biological little human being that his/her insertion in culture is produced. It is not therefore with the becoming human of the little human being that we have to do—it is with the action of culture, constantly, on a little being other than itself, which it transforms into a human being. That is to say that, in reality, we have to do with a phenomenon of investment of which the vector is apparently oriented towards culture, whereas in fact it is culture that constantly precedes itself, absorbing that which will become a human subject.[83]

Althusser certainly is correct that the "inversion of . . . determination" he accurately discerns in Marx (i.e., the above-mentioned reversal of dominance/precedence between first and second natures in a materialist ontology including within its framework human beings) also is to be found in Lacan. However, he passes over in silence Lacan's careful establishment of the biological possibility conditions for this mediation and overwriting of biology by "culture" (an aspect of Lacanian theory I have reconstructed at great length and in meticulous detail on a range of other occasions).[84] If "the cultural" (whether as social structures à la Marx or the big Others of symbolic orders à la Lacan) is a "condition of possibility," a sort of historical materialist transcendental, for the (transformation) of the biology of the human organism, then a dialectical materialist meta-transcendental supplement at the level of the biological itself is mandatory—at least if one desires, as Althusser does, to avoid lapsing into an idealism of "culture," a spiritualist dualism in which the socio-symbolic "always already" exists as inexplicably, mysteriously different-in-kind from material nature (i.e., a macro-subjectivism with culture as the *res cogitans* collectively transcending natural matter). Without taking this additional supplementary step, Althusser himself risks just such a lapse.[85] Here, in a reversal of psychoanalysis needing Althusserian materialism as an undergirding theoretical basis (as Althusser asserts in 1966's "Three Notes on the Theory of Discourses"),[86] it is, instead, Althusser who needs a Lacanian materialism in order to secure a solid materialist standing for himself.

Lacan's own combinations of psychoanalytic and life-scientific elements (as crystallized in such Lacanian conceptual themes as human prematurational helplessness, the body-in-pieces [*corps morcelé*], the corporeal Real, the cerebral cortex as "intra-organic mirror," need in relation to demand and desire, anti/counter-nature [*antiphusis, contre-nature*], rotten [*pourri*] nature, nature as "not one," etc.) point precisely in the direction of the kind of dialectical materialism Althusser has a sense he needs and wants (with Lacan explicitly self-identifying as a dialectical materialist).[87] Several times, Althusser indeed invokes the protracted infantile *Hilflosigkeit* central to both Freud and Lacan. He rightly sees in the biological fact of this anatomical and physiological condition distinctive of the human species the (pre)determinant of social labor as itself humanity's *Gattungswesen*. Indeed, intersubjective and trans-subjective sociality as well as laboring practices inextricably intertwined with such sociality are the inescapable destinies of beings thrown at birth into utter and complete dependence on significant others as nurturing caretakers and who remain thereafter for the rest of their lives reliant upon broader and deeper networks of cooperatively working conspecifics (with the entire species's permanent, insurmountable dependence upon material nature).[88]

In 1975's *Initiation à la philosophie pour les non-philosophes*, Althusser presciently anticipates possible future life-scientific reinforcements of the Lacanian metapsychology presently under discussion.[89] Such reinforcements are requisite if the psychoanalytic and historical materialist prioritization of cultural second nature over biological first nature is to be, as Althusser and Lacan both mean it to be, a properly materialist gesture as supported by a dialectical materialism with a *Naturdialektik* exhibited in and through the natural sciences themselves. That is to say, such realities and phenomena as prolonged prematurational helplessness and the myriad hypothesized effects of this condition demand explanatory anchoring in evolutionary theories of natural history, the biology of the human organism generally, and human neurobiology especially. In particular, if the psychoanalytic and historical materialist thesis of childhood *Hilflosigkeit* resulting in social labor becoming the immediately mediated (non)essence of the human being is to be accounted for in an exhaustively materialist manner—this manner would involve a quasi-naturalism "not without" (*pas sans*) natural scientific "determination in the last instance" (to employ a hybrid of Lacanian and Althusserian parlance)—then, as Althusser insightfully appreciates in 1975, one must hope for and await the natural sciences eventually arriving on their own at evidence and theories of human nature as involving an endogenous openness and receptivity to exogenous acculturations, mediations, overwritings, socializations, and so on. Along with Catherine Malabou, I would claim that Althusser's expectations along these lines indeed have been fulfilled by developments in biology over the course of the past several decades (i.e., the very "Recent Discoveries" I listed earlier here: punctuated equilibrium, epigenetics, neuroplasticity, mirror neurons, affective neuroscience, and neuro-psychoanalysis). A dialectical materialism of human self-denaturalizing nature arising from these biological advances promises to ground historical materialism qua materialism by providing an account of the natural history as well as natural-organic structures and dynamics making possible the nature-immanent denaturalizations of both the phylogeny of human social history and the ontogeny of idiosyncratic subject formation. Human histories and subjects thereby no longer are left to hover magically over an enigmatic gap between themselves and nonhuman natural matters.

At the same time, for such a dialectical materialism to be appropriately dialectical, it and the sciences out of which it forges its theories must not be mechanistic, reductive, eliminative, epiphenomenalist, or the like. Althusser's acute awareness of exactly this comes through loud and clear in the fourth session of the seminar on *Philosophy and the Spontaneous Philosophy of the Scientists* ("Appendix: On Jacques Monod"). Taking the opportunity afforded by Nobel laureate Monod's contemporaneous inaugural lecture at the Collège de France (published in *Le Monde* on November 30, 1967), Althusser glimpses in the figure of Monod, not without good reasons,[90] a spontaneously dialectical materialist biology in which objectively real "emergences" in nature resembling the dialectics of "quality" and "quantity" in Hegel's *Logik*[91] (a feature of Hegelian Logic precious to Marxists)[92] hint at a biological explanation for the arising and subsequent autonomy of the irreducibly non/more-than-biological social and historical entities and happenings of concern to historical materialism.[93] Notwithstanding both Althusser's various criticisms of Monod's text as well as the multiple mutual misunderstandings between the two of them,[94] an emergentist biology accounting for the biomaterially immanent genesis and subsequent irreducibility of the sociohistorical is equally valuable and pivotal for Althusser and Monod alike.

In closing, I readily would concede that there is much to the thesis of Marx's epistemological break, with Althusser thereby brilliantly capturing many key aspects of historical materialism. However, if there also indeed is something to my reworking of Marx's pre-1845 equation of the species-being of human nature with social laboring—this "retrospective" reworking is inspired partially by Althusser himself (especially "The Humanist Controversy") and informed by benefits of hindsight deriving from the Marxist tradition after Marx, Freudian-Lacanian psychoanalysis, and the life sciences of the past half-century—then an ambivalent revisitation of Althusser's (in)famous thesis, one simultaneously for and against it, becomes possible and, in fact, imperative. Specifically, the apparent disappearance of the *Gattungswesen* of the 1844 *Manuscripts* starting in 1845 is the effect not of the actual jettisoning of a concept but, rather, of the Real designated by this concept self-sublating by passing over into its sociohistorical determinations (admittedly, reading Marx in this way is somewhat in tension with the emphasis in *Reading Capital* on strictly holding apart the objective being of real structures and phenomena from the subjective thinking of conceptually knowing said structures and phenomena).[95] Put differently, Marx's "break" with humanity's species-being is made possible by this very same *Gattungswesen*. These assertions of mine also help to explain the recurrent invocations of both naturalism and human essence/nature in such post-1845 contexts as the *Grundrisse* and *das Kapital*,[96] invocations otherwise glaringly problematic for an unqualified version of the Althusserian thesis of the 1845 rupture as neat, clean, and absolute.

Entirely consistent with the Hegelian-Marxian dialectics of continuity and discontinuity, one could claim with respect to Althusser circa 1965 that, on the one hand, a discontinuity admittedly punctuates Marx's intellectual itinerary starting in 1845 but that, on the other hand, this discontinuity is based on a sort of speculative identity-in-difference between indeterminate human nature as social labor in the abstract (1844) and this same nature as self-denaturalizing and auto-propelling of itself into sociohistorical determinations (1845 and after). A dialectical materialist *Naturdialektik*, one appropriately tethered to a biology of ruptures in which there are revolutions as well as evolutions, has been lurking in the shadows for fifty years now. In the (unconscious, latent) spirit if not also the (conscious, manifest) letter of Althusser's corpus, perhaps it is time finally to bring it to light and to realize this dream.

Notes

I would like to thank Agon Hamza for his very helpful recommendations regarding this piece.

1. Louis Althusser, "Reply to John Lewis," in *Essays in Self-Criticism*, trans. Grahame Locke (London: New Left Books, 1976), 67–68, 71–72; "Elements of Self-Criticism," in *Essays in Self-Criticism*, 106, 129–32, 141, 146–50; "Is It Simple to Be a Marxist in Philosophy?," in *Essays in Self-Criticism*, 172, 187; "Letter to Merab Mardashvili, January 16, 1978," in *Philosophy of the Encounter: Later Writings, 1978–1987*, ed. François Matheron and Oliver Corpet, trans. G. M. Goshgarian (London: Verso, 2006), 3; and "Philosophy and Marxism: Interviews with Fernanda Navarro, 1984–87," in *Philosophy of the Encounter*, 257–58.

2. Louis Althusser, "The Object of *Capital*," in Louis Althusser and Étienne Balibar, *Reading Capital*, trans. Ben Brewster (London: Verso, 2009), 160–61; "The Transformation of Philosophy," trans. Thomas E. Lewis, in *Philosophy and the Spontaneous Philosophy of the Scientists and Other Essays*, ed. Gregory Elliott (London: Verso, 1990), 243; "Marx in His Limits," in *Philosophy of the Encounter*, 45; "Correspondence about 'Philosophy and Marxism': Letter to Mauricio Malamud, March 8, 1984," in *Philosophy of the Encounter*, 209–11.

3. Louis Althusser, "Introduction: Today," in *For Marx*, trans. Ben Brewster (London: Verso, 2005), 34–36, 39; "From *Capital* to Marx's Philosophy," in Althusser and Balibar, *Reading Capital*, 32–33, 42; "The Object of *Capital*," 80.

4. Louis Althusser, "The Historical Task of Marxist Philosophy," in *The Humanist Controversy and Other Writings*, ed. François Matheron, trans. G. M. Goshgarian (London: Verso, 2003), 188–89; "Une question posée par Louis Althusser," in *Écrits philosophiques et politiques, Tome I*, ed. François Matheron (Paris: Stock/IMEC, 1994), 346–47, 353–56); "The Transformation of Philosophy," 262–64; "Marxism Today," trans. James H. Kavanagh, in *Philosophy and the Spontaneous Philosophy of the Scientists*, 276–77; *Initiation à la philosophie pour les non-philosophes*, ed. G. M. Goshgarian (Paris: Presses Universitaires de France, 2014), 379–81; *22ᵉ congrès* (Paris: François Maspero, 1977), 30–31; *Ce qui ne peut plus durer dans le parti communiste* (Paris: François Maspero, 1978), 91, 96; "Correspondence about 'Philosophy and Marxism': Letter to Fernanda Navarro, 10 July 1984," 217; "Correspondence about 'Philosophy and Marxism': Letter to Fernanda Navarro, 8 April 1986," 242; "Philosophy and Marxism," 253–55.

5. Louis Althusser, "Réponse à une critique," in *Écrits philosophiques et politiques, Tome II*, ed. François Matheron (Paris: Stock/IMEC, 1995), 368–69, 378–79; "The Humanist Controversy," in *The Humanist Controversy and Other Writings*, 281–82; "On

Theoretical Work: Difficulties and Resources", trans. James H. Kavanagh, in *Philosophy and the Spontaneous Philosophy of the Scientists*, 60; "Philosophy and the Spontaneous Philosophy of the Scientists," trans. Warren Montag, in *Philosophy and the Spontaneous Philosophy of the Scientists*, 117; "Notes sur la philosophie," in *Écrits philosophiques et politiques, Tome II*, 303; "The Transformation of Philosophy," 246–47.

6. Althusser, "Réponse à une critique," 379.

7. Althusser, "The Transformation of Philosophy," 264–65; "Philosophy and Marxism," 259.

8. Louis Althusser, "On the Materialist Dialectic: On the Unevenness of Origins," in *For Marx*, 162, 167–68.

9. Louis Althusser, "Sur l'objectivité de l'histoire: Lettre à Paul Ricœur," in *Solitude de Machiavel et autres textes*, ed. Yves Sintomer (Paris: Presses Universitaires de France, 1998), 24; "La problématique de l'Histoire dans les œvres de jeunesse de Marx," in *Politique et Histoire de Machiavel à Marx: Cours à l'École normale supérieure de 1955 à 1972*, ed. François Matheron (Paris: Éditions du Seuil, 2006), 165–71, 174, 179–80.

10. Althusser, "Introduction: Today," 33–34; Althusser, "On the Materialist Dialectic," 166–67; "Philosophie et sciences humaines," in *Solitude de Machiavel et autres textes*, 49–50; "Theory, Theoretical Practice and Theoretical Formation: Ideology and Ideological Struggle," trans. James H. Kavanagh, in *Philosophy and the Spontaneous Philosophy of the Scientists*, 11–13; "The Historical Task of Marxist Philosophy," 206; "Notes sur la philosophie," 301–2.

11. Althusser, "Réponse à une critique," 361–62; "The Object of *Capital*," 84; "Theory, Theoretical Practice and Theoretical Formation," 7–8, 18–19; "The Philosophical Conjuncture and Marxist Theoretical Research," in *The Humanist Controversy and Other Writings*, 15; "The Historical Task of Marxist Philosophy," 168–70, 172–74, 181; "The Humanist Controversy," 229–30; "To My English Readers," in *For Marx*, 14; "The Transformation of Philosophy," 246–47, 261.

12. Althusser, *Initiation à la philosophie pour les non-philosophes*, 373–74; "Philosophy and Marxism," 264.

13. Louis Althusser, "Philosophie et Marxisme: Entretiens avec Fernanda Navarro 1984–1987," in *Sur la philosophie* (Paris: Gallimard, 1994), 31–32; Althusser, "Philosophy and Marxism," 253–55; "Portrait du philosophe matérialiste," in *Écrits philosophiques et politiques, Tome I*, 582; "Portrait of the Materialist Philosopher," in *Philosophy of the Encounter*, 291.

14. Althusser, "Philosophy and Marxism," 258–59.

15. Louis Althusser, "Correspondence about 'Philosophy and Marxism': Letter to Fernanda Navarro, 18 July 1984," 221.

16. Althusser, "From *Capital* to Marx's Philosophy," 16, 20, 22, 25–31, 57; "The Object of *Capital*," 112, 114; "Correspondence with Jacques Lacan, 1963–1969: Louis Althusser to Jacques Lacan, 11-7-66," in *Writings on Psychoanalysis: Freud and Lacan*, trans. Jeffrey Mehlman (New York: Columbia University Press, 1996), 170–71; "Avant-propos du livre de G. Duménil: Le concept de loi économique dans 'Le Capital,'" in *Solitude de Machiavel et autres textes*, 263–64.

17. Jacques Lacan, *The Seminar of Jacques Lacan*, book 7: *The Ethics of Psychoanalysis, 1959–1960*, ed. Jacques-Alain Miller, trans. Dennis Porter (New York: W. W. Norton, 1992), 139; *The Seminar of Jacques Lacan*, book 11: *The Four Fundamental Concepts of Psychoanalysis, 1964*, ed. Jacques-Alain Miller, trans. Alan Sheridan (New York: W. W. Norton, 1977), 268; *Le Séminaire de Jacques Lacan*, livre XVI: *D'un Autre à l'autre, 1968–1969*, ed. Jacques-Alain Miller (Paris: Éditions du Seuil, 2006), 224–25, 249.

18. Althusser, "Theory, Theoretical Practice and Theoretical Formation," 9; "Reply to John Lewis," 54; "Elements of Self-Criticism," 179.

19. Althusser, "Elements of Self-Criticism," 115.

20. Althusser, "The Object of *Capital*," 205; "To My English Readers," 14; "Theory, Theoretical Practice and Theoretical Formation," 10; "Du côté de la philosophie cinquième Cours de philosophie pour scientifiques," in *Écrits philosophiques et politiques, Tome II*, 257–60; "Notes sur la philosophie," 301, 306, 318, 323–24; "The Historical Task of Marxist Philosophy," 172–74; "The Humanist Controversy," 229–30; "Philosophy as a Revolutionary Weapon: Interview conducted by Maria Antonietta Macciocchi," in *Lenin and Philosophy and Other Essays*, trans. Ben Brewster (New York: Monthly Review Press, 2001), 4; "Lenin and Philosophy," in *Lenin and Philosophy*, 22; "Preface to *Capital* Volume One," in *Lenin and Philosophy*, 45–46; *Politics and History: Montesquieu, Rousseau, Marx*, trans. Ben Brewster (London: Verso, 2007), 166–68; *On the Reproduction of Capitalism: Ideology and Ideological State Apparatuses*, trans. G. M. Goshgarian (London: Verso, 2014), 15–16; *Initiation à la philosophie pour les non-philosophes*, 132–33, 327; "Philosophy and Marxism," 266–67.

21. Althusser, *Philosophy and the Spontaneous Philosophy of the Scientists*, 108.

22. Althusser, *Philosophy and the Spontaneous Philosophy of the Scientists*, 109.

23. Karl Marx, "Letter to Ferdinand Lassalle, January 16th, 1861," www.marxists.org/archive/marx/works/1861/letters/61_01_16.htm, and "Letter to Frederick Engels, December 7th, 1867," www.marxists.org/archive/marx/works/1867/letters/67_12_07.htm; Friedrich Engels, "Letter to Karl Marx, December 11th or 12th, 1859," www.marxists.org/archive/marx/works/1859/letters/59_12_11.htm, and "Speech at the Grave of Karl Marx," March 17, 1883, www.marxists.org/archive/marx/works/1883/death/burial.htm; Friedrich Engels, *Ludwig Feuerbach and the Outcome of Classical German Philosophy*, trans. C. P. Dutt (New York: International Publishers, 1941), 25–27.

24. Adrian Johnston, "Repeating Engels: Renewing the Cause of the Materialist Wager for the Twenty-First Century," *Theory @ Buffalo*, special issue: "animal.machine.sovereign," no. 15, 2011, 141–82; "From Scientific Socialism to Socialist Science: *Naturdialektik* Then and Now," in *The Idea of Communism 2: The New York Conference*, ed. Slavoj Žižek (London: Verso, 2013), 103–36; "This *Is* Orthodox Marxism: The Shared Materialist *Weltanschauung* of Marx and Engels," "On Sebastiano Timpanaro," special issue, *Quaderni materialisti* (2015); *Prolegomena to Any Future Materialism*, vol. 2: *A Weak Nature Alone* (Evanston, IL: Northwestern University Press, 2016).

25. Louis Althusser, "The Underground Current of the Materialism of the Encounter," in *Philosophy of the Encounter*, 194–96; Catherine Malabou, "Whither

Materialism?: Althusser/Darwin," in *Plastic Materialities: Politics, Legality, and Metamorphosis in the Work of Catherine Malabou*, ed. Brenna Bhandar and Jonathan Goldberg-Hiller (Durham, NC: Duke University Press, 2015), 47–60.

26. Althusser, "La problématique de l'Histoire dans les œvres de jeunesse de Marx," 165, 179; "The Discovery of Dr. Freud," in *Writings on Psychoanalysis*, 97.

27. Alexandre Koyré, *From the Closed World to the Infinite Universe* (New York: Harper Torchbooks, 1958), 99, 278.

28. Louis Althusser, "On Feuerbach," in *The Humanist Controversy and Other Writings*, 134–35, 154; "The Historical Task of Marxist Philosophy," 206.

29. Althusser, "The Discovery of Dr. Freud," 107.

30. Althusser, "The Humanist Controversy," 281–82.

31. Althusser, "The Humanist Controversy," 283.

32. Althusser, *Philosophy and the Spontaneous Philosophy of the Scientists*, 111.

33. Althusser, *Philosophy and the Spontaneous Philosophy of the Scientists*, 134.

34. Michel Foucault, *"Society Must Be Defended": Lectures at the Collège de France, 1975–1976*, ed. Mauro Bertani and Alessandro Fontana, trans. David Macey (New York: Picador, 2003), 239–63; Michel Foucault, *The History of Sexuality*, vol. 1: *An Introduction*, trans. Robert Hurley (New York: Vintage Books, 1990), 135–59; Giorgio Agamben, *Homo Sacer: Sovereign Power and Bare Life*, trans. Daniel Heller-Roazen (Stanford, CA: Stanford University Press, 1998), 3–7, 87, 111, 119, 187; Alain Badiou, *Logics of Worlds: Being and Event 2*, trans. Alberto Toscano (London: Continuum, 2009), 1–9.

35. Althusser, "Theory, Theoretical Practice and Theoretical Formation," 12–13; *Philosophy and the Spontaneous Philosophy of the Scientists*, 88.

36. Althusser, "The Humanist Controversy," 268.

37. Althusser, "The Humanist Controversy," 270.

38. Althusser, *Initiation à la philosophie pour les non-philosophes*, 172–73.

39. Althusser, "Introduction: Today," 22; "Reply to John Lewis," 78–79; "Elements of Self-Criticism," 120; "Avant-propos: Histoire terminée, histoire interminable," in Dominique Lecourt, *Lyssenko: Histoire réelle d'une "science prolétarienne* (Paris: François Maspero, 1976), 9–19; *Initiation à la philosophie pour les non-philosophes*, 366.

40. Friedrich Engels, "The Part Played by Labour in the Transition from Ape to Man," in *Dialectics of Nature*, trans. C. P. Dutt (New York: International, 1940), 279–96; Johnston, "From Scientific Socialism to Socialist Science," 103–36; Althusser, "The Humanist Controversy," 284–92, 294.

41. Althusser, "The Humanist Controversy," 304.

42. Althusser, "The Humanist Controversy," 281–82, 284–85, 291–92.

43. Althusser, "The Humanist Controversy," 286, 294.

44. Althusser, "Introduction: Today," 31, 35–38; "Feuerbach's 'Philosophical Manifestoes,'" in *For Marx*, 45–48; "'On the Young Marx': Theoretical Questions," in *For Marx*, 65–66, 68–69, 83–86; "The '1844 Manuscripts' of Karl Marx: Political Economy and Philosophy," in *For Marx*, 155–56, 160; "Marxism and Humanism," in *For Marx*, 223–27,

229–31, 243; "To My English Readers," 11; "The Humanist Controversy," 253; "Marx's Relation to Hegel," in *Politics and History*, 176–80; "Reply to John Lewis," 66, 98.

45. Althusser, "The Humanist Controversy," 288–89, 294.

46. Althusser, "From *Capital* to Marx's Philosophy," 17; "The '1844 Manuscripts' of Karl Marx," 155–56; "Marxism and Humanism," 225–27; "To My English Readers," 10; "On Feuerbach," 89; "The Humanist Controversy," 241–42; "Lenin before Hegel," in *Lenin and Philosophy*, 81; "Ideology and Ideological State Apparatuses: Notes towards an Investigation," in *Lenin and Philosophy*, 110–11; "Reply to John Lewis," 67, 98.

47. Althusser, "Marxism and Humanism," 229; "Elements of Self-Criticism," 109.

48. Althusser, "The Humanist Controversy," 289–90.

49. Louis Althusser, "La querelle de l'humanisme," in *Écrits philosophiques et politiques, Tome II*, 507; "The Humanist Controversy," 285–86.

50. Althusser, "La querelle de l'humanisme," 509–10; "The Humanist Controversy," 287–88.

51. Althusser, "The Humanist Controversy," 291.

52. Althusser, "On the Materialist Dialectic," 198, 214; "Letters to D.: Letter 1, 18 July 1966," in *Writings on Psychoanalysis*, 41; "Marx's Relation to Hegel," 173, 184; "Elements of Self-Criticism," 135; *Initiation à la philosophie pour les non-philosophes*, 64–67, 71–72; "The Underground Current of the Materialism of the Encounter," 169–71, 188–90; "Correspondence about 'Philosophy and Marxism': Letter to Fernanda Navarro, June 11, 1984," in *Philosophy of the Encounter*, 217–18; "Philosophy and Marxism" 272–73; "Portrait of the Materialist Philosopher," 290–91.

53. Althusser, "Introduction: Today," 30–31; "Lenin and Philosophy," 25–26; "Lenin before Hegel," 81–83; "Reply to John Lewis," 70; "Elements of Self-Criticism," 115; "Is It Simple to Be a Marxist in Philosophy?," 186.

54. Georg Lukács, "What Is Orthodox Marxism?," in *History and Class Consciousness: Studies in Marxist Dialectics*, trans. Rodney Livingstone (Cambridge, MA: MIT Press, 1971), 24; "Reification and the Consciousness of the Proletariat," in *History and Class Consciousness*, 88–91, 98–99, 102–4, 109–10; "The Changing Function of Historical Materialism," in *History and Class Consciousness*, 234; "N. Bukharin: Historical Materialism," in *Tactics and Ethics: Political Writings, 1919–1929*, ed. Rodney Livingstone, trans. Michael McColgan (London: New Left Books, 1972), 136, 139–42; "Karl August Wittfogel: The Science of Bourgeois Society," in *Tactics and Ethics*, 144–45; "Tailism and the Dialectic," in *A Defense of History and Class Consciousness: Tailism and the Dialectic*, trans. Esther Leslie (London: Verso, 2000), 100, 102.

55. Adrian Johnston, "Confession of a Weak Reductionist: Responses to Some Recent Criticisms of My Materialism," in *Neuroscience and Critique*, ed. Jan De Vos and Ed Pluth (New York: Routledge, 2015).

56. Althusser, *Initiation à la philosophie pour les non-philosophes*, 184–85.

57. Karl Marx, "Theses on Feuerbach," trans. S. Ryazanskaya, in Karl Marx, *Karl Marx: Selected Writings*, ed. David McLellan (Oxford: Oxford University Press, 1977), 156–58; Adrian Johnston, "Points of Forced Freedom: Eleven More Theses on Materialism," *Speculations: A Journal of Speculative Realism*, no. 4 (June 2013): 91–99; Adrian

Johnston, *Prolegomena to Any Future Materialism*, vol. 1: *The Outcome of Contemporary French Philosophy* (Evanston, IL: Northwestern University Press, 2013), 176; Adrian Johnston, *Adventures in Transcendental Materialism: Dialogues with Contemporary Thinkers* (Edinburgh: Edinburgh University Press, 2014), 6, 18–19, 30, 77–78, 102, 116, 315–16; Adrian Johnston, "An Interview with Adrian Johnston on Transcendental Materialism [with Peter Gratton]," *Society and Space*, 2013, http://societyandspace.com /2013/10/07/interview-with-adrian-johnston-on-transcendental-materialism/; Adrian Johnston, "Interview about *Adventures in Transcendental Materialism: Dialogues with Contemporary Thinkers* with Graham Harman for Edinburgh University Press," Edinburgh University Press, April 2014, http://www.euppublishing.com/userimages /ContentEditor/1397840563624/Adventures%20in%20Transcendental%20Real- ism%20-%20Author%20Q%26A.pdf; Adrian Johnston, "Transcendentalism in Hegel's Wake: A Reply to Timothy M. Hackett and Benjamin Berger," in "Schelling: Powers of the Idea," ed. Benjamin Berger, special issue, *Pli: The Warwick Journal of Philosophy*, no. 26 (fall 2014): 204–37.

58. Althusser, "Reply to John Lewis," 57.

59. Althusser, "Elements of Self-Criticism," 156.

60. Karl Marx, *Capital: A Critique of Political Economy*, vol. 1, trans. Ben Fowkes (New York: Penguin, 1990), 103.

61. Johnston, "Confession of a Weak Reductionist."

62. Althusser, "Marxism and Humanism," 223–29.

63. Karl Marx, *Economic and Philosophical Manuscripts*, *Early Writings*, trans. Rodney Livingstone and Gregor Benton (New York: Penguin Books, 1992), 326–31, 350; Karl Marx and Frederick Engels, *The German Ideology*, ed. C. J. Arthur (New York: International Publishers, 1970), 42; Marx, "Wage-Labour and Capital," in *Karl Marx: Selected Writings*, 250–51, 259; Marx, "Preface to *A Critique of Political Econ- omy*," in *Karl Marx: Selected Writings*, 389–90; Marx, *Grundrisse: Foundations of the Critique of Political Economy Rough Draft*, trans. Martin Nicolaus (New York: Penguin Books, 1993), 84, 243, 323, 496; Marx, *Capital*, vol. 1, 1021–22, 1053, 1068.

64. Marx, "Preface to *A Critique of Political Economy*," 389; Marx, *Grundrisse*, 496.

65. Adrian Johnston, "Man, That Sickness: The Helplessness of Hegelian Philoso- phy, Lacanian Psychoanalysis, and Althusserian Marxism," *Crisis and Critique*, 2015.

66. Johnston, "This *Is* Orthodox Marxism"; *Prolegomena to Any Future Material- ism*, vol. 2.

67. Alain Badiou, *The Century*, trans. Alberto Toscano (Cambridge: Polity, 2007), 165–78.

68. Giovanni Pico della Mirandola, "On the Dignity of Man," in *On the Dignity of Man*, trans. Charles Glenn Wallis, Paul J. W. Miller, and Douglas Carmichael (In- dianapolis: Hackett, 1998), 4–5; Lucio Colletti, *Marxism and Hegel*, trans. Lawrence Garner (London: Verso, 1979), 234, 238–41, 243–46; Giorgio Agamben, *The Open: Man and Animal*, trans. Kevin Attell (Stanford, CA: Stanford University Press, 2004), 29–30; Johnston, *Adventures in Transcendental Materialism*, 159–60.

69. Althusser, "On Feuerbach," 137; "The Humanist Controversy," 263–65.

70. Althusser, "On Feuerbach," 88–89; "The Humanist Controversy," 234, 241–42; "Reply to John Lewis," 54, 56.

71. Karl Marx and Friedrich Engels, *The German Ideology* (Amherst, NY: Prometheus, 1998), 47.

72. V. I. Lenin, "The Three Sources and Three Component Parts of Marxism," in *The Lenin Anthology*, ed. Robert C. Tucker (New York: W. W. Norton, 1975), 640–44.

73. Althusser, "Réponse à une critique," 378; "On Feuerbach," 88–89.

74. Althusser, "Réponse à une critique," 376–77; "On Feuerbach," 103–4, 149; "The Humanist Controversy," 237–42.

75. Althusser, "Reply to John Lewis," 61; "Elements of Self-Criticism," 144–46; *Initiation à la philosophie pour les non-philosophes*, 96, 323–25; "Correspondence about 'Philosophy and Marxism': Letter to Fernanda Navarro, 11 June 1984," 218; "Correspondence about 'Philosophy and Marxism': Letter to Fernanda Navarro, 19 July 1984," in *Philosophy of the Encounter*, 222; "Philosophy and Marxism," 268–70.

76. Althusser, *Initiation à la philosophie pour les non-philosophes*, 321; "Correspondence about 'Philosophy and Marxism': Letter to Fernanda Navarro, 19 July 1984," 223; "Philosophy and Marxism," 267–68.

77. Althusser, *Initiation à la philosophie pour les non-philosophes*, 95–96, 324–25, 342; "Correspondence about 'Philosophy and Marxism': Letter to Fernanda Navarro, 19 July 1984," 223–24; "Philosophy and Marxism," 269–70.

78. Althusser, "Reply to John Lewis," 37–38, 58, 72; "Elements of Self-Criticism," 142–44, 150; "The Transformation of Philosophy," 261; *Initiation à la philosophie pour les non-philosophes*, 50–51, 322–23, 326–27, 359, 383; "Philosophy and Marxism," 270–71.

79. Marx and Engels, *The German Ideology*, 34; Marx, *Capital*, vol. 1, 133, 310; Marx, "Critique of the Gotha Programme," trans. Joris de Bres, in *The First International and After: Political Writings*, vol. 3, ed. David Fernbach (Harmondsworth, UK: Penguin, 1974), 341.

80. Althusser, *Initiation à la philosophie pour les non-philosophes*, 184–85.

81. Althusser, "Theory, Theoretical Practice and Theoretical Formation," 8.

82. Althusser, "Theory, Theoretical Practice and Theoretical Formation," 8–9.

83. Louis Althusser, "*Psychanalyse et psychologie*," *Psychanalyse et sciences humaines: Deux conférences (1963–1964)*, ed. Olivier Corpet and François Matheron (Paris: Librairie Générale Française/IMEC, 1996), 91.

84. Adrian Johnston, *Time Driven: Metapsychology and the Splitting of the Drive* (Evanston, IL: Northwestern University Press, 2005), xxxvi–xxxviii, 293–99, 335–37, 340–41; *Žižek's Ontology: A Transcendental Materialist Theory of Subjectivity* (Evanston, IL: Northwestern University Press, 2008), 270–73; "The Weakness of Nature: Hegel, Freud, Lacan, and Negativity Materialized," in *Hegel and the Infinite: Religion, Politics, and Dialectic*, ed. Slavoj Žižek, Clayton Crockett, and Creston Davis (New York: Columbia University Press, 2011), 159–79; "Reflections of a Rotten Nature: Hegel, Lacan, and Material Negativity," in "Science and Thought," ed. Frank Ruda and Jan Voelker, special issue, *Filozofski Vestnik* 33, no. 2 (2012): 23–52; *Prolegomena*

to *Any Future Materialism*, vol. 1, 13–77, 175–78; "Drive between Brain and Subject: An Immanent Critique of Lacanian Neuro-psychoanalysis," in "Spindel Supplement: Freudian Future(s)," special issue, *Southern Journal of Philosophy* 51 (September 2013): 48–84; *Adventures in Transcendental Materialism*, 65–107; *Prolegomena to Any Future Materialism*, vol. 2.

85. Althusser, "Freud and Lacan," in *Writings on Psychoanalysis*, 22–23; "Letters to D.: Letter 1, 18 July 1966," 52–53; "Letters to D.: Letter 2, 22 August 1966," in *Writings on Psychoanalysis*, 57–58, 68; *On the Reproduction of Capitalism*, 192–93.

86. Louis Althusser, "Three Notes on the Theory of Discourses," in *The Humanist Controversy and Other Writings*, 38–41, 43–46, 53–68, 80–82; "Lettre à Franca: 13 septembre 66," in *Lettres à Franca (1961–1973)*, ed. François Matheron and Yann Moulier Boutang (Paris: Stock/IMEC, 1998), 711–12.

87. Johnston, *Adventures in Transcendental Materialism*, 65–107.

88. Althusser, *Initiation à la philosophie pour les non-philosophes*, 82–83; "Philosophy and Marxism," 284.

89. Althusser, *Initiation à la philosophie pour les non-philosophes*, 296–97, 303.

90. Jacques Monod, *Chance and Necessity: An Essay on the Natural Philosophy of Modern Biology*, trans. Austryn Wainhouse (New York: Alfred A. Knopf, 1971), xi, 42–44, 87, 94–98, 112–19, 128–30, 145–46, 148, 154, 162–63.

91. G. W. F. Hegel, *Science of Logic*, trans. A. V. Miller (London: George Allen and Unwin, 1969), 331, 334–36, 369–70; *The Encyclopedia Logic: Part I of the Encyclopedia of the Philosophical Sciences with the Zusätze*, trans. T. F. Geraets, W. A. Suchting, and H. S. Harris (Indianapolis: Hackett, 1991), §105 [168], §107–108 [170–71], §111 [173].

92. Friedrich Engels, "Dialectics," in *Dialectics of Nature*, 26–27; Engels, *Anti-Dühring: Herr Eugen Dühring's Revolution in Science*, 2nd ed. (Moscow: Foreign Languages Publishing House, 1959), 164–77; V. I. Lenin, "Conspectus of Hegel's Book *The Science of Logic*," in *Collected Works*, vol. 38: *Philosophical Notebooks*, ed. Stewart Smith, trans. Clemence Dutt (Moscow: Progress Publishers, 1976), 122–25; Althusser, "Une question posée par Louis Althusser," 346–47, 353–56.

93. Althusser, *Philosophy and the Spontaneous Philosophy of the Scientists*, 147–49, 152–56.

94. Althusser, *Philosophy and the Spontaneous Philosophy of the Scientists*, 150–56, 160, 162–64; Althusser and Jacques Monod, "Correspondence," IMEC/Fonds Althusser (unpublished dossier); Monod, *Chance and Necessity*, 37, 39–40, 79, 110–11, 169, 179–80; Maria Turchetto, "Althusser and Monod: A 'New Alliance?,'" trans. Peter Thomas, *Historical Materialism*, no. 17 (2009): 61–79; Stéphane Tirard, "Monod, Althusser et le marxisme," in *Une nouvelle connaissance du vivant: François Jacob, André Wolff et Jacques Monod*, ed. Claude Debru, Michel Morange, and Frédéric Worms (Paris: Éditions Rue d'Ulm, 2012), 75–88.

95. Althusser, "From *Capital* to Marx's Philosophy," 42–46, 49–51, 60; "The Object of *Capital*," 95–96, 130, 210.

96. Marx, *Grundrisse*, 85, 92, 109–11, 243, 320, 325, 398, 400, 462–63, 496–97, 540; *Capital*, vol. 1, 207, 283, 323, 447, 461.

PART III

Reading Capital Today

CHAPTER 9

Reading Social Reproduction into
Reading Capital

NINA POWER

One of the main problems with the disciplinary quality of contemporary academia is the way in which the fragmentation of disciplines carries over into a fragmentation of analysis. Despite the best efforts of well-intentioned intellectual laborers everywhere, "interdisciplinarity" rarely succeeds in its aims, often remaining little more than the sum of its parts. Largely forbidden from the standpoint of today's academia is an approach that totalizes and synthesizes, that addresses the global hidden domains of contemporary knowledge production and contemporary political action. While a theory of reading may not immediately seem to be the most obvious solution to the fragmentation of disciplines, it is clear that the concept of reading proposed by Althusser in *Reading Capital* is of enormous importance in the identification of "oversight" as a constitutive feature of intellectual practice—the identification of the process through which "one sees," or understands *as such*. Any such attempt to identify what might be usually passed over in silence or simply missed is necessarily more open to criticisms along the same vein—this theory claims to identify the unconscious of the text but is itself unconscious of something else.

Yet for all the importance of *Reading Capital* in its attempt to identify the very way in which "incorrect" theories of reading have been unconsciously presupposed in earlier ways of approaching Marx's *Capital*, it can certainly be said of the authors of *Reading Capital* that they too neglect, as Marx himself did, certain crucial concepts that in fact alter completely the way in which we might understand capitalism itself. While we might accept with Althusser that all readings are "guilty," and not least guilty in the oversights of their own historical contingency, we might say that the time has come for a reading of *Reading Capital* that explicitly draws out the "absent" question of feminism.

This is of course not to suggest that much work hasn't already been done, both in terms of a feminist reading of Marx and a feminist critique or, more positively, use of the work of the various authors of *Reading Capital*. But there is much, positively, that can be done with the theory of reading presented in the text that allows for a more interesting double-reading of both Marx and *Reading Capital*. In this sense, then, the work of Ellen Rooney, which takes a polemical approach to the question of ideology, provides us with a useful model to ultimately move beyond the stasis of guilt. My brief chapter will attempt to adhere to Rooney's description of "the irreducible difference of view, of terrain, that is reading," an approach that "discloses double-reading as a hopelessly political and historical process, one that no text can escape, foreclose, or defend itself against."[1] Rooney's emphasis on the politics of reading informs here the suggestion that it is possible to read the gaps of *Reading Capital* as full gaps, rather than empty spaces.

This essay, while siding with the position that emphasizes the importance of Althusser's theory of reading, seeks to examine both the possibilities the text opens up for a feminist reading of Marx via the use it has been made by feminist theorists since its publication, but also to point to oversights of the text itself, particularly concerning the concept of social reproduction. This latter point will be made of both Althusser and, to a lesser extent, Marx himself, based on a reexamination of feminist responses to *Reading Capital* and of my own argument in direct response to the text. The chapter will be divided into two sections. The first will examine previous feminist responses to Althusser and *Reading Capital*, particularly the work of Rooney, the second to identifying the conceptual areas neglected by the text directly. It is a short intervention into thinking about the limitations of the model of reading and the model of reproduction proposed by *Reading Capital*, but hopefully something minor will have been opened up here.

Feminist Responses to *Reading Capital*

The relative (or rather complete lack) of references to feminism, gender, or women in *Reading Capital* has nevertheless not prevented some feminists taking up ideas from the text, particularly regarding a theory of reading. Nevertheless, as Rooney notes, by far the dominant use of Althusser stems from a feminist rereading of his theory of ideology, neglecting the framework and resources of *Reading Capital*: "The reception of Louis Althusser's work has fetishized his theory of ideology and virtually overlooked, left unread, his theory and his practice of reading" (183). It is this theory of reading that Rooney (and I too here) wish to resurrect, with certain feminist caveats. We can certainly find much evidence of Rooney's claim as regards the use of ideology. Hennessy's work in the early 1990s for example, makes a positive case for understanding Althusser's ideas in relation to feminist standpoint theory, avoiding the pitfalls of a transparent appeal to experience without understanding the constructed aspects of subject positions: By "foregrounding the material and productive role of ideology in social arrangements, Althusser's theory of ideology stimulated developments in postmodern Marxist and feminist formulations of the discursive construction of the subject."[2] Gimenez in the 2000s gets closer to *Reading Capital* than other feminist readings, pointing to the usefulness of the methodological insights of this collective work for a sociological understanding of Marx's methodology: "I have explored the relevance of Marx's method as developed by Marx and elaborated by Althusser and Godelier, to identify the non-observable structures and social relations underlying the invisible patterns of interaction between men and women that place the latter in a subordinate position."[3] The work on ideology and the project of *Reading Capital* is thus seen as a useful supplement to a feminist approach that seeks to approach social interactions in a materialist way. But how might a return to the claims about reading be put in the service of a contemporary Marxist-feminist project?

Rooney's work provides a highly fruitful way of understanding both how Althusser's theory of reading is useful on its own terms (particularly for avoiding ideological conceptions of his own theory of ideology as she suggests happened in the reception of his work),[4] but also how the theory can be turned against itself, not merely for the sake of some of sort of twist-in-the-tale game, but as a genuine attempt to reinsert, to revive, a particular concept, namely *reproduction*, back into a Marxist and materialist conception of capitalism itself. She is, along the way, critical of other types of feminist attempts to "use" Althusser, particularly if their focus is primarily on the problem of ideology (she identifies "those elements within feminist and Marxist-feminist discourse that have found ideology a useful way to speak about gender and the Althusserian subject of ideology a plausible figure for woman" [192n12]). We must understand reading here as a broader political process, not the bourgeois model of the individuated reader, sitting alone with a book. It is reading that permits access to knowledge, because it allows access to its own effect, however open-ended and historically specific that process is:

Knowledge is produced only as an effect of reading practices, and this most emphatically includes knowledge of ideology. Althusser's theory (and his own practice) of reading makes it painfully clear that this is a task that we may very well fail (will repeatedly fail) to complete. (186)

Reading is a "guilty, dynamic, flawed, open-ended, historically contingent, and wholly political practice of displacements reading as antifetishism" (185). What is clear about the *Reading Capital* project for all its confessionals, is its neglect, even relative to Marx, of the concept of social reproduction. Rooney touches on this when she notes that the stress on ideology as form, as eternal, serves to obscure the materialist emphasis on actual reproduction (in the broadest sense—everything it takes to keep capitalism going, from the reproduction of the species, to feeding, clothing, and healthcare, all the work that forms the backdrop to waged labor). By speaking purely of the reproduction of ideology we run the risk of neglecting the major processes that sustain capitalism: "The erasure of the feminine contribution to this process [the reproduction of labor power as such] is far from trivial; the history of Marxist feminist discourse on the family wage, domestic labor, and class itself is the arduous history of rethinking [the] proletarian and his children to the nth power" (190). Rooney argues that Althusser "ironically" was indeed precisely attempting to move away from such empirical questions in his discussion of ideology as a more psychoanalytically inflected framework for understanding the impossibility of getting beyond certain structures. But we can argue that the emphasis on ideology alone goes too far—a return to reading at least leaves open the possibility that we are reading from *within* antagonism, guiltily, problematically:

> The articulation of an "unposed" or "absent" question, the question that the reading (the reader) establishes as unthinkable within the text's own problematic. "Symptomatic" reading is precisely the production of this absent question, which figures the political and rhetorical relation—or more accurately, conflict—between a text and its reader, between readers, between positions. To read is to give form to this conflict, to pose the question that gives the problematic its structure. But the symptom is not something that afflicts only the texts of our opponents; our own symptom is visible as our guilt, the guilt that our reading will expose rather than conceal, the guilt that opens the text. Therein lies the very possibility of a politics of reading. (187)

Reading in this sense is unnatural. It cuts against Hegelian and biblical wholes, teleology, expressionist kernels. A feminist "reading" of capitalism is unnatural because it identifies both its own position as one taken against usual accounts of reproduction, but also because it articulates what is not said: the absent question of capitalism in this sense is the question of reproduction. It is reading conceived in the broad sense that, as Rooney concludes: "reading is risky because it is always a relation among readings and readers, a productive and political relation, but productive precisely in that it intervenes in the process of reproduction and thus cannot be guaranteed" (194). While Rooney precisely identifies that it is on the question of reproduction that the relationship between reading and ideology turns, there is much more to be said about what Althusser and indeed much of Marxism itself doesn't say about the role of women and gender in the formation and perpetuation of capital. This requires a doubling, maybe even tripling of the reading (the absence within an absence within an absence), of rethinking countertraditions that have themselves become traditions.

The Ghosts of *Reading Capital*

So, guilty reading in mind, what unposed and absent question are we asking of *Reading Capital* here? We are perhaps dealing here with questions that are semiposed and barely answered on multiple levels. Althusser asks, in a discussion of the classical economists and Marx on the value of labor the following: "what is the maintenance of labour? What is the reproduction of labour?"[5] Althusser argues that Marx precisely sees what the classical economists do not see, namely that the entire terms of the question need to be altered: "Marx can pose the unuttered *question*, simply by uttering the concept present in an unuttered form in the emptiness in the *answer*, sufficiently present in this answer to reproduce and reveal these emptinesses as the emptiness of a presence" (RCC 21). Marx's reposed question, based on a complete restructuring of the entire framework, is, according to Althusser, "what is the value of labour-power?" (RCC 22). But while it is true that the classical economists obscured the question of labor, they at least raised in the abstract the question of reproduction itself, outside of the epistemological concept of production (the production of knowledge by different domains) that Althusser wants to interrogate. Oddly then, the vaguer question about how labor is maintained and reproduced might in fact be the harder one to answer, not because it is misposed, but because the level on which it is asked is frequently misidenti-fied. Reproduction is a question often unseen precisely because it suffers from an overabundance of meanings. As Lise Vogel puts it in *Marxism and the Op-pression of Women*:

> Problems in defining the concept of reproduction derive from its wide range of potential meanings. Felicity Edholm, Olivia Harris and Kate Young suggest that three levels of analysis might be distinguished: social reproduction, or the reproduction of the conditions of production; repro-duction of the labour-force; and human or biological reproduction. While the suggestion has been helpful, the issue of the relationship among the different aspects remains.[6]

A Marxist answer to the question of reproduction has to attempt clarity on this question. Althusser's reposing of the ground of the classical economists arguably restricts the question of reproduction to the second of these aspects, reproduction of the labor force. But this is precisely to ignore all the work that exists in order to keep life going, waged and unwaged. The erasure and under-mining of women's role in this is a central feature of capitalism. As Silvia Fed-erici puts it: "Through my involvement in the women's movement I realized that the reproduction of human beings is the foundation of every economic and political system."[7] "Reproduction" here should be read in the broadest possible sense as the "complex of activities and relations by which our life and labour are daily reconstituted,"[8] that is to say, everything that makes life possi-ble in the first place and everything that continues to sustain it. Reproduction in this broad sense is where the contradictions inherent in alienated labor are "most explosive," according to Federici.

In Lise Vogel's *Marxism and the Oppression of Women*, she describes the convoluted and intense struggles over determining whether unwaged or domestic labor produced value, and could therefore be considered "produc-tive" or "unproductive."[9] The wages for housework debates raised the broader question of social reproduction and questioned Marx's position on the estab-lishment of the wage level. It seems that today at least two of the positions that were staked in this debate have some kind of strange genealogical resonance today. On the one hand, the autonomist Marxist idea that domestic labor cre-ates surplus value, either "directly or indirectly" as Kathi Weeks puts it in her recent *The Problem with Work*,[10] and the related claim that there should be economic recognition of the value this work produces, not in order to valorize housework as such, but to make a broader point about how the wage relation operates within capitalism, and how it depends on vast quantities of unpaid female labor. As Federici puts it in *Caliban and the Witch*, summing up the earlier debates:

> A social system of production that does not recognise the production and reproduction of the worker as a social-economic activity, and a source of capital accumulation, but mystifies it instead as a natural resource or a personal service, while profiting from the wageless condition of the labour involved.[11]

But how might we put Federici and others' insights regarding the definition of reproduction in a Marxist-feminist way back in contact with the Althusserian project? A useful clue comes from a review of one of Althusser's books, *Montesquieu, la politique et la histoire*, by Federici. The review is from 1969, slightly before we position many of the debates around social reproduction, but already Federici is very clear. She writes: "The question here is: how do we handle the past? If it is true, as Althusser reiterates, that prior to Marx every 'production' is merely ideological, why should we study it at all?"[12] Federici's criticism of Althusser's reluctance to historicize reproduction is crucial to the feminist attempt to move away from the kind of analysis presented in *Reading Capital*, and Federici makes it very clear that Althusser's attempt to make Marxism a "science," by appealing to forerunners in the shape of Montesquieu and others, is predicated on false, generalizing assertions: "Althusser fails first and foremost because he chooses only a part of Montesquieu's assertions to constitute his theoretical 'praxis.'"[13] What impact do these generalizing, non- or ahistorical claims mean for any understanding of the relationship between production and reproduction, labor and sex? Federici claims that Althusser's inability to determine what the motor of the dialectic might be for Montesquieu (for example, does law precede justice or vice versa?) leads to a curiously non-Marxist approach to the problem, and thus Althusser wastes "valuable space and ink on a problem which, for a Marxist, could easily find its solution in the 3rd thesis of Feuerbach."[14] "Structuralist-Marxists," of which Althusser is the leading light, suffer, thinks Federici, from reading everything "within their own context."[15] This closed reading is very clearly in tension with the model of reading complicated in the discussion of the topic in *Reading Capital*. Are there resources in yet another theory of reading that could reconcile the structuralist-Marxist and Marxist-feminist readings?

In the meantime, I am suggesting, via Federici and Federici's reading of Althusser, that the question of reproduction, reposed by Althusser via Marx, does not solve the complex interaction between social reproduction, the reproduction of labor power and biological reproduction, and indeed, perhaps further confuses the question. In *Reading Capital*, Étienne Balibar devotes an entire section to reproduction, but remains strangely opaque on the relationship between these kinds of reproduction, all crucial to the reproduction of capital. In his analysis, there are three ways in which a theory of reproduction ensures a triple continuity: firstly, the link between different economic subjects, which in fact move together and are intertwined, where the parts of the whole are more than their sum; secondly, "the permanence of the non-economic conditions of the production process," where law is especially singled out, and thirdly, reproduction that ensures the "successive continuity of production itself" (RCC 426–27), which is the basis for all the rest. It is on the third point that Balibar slightly mystifies the question, although unconsciously referring to it on another level:

> Production cannot be stopped . . . it is the materiality of the elements which supports the continuity, but it is the concept of reproduction which expresses its specific form, because it envelops the different (differential) determinations of the material. Through each of the aspects that I have invoked, the concept expresses merely one and the same pregnancy of the structure which presents a "well-bound" history. (RCC 425)

Taking a quote from Rosa Luxemburg's *The Accumulation of Capital*, Balibar agrees that "reproduction appears to be the general form of permanence of the general conditions of production, which in the last analysis englobe the whole social structure." What Marxist feminists strove to do was to begin from this question of the "whole social structure," but here Balibar points to this as a potential site of analysis before retreating back toward a more narrowly economic reading. Even in the section "The Reproduction of the Social Relations," Balibar avoids the possibility of beginning with the discussion of what is at stake in the "perpetuation" of the worker, that "absolutely necessary condition," as Marx puts it, for the capitalist mode of production to function:

> The concept of reproduction is thus not only the concept of the "consistency" of the structure, but also the concept of the necessary determination of the movement of production by the permanence of that structure; it is the concept of the permanence of the initial elements in the very functioning of the system, hence the concept of the necessary conditions of production, conditions which are precisely *not created by it*. This is what Marx

calls the *eternity* of the mode of production: "This incessant *reproduction*, this *perpetuation* (*Verewigung*) of the worker, is the *absolutely necessary* condition for capitalist production." (RCC 440, citing *Capital* vol. 1, 716)

Perhaps what is ultimately missing in the entire approach or reading in *Reading Capital* is an openness to the question of what "comes first" and what is and is not "eternal." Marxist-feminism, by opening up the question of sex *historically* and pointing out that reproduction can be understood "in the last instance" not only in an economic way, but in a way that takes into account the entire conditions for the "perpetuation of the worker."

Coda

The concept of reading that *Reading Capital* announces is an enormously productive one for feminist readings of Marx that seek to supplement and expand on Marx's analysis while not remaining hidebound by its gaps and absences. The closeness of *Reading Capital*'s "guilty" reading disguises what is perhaps most productive about its model of reading. As Vogel puts it: "Scattered throughout the pages of *Capital*, Marx's comments on women's situation, on the family, on divisions of labour according to sex and age, and on the reproduction of the working class have never been sufficiently appreciated by students of the so-called woman-question."[16] What the discussion of social reproduction does is open up the possibility, once again, of a true meeting of Marxism and feminism to begin again to answer the complex questions of sex and value, and the relationship between structure and history, in the twenty-first century.

Notes

1. Ellen Rooney, "Better Read Than Dead: Althusser and the Fetish of Ideology," in "Depositions: Althusser, Balibar, Macherey, and the Labor of Reading," special issue, *Yale French Studies*, no. 88 (1995): 183–200. Further page references are cited in the text.

2. Rosemary Hennessy, "Women's Lives/Feminist Knowledge: Feminist Standpoint as Ideology Critique," *Hypatia* 8, no. 1 (winter 1993): 14–34, quotation on 21.

3. Martha E. Gimenez, "Capitalism and the Oppression of Women: Marx Revisited," in "Marxist-Feminist Thought Today," special issue, *Science and Society* 69, no. 1 (January 2005): 11–32, quotation on 13n5.

4. Rooney, "Better Read Than Dead," 183: "His theory of reading actually helps to resolve some of the very theoretical and political difficulties that many commentators on his theory of ideology find so troubling."

5. Louis Althusser, Étienne Balibar, Roger Establet, Pierre Macherey, and Jacques Rancière, *Reading Capital: The Complete Edition*, trans. Ben Brewster and David Fernbach (London: Verso, 2016), 20. All further references will be given in the text.

6. Lise Vogel, *Marxism and the Oppression of Women: Toward a Unitary Theory* (Leiden: Brill, 2013 [1983]), 28.

7. Silvia Federici, Preface, *Revolution at Point Zero: Housework, Reproduction, and Feminist Struggle* (Oakland, CA: PM Press, 2012), 2.

8. Federici, *Revolution at Point Zero*, 5.

9. Vogel, *Marxism and the Oppression of Women*, 22.

10. Kathi Weeks, *The Problem with Work: Feminism, Marxism, Antiwork Politics, and Postwork Imaginaries* (Durham, NC: Duke University Press, 2011), 97.

11. Silvia Federici, *Caliban and the Witch: Women, the Body and Primitive Accumulation* (New York: Autonomedia, 2004), 8.

12. Silvia Federici, "Review of Louis Althusser, *Montesquieu, la politique et la histoire*," *Telos*, no. 4 (fall 1969): 236–40, quotation on 237.

13. Federici, "Review of *Montesquieu, la politique et la histoire*," 238.

14. Federici, "Review of *Montesquieu, la politique et la histoire*," 239.

15. Federici, "Review of *Montesquieu, la politique et la histoire*," 239.

16. Vogel, *Marxism and the Oppression of Women*, 62.

CHAPTER 10

Value as Symptom

NICK NESBITT

> I heard this silence as the possible weakness of a discourse under the pressure and repressive action of another discourse, which takes the place of the first discourse in favour of this repression, and speaks in its silence: the empiricist discourse.
> —LOUIS ALTHUSSER, *Reading Capital*

> The capitalist mode of production comes up against a barrier to the development of the productive forces *which has nothing to do with the production of wealth as such*; but this characteristic barrier in fact testifies to the restrictiveness and the solely historical and transitory character of the capitalist mode of production.
> —MARX, *Capital, Vol. III* (emphasis added)

> Marxism is the set of misinterpretations that have been made of Marx.
> —MICHEL HENRY, *Marx*

In what follows I propose to analyze the concept of value in *Reading Capital* following Althusser's own protocol: not in the fullness of its presence, but instead in its symptomatic status in *Reading Capital*. As is well known, Althusser famously neglects and even derides Marx's first, most abstract chapter of *Capital*, in which he initially constructs the concept of value in its most abstract form.[1] "If," as Michele Cangiani quite rightly asks, "knowledge is conceived [by Althusser] as a structure, how is it possible to amputate Marxian theoretical structure from its starting point, its basis, its 'most abstract determinations'?"[2] Though Althusser twice lists value first among the key concepts of Marx's "theoretical revolution," its relative nonexistence in the abridged translation—as well as its marked underdevelopment in the original essays of *Lire le Capital*—delineates, I will argue, the limits of Althusser's critique of Marxist empiricism and humanism.

On the one hand, the authors of *Lire le Capital* each clearly distinguish Marx's novel conception of the value-form as a social relation from the quantitative concept of value found in the classical economics of Smith and Ricardo ("The value of a commodity," writes Ricardo, "depends on the relative *quantity* of labour which is necessary for its production").[3] At the same time, however, this relational understanding of the value-form arguably continues to rely upon an ontological, transhistorical understanding of the place of living labor in capital, thus reintroducing at the level of the forces of production the essentialist humanism Althusser had critiqued so powerfully elsewhere. In this view, the social relation of value Althusser and his collaborators conceptualize is not a critique of the capitalist mode of *production* but of the relations of the exploitation of the proletariat at the level of the *distribution* of the wealth the latter has produced.

Among the various contradictions of capitalist production that Marx identified, the simultaneous drive to expel living labor from the production process while retaining abstract labor as the source of value—a process he called capitalism's "moving contradiction"—remains obscure in *Reading Capital*, to say nothing of the tendency toward an eventual collapse of the valorization process this contradiction identifies:

> Capital itself is the moving contradiction, in that it presses to reduce labour time to a minimum, while it posits labour time, on the other side, as sole measure and source of wealth. . . . As soon as labour in its immediate form has ceased to be the great source of wealth, labour time ceases and must cease to be its measure, and hence exchange value [must cease to be the measure] of use value. . . . With that, production based upon exchange value collapses.[4]

Indeed, the concept of a collapse of valorization is never fully developed in the four volumes of *Capital* itself.[5] This dimension of the structure of capitalism names a long-neglected yet absolutely crucial dimension of Marx's critique: a terminal structural dynamic arising from a limit inherent to the expansion capacity of capital, or, more precisely, in the capacity of capitalism as a whole to continuously expand the production of surplus value in totality.

In the "Fragment on Machines" at the end of Marx's Notebook 6 and beginning of Notebook 7 of Marx's preliminary studies for *Capital*, Marx describes the historical dynamic of what he will come to place under the concept of the "organic composition" of capital, as the contradiction between living labor and the machine automation of the production process. In the

Grundrisse, Marx emphasizes the domination of automation processes as the "culmination" of "the production process of capital," in which the human is displaced from production to become the mere "watchman and regulator" of the "virtuoso" machine, such that machinery "confronts [the human laborer's] individual, insignificant doings as a mighty organism, . . . a power which rules" over living labor (694, 705). Crucially, Marx identifies this as a universal tendency toward the development of automation in capitalism, its "most complete, most adequate form, . . . the necessary tendency of capital" (692).

While Marx will elaborate on the structural dynamic of organic composition at length in various sections of *Capital,* the crucial feature of the condensed, dramatic rather than analytical presentation of this contradiction in these pages of the *Grundrisse* is the way in which a general and universal (if always uneven) logic of a tendency of development, presented in abstraction from the various countervailing forces that can serve to restore profitability, implies an inherent structural limitation to the creation of surplus value, understood not merely as empirical and perpetually correctable *falling rate of profit* but as a diminishing *total aggregate mass.*[6]

Crucially, to call this concept a structural tendency is not to invoke a historical determinism or teleology of the *necessary* collapse of capitalism, the movement of the whole expressed in a putative unity of its contradictory tendencies. Instead, to conceptualize the "moving contradiction" of capitalism as what I am calling a "terminal" dynamic requires, as Althusser demanded, sustaining the immensely complex, overdetermined coexistence of this dynamic with the multitude of other factors and tendencies Marx conceptualizes and analyzes in the three volumes of *Capital.* Like all the laws Marx conceptualizes, capitalism's "moving contradiction" does not and cannot predict empirical events and movements. Instead, like the concept of the falling rate of profit, it names the *law* of a "tendency," one which may or may not confront counteracting tendencies at various conjunctures in the development of global capital.

In this case, and in contrast to Marx's Law of the Tendency of the Profit Rate to Fall, the tendency of the "moving contradiction" is of a unilinear, and not cyclical, decline in the capacity to valorize value.[7] In this "moving contradiction" of capitalism, machines continuously appear as the fruit of science and industry under the control of capital, displacing humans from newly invented and reconfigured processes of automation in the struggle to achieve increases in relative surplus value. This factor or tendency nonetheless exists within a complex, contingent, temporally dynamic structure, in which, as Althusser writes, "each of the different levels of the whole . . . does not have the same type of historical existence" (RCC 247).[8] Arguably, it is only in the contemporary conjuncture in the decades following the publication of *Reading Capital*, with the collapse of Fordism in the 1970s and the expansion of automated, posthuman production to virtually every realm of global capital in the twenty-first century, that this substructure of capital has become structurally predominant.[9] Crucially, this general tendency of capitalism in the present conjuncture now proceeds unchecked, encountering no countervailing tendencies that would restore the centrality of living labor power to production—and thus reanimate the creation of surplus value—the introduction, in other words, of new production processes requiring intensive living rather than machinic labor.[10] Though I am arguing on the one hand that this dynamic remained invisible to the authors of *Lire le Capital,* at the same time I will maintain in what follows that the adequate conceptualization of this novel, post-Fordist conjuncture and its attendant collapse of valorization, absent all teleology and determinism, requires bringing *Reading Capital's* logic of structural causality and historical contingency to bear upon this underdeveloped dimension of Marx's categorial critique of capitalism.

Value . . .

The concept of value is assuredly the single most essential Marxian category to be developed for any contemporary critique of the limits of global capitalism in the twenty-first century. Few of the various Marxist-Leninist categories of analysis and militancy that dominated the twentieth century, from labor, socialism, nationalization, modernization, the proletariat, and the state, to the very category of revolution—traditionally understood—itself, have retained their critical valence in the decades since the fall of Eastern European "socialism." This can be affirmed not subjectively but as a categorial tendency of late capitalism: the very real successes and advances of the modernizing revolutions from the French, Haitian, and even American to the Bolshevik and anticolonial, those two and a half centuries of development in the form of modernization are to a great extent simply no longer available, for better and worse, in a world in which industrial production, and human labor more generally, produces ever less surplus value.[11] Moreover, both the anticolonialist revolutions from Vietnam and Algeria to China itself, alongside the Bolshevik Revolution and its Central and Eastern European offshoots from Poland to Yugoslavia, while often instantiating real advances in social justice (as in postslavery Haiti, including the first postcolonial land reform) and the distribution of wealth (as in the former Eastern bloc), arguably never extracted themselves from the telos of global capital, the universal compulsion to valorize value. Such was the destiny of so-called orthodox or "traditional" Marxism as Moishe Postone analyzed it two decades ago in *Time, Labor, and Social Domination.*

Postone abstractly and reductively rejected as an undifferentiated, wrongheaded totality, a 150-year revolutionary movement oriented toward what he called social critique from the standpoint of labor, rather than a critique of labor itself.[12] In this view, labor, along with its fundamental secondary products from the proletariat and its dictatorship to the state itself, stand not as the antithesis to capital, not even, as Tronti, Negri, and the contemporary antiwork movement inspired by Operaismo would have it, as fundamentally antagonistic to capital, but rather as features of the social objectivity of capital, as constitutive elements in the growing perfection of capital toward what Marx called, objectively but with no small irony, its most "adequate," automated, and posthuman form.[13] Class struggle, identifying from the perspective of the Left the historical fight for a more just redistribution of wealth in a context in which brutal inequality expands unbridled, nonetheless remains a category internal to the dynamics of capitalism itself. In its antagonism to work, in this view, class struggle—even as it achieves ephemeral, if vital, advantages in the redistribution of wealth to labor—drives forward the organic composition of capital, relentlessly reducing the value of labor power, before imposing the verdict we witness everywhere today, of the global superfluity of humans to capital in a planet of slums.[14]

Already in 1966, Mario Tronti, in *Workers and Capital,* underscored the manner in which "the pressure of labor power is capable of obligating capital to modify its very internal composition [to realize increases of relative—and not merely absolute—surplus value]," and the fundamental nature of class struggle as "an essential component of capitalist development, that it pushes forward, from within," if only to draw precisely the opposite—I think mistaken—conclusion regarding the putatively revolutionary powers of so-called "labor" (2016: 64, see also 75).[15]

To this eternal illusion of Operaismo stands in contrast Foxconn founder Terry Gou's plan to replace his all-too-human, underpaid, suicide-prone iPhone assemblers with a million robots.[16] Though more difficult to implement than he had originally foreseen, Gou's explicit drive for massive automation at the expense of living labor is not even cynical, but merely casts in contemporary terms the eternal response of capital to class struggle: automate to seek out transient increments of relative surplus value, and as the prices fall for the means of production and commodities necessary for the reproduction of labor power, so will the global, socially necessary value of that labor power decrease, till eventually it (living labor) is rendered superfluous and displaced from the production process itself, while an immiserated humanity nonetheless remains ever dependent upon capital for its mere survival.[17] The point is not to dismiss Tronti in hindsight, but instead to underscore the degree to which the process of the massive and global expulsion of living labor from industrial production that is visible—if not coherently understood—by everyone today was historically neglected in the late-Fordist 1960s, invisible as a theoretical problem even for those Marxist philosophers like Tronti and Althusser who were most critical of traditional Marxism.

The object of Marx's concept of value, in its details the subject of an enormous and contentious literature, is in fact quite straightforward. Marx insists on the tripartite distinction between use value, exchange value, and value as the fundamental starting point to his conceptual analysis and critique of capitalism in order to determine the basis on which incommensurate commodities or use values can be measured as equivalent exchange values (i.e., x yards of linen$=y$ lbs. of steel$=z$ dollars), or, as Marx repeatedly formulates the matter, to answer the question of what forms the common "substance" of capital. That is to say, it is not fundamentally the numerical quantities of exchange values and their relations that interest him, but rather the underlying basis upon which any such relation can be measured; what, Marx asks, are relative values, for example in the form of prices, actually measuring?[18] As Pierre Macherey writes in his contribution to *Reading Capital*, "The equality of the relation [between exchange values] can only be constituted and determined on the basis of a measurement, or rather *a possibility of measuring*, in itself distinct from all particular relations" (RCC 201, emphasis added).

Marx's concept of value expressly refuses the most familiar, empirical, and subjective answer to this question offered from Adam Smith to today: that the substance of exchange values lies in the subjective utility or satisfaction offered by a commodity for its consumer. Instead, the entire analysis of volume 1 of *Capital* elaborates Marx's contention that the substance of capital is instead abstract labor power; Marx conceptualizes the substance of value in capitalism not in terms of subjective or even implicit judgments of equivalence by commodity owners, but as a system that confronts subjects as a socially constituted objective fact and necessity (subjects cannot simply "opt out" of capitalism), the structural logic of which is not immediately apparent and must instead be elucidated through critique.[19]

Marx's analysis of the value-form contains three principal dimensions subtending this primary affirmation. The first, most familiar dimension, describes the realization of relative (as opposed to absolute) surplus value, articulated in volume 1 of *Capital*, while the second, the Law of the Tendential Fall in the Rate of Profit that Marx repeatedly reaffirmed as "the most important law of political economy" and the very key to all of political economy since Adam Smith, is developed in chapters 13–15 of volume 3. The third and least familiar element of the theory of value, that of surplus value understood as a global mass or totality, is furtively and even incompletely developed in Marx's mature work, finding its most concise, formulaic expression in the concept of the "moving contradiction" discussed above.

The distinction between the latter two categories is key to the conceptualization of value to be developed below: while the former primarily addresses an *empirical* dimension of capital manifest in the monetary values and rates of profit of *individual capitals* of various sizes and compositions, the concept of surplus value as a totality is of an entirely different order, specifically, that is, of the order of *concepts* rather than the empirical. The global mass of surplus value cannot be apprehended empirically precisely because it is not an empirical given, but the concept of a (nonetheless entirely real and effective) systemic relation and structural logic.[20] As such, this notion requires the development of an adequate conceptual understanding of value, precisely the intellectual operation Althusser and above all Pierre Macherey call for more generally in *Reading Capital*, without, however, sufficiently addressing in their respective contributions to the volume the implications of this demand for Marx's concept of value specifically.

The development of the concept of value along these lines points beyond the dependence of capital as a whole upon increases of relative surplus value among competing individual capitals, to address the structural limitations to the accumulation of surplus value (a dynamic that, following Marx, is to be rigorously distinguished from increases in the empirical number of humans employed). It is this expansion of value production as an aggregate mass, rather than the profitability of individual capitals per se, that in this view has stalled since the end of the Fordist expansion of labor-intensive industrial production processes, with the exponential expansion of fictive capital not a cause, but rather the only significant countervailing factor still deferring a global collapse of valorization.[21]

Marx articulates this distinction between cyclical, recurrent crises in profits and a fundamental limit to expansion via the Hegelian distinction between, respectively, the limit ("*Grenze*") and the finite boundary ("*Schranke*").[22] If the former, as in a territorial limit, is potentially overcome in the act of its posing, the *boundary* (as in the case of the absolute bounds of jurisdiction [*beschränkte Zuständigkeit*]) constitutes an absolute block that capital cannot overcome without imperiling its very existence. Capitalism, in this view, should be understood not only in its historical tendency to the self-overcoming of limited crises, but also as a bounded (*beschränkte*) finite entity. [23]

At some point as we approach the total automation of labor, in the absence of new production processes requiring living rather than automated labor, the accumulation of surplus value, Robert Kurz long argued, will begin to collapse.[24] To point ahead to my conclusion, it is precisely this contradiction between human and machinic labor that Marx termed the development of the organic composition of capital that remains utterly invisible in the all-too-humanist reading of *Capital* in *Lire le Capital*, to say nothing of orthodox twentieth-century Marxism as a whole.

... As Symptom

Value—along with its component concepts, including ideology—stands revealed in the twenty-first century, in light of the becoming-infinitesimal of the value of living labor, as what Marx always said it was, the key to any critique of the political economy of capitalism. If this is the case, it seems essential to interrogate the symptomatic status of the concept of value in one of the key theoretical interventions of twentieth-century Marxism, that of Althusser and his collaborators Rancière, Balibar, Macherey, and Establet, published as *Lire le Capital* fifty years ago in 1965 by François Maspero.

The concept of value bears a paradoxical character in *Lire le Capital*, insofar as, on the one hand, Althusser points on two occasions to Marx's labor theory of value as the single most important concept in *Capital*, while, remarkably, the construction of the concept of value is rudimentary and even superficial, particularly in the much better-known, truncated second edition of *Lire le Capital* from which Rancière, Macherey, and Establet's essays were eliminated. Beyond Althusser's brief mentions of the concept in his famous essay "The Object of Capital," only two brief but key sections in Rancière's essay (259), and especially the third section of Macherey's long-overlooked contribution "Analyse de valeur" treat the concept in more than passing detail. Even when one reads the restored complete volume of essays in the PUF Quadrige edition, however, the treatment of value remains highly problematic, or rather, in Althusser's own terms, symptomatic: symptomatic from the contemporary perspective outlined above of a categorial critique of value. Symptomatic, that is to say, not only of the limits of Althusser's own antihumanism circa 1965, but more generally of the humanist ontology of labor that characterized orthodox Marxism itself.

Althusser had first articulated his concept of "theoretical antihumanism" in the final essay of *Pour Marx*, "Marxisme et humanisme." The essay has generally been read for its sweeping conception of ideology as necessarily inherent to all societies, including socialist and communist, as well as for its relation to Althusser's subsequent, better-known critique of ideology in "Ideology and Ideological State Apparatuses."[25] Althusser's analysis of ideology in this 1963 essay, however, is secondary to his main concern: the critique of Marxist humanism based on a categorical opposition between two terms, humanism and socialism: "the concept of 'socialism' is in fact a scientific concept, but the concept of humanism is a merely ideological concept" (229). Humanism, Althusser affirms, is characterized by two interdependent beliefs: that there exists "a universal essence of man" and, secondly, that this essence is the attribute of real subjects, concrete individuals. Together, these beliefs constitute for Althusser an "empiricism of the subject" and an "idealism of the essence" of humanity (234). After 1845, in this reading, Marx eliminates these specters of humanist empiricism, idealism, and the subject, to replace them with what Althusser calls a new *problématique* (historical materialism) and a critical conceptual apparatus of "scientific" concepts ("forces of production, relations of production").

Althusser's critique of humanism in the essay is brilliant and penetrating, perhaps the founding document of the so-called poststructuralist critique of the subject soon to be developed by Foucault and Derrida in particular. Relatively little attention, however, has been paid to the term Althusser casts as the putative other of this humanism, "socialism." Understandably so, since Althusser the steadfast PCF militant here sings the praises of the USSR without moderation, as a socialist paradise realized, and this precisely in the period of the waning of prestige of actually existing socialism that in France would culminate in May '68 and the subsequent rise of the Nouveaux philosophes in the 1970s: "The communism the Soviet Union has undertaken [to develop via its 1961 renunciation of the socialist doctrine of the dictatorship of the proletariat] is a world without economic exploitation, without violence, without discrimination—

a world opening before the Soviets the infinite space of progress, of science, of culture, of bread and freedom, of free development—a world that can be devoid of shadows and dramas" (245).[26]

Rather than dismissing in hindsight this mawkish encomium as mere embarrassment in light of the decline of Soviet society in the years leading to 1989, the concept of socialism in the essay should be subjected to precisely the critique Althusser makes of its supposed other, humanism, that it is, in other words, profoundly ideological not only in the neutral sense of a "system of mass representations indispensable to any society in the formation of men" (242), but in the mystified, precritical sense of the term that Althusser brings to bear against the concept of humanism, that it constitutes, in other words, both an *empiricism of the subject* and an *idealism of the essence of labor*.

More specifically, this Manichean opposition that casts socialism as a scientific, non-ideological concept precisely locates the limit of Althusser's antihumanism: Althusser's presentation of "socialism" in the essay should be critiqued, I wish to argue, precisely for its unrecognized *humanism*. The very substance of socialism as Althusser defines it in the opening page of the essay, human labor,[27] constitutes in the essay a precritical absolute, quite literally, an article of *faith* presumed without question to stand in *antagonistic opposition* to capitalism. "*It is beyond doubt*," writes Althusser, "that the communists are right to *oppose* the economic, social, political, and cultural reality of socialism to the 'inhumanity' of imperialism" (246, my italics). Whether in fact socialism actually stood in opposition to capitalism or was simply an alternative (statist) mode of the distribution of wealth structured upon the general obligation to valorize value was precisely the question that needed to be asked of actually existing socialism in a critical, systematic (scientific) fashion.

This was, however, a question that traditional Marxism, caught up in the process of recuperative modernization, found impossible to entertain. Instead, locating the critique of capitalism at the level of the distribution of wealth, the capitalist mode of *production,* with its fundamental dependency on the real abstraction of living labor for the creation of surplus value, was understood as a transhistorical absolute (an essence), and the various ways that abstract labor is actually constituted prior to exchange in the production process itself, along with its attendant forms of subjectivation (as competition, productivity, performance, cold-heartedness, self-interest, rationalization, and the like for both liberal capitalism and Stakhanovite socialism) all remained studiously unanalyzed, both in Althusser's essay and traditional Marxism more generally.

Like that of his contemporary Tronti discussed above, Althusser's analysis of socialism and humanism constitutes in this view a classic example of a critique of capitalism from the transhistorical standpoint of labor, rather than a critique of labor itself as a constituent and necessary element in the valorization process. Althusser—like traditional Marxism more generally and its Leninist tradition of industrial productionism—thus celebrates the unalloyed "development of the forces of production" to be mitigated only by the Soviets' "socialist" redistribution of this wealth (as "socialist relations of production" and the dictatorship of the proletariat) (*Pour Marx*, 244).

It is not only that "socialism" remains an article of faith for Althusser, standing in unquestioned opposition to capitalism, but, more to the point, that faith is precisely a *humanist* one: human labor constitutes for Althusser in "Marxism and Humanism," as it will in *Reading Capital*, the unproblematic essence of socialism as well as that of the production process more generally (whether as wage labor for liberalism or in its equally fetishistic, Stakhanovite forms in socialism). If living labor, in its real abstraction as labor power, is both a product of capitalism and by definition the unique substance of valorization in any and all forms of capitalism, this in itself constitutes for Marx not just a fact, but a *problem* for the capitalist mode of production.

This is the case insofar as labor is only one of two forms of capital that constitute the means of production. In Marx's categorial analysis, the working class, "labor," stands not opposed to capital, but, quite to the contrary, *is itself one form of capital*, what he called "variable" (as opposed to constant) capital.[28] If variable capital—the empirical forms of which include wage labor in liberal capitalism and state-remunerated labor in socialist state-capitalism[29]— contributes value to the commodity in the process of production, constant capital (including not only machines, but slaves, mules, raw materials, in short, all means of production beside living labor) merely transmits previously existing value in the production process.[30] The relative weights of these two forms of capital, variable and constant, constitute for Marx the organic composition of capital.[31]

It is the former, constant capital, that tends unrelentingly to displace variable capital in the unilinear "moving contradiction" of capital's historical development. At the same time, however, capitalism continues to and can derive surplus value only from living, wage labor. This dynamic, "moving" contradiction can be termed, in light of Althusser's dedication to theoretical antihumanism, "posthuman," in contrast to a more familiar, "humanist" substructure or contradiction of capitalism. The phenomenology of cyclical crises and exploitation that forms the substance of traditional Marxist analyses is humanist, in this view, insofar as it locates the system's dynamic in the class struggle to control the wealth of society and its mode of production and, above all, distribution. This humanist contradiction pits capitalists against workers in the fight against exploitation and for universally humane and egalitarian wealth distribution. It is fundamentally cyclical insofar as it is manifest in the theoretically unending struggle within capitalism between its two principal actors, capitalists and wage laborers, over empirical categories such as wages, profits, and working conditions.

In contrast, in what Marx called the "moving contradiction" of capitalism (a substructure or subcontradiction that I am arguing has today become dominant within the contingent, moving totality that is capitalism), machines continuously appear as the fruit of science and industry under the control of capital, displacing humans from newly invented and reconfigured processes of automation in the struggle to achieve increases in relative surplus value. The development of this contradiction is tendentially "posthuman," I am arguing, in that it enjoins a historically unilinear, if fitful and overdetermined, elimination of humans from the production of wealth, while capitalism as a general and predominant social relation continues to depend upon living labor as the substance of value.

Althusser's failure to subject the concepts of labor and value to Marx's categorial critique in "Marxism and Humanism" merely points to his own inability to call into question an unwavering fidelity to the PCF and through it the Soviet Union. In *Lire le Capital*, however, this limitation will become a more fundamental limitation to the ability to adequately articulate the essential structural concept of capitalism, the contradictory, historical dynamic of valorization.

As Robert Young points out elsewhere in this volume, Althusser understood as a "symptomatic [*symptomale*]" reading of Marx dedicated not to revealing a truth hidden within the depths of a text, but rather, as Marx had argued of Ricardo, to the articulation of questions to which *Capital* gives answers, without at the same time being capable of formulating those very questions. My own question is whether the treatment of value in *Lire le Capital* even achieves this level of symptomaticity, or if the concept instead remains quite simply invisible as a *problem*, a problem confronting global capital in the very laws of its development, a problem that has only today become perceptible and even crucial for any contemporary critique of political economy.

From one perspective, the symptomatic underdevelopment of the concept of value in *Reading Capital* is readily comprehensible: the enormous literature on the labor theory of value, from Engels to I. I. Rubin's pathbreaking 1924 study *Essays on Marx's Theory of Value*, long understood Marx's labor theory of value in *empiricist* and above all *humanist* terms, to adopt Althusser's terminology. Empiricist insofar as, for orthodox Marxism, socially necessary labor inputs to production, and thus the value of commodities, were thought to be quantifiable, as Engels (in)famously claimed in his appendix to volume 3 of *Capital*, and through this calculation, as Rubin summarized, "the value of commodities is directly proportional to the quantity of labor necessary for their production."[32]

Above all, value remained in twentieth-century Marxist philosophy deeply inscribed within a humanist horizon that could only make it unpalatable to Althusser's self-proclaimed antihumanism. The dynamic of the growing organic composition of capital that Marx described remains completely invisible within the Leninist ontology of labor, of recuperative modernization, class struggle, the dictatorship of the proletariat, and nationalization (in a word, electrification plus soviets), a transhistorical ontology from which Althusser never exited (and in fact reinscribed himself within ever more fully as the so-called class struggle in theory of the 1970s). In this sense, *Reading Capital* falls behind even the thought of the Russian bourgeois economist Vladimir Dmitriev, whose 1904 *Economic Essays* at least attempt to formalize the implications for the rate of profit of the completely automated, posthuman economy that Marx's theory implicitly predicts.[33] In fact, I would argue that the labor theory of value has remained unable to this day to transcend this anthropocentric horizon, even in its most recent developments in the thought of writers as diverse as Postone and Chris Arthur. Instead, value continues to be grasped, in Rubin's phrase, uniquely as a "social relation among people" rather than, in addition, as the contradictory relation between humans and machines that Marx describes.

When Althusser, Rancière, and Macherey do address the concept of value in *Reading Capital*, they only ever critique it in terms of the *empiricism* in which it had been understood since Engels, for example via the long-standing debate on the transformation problem. Althusser initiates his analysis by listing the fundamental concepts to be taken from Marx's critique of political economy, beginning with value: "the concepts which contain Marx's basic discoveries are: the concepts of *value* and *use-value*; of *abstract labour* and *concrete labour*; and of *surplus-value* " (RCC 224).[34] In line with the general protocol of

Reading Capital as a whole, Althusser's point is to describe and celebrate value in nonempirical terms as "non-measurable and non-quantifiable," against which familiar critiques of its "imaginary" or "metaphysical" status are simply a "misunderstanding" (225). Althusser quickly ends his discussion with a rejection of Engels's mistaken "empiricist" and transhistorical understanding of the concept of value as "a troubling example [of] the empiricist ideology of knowledge" (265). At this point, Althusser abandons his discussion of value, though one might argue that it continues to operate silently beneath his critiques of historicism and structural causality; these critiques must be brought to bear, in a way *Lire le Capital* never consciously undertakes, on the contingent, immanent contradiction of the organic composition of the forces of production central to the expansion of capital. To develop this defining dimension of Marx's concept of value requires a symptomatic reading of *Lire le Capital* itself, a reading in which, as Althusser says of reading *Capital*, "a mere literal reading of Marx's text, even an attentive one, will leave us unsatisfied or even *miss the question altogether*, dispensing us from the task of posing this question, even though it is essential to an understanding of Marx" (218).

Following Althusser's truncated discussion of value, Rancière, in the section of his essay entitled "Value and Value-form," points precisely the conceptual status of value, focusing on *abstract labor* as determinate abstraction and, furthermore, to value in its non-empirical, structural dimension as form, that is, as the "value-form" (RCC 128–29). "The law of labor-value is a theoretical law . . . Marx's revolution does not consist in historicizing the categories of political economy. It consists in the construction of a system . . . through its scientific exposition" (160, 170). Notably, labor, as throughout *Reading Capital,* is always presupposed, here quite explicitly and repeatedly, to be *living* labor ("the determination of value by the time of labor"; "the human labor [*travail humain*] of which it is here a question") (116, 122).

Crucially, Rancière returns to the problem of value in relation to prices of production and briefly, almost in passing, mentions the key concept that would have allowed for the exploration of value as a *problem* for the critique of political economy: the organic composition of capital.[35] No sooner does he mention it, however, than Rancière immediately shifts his focus from the contradiction between living and automated labor implicit in Marx's concept to critique the empiricism of the so-called transformation problem (the problem, that is, of determining the transformation of empirical quantities of living labor-time into commodity prices) that had endlessly preoccupied traditional Marxist theory since Engels's mechanical quantification and transhistorical ontologization of value in his 1895 "Supplement" to volume 3 of *Capital*, the last piece he wrote before his death, where he claimed that "the Marxian law of value has a universal validity for an era lasting from the beginning of the exchange that transforms products into commodities down to the fifteenth century of our epoch."[36] Rancière again insists on the nonempirical nature of the concept of value: "Marx's revolution does not consist in historicizing the categories of political economy. It consists in making of them a system, and we know that the critique of the system is made by its scientific exposition, that is to say that this system makes apparent a structure that can only be understood in the theory of the development of social formations" (RCC 170).

Finally, in his closing "Remarks," Rancière fleetingly returns to two related critical concepts that allow Marx to develop a theory of the historically developing organic composition of capital, only again to fail to perceive them as in any sense problematic. Rancière argues that if the relation between variable and constant capital (i.e., its organic composition) had constituted a problem for *classical* economy, it is one that Marx resolved definitively, such that it no longer constituted a problem when properly (i.e., "scientifically") understood: "There is an *absent* distinction from the entire discourse of classical economy, the distinction between *variable capital* and *constant capital*" (RCC 195). In words that could rightfully be returned against the entire volume of *Lire le Capital* itself, Rancière concludes, "There is something that it [classical economics] *cannot see*" (195).

It is, however, Pierre Macherey's brilliant and long-overlooked contribution "A propos du processus d'exposition du *Capital*" that contains in its third section the single most incisive and original exposition of the concept of value not only in *Reading Capital*, but, I would argue, in Marxist philosophy of the 1960s and 1970s. It is undoubtedly, from the perspective of the contemporary critique of value developed in these pages, an unsuspected gem of theoretical investigation suddenly revealed by the republication of the complete volume of *Reading Capital*.[37] Macherey's precocious genius in these pages, however, pushes Althusser's Cavaillèssian epistemology to its most extreme and rigorous formulation imaginable.

The object of Macherey's brief chapter is to investigate Marx's conception and practice "of the scientific exposition" of his principal concepts in the initial five pages of *Capital* volume 1, chapter 1, section 1.[38] The essay, which expands on the form of the *explication de texte* that every French *normalien* is trained to master by the "*caïmans*" such as Althusser who prepared them for the rigorous *agrégation*, does in fact possess a formulaic quality.

Macherey's brief exposé nonetheless brings a discerning, analytical precision to bear upon the opening lines of *Capital*, to make a fundamental analytical division between the concepts with which Marx begins his critique of political economy: wealth (*la richesse/Reichtum*) and the commodity (*la marchandise/Ware*), along with the two contradictory aspects of its nature, use- and exchange-value, and, finally, value itself (*la valeur/Wert*). If the first of these, wealth, is only fleetingly presented in the opening sentence of *Capital* ("The wealth of societies in which the capitalist mode of production prevails appears as an 'immense collection of commodities'"),[39] Macherey argues that this is due to its extreme conceptual poverty. Wealth, in this reading, is a purely, reductively empirical category, the mere semblance of facticity that any and all things take as products of production. This form of any given object that constitutes an object of wealth is "the empirical mode of existence of the thing," says Macherey, continuing in distinctly Heideggerian terms: "its manner of appearing, showing itself, manifesting itself" (RCC 191).

In contrast to *value*, a much richer concept that, above all, "does not show itself, does not appear," wealth is "empirically very thin [*maigre*]: transparent" (RCC 192). The concept of wealth serves to initiate the conceptual analysis of *Capital* primarily, Macherey argues, as a "reminder," in its capacity to refer back to the origins of classical economy, to its arbitrary and precritical status in Smith and Ricardo. Consequently, this implies for Macherey two key points he will develop intensively: first, that the array of concepts Marx deploys in *Capital* are not equal; wealth is an impoverished, "sterile," concept, referring merely to the empirical appearance of things, rather than being adequate to its object (RCC 190). It is never anything more than the empirical definition Marx gives it: "a mass of commodities." In contrast, the endpoint of Macherey's exposition, value, is a rich concept, one that arguably will take the entire, incomplete labor that is *Capital* volumes 1–4 as we have it, to unfold. Secondly, however, Macherey argues that wealth, for all its superficiality and brevity of appearance in Marx's analysis, is nonetheless purely a *concept*. Wealth can never be confused with any of its empirical manifestations (from gold to grain, missiles to mansions); it is and remains purely a concept.

Macherey's analysis attends closely to the logical components and operators he identifies in the opening pages of *Capital*. These constitute what he terms "intermediaries," the "instruments of rationality" that allow for the construction of a rigorous demonstration. Macherey's assertion that the various concepts laid out in these opening lines of *Capital* are fundamentally and necessarily heterogeneous is a point that will be sustained and developed step by step; the notion of conceptual heterogeneity constitutes, moreover, "one of the fundamental conditions of scientific rigour." The system of Marx's concepts, and the system of rational operators more generally, in this view, consists of various components that do not coexist "on one and the same level of intelligibility," but which instead inhabit multiple, incommensurable planes (RCC 188).

This assertion leads Macherey to consider the relations of heterogeneity between the five concepts under consideration: the "empirical form" of wealth, the contradictory pair of "factors" of the commodity that are use- and exchange-value, and, finally, the purely relational concept of value. If use-value, like wealth, remains tied to the empirical, but as "the notion of a thing" and not that empirical thing itself, exchange-value only exists as a relation *between* commodities (RCC 194). This contradictory, dual nature of the commodity, as both thing and relation, is for Macherey a primary contradiction or aporia of capital that is not "resolved" in a Hegelian *Aufhebung*, but which is instead "suppressed" (195). This contradiction between use- and exchange-values exists, furthermore, purely at the level of Marx's concepts, and leads to "a break in the treatment of these concepts . . . and in no way refers to a real process . . . The concepts that sustain the scientific exposition are not of the same kind" (196).

A principled rejection of empiricism, Macherey's analysis simultaneously rejects phenomenological *experience;* value, in this view, is a category invisible to immediate experience of the commodity in its phenomenological appearance. In terms perfectly congruent to the antiphenomenological hermeneutical principles that *Reading Capital* adapts and reorients from the work of Cavaillès and Canguilhem,[40] value for Macherey is to be located neither on the surface of phenomena (in their appearance as use-values), nor in their empirical relation to one another (as exchange-values); but for all that, nor can value be said to lie hidden within the depths of that relation, to stand revealed in a moment of Hegelian *aufhebung*. Instead, the concept of value exists in a relation of "rupture" to commodities in the form of both use-values and of exchange-values. "The paradox of the analysis of exchange is that value is neither *in* the terms of exchange, nor *in* their relation. Value is not given, or revealed [*dégagée*], or displayed [*mises en évidence*]: *it is constructed as concept*" (RCC 203, italics in original). The object that is value "is more hidden than revealed" in the act of exchange. Thus the necessity for Marx's categorial, "scientific" critique of political economy: "Without the rigor of scientific exposition, which alone is able to produce knowledge, the *concept* of value would have no meaning: that is to say, it would not exist" (205, translation modified, italics in original).

The aporetic structure of the commodity, its dual nature, thus leads to the heart of Macherey's analysis. Althusser, I argue in this volume's introduction, ultimately regresses from an absolute distinction between real and conceptual orders into a vocabulary of "appropriation" of the real by the conceptual. Macherey, by contrast, identifies in the *relation* between two equivalent commodities under conditions of exchange the determinant condition of a concept *devoid of all empiricism*. To approach value itself, he writes, "the analysis must no longer be conducted in terms of experience." Instead, the concept of a relation of exchange, like that of an infinite set for Cavaillès, Macherey provocatively asserts, *has no empirical content*.[41] Unlike wealth or the commodity, value, the concept of the measure allowing for the equality of empirically nonidentical commodities, is purely and only that, a concept. Like any other concept, it is real, but, we might say in the Spinozist terms underlying Macherey's analysis, it is a reality in the conceptual, rather than empirical mode of being.

The conceptual relation that is value, moreover, poses the equality of two commodities as a formula, $a = b$; it is, in other words, "defined as a *relation of expression*" (RCC 200, emphasis in original). Unlike the qualitative, empirical relation of two use-values standing side by side in the market, the relation of exchange-value is characterized by the extinction of all qualities. Fungibility is thus more precisely represented as the purely quantitative expression of relative value: "$ax = by$ (a is so much of b)." It is this reduction to pure quantitative relation that then definitively displaces Macherey's analysis in its final step, toward the concept of value itself: Marx's "new analysis [now addressing of the concept of value] begins with a decisive choice: the refusal to study the exchange relation as a qualitative relation, to only consider it in its quantitative content" (200). It is this pure conceptualization, then, that will allow for the adequate construction of the concept of value, "the structure of the relation" of exchange itself (201).

The heterogeneous, nondialectical series of logical steps Macherey identifies in Marx's exposition then suddenly culminates in a parenthetical gesture of pure conceptual abstraction, momentarily abstracting, that is, from Marx's exposition itself to articulate a pure axiomatic statement of conceptual nonempiricism. It is possible, Macherey provisionally concludes from this exposition, to "formulate a general rule: . . . to compare objects non-empirically, it is necessary as a preliminary to determine the general form of this measurement . . . It is not possible to make a relation of expression say what it expresses if it is examined only in its empirical reality" (RCC 201). The concept expressing the nature of any relation whatsoever is of a different nature, "another kind," than empirical experience. "To know what a relation expresses," Macherey concludes, "it is also necessary, even first of all, to know what is expressing it" (201).

Macherey's demonstration advances not in a progressive, dialectical spiral, but rather via a series of quantum-like leaps from one discrete, bounded concept to another, each shown to occupy a singular, heterogeneous orbital. Macherey's analysis to this point has traced the systematic elimination of all empirical qualities (of wealth, and the use-value aspect of commodities) in the analytical passage to exchange-value and then value, arguing that just as "the area of a triangle is not in itself triangular; in the same way too, the notion of value is not exchangeable" (RCC 205). At this point, however, the previously abandoned notion of quality suddenly returns, now, however, residing in a state of pure nonempirical conceptuality, a state in which we find that "the notion of value *qualifies* commodities as the notion of area qualifies areas"; only here, it is abstract labor power, a purely relational, nonempirical notion, that constitutes "a new quality," the substance of value itself.[42] As Macherey quotes Marx, at this culminating point in the initial conceptual exposition of these pages from *Capital*, "there remains only a quality," the abstract, nonquantifiable concept of the substance of value (206). The logic is implacable and unyielding, the density of Macherey's argument in these seven pages formidable, brilliant, original, in itself as daunting as the five introductory pages of *Capital* it theorizes, in its Cavaillèsian rigor constituting a culminating and bravura theoretical gesture of *Lire le Capital* in its totality.

That said, read today, the rigorous, nondialectical conceptual divisions between wealth, use and exchange value, and value itself that Macherey produces in his analysis of the opening section of *Capital* nonetheless remain, as does the problem of value and the organic composition of capital more generally, imperceptible as a historical—and not merely epistemological—problem. Marx's distinction between wealth and value, constructed in itself as a nondialectical concept of relationality, remains a purely formal one for Macherey, never rising to the status of a problem. Value and the value-form, that is to say, will come to constitute a problem that, in the wake of the suppression of Macherey's essay, will arguably remain invisible until Moishe Postone's 1996 analysis of the value form in *Time, Labor, and Social Domination*.[43] In fact, the distinction between wealth and value, already present in Ricardo, rigorously developed by Marx and underscored by this purely formal division of

Macherey's analysis, will constitute one of the fundamental interventions in Postone's critique of what he called "traditional Marxism" and its critique of society from "the standpoint of labor."

Despite this limitation—and I can only suggest in passing what remains the object of future research—Macherey's essay sketches out a highly suggestive and novel interpretation of *Capital* and Marx's theory of value via what might be called an arithmetical ontology and logic. While Alain Badiou has convincingly argued that it is mathematics that most adequately articulates what can be thought and expressed of being itself, in subtraction from all specific empirical qualities and experience, he has limited his phenomenological investigations (his "logics of worlds") to the fields or "conditions" he identifies as politics, science, art, and love.[44] Within this disposition of categories, the science that interests him is predominantly mathematics, while his discussion of Marx is largely limited to the latter's historico-political analyses of revolutionary events (1848, the Commune) and the notion of communism; as such, Badiou almost entirely forsakes critique of the dominant logic of modernity, capitalism.[45]

In his 1965 text, however, Macherey argues that production of the concept of value, if it is to adequately conceptualize the enabling conditions of exchange, can only occur through the extinction of the illusory, empirical concrete: "Exchange manifests itself first of all (although indirectly) as the suppression of every quality and on the basis of this disappearance it brings to light a proportion: value can only be distinguished on the basis of a quantitative (and no longer qualitative) diversity" (RCC 206). In this sense, he precociously identifies a mathematico-ontological operation (schematically analogous to Badiou's numerical ontology) in Marx's passage from the empirical concept of "wealth" to the purely "quantitative" relation of exchange, "reduced to an equation."

Furthermore, Macherey argues in turn that "it is the equation that provides the means of escaping from the exchange relation and seeing the concept of value" (RCC 202). In this view, it is the nonempirical, "general form of measurement" (value and its substance, labor power), Macherey argues, that *enables* the relation of exchange (as "the conditions of its appearance") (201).[46] From this I would conclude that while I have argued that the abstract level at which Macherey carries out his study of value obscures the historical becoming-infinitesimal of value production in late capitalism, it is paradoxically this same, intensive degree of abstraction that retrospectively announces—in the wake of Badiou's two-volume ontology, *Being and Event* and *Logics of*

Worlds—the possibility of conceptualizing an ontology of pure multiplicity to account for the logic of capitalism: the nonempirical, conceptual structure of the value-form itself as a (dominant) transcendental structuring principle contingently articulated in a multipart, overdetermined complex or conjuncture containing various secondary, subordinate substructures. Such a project, however, were it to address the totality of *Capital*, and not simply, as for Macherey, its first five pages, lies far beyond the compass of this chapter.

In the wake of *Lire le Capital*, following the suppression of Macherey's brief but incisive essay, the confusion of wealth (in the form of commodities) and value remained a fundamental stumbling block of critical theory. Postone shows how Habermas's proposition in *Theory and Practice* (1973) that "the scientific development of the technical forces of production are to be considered as a possible source of value" fails to comprehend Marx's basic, liminal distinction between wealth, as the production of commodities, and the abstract relation that is the concept of value.[47] Habermas instead reverts to a precritical understanding of value as equivalent to wealth "and thus conflates what Marx had distinguished," making vanish by rhetorical sleight of hand the contradictory nature of the organic composition of capital that Marx had first identified in the *Grundrisse*'s "Fragment on Machines."[48]

Similarly, one might extend Postone's critique of Habermas to the moment in *Anti-Oedipus* when Deleuze and Guattari posit the spurious, "willfully incompetent" category of so-called machinic surplus value (*plus-value machinique*). The iconoclastic authors observe with feigned simplicity that "machines also 'work' or produce value, . . . and there is thus [as though by this putative 'fact' something had in fact been demonstrated] a machinic surplus-value produced by constant capital that develops with automation and productivity," demonstrating in so doing little more—in marked contrast to Macherey's 1965 analysis—than the authors' lack of understanding of Marx's rigorous analysis of the concepts of labor/work, value, and surplus value in the system of commodity production, as though they could be applied to anything that may subjectively be judged to have "value."[49]

Though equally "symptomatic" of this general tendency of *Lire le Capital*, most striking and suggestive of all are undoubtedly Étienne Balibar's concluding remarks to the entire volume on the dynamic temporality of the development of the forces of production (RCC 470–80). These focus on the development of crises of profitability resulting from "the increase of constant capital with respect to variable capital" (470). In Balibar's analysis, this dynamic constitutes only a "movement," rather than a structural limit to the implicitly infinite expansion of capital; in Balibar's final comments, organic composition does in fact rise to the status of a problem, but merely in the form of the *empirical* problem of *consumption* (one that would imply the possibility of ameliorist solutions such as a guaranteed minimum income, rather than the surpassing of the value form itself).[50]

In these closing comments, Balibar formulates the problem of the organic composition of capital in relation to what he terms the "'age' of capitalist production, [which] is to be measured precisely by the relative level of the relation between constant capital and variable capital" (RCC 470).[51] With this fascinating suggestion, Balibar gestures, I would argue, toward a novel and still-today untheorized *categorial* understanding of the problem of development that Bruno Bosteels analyzes elsewhere in this volume. Drawing on Bosteels's analysis of the problem of combined and uneven development from Trotsky to Althusser, an analysis that culminates in Bosteels's reading of this same passage of Balibar's, I would suggest that these two closing pages of *Reading Capital* announce, if only to postpone, an essential project still awaiting contemporary Marxian thought: the reformulation of the theory of uneven and combined development—perhaps the central enabling concept for peripheral Marxist militancy throughout the twentieth century—from the standpoint not of labor and industrialization, but in relation to the categorial critique of valorization and its limits in global capitalism in the twenty-first century.

In traditional Leninist Marxism, the process of "development" contained within Trotsky's concept of Uneven Development—in Trotsky's original, pre-1917 formulation, as well as for Lenin from the point of the "April 1917 Theses" that rally to Trotsky's formulation, and what Bosteels points to as the late, "metaphysical" Trotsky alike—remained unquestioned.[52] If I have argued in this essay that the concept of value remains symptomatically "underdeveloped" in *Lire le Capital*, Balibar's suggestions point to the final, paramount implication of this underdevelopment.

The concept of development (as socialist industrialization) arguably remains a precritical normative horizon, both for Trotsky and Lenin's appropriation of the concept of uneven development. The perspective of "development" in this view then travels throughout the century, as Löwy shows, to serve a plainly ideological function in "third world" industrializing socialist revolutions.[53] The theory of uneven and combined development, in this view, serves as the primary ideological justification for peripheral socialist revolutions as the struggle for recuperative modernization, without ever calling into question the norm of development itself, but merely that of the social distribution of wealth resulting from industrial development.[54] Cultural and humanistic development, while obviously of concern to anticolonial intellectuals, remained historically overdetermined by the drive for industrial economic development.[55] In this view, whether development was taken as an unquestioned norm, as in classic development theory, or critiqued in its uneven deployment in dependency and underdevelopment theory, or even when supplemented by attention to other, cultural categories such as gender, sustainability, or rights, as in critical and postdevelopment theory, the historical and social obligation to valorize value was never questioned, but merely, the unequal global distribution of wealth and accumulation.[56]

If this is the case, does Marx suggest a critique of uneven development analogous to the categorial critique of labor and valorization that Postone identifies in his critique of political economy? What, in other words, can a reading of *Capital* today—in contrast to the labor-centric perspective of Trotsky's theory and its traditional, peripheral reception—bring to bear on the concept of uneven development? While I can here only suggest the mere sketch of an answer, it might be possible to distinguish on this point exoteric and esoteric dimensions of Marx's understanding of the concept of development.[57] On the one hand, Marx repeatedly refused the various Luddite and antiprogressive critiques of industrial "development" of his time, to distinguish the production of surplus value in capitalism from the technical, scientific, social, and intellectual development of human powers more generally, of what he called species-being (*Gattungswesen*), famously celebrated in the *Grundrisse*'s "Fragment on Machines." There he evokes the possibility of a general, post-capitalist development of human powers understood as a common social force: "The appropriation of [man's] own general productive power, his understanding of nature and his mastery over it, by nature of his presence as a social body—it is in a word, the *development of the social individual.*"[58]

At the level of Marx's analysis of the categorial structure of capitalism, *development* refers neither to empirical industrialization nor to human essence, even understood as contingency, as a Rousseauian perfectibility deployed within social relations, as the Sixth Thesis on Feuerbach had argued.[59] Instead, for this esoteric Marx, the "development" in uneven development is an analytical, categorial ("scientific") measure of the "development" of the structural components and relations of capital such as its organic composition, rate of profit, and, above all, the differing values of labor power across the globe. It is precisely this structural conceptualization of uneven development that is manifest in the very passage from the third volume of *Capital* that Balibar cites in the final section of his essay, lines in which he (Balibar) evokes an "internal limitation" to capitalist production and suggestively hints at the persistence of various "forwardness or backwardness of development" reflecting "the uneven development implied by the unevenness of the organic composition between competing capitals" (RCC 471).

Tantalizingly, the fundamental conceptual elements inherent to the central claim of this essay—that capitalism, understood conceptually rather than empirically as a contingent structure of structures, bears an overdetermined contemporary tendency toward the collapse of valorization—are copresent in Balibar's final observations:

1. That of the contingent (and implicitly bounded) historicity of capitalist development, what Balibar terms the "'age' of capitalist production."

2. That this age is to be determined conceptually rather empirically, "by the level of the relation between constant capital and variable capital, i.e., by the internal organic composition of capital."

3. That this historicity or "age" of capitalism can, moreover, be conceptually grasped as a singular tendency, overdetermining the development of the totality of a structure of structures.

4. Finally and crucially, we read Balibar's lapidary conceptual restatement and reduction of Marx's formulation of capital as the "moving contradiction," as the assertion that the contingent tendency of capitalism bears an element of unilinear necessity in its development: "The necessary orientation of the development consists in the increase in constant capital with respect to variable capital"[60] (RCC 470). If these provocative closing fragments never coalesce into a theory of collapse, this is not merely because Balibar's focus is instead the problem of historicity ("several concepts of time which differ in function"), but above all because the tendency Balibar names (of a unilinear "increase in constant capital with respect to variable capital") here as throughout *Reading Capital* remains invisible as a historical problem, one that instead demands only clear conceptual demonstration. Indeed, no sooner, has Balibar intimated the enormous implications of such a refounding of the concept of uneven development, than he tantalizingly suspends this provocative closing parenthesis: "Obviously this is not our object here. I am only suggesting it as a possibility" (RCC 530).

To pursue Balibar's conceptual reformulation of uneven development would undoubtedly require a project analogous to the categorial critique of the so-called perspective of labor Postone identifies in traditional Marxism, a critique that would push beyond all productivist and empiricist humanism of "development" (whether liberal or socialist). Following Balibar's suggestions, uneven development arguably indicates for the esoteric Marx, unlike Trotsky and traditional, peripheral Marxism, the conceptualization of uneven levels of organic compositions of capital and values of labor power globally. These differences allow for the crucial recovery of the profitability of individual capitals as they engage "underdeveloped" sites across the globe in which the value of labor-power has been forcibly and violently reduced to levels below North Atlantic standards. In this view, the obfuscating, even cynical neoliberal notions of so-called factor endowments and labor arbitrage mask the ways in which various forms of social violence forcibly drive down the value of labor power in peripheral sites such as Bangladesh or Haiti.[61]

From the perspective of a categorial analysis of global capitalism, a description of the so-called superexploitation of labor power can only explain how individual capitals (such as Levi's or Polo in Haiti) seek to ensure profitability; such an analysis says nothing about the question of whether and the degree to which contemporary imperialist superexploitation of labor power contributes to the production of *surplus value*. While it is certainly true, as John Smith argues, that "*all* of the labor-power expended by workers employed in less productive capitals counts *equally* [compared with more productive, typically North Atlantic, production] toward total value," or, stated differently, that though "workers using advanced technology will produce more use-value, the quantity of value and of surplus-value generated by their living labor will be no different than if the same labor was performed in a less advanced firm in the same branch of production,"[62] such statements say nothing about whether in fact anything more than vanishingly infinitesimal amounts of surplus value are in fact being produced by the billions more workers employed globally by capital since the 1980s, implying instead that the arithmetic increase in workers employed worldwide corresponds directly to matching increases in surplus value.[63]

This is to ignore completely, however, the contradictory dynamic of capital described above, in which the production of *value* (though not necessarily profits) for any given unit of capital continuously diminishes with the minimization of living labor's contribution to production. The miserable salaries and working conditions of billions of exploited laborers do not at all indicate increased masses of surplus value production. An identical commodity produced in Germany or Bangladesh is subject to the same standard of socially necessary production times; longer production times do not mean increased production of value.[64] To take an actual example, a kilo of cotton could in

2010 be harvested by machine at a rate three hundred times that of human laborers in India or Africa.[65] In other words, the labor of the driver of one John Deere 7460 Cotton Stripper is equivalent to that of three hundred laborers harvesting cotton by hand in India or Mali; even after factoring costs of production, maintenance, fuel, and repair of the machine, the stripper still requires only 1/150th of the time required by a hand laborer in India.[66] To be competitive on the world cotton market, Indian and Africans' labor power must sell at something approaching 1/150th of the value of labor power of the driver of a John Deere stripper in Texas. When in the near future such machines will drive themselves autonomously, even that last bit of living labor, along with the infinitesimal value creation it contributes to the cotton picking process today, will vanish.

If the cotton stripper, thanks to its patented mechanisms, can harvest cotton in less than the socially necessary labor time, its owner can capture a greater share of the global value of cotton harvesting in the form of profits, while, conversely, such technical innovations continuously drive down the value of labor power of the millions of Indian and other impoverished hand laborers who must compete with its powers.[67] Compared to the period prior to the introduction of the first mechanical cotton strippers after 1945, a period when cotton was universally harvested by hand, the value creation of a single manual laborer has today shrunk to some 1/150th of its prior magnitude.

The value of these workers' slave-like production is determined and continuously devalued by improvements in the North American machines with which they compete for employment on the contemporary global market. In this manner more generally, the value of superexploited labor power is continuously depressed as evermore categories of production become automated, and humans must compete for employment with machinic production processes that drive down socially necessary labor time, and thus the value of living labor, incessantly.

If, I have so far argued, the concept of value and that of organic composition more specifically in *Lire le Capital* are "symptomatic" insofar as they never come to constitute a fundamental *problem* for the historical destiny of capital as Althusser, et al. analyze it, the book's truncated conceptual analysis of the value form finds unexpected—if antagonistic—completion in what is perhaps its nearest analogue in the canon of postwar French Marxist philosophy, Michel Henry's thousand-page 1976 study of Marx's philosophy.

Superficially, Henry's inquiry explicitly casts itself as a refutation of *Lire le Capital*, identifying the phenomenological category of *"la vie"* as the ineradicable ground and "foundation" of valorization (as living labor), as against the primary assertion made in *Reading Capital*, by Rançière, Balibar, and Althusser alike, that the subject is a mere effect or support (*Träger*) of capital (507).[68] In contrast to the richly complex, Lacanian notion of the subject informing *Lire le Capital*, Henry's axiomatic assertion of "life" as the unproduced foundation of the creation of surplus value depends crucially upon a precritical notion of the subject as *"naturant du naturé,"* life as the unmoved mover (830, 819), the unproduced force that can only be brought within the compass of capital through the violence of primitive accumulation and the reduction and mere representation of its creative powers as the real abstraction of value, as labor power measured by time (827).[69] Henry's critique of Althusserian structuralist Marxism and *Lire le Capital* more specifically depends on a reductive and specious presentation of the latter as amounting to no more than the "ideology of capitalism" itself, insofar as Henry takes the absence of a foundational, absolute notion of the subject in *Lire le Capital* merely to reinstate the illusion of capital as self-valorizing value within a self-contained system or totality (827).

Indeed, Henry's study constitutes a singularly unique combination of a systematic presentation of Marx's categorial critique of political economy combined with a precritical assertion of "life" as a phenomenological ground claimed to be ontologically heterogeneous, yet essential, to the process of valorization. Henry's argument relies, moreover, upon a series of related ahistorical, underived, ontological categories that stand in absolute, immaculate externality to the realm of the "economic": "man," "praxis," "subjectivity," "the individual," "reality," "human activity," labor (*travail*), and, towering above all others, *la vie* itself (25; see also 667, 770). In Henry's neo-Sartrean philosophy of "praxis," life and labor are eternally, ontologically selfsame ("en soi"), the "fragile power of life, the burning fire that bends matter and gives it the form that preserves and conserves it" (635, 688, 750; see also 869). This transhistorical ontology of life as creative labor or "praxis" culminates in Henry's stupefying celebration of what surely constitutes one of Engels's most disastrously confused misinterpretations of Marx's theory of value, the appendix to volume 3 of *Capital*, in which he (Engels) claims that value constitutes a transhistorical absolute common to all human epochs and in no way limited to capitalism (479).

Henry's explication of Marx's logical, categorial analysis of capitalism grounds its authority, in the grand tradition of Husserlian phenomenology so powerfully critiqued by Cavaillès, on the notion of "la vie."[70] This category remains entirely untheorized by Henry, presupposed and accepted in its putative obviousness. It is, to quote Cavaillès, "the universal soil of experience, its [basis] constantly presupposed as the concordant unity of possible experience."[71] Living labor is for Henry the subjective, productive human creativity that founds, while always remaining external to, the objectivity of the structure of capitalism. If Husserl had subsumed the science of physics within the intuition of vitalism, what he terms "the intuition of the vital," Henry, in contrast, maintains a strict dualism between a nonsubsumable "life" and the false totality that is capitalism, relentlessly driven forward by the compulsion to valorize value, a false totality founded upon the illusion that it could subsume the productive power of life, rather than its mere abstract semblance as "labor power."[72]

Henry's analysis willfully and explicitly affirms nearly every category of analysis that Althusser had so powerfully critiqued in *For Marx* and *Reading Capital*: phenomenology, the existence of a single unifying and ahistorical principle of analysis in Marx's thought (life as praxis), a principle that in this view allows Marx's philosophy to be understood in its "general unity" and teleology as a process of "genesis" (31, 26). Henry's exposition of Marx's philosophy constitutes in the author's own terms a "transcendental inquiry" into the historical genesis of the "possibility" of the economic as an "eternal truth" and pure essence (614). In this view, the "transcendental genesis of the economic" (the title of the book's central chapter) derives from the historical production of the "abstraction" of individual, living labors as identical *labor power* quantifiable as units of time. While this "genesis" is a contingent, historical fact that Marx analyzes, following Adam Smith, as the violence of primitive accumulation, it depends in this view upon the (eternal) categorical possibility of labor to be construed as a dualism: living labor, producer of use values, over and against abstract labor, producer of exchange and surplus value (627–628).[73]

Henry's reconstruction of Marx's theoretical apparatus, self-consciously styled as a purely antagonistic rebuttal to *Lire le Capital*, in fact stands in much more ambiguous relation to its immediate predecessor. At the very moment Althusser asserted the ultimate preponderance of relations of production over the forces of production via the slogan of "class struggle in theory," Henry scandalously (and no doubt correctly) affirmed the concept of class as entirely secondary and derived in Marx, in contrast to the primary category of valorization and living labor as its substance (9). Class relations, in Henry's critique of Althusser and traditional, Leninist Marxism more generally, constitute a relation interior to capital itself, labor being produced by the ever-renewed violence of primitive accumulation (724; see also 934). In contrast to his pre-critical celebration of life as praxis, Henry simultaneously demonstrates in all its complexity the process by which living labor is historically produced by capital itself and violently integrated into the process of valorization as an abstraction. In other words, while life as praxis is merely affirmed without adequate demonstration on nearly every page of *Marx*, and affirmed furthermore as irreducibly heterogeneous to the process of valorization (while constituting its necessary substance), Henry at the same time shows how the historical process of abstraction reduces living labor to its mere representation as measured time. At the same time, he does so without ever theorizing the myriad ways in which so-called life, and not merely its representation, is always constituted and instantiated as *a* life, and, within capital, is preformed as the substance of valorization determined in myriad ways, both subjectively (as attitudes and desires coherent with the social compulsion to valorize value) and objectively (through the structuration of work processes such as the assembly line or the demands for generalized labor to extend throughout the waking day).[74]

That said, Henry's analysis of the incorporation of living labor within capital is truly unparalleled in its subtlety: as use value for capital, the substance of valorization, living labor, creates both use values (commodities) and surplus value, the latter *the* use value for the capitalist himself, the variable M that justifies his investment in production and the purchase of labor power as commodity. At the same time, Henry points out that living labor can never itself be reduced to an exchange value, insofar as it is not and cannot be a commodity itself (living labor is not produced by living labor, but is pure, underived "life").[75] Instead, capital must resort to a subterfuge, purchasing not living labor, but the *commodities* that the laborer will use to restore her life (720).[76]

Despite its manifest antagonism, Henry's *Marx* reaffirms and further develops a series of initiatives characteristic of *Lire le Capital*. Henry's study is explicitly cast as an attempt to analyze "the concepts of Marx's thought," and these as a totality or structure, "that of the determination of the fundamental concepts and the relation that is established between the different concepts as a philosophically founded relation" (28). Henry's *Marx* is a work of categorial analysis, fundamentally, moreover, as much a work of antiempiricism as its Althusserian predecessor.[77] Its explicit, Spinozist goal, in turn, is "to construct the adequate concept of exchange . . . that *Capital*, it is true, produced for the first time" (615).

Where *Marx* constitutes an enormous leap forward from *Reading Capital* is precisely in its identification of the organic composition of capital not merely as a structural element of the historical *functioning* of capital, but also and even more crucially, as the fundamental contradiction and *problem* that historically, in allowing for the ongoing process of valorization, drives capital forward, while at the same time impelling it toward an eventual collapse in its capacity to create surplus value. Here, Henry unambiguously (and decades before the work of Postone and Kurz) formulates this unilinear historical dynamic—a process in this view more fundamental than any cyclical capacity to recover mere profitability—as what he terms the historical disassociation of production and labor (927).

If capitalism, for Henry, must be defined, categorially, as "the system of value, of its development and maintenance," in consequence "the destiny of capital is that of labor [its substance]" (926). After nearly a thousand pages of painstaking analysis, decades before Robert Kurz and the *Wertkritik* school would draw identical conclusions, Henry's theoretico-historical deduction comes like a bombshell launched against the faith of traditional Marxism that capital, based only upon its past historical performance, will perpetually recover profitability in the wake of recurrent cyclical crises: the progressive reduction of variable capital (abstract labor power) within the production process, Henry concludes, "confronts us with the event that will determine modern history, even if this is a history to come, even if still today we are only beginning to perceive it: *the dissociation, at the core of social existence [au sein de la réalité], of the process of production and the process of labor*" (927, italics in original).

Henry focuses his conclusion in this manner on the dynamic of the organic composition of capital as the "adequate concept" of valorization (759). This analysis culminates in a simple thought experiment : "If we imagine a material production process from which living labor were excluded, this process is no longer a process of valorization, no system of value will or can result from [such a situation]; capitalism is henceforth impossible." Posed in absolute theoretical purity, the historical destiny of capitalism is "a process in which the element [of living labor] ceaselessly shrinks and tends at its limit toward zero, [a process that can be expressed as] an essence, cv [variable capital] $= 0$." This point, Henry concludes, constitutes "the insurmountable theoretical limit of the market economy and *a fortiori* of capitalism" (726). Henry thus concludes from his monumental categorial exposition that total automation constitutes both the historical "destiny" and "self-destruction of capitalism," the inner dynamic leading to its "decline," "collapse," and "end" (959, 766, 940, 932, 933). In this view, the approach to total automation ("$cv=0$") constitutes not a merely contingent political platform, but rather the formal deduction of the historical passage from capitalism to socialism.

In drawing this conclusion, however, Henry's critical faculties fail him, and the final pages of *Marx* evince a philosophical idealism in the form of a faith in the mechanistic necessity of this transition to a true socialism. Henry implies that this passage to socialism, as cv approaches the value of 0, will be automatic, a "consequence" of capital as "moving contradiction," claiming that this transformation will mark "a mutation in the 'history of humanity,' the beginning of a new state that one could precisely characterize as 'social.' This must be understood in the sense of a revolution in being itself" (932, 943).[78] At least as likely as this automated and automatic utopia, it seems, would be the advent of a terrifying age of postcapitalist barbarity.

It is arguably only with the rise of a critique of the capitalist valorization of value as a whole, undertaken by thinkers such as Moishe Postone and Robert Kurz, that Marx's single most important critical concept, that of value, has today begun to displace the twentieth-century critique of the distribution of wealth from the standpoint of labor as the fundamental category of any substantial critique of political economy. Theorists including Moishe Postone, Guglielmo Carchedi, Andrew Kliman, and David Harvey continue to maintain that global capital still possesses the capacity to restore profitability through remedies such as financialization, exploitation of global inequalities in the value of labor power, and massive devaluation.[79] In contrast, Robert Kurz has put forward the much more radical thesis that the second machine age of the digitalization, robotification, and dematerialization of virtually all labor processes has already brought global capital, via the unilinear, historical diminution of socially necessary levels of labor, past a point of a collapse in the global production of surplus value (as an absolute mass).[80] Though capital is destroyed and devalued in crises, allowing the recovery of rates of profit, socially necessary levels of productivity do not regress (failing global catastrophe). While it is beyond the scope of the present essay to defend this thesis, it becomes ever more apparent that we now live in a world in which living labor has become, as Marx long ago predicted in the *Grundrisse*'s Fragment on Machines, an "infinitesimal, vanishing" component of production, with this fundamental, "moving contradiction" of capitalism leading toward the gradual collapse of the capacity for global capital in aggregate to realize surplus value.[81]

Perhaps the absolute collapse of valorization predicted by Kurz is no more than the dominant *tendency* of contemporary capitalism, not its teleological destiny, one that remains decades ahead of us, as automation continues its course and the various palliatives Marx listed in his discussion of the Tendency (*Capital*, vol. 3, chap. 15), from financialization and the expansion of global markets, to the depreciation of the value of labor, lose their effect. While the absolute mass of humans working has indeed increased in recent decades—by one measure rising from 1.9 billion "economically active" in 1980 to 3.1 billion workers in 2006, amounting to a 63 percent increase[82]—their *relative* contribution to the creation of surplus value tends to decrease with the progress of socially necessary levels of productivity. As the global economy approaches this point of merely "infinitesimal" levels of surplus value creation, the collapse of valorization comes to overdetermine the contingent structure of structures in twenty-first century capitalism.

———————

Ultimately, in contrast to Michel Henry's deduction of the necessary decline and collapse of capital resulting from its structural contradictions, the concept of labor, by definition the key component of Marx's labor theory of value, remains mystified in *Lire le Capital*. If the original volume as a whole manages to construct a nonempirical, antiphenomenological concept of value in the somewhat erratic fashion described above, labor itself remains utterly encapsulated in *Reading Capital* within the humanist horizon of living labor and the labor-ontological dialectic of the class struggle of the proletariat. The contradiction between variable and constant capital ironically remains, in its very invisibility as a *problem*, "an absent distinction," not just from classical economy, as Rancière points out, but from *Lire le Capital* itself (RCC 195). "There is something it cannot see," Rancière says of classical political economy, a blindness that is itself, paradoxically, characteristic of the symptomatic status of value in *Reading Capital*.

In the various moments when *Reading Capital* mentions labor, it is always presupposed as living, *human* labor, as though Marx's formal description of the logic of capital as "the moving contradiction" between the living and the machinic, variable and constant labor, did not actually pose a boundary to valorization. *Reading Capital* proceeds as though once value is summarily reconstructed as a *concept* rather than an empirical given—work that Althusser delegates to his student researchers, then summarily excises from subsequent editions—labor and the organic composition of capital more generally cease to pose a problem in the conceptual economy of *Reading Capital*. Even within this most sophisticated and original monument of twentieth-century Marxist philosophy, the humanism of living labor substantiates not a political program, but the ontological horizon of the conceptual analysis of the 1965 seminar papers that constitute *Reading Capital*. Althusser's subsequent self-critique, culminating in his doctrine of "class struggle in theory" and that of the proletarian state in the 1970s only exacerbated this problem.

And yet, *Reading Capital*, in its theoreticist insistence on the construction of concepts as the primary operation of Marx's critique of political economy, years before the Neue Marx-Lektüre in Germany, decades before the return to Marx's categorial critique in the work of Henry, Postone, and Kurz, remains the founding methodological document for a critique of value and the dominant tendency of a collapse of valorization in the twenty-first century.[83] Despite his dogmatic and uncomprehending anti-Althusserianism, Postone's 1996 *Time, Labor, and Social Domination* might superficially appear in light of the above analysis as something like a missing second volume of *Reading Capital*, a critique that could only be written three decades later, when the previous century's Leninist and neoliberal ontologies of labor had been shattered by the foundering of capital's capacity to valorize value on a global scale. Both Postone's categorial analysis of the logic of *Capital* and Henry's phenomenological account of its vitalist ground (*la vie*), however, for all their originality and penetration of Marx's conceptual apparatus, each fail to attend to the Marxian concept of value according to the rigorous logical criteria set forth in *Lire le Capital*.

It is true that Postone's categorial analysis compellingly demonstrates the extrinsic conditions determining Marx's fundamental distinction between wealth and value, moving beyond both the neoliberal empiricism that remains enthralled to categories of immediate experience (as price, profit, GDP, employment, and the like), eternally referenced to the transcendental primacy of a human subject as well as the subjective reference to the critique "from the standpoint of labor" in traditional Marxism. The categories of this critique, however, ultimately remain formalistic, unable, crucially, to account for the movement of historical contingency at a structural level; nor do they attend to the development of the *idea* of value as a purely conceptual object, the idea of an idea, the true and adequate idea that Marx produced from the idea of value in the thought of Smith and Ricardo.

Alternatively, in Michel Henry's analysis, Marx's categorial analysis always remains subtended by an exterior, vitalist phenomenological ground ("life"). At the same time, Henry's categorial analysis culminates in a mechanistic prediction of the necessary collapse of capitalism and attendant passage to communism as the contribution of living labor to valorization approaches its zero point, $cv=0$. This determinist, mechanistic teleology is even more pronounced in the writings of Robert Kurz, in which the structural dynamic of Marx's "moving contradiction" becomes the single cause expressing the historical totality of capitalism, read obsessively by Kurz as the mechanistic necessity of actually unfolding collapse.[84] Instead, it should be possible to reject all teleological mechanism and to conceptualize contemporary capitalism and its crises as a complex yet contingent structure of structures, one whose contemporary conjunctural form, nonetheless, has come to be characterized in the twenty-first century by the overdetermined dominance of the crisis of valorization and the terminal dialectic of its moving contradiction.

The program Althusser sets forth in *Reading Capital*, in contrast to the theorizations of Henry, Postone, or Kurz, understands the production of concepts as a contingent process purely immanent to itself, in which the truth of a concept never depends upon its external verification, whether historical (as the politics of class struggle) or empirical (as neoliberal enthrallment to the factical). Instead, the truth of Marx's conceptual apparatus resides in its structural integrity as the critique of a totality (capitalism) understood as a diversely articulated, contingent yet overdetermined structure, a system in which the concept of value and the process of valorization more specifically constitute the structures in dominance from which all other concepts are produced.

If in his earlier essay "Marxism and Humanism" Althusser retained a teleological rump in the form of the historical horizon of "socialism," the essential virtue of the radical theoreticism of *Reading Capital,* in this view, is to have completely jettisoned the last remnants of empiricism and phenomenological, humanist vitalism subtending the political horizon of labor and class struggle, and to have focused on Marx's idea of an idea, the pure and self-legitimating logic of *Capital*. If Althusser and his collaborators ultimately, as I have argued above, remained unable to carry through a *critical* construction of Marx's central concept, value, *Lire le Capital* nonetheless set forth the criteria for such an impending project.

Instead of attempting to transcend Marx's labor theory of value, to argue for example that machines can in fact create value in the face of the collapse of human labor—as both Habermas and Deleuze and Guattari misguidedly suggested—the crisis of value in the twenty-first century impels us, as it did Althusser a half-century ago, to return again to Marx, to leap over the twentieth century and to construct a nonanthropocentric and neostructuralist concept of value. Althusser, to the end, continued to affirm the necessity of a return, once again, to Marx:

> At a time when the leading "hair-splitting" philosophy—as Marx described the decomposition of Hegelian philosophy—considers Marxism dead and buried, when the craziest ideas based on the most implausible eclecticism and feeble-minded theory are in fashion, under the pretext of so-called "post-modernism,"... Marxist thought will survive.... The feebleness of current theoretical thinking is such that the mere reappearance of those elementary but necessary ingredients of authentic thought—rigor, coherence, clarity—will, at a certain point, contrast so markedly with prevailing intellectual attitudes that all those who are bewildered by what has happened are bound to be struck by them. (Althusser, 1993 [1985]: 223)

When, as in the current and near-future context, human labor—not empirically, but in its capacity to produce surplus value—becomes vanishingly infinitesimal, the system itself necessarily enters into crisis. Faced with the enormous empirical complexity and even obscurity of this dynamic, only a posthuman, categorial understanding of the labor theory of value can begin to construct a critique of the quantum economy of massive inequality and global slums that lies ahead. Bringing the radical epistemology of Spinoza and Cavaillès to bear upon the structural logic of *Capital* to articulate an adequate understanding of the concept of value as the contradictory inner logic of capital: such a process can hope to overcome the historical impasse of the politics of proletarian class struggle and the phenomenology of living labor.

Instead, the promise of *Lire le Capital* in the twenty-first century is to apprehend the structural dynamic of capital as the necessity of contingency, as the moment in which humanity's enthrallment to valorization as unsurpassable horizon gives way before an adequate understanding of capitalism as the "moving contradiction." If capitalism itself poses the conditions of its tendential collapse in the current conjuncture of terminal crisis, what Althusser called the "real production" of its overcoming, the struggle over the precise modality of a future society without valorization, nonetheless remains all the more a matter of politics.[85] Devoid of adequate conceptualization, the contemporary crisis of capital is left dependent upon hollow, empiricist neoliberal categories such as so-called secular stagnation, while the unthought, inchoate impression of inexorable collapse manifests as universal anxiety and terror, to be sutured by recourse to reactionary, populist demagogues. As global capitalism, mired in debt—to stave off collapsing from its inner contradictions—puts every last bit of living labor to work in ever more miserable conditions, to produce ever less surplus value, politics is fast being reduced to an accelerated descent into global barbarism, a future rapidly displacing any residual image of communism. Any politics more adequate to the imperative of universal emancipation and justice as equality will surely have to address the necessity of intervention within the contingent development of late capitalism, via a politics rightly directed toward the utterly unpredictable yet imperative collapse of capital, of the *sujet automate* under whose spell humanity remains miserably entranced.

Notes

1. In his 1969 preface to *Capital*—among the most regrettable, condescending moments in his protracted mea culpa for the sin of so-called theoreticism—Althusser infamously goes so far as to recommend that first-time readers of *Capital* not even bother reading its first section, dismissing its abstract form of presentation as "Hegelian prejudice" (*Lenin and Philosophy, and Other Essays*, trans. Ben Brewster [London: New Left Books, 1971], 90). I would argue moreover that Althusser's simplistic dismissal of the value-form (culminating in his last writings as what he termed "the wooly and literally untenable labor theory of value") leads directly to Althusser's similarly impoverished, distribution-based notion of communism ("I believe the only definition of communism—if one day it were to exist in the world—is the absence of relationships based on the market") (1993: 211, 225). It must be said, however, that this perception of neglect of the concept of value in *Reading Capital* is one of the many unfortunate consequences of the book's subsequent abridged form, since Macherey's contribution (to be discussed below) in fact discusses the first section of *Capital* in painstaking detail. I would like to acknowledge the degree to which discussion in Prague with Petr Kužel, Michael Hauser, Jan Mervart, Jiří Ružička, and Joe Grim Feinberg in the Czech Academy of Sciences' Departments of Contemporary Continental and Modern Czech Philosophy, as well as with Norbert Trenkle, Ernst Lahoff, and Moishe Postone, and, in Princeton, Max Tomba, all proved crucial to the conceptualization of the issues discussed in this chapter.

2. Michele Cangiani, "Althusser and the Critique of Political Economy," in *Encountering Althusser: Politics and Materialism in Contemporary Radical Thought*, edited by Katja Deifenbach, Sara R. Farris, Gal Kirn, and Peter D. Thomas (London: Bloomsbury, 2013), 238.

3. David Ricardo, *On the Principles of Political Economy, and Taxation*, 3rd ed. (London: John Murray, 1821), 1, my emphasis; see also John Milios, "Rethinking Marx's Value-Form Analysis from an Althusserian Perspective," *Rethinking Marxism* 21, no. 2 (April 2009): 262. While he only considers Althusser's contribution to *Reading Capital*, Milios clearly delineates the specificity of Marx's relational concept of value, as presented by Althusser, from the quantitative notion to be found in both Smith and Ricardo, as well as in Lenin, Gramsci, and traditional Marxism more generally.

4. Karl Marx, *Grundrisse: Introduction to the Critique of Political Economy*, trans. Martin Nicolaus (New York: Vintage, 1973), 706, translation modified.

5. On the fragmentary and incomplete nature of Marx's conceptualization of the structural limits of capital and his theory of crisis more generally, see Robert Kurz, *Dinheiro sem valor: Linhas gerais para uma transformação da crítica da economia política*, trans. Lumir Nahodil (2012; Portuguese translation, Lisbon: Antígona, 2014), chap. 13, "O carácter fragmentário e a recepção redutora da teoria marxiana da crise." Marx's presentation of this fundamental contradiction of capitalism in the drafts edited by Engels as volume 3 of *Capital* is much less incisive, as for example when he writes that "the capitalist mode of production tends towards an absolute development of the productive forces irrespective of value and the surplus value this contains . . . The true barrier to capitalist production is *capital itself*" (*Capital*, vol. 3 [London: Penguin, 1991], 357–58).

6. In its opening pages, Marx underlines the superficial (though nonetheless real, significant, and necessary) nature of the empirical phenomena such as profit he will analyze in volume 3, including their culmination in the Law of the Tendency of the Rate of Profit to Fall: "The configurations of capital developed in this [third] volume, thus approach step by step the form in which they appear on the surface of society . . . and in the everyday consciousness of the agents of production themselves" (1981: 117). On the primacy and centrality (as well as historical neglect) of Marx's theory of surplus value conceptualized as a total aggregate, as distinct from its (logical, rather than empirical) secondary distribution among competing individual capitals as profit, see Moseley, in particular chapter 3, in which the author traces this primacy and growing conceptual complexity across all four drafts of *Capital* (Fred Moseley, *Money and Totality: A Macro-Monetary Interpretation of Marx's Logic in* Capital *and the End of the 'Transformation Problem'* [Leiden: Brill, 2016]). Roger Establet already makes this point in his contribution to *Reading Capital*, where he cites Marx's assertion in volume 2, that "the theoretical object whose laws volumes 1 and 2 construct, so as to completely resolve this problem, is that of 'a fraction of the total social capital that has acquired independence'" (RCC 500). See also RCC 400, 454–63.

7. On the notion of the "law of a tendency" in Marx, see Ben Fine and Alfredo Saad-Filho, *Marx's Capital*, 6th ed. (London: Pluto, 2016), chapter 9.

8. For a brilliant exposition of contingency in its fundamental relation to the concept of structural causality in Althusser's thought and *Reading Capital* specifically (an argument that informs the tenor of this chapter as a whole), see Stefano Pippa,

"The Necessity of Contingency: Reading Althusser on Structural Causality," *Radical Philosophy* 199 (September–October 2016), 15–25.

9. This historical displacement and rearrangement of subsidiary structures within capitalism identifies what Althusser calls in "On the Materialist Dialectic" a "structure in dominance": an overdetermined structure of structures susceptible to constant reorganization but continuously, by definition, dominated by, in the case of capitalism, the social and objective obligation to increase the production of surplus value: "If the structure remains constant, the disposition of the roles within it changes; the principal contradiction becomes a secondary one, a secondary contradiction takes its place" (Althusser, "On the Materialist Dialectic [On the Unevenness of Origins]," in *For Marx*, trans. Ben Brewster [London: Verso, 2005], 211).

10. See Trenkle and Lohoff, *La grande dévalorisation*, 45–54, and Kurz, *Dinheiro sem valor*, 262–67.

11. Dani Rodrick has argued that the process of deindustrialization has become global, and not merely limited to the postindustrial North Atlantic states. "Countries are running out of industrialization opportunities sooner and at much lower levels of income compared to the experiences of earlier industrializers . . . The evidence suggest both globalization and labor-saving technological progress have been behind these developments" (2). The logic of Rodrick's conclusion remains circular, however, encapsulated within the horizon of valorization, shying away from the enormous implications for global capitalism of the process he identifies (Dani Rodrick, "Premature Deindustrialization," NBER Working Paper No. 20935, February 2015, 27, http://www .nber.org/papers/w20935).

12. This is the point of Postone's abstract, underdocumented dismissal of "traditional" Leninist and Stalinist Marxism, based upon a painstaking reconstruction of Marx's protostructuralist critique of value in the *Grundrisse* and *Capital*. The classic statement of this productivist orientation is undoubtedly Lenin's famous assertion that "Communism is Soviet power plus electrification [. . . For this we must] place the economy of the country, including agriculture, on a new technical basis, that of modern large-scale production . . . Only when the country has been electrified, and industry, agriculture and transport have been placed on the technical basis of modern large-scale industry, only then shall we be victorious" (V. I. Lenin, "Address to the Eighth Congress of Soviets, December, 1920," in *The Lenin Anthology*, ed. Robert C. Tucker [New York: W. W. Norton, 1975], 494). Lenin's political and theoretical thought is vast and protean, to be sure. For the purposes of this essay, I would define *Leninism* as the seizure of state power toward the end of redistributing material wealth in the interests of the working class, while leaving uncriticized and, indeed, striving by all means available actually to *expand* industrial forms of production that continue to be structured by the demands of valorization.

13. The most theoretically advanced and uncompromising statement of such a critique of capital "from the standpoint of labor" (Postone, *Time, Labor, and Social Domination*) is undoubtedly Tronti's 1966 *Workers and Capital* (*Operai e capitale*). Tronti argues repeatedly that the theory of "Marx has been and remains the *workerist*

point of view on *bourgeois* society" (*Ouvriers et capital*, trans. Yann Moulier-Boutang [Paris: Editions Christian Bourgois, 1977]), 44, 47, www.multitudes.net/category /archives-revues-futur-anterieur-et/bibliotheque-diffuse/operaisme-autonomie /tronti-ouvriers-et-capital/). Surprisingly, Postone seems not to have read Tronti in preparing *Time, Labor, and Social Domination*. Étienne Balibar discusses the theoretical *rencontre manqué* of Tronti and Althusser in his contribution to this volume.

14. Although Massimiliano Tomba and Ricardo Bellofiore offer a convincing critique of the Workerist and Post-Workerist faith in the infinite capacity of living labor to produce value beyond measure (focusing on Negri and Virno in particular), the authors themselves steadfastly maintain a transhistorical, ontological conception of "labor" and "labor-power," while failing to take into account, in their sophisticated conceptualization of uneven development, the unilinear, if uneven, historical tendency to increases in productivity and, thus, to ever-decreasing levels of socially necessary labor in the production of surplus value under capitalism. See Massimiliano Tomba and Ricardo Bellofiore, "The 'Fragment on the Machines' and the *Grundrisse*: The Workerist Reading in Question," in *Beyond Marx: Theorising the Global Labour Relations of the Twenty-First Century*, ed. Marcel van der Linden and Karl Heinz Roth (London: Brill, 2014), 345–67.

15. Tronti's initial argument in *Workers and Capital* is predicated upon the precritical assertion of "labor" as a transhistorical category that is in this view "integrated" as such within capital, never pausing to question the degree to which the category and determinate forms of labor are themselves products of the historical demands of valorization, precisely, that is to say, abstract labor power (labor as such), required by and appearing only within the social relations of capitalism (*Ouvriers et capital*, 56). That Tronti goes on to analyze the historical nature of the abstraction "labor" and Marx's discovery of labor power (*Arbeitskraft*) changes nothing, since this insight into the development of abstract labor in capitalism remains theoretically isolated from the transcendental assertion of the putatively revolutionary powers of the working class circa 1966: "We discover at the heart of the system that it is the working class that constitutes the articulation of the entirety of the capitalist mechanism, that it is henceforth the arbitrator of its future development or of its definitive crisis . . . What happens when [the workers' organization] refuses to serve as *bearer* of the needs of capital via workers' demands? The answer is that at this moment we witness the complete blockage of the mechanism of the development of the system" (*Ouvriers et capital*, 113, 335; see also 164–67, 219, 292, 317).

16. "Foxconn's Robot Army Yet to Prove Match for Humans," *Wall Street Journal*, May 5, 2015. "Hon Hai [Foxconn]," Gou was famously quoted as saying, "has a workforce of over one million worldwide and as human beings are also animals, to manage one million animals gives me a headache." Cited in *Business Insider*, January 19, 2012. For a fuller exploration of the contemporary dimensions of this fundamental dynamic of capitalism, see Martin Ford, *The Rise of the Robots: Technology and the Threat of Mass Unemployment* (London: Oneworld, 2015). See also Postone, 314–24.

17. If Gou was not immediately able to implement his fully dehumanized factories, the number of industrial robots sold nonetheless grew by some 27 percent in 2014, and is expected to continue increasing at a rate of 10 percent in the coming decade to 2025. A recent article confirms that Foxconn is as of this writing in fact approaching such results, to the point that one "Foxconn factory has reduced its employee strength from 110,000 to 50,000, thanks to the introduction of robots." "The Rise of the Robots: 60,000 Workers Culled from Just One Factory as China's Struggling Electronics Hub Turns to Artificial Intelligence," *South China Morning Post*, May 21, 2016. The process that Gou calls attention to is accelerating such that, in China, it now takes only a single year to amortize the cost of an industrial robot, in marked contrast to the twelve years the process required as recently as 2008. "L'industrie attend une invasion de robots," *Le Monde*, September 30, 2015.

18. As Diane Elson writes, "If we treat the equivalence of commodities in terms of a numeraire commodity, we must presuppose the equivalence of commodities, but we still have not answered the question 'As what do they become exchangeable?'" ("The Value Theory of Labor," in *Value: The Representation of Labor in Capitalism*, ed. Diane Elson (London: Verso, 2015), 195. Macherey's contribution to *Reading Capital*, to be discussed below, constitutes a minute and rigorous analysis of the passage in the opening pages of *Capital* from an empirical analysis (of wealth), to that of a contradiction (of the commodity), and finally to the problem of measurement and its substance: "The analysis of value is thus based on a material logic that . . . no longer has anything in common with the empirical method of decomposition nor with the formal method of contradiction . . . The relation [between commodities] is essentially the place where *measurement* appears" (RCC, 201).

19. Diane Elson, "The Value Theory of Labor," in *Value: The Representation of Labor in Capitalism*, ed. Diane Elson (London: Verso, 2015).

20. "Everything takes on a completely different form when we contemplate the value of capital in its global form [*o plano do valor do capital global*]—which is not susceptible to immediate, empirical apprehension" (Robert Kurz, *Dinheiro sem valor*, 287). See also Kurz, *Vies et mort du capitalisme* (Paris: Lignes, 2011); Anselm Jappe, *Crédit à mort* (Paris: Lignes, 2011); and, for an English-language selection of the work of Kurz, Jappe, Trenkle, and other members of the Value Critique school of thought (*Wertkritik*), see Larsen et al., *Marxism and the Critique of Value*. For a lucid overview of Kurz's thought, see Anselm Jappe, "Kurz: A Journey into Capitalism's Heart of Darkness," *Historical Materialism* 22, nos. 3–4 (2014): 395–407; see also Frank Engster, "Krisis, What Krisis?" (review of Larsen et al., *Marxism and the Critique of Value*), *Radical Philosophy* 195 (January–February 2016): 48–51. Michael Heinrich's offhand dismissal of Kurz is simplistic and misguided. He wrongly equates Kurz's theory of collapse with the only preexisting theories in traditional Marxism, those of Luxemburg and Grossman, both of which Kurz repeatedly and extensively critiques, most recently in *Geld Ohne Wert*. More significantly, Heinrich wrongly and without basis asserts that Marx "implicitly rejected his former arguments for [the] collapse" of surplus value production sketched out in "The Fragment on Machines" (*An In-*

troduction to the Three Volumes of Karl Marx's Capital [New York: Monthly Review Press], 176). To claim that "the fact that increasingly less labor must be expended in the process of producing a commodity is not regarded in *Capital* as a tendency toward collapse but as the foundation for the production of relative surplus value" simply begs the question and disproves nothing (177).

21. The analysis of Trenkle and Lohoff is on this point definitive, in the view of this reader. They argue that "the decisive factor [in the postwar Fordist boom] was the *absolute* enlargement of the base of labor and value" in new, labor-intensive production processes of consumer goods and the industrial machinery to produce them, while increases in relative surplus value only served to "amplify" this basic dynamic. From the 1970s on, the third industrial revolution—which put an end to Fordism and is culminating in the twenty-first-century automation of the vast majority of industrial production processes—witnesses "the expulsion of humans from the production process. [. . . It culminates in] the displacement of productive power from the expenditure of immediate labor toward the level of general social knowledge, an evolution that is in the last instance incompatible with the restrictive laws of the abstract form of wealth in capitalism, whose content is constituted by the exploitation of the power of living labor in the production of value." In this context, the exponential increases in financialization seen since the 1970s, Trenkle and Lohoff argue, are not the *cause* of the 2008 crisis but, through the continued creation of fictive capital as speculation on (perpetually deferred) future valorization, the only remaining means of avoiding collapse (Norbert Trenkle and Ernst Lohoff, *La grande dévalorisation: Pourquoi la speculation et la dette de l'état ne sont pas les causes de la crise* [French translation, Fécamp: Post-éditions, 2014], 45, 64).

22. Trenkle and Lohoff, *La grande dévalorisation*, 18. See also Hegel's *Science of Logic*, where he distinguishes between "the [determinate] something, which is now only in its limit, equally separates itself from itself, points beyond itself to its non-being and declares it to be its being, and so passes over into it," versus finite things, the determination of which "does not go past their end" (Hegel, *The Science of Logic*, trans. George Di Giovani [Cambridge: Cambridge University Press, 2010]), 99, 102.

23. It is important to note that when in four instances in volume 3 of *Capital* Marx speaks of an "absolute" or "quantitative limit," this refers in each case not to a limit to the expansion of total surplus-value, but rather to the limit a given total surplus-value (whatever its size) sets for the various rates of profit among the individual capitals into which it is subdivided: "The size of the [total] surplus-value sets a quantitative limit for the parts it can be broken down into" (Marx 1981, 971; see also 961, 998, as well as the initial paragraphs of Marx's 1864–65 manuscript that Engels suppressed and which Moseley (2016) analyzes, now translated in Marx 2016, 7–11). Marx, in other words, is not analyzing in these passages whether and under what conditions total surplus-value, in the course of capital's historical development, can continue to be produced as anything more than what the *Grundrisse* called an "infinitesimal, vanishing quantity," but instead, in this later manuscript, he simply

presupposes the continued existence of this aggregate mass as a given magnitude x. This is further evidence of the underdevelopment of this aspect of his theory, after having first posed it impressionistically and in passing in the *Grundrisse*'s "Fragment on Machines."

24. Kurz, *Vies et mort du capitalisme*, 16, 82, 92, 96, 140; see also Ernest Mandel, *Late Capitalism* (London: New Left Books, 1975), 198, 204. Both Kurz and Mandel fail to distinguish clearly, as Marx did, between the number of human beings actually working (if in conditions of ever increasing misery)—which has indeed continued ineluctably to rise since the 1960s, and the contribution of that mass of living labor to the creation of *surplus value*, which continues to fall with increasing automation and (what amounts to the same) a rising organic composition of capital, relative to a given total mass of capital.

25. Warren Montag contextualizes and situates "Marxisme et humanisme" within Althusser's corpus and gives a detailed and nonteleological reading of its singular conceptualization of ideology in *Althusser and His Contemporaries* (Durham, NC: Duke University Press, 2013), 104–6.

26. On the historical fate of the PCF, see George Ross, "Communism," and Roland Quillot, "Marxism," both in *The Columbia History of Twentieth-Century French Thought*, ed. Lawrence Kritzman (New York: Columbia University Press, 2006).

27. "Les travailleurs, ouvriers," which Althusser understands empirically, as an actually existing, material social class that takes power in a socialist society, rather than a universal subject, "l'essence humaine elle-même" (*Pour Marx*, 228n1).

28. This distinction between constant and variable capital constitutes a secondary symptomatic blindness of *Reading Capital*: Just as Marx critiques Adam Smith, who, in Althusser's words, "did not *see* what was, however, staring him in the face," that is, precisely "the confusion of constant capital and variable capital" and even more, the "necessary invisible connection between the field of the visible ['*labor*'] and the field of the invisible ['*labor power*']" that Marx distinguishes for the first time, so we can say of Althusser that while he explicitly points to this distinction between constant and variable capital, calling attention to its fundamental status in Marx's conceptual apparatus, Althusser nonetheless never draws the obvious conclusion from this distinction, i.e., that labor power (and what Marx calls its "phenomenal form," labor *tout court*), is not *opposed* to capital, but rather constitutes one of the primary forms of capital, *even in its recalcitrance to fulfill its contractual function* (laboring in its form as concrete abstraction, what Marx calls the "expenditure of human brains, muscles, nerves, hands, etc." [*Capital*, vol. 1 (New York: Penguin, 2004), chap. 2.1]).

29. The concept of variable capital is both of critical importance and enormous complexity in Marx's theoretical edifice. It cannot simply be equated with the salary paid to a wage laborer (this, Marx argues in volume 2 of *Capital*, was one of Adam Smith's fundamental errors; see Michel Henry, *Marx* [Paris: Gallimard, 1976], 768), but instead, as Michel Henry shows in one of the most brilliant and original analyses of his *Marx*, encompasses in its dialectical mutations the total value of labor power in any commodity, including and especially its surplus value beyond any paid wage.

To equate variable capital with mere salary alone is to succumb to one of the founding illusions of capital itself, Marx argues repeatedly (Henry, *Marx*, 756). Though the concept of state capitalism was forged by Wilhelm Liebknecht, it was first deployed by Lenin in 1918 as a "step forward" in which the state would temporarily run the economy until it could be taken over by workers: "If in a small space of time we could achieve state capitalism, that would be a victory" (Lenin, "Left Wing Childishness," in *Collected Works*, vol. 27, www.marxists.org/archive/lenin/works/1918/may/09.htm).

30. In slavery, slaves are of course considered in both a practical, economic, and, quite frequently, literal sense, to be subhuman, animalistic machines of production, to be used up unto death as depreciating constant capital that will be replaced at will on the market.

31. Marx develops these two concepts in chapter 8 of *Capital*, vol. 1, "Constant Capital and Variable Capital."

32. I. I. Rubin, *Essays on Marx's Theory of Value* (1928; reprint, Delhi: Aakar Books, 2008], 65.

33. V. K. Dmitriev, *Economic Essays on Value, Competition, and Utility* (1904; reprint, Cambridge: Cambridge University Press, 1974): "It is theoretically possible to imagine a case in which all products are produced exclusively by machines, so that no unit of *living labour* (whether human or of any other kind) participates in production, and nevertheless an industrial profit may occur" (64). This is a totally automated economy, in which machines produce all commodities, including the machines of production itself (machines producing further "machines of an even higher order").

34. Althusser's strange pairing of value with use value, while excluding Marx's third key concept of exchange value, overlooks the way Marx carefully distinguishes the three in the opening chapters of *Capital*.

35. From its initial elaboration in the *Grundrisse*, Marx names and develops his concept of the value- or "organic"-composition of capital in chapter 25, section 1, of volume 1.

36. *Capital*, vol. 3, 1037; cf. *Lire le Capital*, 160.

37. To be sure, the second edition of *Lire le Capital* that appeared in two volumes in 1968, comprised only of Althusser and Balibar's texts (and which served for the various international translations of the book), was eventually completed in 1973 with a third and fourth volume, containing the original contributions of Rancière (vol. 3) and Macherey and Establet (vol. 4). That said, even among Francophone readers, who save a few specialists actually went so far as to read that obscure fourth volume in the twilight of Althusserianism in the 1970s?

38. Macherey has offered a surprisingly modest appraisal of his contribution to *Lire le Capital*: "When, with fifty years' distance, I reread [my] contribution, I see all of its imperfections . . . When, subsequently, I was addressed as a 'coauthor' of *Reading Capital*, I could not prevent myself feeling a certain *malaise* . . . In reality, *Reading Capital* has only one author: it is Althusser who, when he constructed this book on the basis of the working documents [we] provided him with, made a work unto itself,

for which he himself bears responsibility" (Aliocha Wald Lasowski, *Althusser et nous* [Paris: PUF, 2016], 176–77).

39. *Capital*, vol. 1, 125.

40. Cf. the editor's introduction to this volume, and Knox Peden, *Spinoza contra Phenomenology* (Stanford, CA: Stanford University Press, 2014).

41. "In experience, it is possible to conceive that two things stand alongside the other, that they are juxtaposed (like commodities in wealth). But they do not explicitly tolerate any relation; from the standpoint of experience, between two things and one thing there is a quantitative difference, but absolutely no qualitative difference" (RCC 200).

42. "As mere things," Macherey writes, "'objects' are differentiated by their uses, i.e., their irreducibility. If this character is set aside then at the same time as their empirical qualities disappear, there appears, not their quantitative aspect, but *another quality* (of a quite different nature: not directly observable): . . . It will be precisely value whose *substance* it will then possible to determine" (RCC 206).

43. Without developing this point to the level it will attain in Postone, Michel Henry nonetheless clearly expresses this distinction between wealth (as commodities) and value (as surplus value) in his 1976 study *Marx*: "Marx categorically denied that machines are able to create any value whatsoever. To repeat: machines do not work" (907; see also 926).

44. Cf. Peter Hallward, *Badiou: A Subject to Truth* (Minneapolis: University of Minneapolis Press, 2003), chap. 3.

45. On the fraught relation of Badiou's thought to the critique of political economy and Marx's *Capital* more specifically, see Alberto Toscano, "From the State to the World?: Badiou and Anti-capitalism," *Communication and Cognition* 37, nos. 3–4 (2004): 199–224. Note that Toscano seems to affirm without reserve the infinite expansive capacity of capital ("surplus-value is nothing if not the figure of an 'excessive count,' a count that draws, from the socio-economic materials which it indifferently affects, the means whereby to perpetually exceed itself," an assertion that begs the question whether in fact it remains the case today that "surplus-value may [still] be extracted" from living labor, as opposed to mere profit (211, 214).

46. To continue the comparison with Badiou, this enabling condition of exchange is perhaps analogous to what the latter calls, in *Logics of Worlds*, the "transcendental" (*Logics of Worlds: Being and Event, 2*, trans. Alberto Toscano [London: Continuum, 2009], 38: 102–3; 201–4). Alberto Toscano initiates a reading of *Capital* comparable to the one I am calling for here (limited in Toscano's brief article to consideration of Marx's conceptual doublet *formal/real subsumption*) when he writes that "we can consider the key tenets of Marx's socio-economic analysis and critique as resulting precisely from an inquiry into the concrete and identifiable structuring principles of a particular world . . . The jump to real subsumption signals a veritable event in or for the transcendental" ("From the State to the World," 218–19). In Toscano's Badiouian reading of Marx, capital constitutes an "operationally transcendental instance," a "structuring principle" that may become legible via the conceptual apparatus of *Log-*

ics of Worlds (220). This is the case, I would agree, despite Badiou's incredible disregard for the reigning structural compulsion to valorize value, as when the latter claims that "today the enemy is not called Empire or Capital. It's called Democracy" (*Logics of Worlds*, cited at 222).

47. Cited at Postone, *Time, Labor, and Social Domination*, 233. In the *Grundrisse*, Marx articulates what Michel Henry terms his "essential thesis" on this question: "It is easy to form the notion that machinery as such posits value, because it acts as a productive power of labor. But if machinery required no labor, then it would be able to increase the use value; but the exchange value which it would create would never be greater than its own costs of production, its own value, the labor objectified in it. It [machinery] creates value not because it replaces labor; rather, only in so far as it is a means to increase surplus labor, and only the latter itself is both the measure and substance of the surplus value posited with the aid of the machine; hence of labor generally" (*Grundrisse*, 67–68, cited at Henry, *Marx*, 907).

48. This confusion of the concepts of wealth and value reaches a remarkable degree of explicitness, if not theoretical clarity, in Raymond Aron's 1962 "Lessons on Industrial Society," in which Aron, discussing Marx's critique of capitalism as well as Soviet and Western industrial societies, reduces the question of value to a pure problem of the consumption and accumulation of use values: "A modern economy . . . presupposes that the collective does not consume each year the totality of value it produces" (Raymond Aron, *Penser la liberté, penser la démocratie* [Paris: Gallimard Quarto, 2005], 822). The confusion between wealth and value is complete when Aron goes on to assert that this "surplus of value" is purportedly composed, in the form of expenses for a given company, of four elements: salaries, taxes, reinvestment into the firm, and dividends to stockholders (823). Unhindered by any categorial concept of value as distinct from material wealth or profit (whether derived from Marx or his predecessors), Aron is free to assert that "I think that the capitalist regime can continue to function no matter what stage of growth it attains." Though any given industrial capitalist society may in fact be destroyed, in Aron's view this would only occur due to exogenous, non-economic causes (913). Given this theoretical muddle, it is not surprising Aron can finally claim that "the ideal schema of a capitalist society self-destructing is inconceivable and I would similarly say that the ideal schema of a planned economy self-destructing is inconceivable" (938). This confusion was no mere preserve of the ideological right in the culminating decade of the postwar expansion of Fordism. It is astounding to witness as sophisticated a reader of Marx as Adorno utterly oblivious to this inaugural distinction—between wealth and value—of the entire conceptual architecture of *Das Kapital*: "One must concede that capitalism has discovered resources within itself, which have permitted the postponing of collapse *ad Kalendus Graecus*—resources which include the immense increase of the technical potential of society and therein also the consumer goods available to the members of the highly industrialized countries" (Adorno, "Late Capitalism or Industrial Society?" [speech], 1968, www.marxists.org/reference/archive/adorno /1968/late-capitalism.htm).

49. Gilles Deleuze and Félix Guattari, *Anti-Oedipe: Capitalisme et schizophrénie* (Paris: Editions de Minuit, 1972), 279. In *A Thousand Plateaus*, Deleuze and Guattari maintain this unsubstantiated claim (that Marx had "a sense that machines would become productive of surplus value" [492]), but go on to state that "labor (in the strict sense) begins only with what is called *surplus labor*" by which they mean not capitalism per se, and the unique centrality of the value-form to its functioning, but any state apparatus able to accumulate "surplus labor" (490–91). The authors' focus is in this sense not on the structure of capitalism, but of the state, understood as a transhistorical apparatus that constructs "striated" arrangements of social space. They conclude their brief comments with the conceptually confused, impressionistic claim that contemporary capitalism is characterized by "a generalized 'machinic enslavement,' such that one may furnish surplus value without doing any work." Rather than Marx's rigorously developed formulation of capitalism as the "moving contradiction," the categories of surplus-value and labor are reduced by Deleuze and Guattari to empirical, phenomenological ciphers for the experience of work, non-work, and subjection to the social domination of machines in contemporary society. This wandering line of thought culminates in the groundless claim that in contemporary capitalism, value as "quantity of labor" has been replaced by "ways of perceiving and feeling" (492). Deleuze and Guattari, *A Thousand Plateaus: Capitalism and Schizophrenia*, trans. Brian Massumi (1980; reprint, Minneapolis: University of Minnesota Press, 1987).

50. Citing Marx's observation that "the more productive forces develop, the more they enter into conflict with the constrained basis upon which are founded the relations of *consumption*," Balibar comments that "in this '*external*' adventure, capitalist production always meets its own peculiar *internal* limitation, i.e, it never escapes being determined by its own peculiar structure" (RCC 470). Should the reader conclude from this elliptical formulation that this "internal structure," in its fundamental contradictions, describes a degree of automation and becoming-infinitesimal of living labor that implies the collapse of valorization itself? Or, conversely, that the structure of capital is that of an eternal return of crises of devalorization that restore profitability?

51. In Balibar's recent study *La philosophie de Marx* (1993; reprint, Paris: La découverte, 2001), he returns to the problem of organic composition to suggest that if the "growing contradiction" between forces and relations of production is, in Balibar's words, "resolved" by class struggle (thus refuting any economistic inevitability of historical progression toward communism), Marx's more "general declarations" in this sense are nonetheless superseded in *Capital* by a "maximal explication of concepts": specifically, for Balibar, the concepts of absolute and relative surplus value and the analysis of the various forms (manufacture, machinery, large-scale industry) of the industrial revolution (89–90). Even here, however, there is no suggestion by Balibar that Marx's analysis of the historical dynamic of organic composition implies—even logically, much less historically, in the twenty-first century—a becoming "infinitesimal" or point of collapse of the production of surplus value. Instead, Balibar refers to

the *operaismo* tradition of Tronti and Negri, a school of thought in which class conflict between labor and capital arguably remains an open-ended, implicitly infinite process of struggle, one that can only be transformed by the external intervention of political, revolutionary militancy.

52. On the history of the concept of uneven and combined development, see Löwy's penetrating exposition: Michael Löwy, *The Politics of Combined and Uneven Development* (New York: Verso, 1981).

53. While Postone and Kurz's critiques of "traditional Marxism" and "recuperative modernization" (respectively) both remain abstract and historically unsubstantiated, Löwy investigates in detail (in the first English edition of his study) the Yugoslav, Chinese, Vietnamese, and Cuban revolutions, and, unconsciously, as it were, confirms the similar claims of Kurz and Postone. It is telling that, beyond the book's overwhelming focus on the political (as the struggle for proletarian domination of revolution and then state power) rather than the economic (implicitly stigmatized as determinist "economism"), when Löwy *does* mention the economic dimensions of these revolutions, the author sees no need to define what might actually constitute definitions of terms such as "anti-capitalist," "development/underdevelopment," "dependent," and, indeed, "revolution" itself. Instead, these are repeatedly and unquestioningly linked to norms of "industrial growth" vs. "limited industrialization," while revolution as "land reform" and the "nationalization" of capital or "confiscation of property" (i.e., the egalitarian transformation of mere property relations with industrial production processes remaining unquestioned) is presumed to bestow a "socialist character" to the revolutionary process (Löwy, *The Politics of Combined and Uneven Development*, 108, 111).

54. An exception to this is Ruy Mauro Marini (*Sous-développement et révolution en Amérique Latine* [Paris: François Maspéro, 1972]), who in one of the most sophisticated theorizations of uneven development, argues that the historical transition in North Atlantic capitalism from the predominance of absolute to relative surplus value in the process of valorization was crucially facilitated by a third factor, the *super-exploitation* of labor in colonialism and neocolonialism, that is to say, by the historical and continuing exploitation of labor power purchased at less than its value, that sale enforced by various forms of social violence (John Smith, *Imperialism in the Twenty-First Century* [New York: Monthly Review Press, 2016], 216–17). Smith extensively develops Marini's insights to analyze the fundamental role of "super-exploited" labor in contemporary imperialism.

55. Aimé Césaire is paradigmatic of this tendency; while the great Marxist poet-statesman could never be accused of neglecting the importance of the cultural and humanistic dimensions of "development" for the colonized subjects of Negritude, these concerns were systematically subordinated throughout his long political career to repeated calls for the industrial development of Martinique and the redistribution of French capitalist wealth to reflect the interests of what he termed the Martinican "proletariat" (Nick Nesbitt, "From Louverture to Lenin: Aimé Césaire and Anticolonial Marxism" (*Smallaxe* 48 [fall 2015], 129–44).

56. Robert J. C. Young, in his exemplary and exhaustive historical examination of postcolonialism, a study in which he pays particular and salutary attention to the centrality of Marxism to the decolonization movement and postcolonial critique more generally, nonetheless unwittingly reinscribes precisely this limitation of critique within the horizon of the (re)distribution of wealth, disregarding the general social compulsion to valorize value characteristic of capitalism as a whole. Witness his discussion of the various theories of neocolonialism from development to postdependency theory, from which he concludes only that "any readjustment of north-south economic relations would be of very little use without an accompanying social redistribution of wealth and the development of wider constituencies of both production and consumption" (Robert J. C. Young, *Postcolonialism: An Historical Introduction* [Malden, MA: Blackwell, 2001], 54). For an expansive overview of the theories of development, dependency, underdevelopment, critical and postdevelopment theory from a postcolonial perspective, see his chapter on neocolonialism (44–56).

57. I adopt this distinction from Robert Kurz.

58. Marx, *Grundrisse*, 705 (my emphasis).

59. "The human essence is no abstraction inherent in each single individual. In its reality it is the ensemble of the social relations" (Marx, *Economic and Philosophical Manuscripts, Early Writings*, trans. Rodney Livingstone and Gregor Benton [New York: Penguin, 1992], 423).

60. This dynamic is unilinear because, though capital is destroyed and devalued in crises, allowing, à la Schumpeter, the recovery of rates of profit, socially necessary levels of productivity do not regress (failing global catastrophe). Roger Establet makes a similar claim for the fundamental priority of this tendential structure, when he refers to "the elaboration of a fundamental tendential law: the law of the transformation of the organic composition of *capital* (law of the decline in in *variable capital* in relation to *constant capital*)" (RCC 504, emphasis in original). As is the case with the other authors of *Reading Capital*, Establet simply states the law of this tendency as a conceptual object to be clearly demonstrated, rather than a historical problem for late capitalism.

61. See Smith, *Imperialism in the Twenty-First Century*, chapter 7.

62. Smith, *Imperialism in the Twenty-First Century*, 241, 242.

63. Rosa Luxemburg's *The Accumulation of Capital* is the classic example of such a failure to take into account the distinction between empirical numbers of people working across the planet and their capacity to produce surplus value, both individually and in aggregate. When Luxemburg describes the limits of capitalist accumulation as a mere empirical, numerical limit to the subsumption of humans globally to capital, her analysis of imperialism proceeds as if the increasing subsumption of global labor to capital produces equivalent increases in surplus value production: "With the international development of capitalism the capitalization of surplus value becomes evermore urgent and precarious, and the substratum of constant and variable capital *becomes an ever-growing mass—both absolutely and in relation to*

the surplus value" (Rosa Luxemburg, *The Accumulation of Capital* [London: Routledge, 2003], 408, my emphasis). Marx himself, never having systematically developed his theory of crises, at times denied a direct correspondence between empirical numbers of workers and mass of surplus value produced (i.e., *Capital Vol. III* [London: Penguin, 1991], 322–24), while at others he implied precisely a direct correspondence, as for example when he writes, "Capital has absorbed a given amount of unpaid labor. With the development of this process . . . the mass of surplus-value thus produced swells to monstrous proportions" (see Kurz, *Dinheiro sem valor*, 226).

64. See Trenkle and Lohoff, *La grande dévalorisation*, 110–17.

65. Wolfgang Uchatius, "Das Welthemd," *Die Zeit*, December 16, 2010. In this remarkable article, Uchatius analyzes the production costs of a T-shirt sold by H&M for €4.95. Both Smith and Trenkle and Lohoff analyze the article in some depth, though they draw remarkably different conclusions from the facts it presents, the former focusing on the super-exploitation of global labor, the latter on the vanishingly small quantities of value produced in this contemporary production process.

66. Trenkle and Lohoff, *La grande dévalorisation*, 113.

67. Uchatius reports that nineteen thousand cotton harvesters currently work in the United States, versus some 10 million in India and Africa.

68. For Henry, "while Marx's entire philosophical effort went toward substituting for the ideological concept of the individual defined by its consciousness, . . . the concept of the real individual defined by its praxis, the individual as producer, . . . structuralism, in its will to 'evacuate the subject,' accomplishes the inverse substitution" (*Marx*, 507).

69. Spinoza, *Ethics* I, Prop. 29, Schol.: "By *Natura naturans*, we must understand what is in itself and conceived through itself . . . God, insofar as he is considered a free cause" (London: Penguin, 1996).

70. "L'autorité de la logique [Husserlienne]," Cavaillès writes, "a son fondement dans son rapport à la vie" (Jean Cavaillès, *Sur la logique et la théorie de la science* [1942; reprint, Paris: Vrin, 2008], 71).

71. Cavaillès, *Sur la logique*, 73–74.

72. Husserl, cited in Cavaillès, *Sur la logique*, 80.

73. "Doubtless exchange is a transitory phenomenon and the system that rests upon it is destined to history [*voué à l'histoire*], but the possibility of exchange, had there never occurred an instance of which on earth and would there never be such, is a pure essence, [and] the thought that thinks [this essence] derives a transcendental truth or, in other words, an eternal truth; it goes beyond [*dépasse*] the factical science of a factical reality and escapes history: it is philosophy" (Henry: *Marx*, 614).

74. This is where Kurz's analysis of the objective, real abstraction of living labor and Jappe's more recent attention to the subjective dimensions of this process should be brought to bear against Henry's ahistorical and precritical notion of life. See Kurz, *Dinheiro sem valor*; Anselm Jappe, *Crédit à mort* (Paris: Lignes, 2011).

75. "That labor has no value means that it cannot have any. Labor as such is not derived from a process of work; production is not itself the product of any production [process] . . . Exchange can only become possible if one substitutes for the subjectivity of praxis quantifiable, objective equivalents upon which value itself may be quantified . . . In paying for labor or the productive activity of the laborer [in the form of a salary], it [labor] is recognized and assigned a value. But this is impossible. And so a detour is used: what is paid is not this activity but the group of subsistence goods and products it [labor] requires to function, [though] *this work* [required to produce these goods] *is itself subjective*" (Henry, *Marx*, 796, 803, italics in original).

76. "It is not the representation of [an instance of actual] work that can create any value whatsoever; only effective work [*le travail effectif*] that effectively produces an object can produce at the same time the value of that object, *create value* . . . It is remarkable that everywhere that abstract labor seems to compose the substance or source of value, it is in fact nothing more than its measure, the instrument invented by humans to this end" (Henry, *Marx*, 720–21; see also 764).

77. Of Marx's critique of the notion of profit, Henry characteristically writes: "Why is this rate illusory? Because in relating, in the form of profit, surplus value to total capital, it implicitly designates the latter as the source of the former, and the total structure [of capital] as its cause [rather than the true cause of valorization, living labor] . . . The totality of economic phenomena deployed in a system [i.e., that of Smithean and Ricardean political economy] only constitutes the surface of things and their appearance" (Henry, *Marx*, 828).

78. At this point, Henry fails clearly to distinguish between the historically vanishing capacity of living labor to produce surplus value, and the continued (empirical) presence of living labor within the global production process itself (Henry, *Marx*, 932; see above, note 18). Contrast this faith with the skepticism of Robert Kurz (*Vies et mort du capitalisme*) and Anselm Jappe (*Crédit à mort*).

79. Guglielmo Carchedi, *Behind the Crisis: Marx's Dialectic of Value and Knowledge* (Leiden: Brill, 2011).

80. Kurz initially put forward this thesis in his 1986 article "The Crisis of Exchange Value: Science as Productivity, Productive Labor, and Capitalist Reproduction," while Claus Peter Ortlieb offers a detailed analysis of the logic of the collapse of surplus value production in "A Contradiction Between Matter and Form: On the Significance of the Production of Relative Surplus Value in the Dynamic of Terminal Crisis," both translated in Larsen, *Marxism and the Critique of Value*.

81. Marx, *Grundrisse*, 694. The original German in fact refers to the *unendlich Kleines* or "infinitely small" rather than the mathematic and scientific concept of the *infinitesimal* contribution of living labor to the production process in fully developed capitalism; in this case, the English translation arguably improves upon Marx's original draft. For analyses of the contemporary transformation of the organic composition of capital from a neoliberal perspective, see Erik Brynjolfsson and Andrew McAfee, *The Second Machine Age: Work, Progress, and Prosperity in a*

Time of Brilliant Technologies (New York: W. W. Norton, 2014); Martin Ford, *The Rise of the Robots: Technology and the Threat of a Jobless Future* (New York: Basic Books, 2015); and the special report "Technology and the World Economy" in *The Economist*, October 4–10, 2014.

82. Smith, *Imperialism in the Twenty-First Century*, 113.

83. Riccardo Bellofiore and Tommaso Redolfi Riva, "The *Neue Marx-Lektüre*," *Radical Philosophy* 189 (January–February 2015), 24–36.

84. This unyielding desire to affirm the actual imminent end of capitalism culminates on the conceptual level in Kurz's pseudo-distinction, in his final work, *Money without Value,* between so-called real vs. mere theoretical categories. By the latter, Kurz seems to understand a logical "positivism" that he identifies with Michael Heinrich and, lurking behind the latter, (a schematic, spectral) Althusser (*Dinheiro sem valor,* 256). Via this distinction, Kurz invokes an "inevitable mental isolation of the categories relative to the dimension of their real unfolding [*a sua dimensão processual real*]." In contrast, one should affirm against Kurz's tendentious claim, with Cavaillès, Althusser, and Macherey, that some concepts are not more "real" than others, but merely more or less adequately developed; that no concepts exist out in the "real" world like cats and dogs, but that as much as the concept of dog does not bark, no more is, as Macherey writes, the concept of value exchangeable in Kurz's "real" world (RCC 257).

85. This, for example, is the argument of Peter Frase's *Four Futures: Life After Capitalism* (New York: Verso, 2016), where the author delineates four contingent postcapitalist futures in the wake of general automation and ecological catastrophe, which he names in turn communism, rentism, socialism, and exterminism. The book's innovative interrogation of a forthcoming politics of contingency is unfortunately weakened, however, by a truncated, highly simplistic presentation of late capitalism as a mere "system of class power" and unequal distribution of wealth (44).

CHAPTER 11

Vive la Crise!

FERNANDA NAVARRO

First of all I would like to thank the organizers for the invitation to partici-
pate in this project, celebrating Althusser's best-known work. Twenty or thirty
years ago this would have been unheard-of "in the heart of the beast" (the
United States and capitalism)! Now the beast is everywhere; it is global, with no
fixed address. But we are global too, or rather we are all over the globe, in an
age whose atmosphere reminds me of that described by Nicolas de Cusa at the
end of the Renaissance, when "the center is everywhere and the circumfer-
ence, nowhere."

I will begin this essay trying to explain the reasons for its title, well known
to all those familiar with Althusser's work. In order to do so, I will first concentrate only on the word *crisis* without referring it to any particular historical
moment or event. I realize this is a daring approach since I am not limiting it
to Marxism but extending it to a major crisis: the global crisis of today, that
of capitalism—in its neoliberal stage—and its effects, in order to finally close
the circle that intends to give meaning to these pages. I will retain, however,
Althusser's interpretation of the word *crisis* as not necessarily meaning chaos
or death but also catharsis, renaissance, or transformation.

I also want to point out that epochal changes or mutations occur not only
in history, but also in the course of an author's lifetime of work. Outstanding
examples of this are Marx and Althusser himself. In the early Marx we have
the *Economic-Philosophical Manuscripts of 1843–44* and other well-known
titles, culminating with *Das Kapital*, written by a later Marx. In the case of Althusser, the texts which we now are celebrating, *For Marx* and *Reading Capital*, correspond to his maturity, but we cannot forget his last philosophical
period, when he wrote *Aleatory Materialism,* a philosophy of the *encounter*

based on Epicurus's "clinamen." Between those two periods we find not only enormous differences as far as subjects and approaches are concerned, but also a clear turning point.

Having said this, I will concentrate myself on his last period because it coincides with the time in which I had the privilege of meeting and studying with him more directly (1984–89), and also because it provides me with the means to close the circle—as I have in mind—regarding the meaning of *crisis*.

Althusser's Influence in Latin America

Many of us—philosophy teachers and students—in this part of the American continent had concluded that, after 1970, it was impossible to approach Marx or to conceive Marxism in a pre-Althusserian manner. In other words, one could not read Marx without considering Althusser's theses, regardless of one's own position for or against them. The simple fact was that Althusser could not be ignored. Was this due to the clever way in which he updated Marxism introducing linguistics and psychoanalysis in order to rethink Marx? Or due to his project of "returning to Marx," leaving aside all litany and dogmatism and standing out as an unusual thinker capable of questioning Western rationalism as well as its dominating structures? Or was it thanks to the ethical stature of a man engaged with his own time, searching to inaugurate new possibilities for a different society and a different consciousness? Hard to say! The fact is he provoked passionate, polemic discussions that went beyond the normal academic tone reserved for philosophers, from Mexico to Argentina, where his writings were studied intensively from 1967 to 1978, along with his recent revival in many countries.

My *Encounter* with Althusser

This occurred at a time that was referred to as "between his two deaths" (1980–90), when his name passed from that of a myth to a mystery. Yet later on, many had to acknowledge that he had continued rethinking and reflecting, questioning and writing in a period which, despite undoubted suffering, was also rich in new ideas and conceptions. There were also those who regarded the last period in Althusser's life as a turning point in his philosophical writings.

Along these lines, I would like to mention a few of these new ideas and conceptions, since, to my surprise, this occurred at a time when I had the unexpected opportunity to go over his papers and manuscripts directly from his desk, photocopies of which I still keep, due to his generosity.

During my first visits, I started asking him simple questions regarding what he considered the best way to teach philosophy to young students such as my own. Months later, I couldn't believe that this *encounter*, deeper in dialogues every day, would end up in a long interview finally edited as a book (the last one published during his lifetime) now translated into five languages![1] So I also learned that life is full of surprises or *évenements*![2]

The questions continued. I asked him how he explained the fact that among the authors he mentioned as having influenced him there was not one Marxist thinker. I was referring, of course, to Foucault, Lacan, Bachelard, Canguilhem, and Cavaillès. His reply came quickly: "It is simply because what has been done with philosophy in the USSR in recent decades is absolutely appalling. The poverty of theoretical concepts held by socialist realism and dialectical materialism simply proves the surrender of intelligence, whereas the authors to whom I refer to not only allow us to think but also open new ways of thinking. We must remember, he added, that what is important is not the object of reflection but the *mode* of reflection." Among the subjects we touched on was "the difficulty of speaking of a Marxist philosophy: just as it would be difficult to speak of a mathematical or physical philosophy." He finally pointed out that one could not really speak of a Marxist philosophy but of a philosophy *for* Marxism.

The consequences of this position are deep and polemical, since this critical conclusion he reached has to do with Marx's relationship with Hegel's idealism, a point that contradicts what is generally and historically known and taught as the history of philosophy: that Marx freed himself from Hegel, "turning him upside down," causing an absolute cut or breakthrough. But Althusser, in the end, especially after the results of J. Bidet's research published in his book *Que faire du Capital?*, recognized that Marx never totally liberated himself from Hegel, but did so only tendentially, since he remained within the same framework of idealism. Even so, he acknowledged that Marx had moved toward a different domain, the scientific, in which he had founded historical materialism.

If we move to his last writings, we find a clear cut or mutation, in the realization that the late Althusser considered aleatory materialism a possible philosophy for Marxism. This is another reason to concentrate on it, following his own description: "It is a *Materialism of the Encounter* that follows the line of Epicurus—with the image of a disorderly fall of atoms through a vacuum, causing their free encounter or 'clinamen' in order to 'make a new world possible.'" An important point is that it is there that the so-called interstices or open spaces appear (and to which we will come back later).

Althusser included in that same line of thought all the materialist tradition barely acknowledged by the official history of philosophy. All those rare, nonapologetic thinkers who were able to avoid being caught in such dichotomies as materialism-idealism and who claimed no First Cause, no Sense, no Reason (Logos), no End; that is, no teleology, be it rational, moral, political, or esthetic.

He added that this materialism does not call for any subject but posits rather a process *without* a subject, referring to Machiavelli, Hobbes, the second Rousseau, Marx, Nietzsche, and Heidegger and to their respective categories: limit, margin, void, lack of center, and freedom. Aleatory materialism is thus a materialism of chance, of contingency, not in the sense of an absence of necessity but in the sense of necessity conceived as a *devenir*, a becoming necessary for contingent encounters.

This view of contingency is contrary even to one commonly attributed to Marx, Engels, and Lenin, which, as with every materialism of the rationalist tradition, is based on necessity and teleology—in other words, is a disguised form of *idealism*. In this view, materialism need not conform to any idea of a system in order to be considered a philosophy, because what constitutes a philosophy as such is not its discursive justification or demonstration but the position for which it stands in the philosophical battlefield, as in Kant's *Kampfplatz*.

For our author, aleatory materialism represents the highest point of materialism because of the compelling impulse it has to open the world to "the event," *l'événement*, to all living practices, including politics, in an unpredictable way, modifying all fixed premises and data. Here he referred to Wittgenstein's proposition: "Die Welt ist alles was das Fall ist" ("The world is everything that takes place, or is the case," in B. Russell's translation) . . . an astonishing proposition because—as Althusser agrees—there exists nothing but cases, particular situations, singular things in the world that simply fall over us, in spite of us, without any notice, and each of them has a proper name.

What Does Althusser Mean by *Interstices?*

These refer to the social and popular movements and struggles of marginalized, oppressed people that have emerged all over the world, such as the pacifist, ecological, feminist, gay, student, Indian, and immigrant movements, bringing some hope with their different ways of functioning and organizing, with no intention of instituting new pyramids with dominating structures. These movements, he added, have followed the line of Rosa Luxemburg and not that of Lenin. Althusser was convinced of their priority, as opposed to those with rigid, vertical structures like those adopted by political parties, making the practice of democracy difficult, if not impossible. I would like to quote our author, from the notes I still keep from that time, thirty years ago. Among them I found the following, of which I only will quote a few lines:

> Everything in this world is in a constant, unpredictable flow. If we want to give an image of this we must go back to Heraclitus or Epicurus. Yet if we want to give a more recent image of it we must follow Deleuze in order to avoid Descartes' hierarchical representation of the world as a tree but rather as a rhizome: Deleuze's horizontal root. Yet I still prefer Marx's image: "The gods exist in the *interstices* of the world of Epicurus. In the same way that mercantile relations existed already in the interstices of the slave world."

Althusser adds something more: "The proletariat is found in the margins of bourgeois society. The question now is to 'place the margins in the center.'" The difficulty today is the dispersion and lack of connection of the multiple alternative groups or *interstices*. He goes on to make a last, unexpected recommendation that I consider to show a visionary approach to this problem: "In order to open theses *interstices* that announce a more just society, we must to learn—from and with the people—a language in which they may recognize themselves . . . thus ending up in a new conception of a real materialist and aleatory history." He then summed this up precisely: "In order to change the world, from its basis, we must think differently, speak differently, in order to act differently and conceive the horizon of our actions in a different manner, in order to reach and propose a different conception of history: materialist and aleatory." This was an obvious refusal of today's official political practices, so degenerated and sealed by corruption and violence. How to overcome this? *Organization* was the key word.

In his *Theses de Juin* (still unedited) he made the following brilliant assertions:

"To think in an international liberation movement would be utopian. The most we can conceive of is an International Center of Ideological Convergence for Liberation, capable of unifying alternative and revolutionary movements that are appearing everywhere, searching a new strategy and new practices and principles as well as communitarian forms with transversal relations. A Center of Information without the pretention of directing or taking decisions, since this belongs to the militants of each region or country: in short, a *Center of/for Encounters* where the interchange of ideas, positions, and experiences can take place. This will first come true in the Third World countries. He considered this the possibility of a truly materialist and aleatory history."

In 1994, four years after Althusser's death, an unexpected *interstice* with an alternative way of organizing and expressing a total refusal to integrate to the capitalist values and ways of life—appeared in my country, Mexico, in the southern state of Chiapas, as if our visionary author had had an intuition of its possibility when he stressed the fact that if this ever happened, it would be in the Third World. Its name is the Zapatista movement.

The Link between the Zapatista Movement and Althusser: An Identity and a Philosopher's Name Revealed

In February 1995, Subcomandante Insurgente Marcos, one of the leading figures of the Zapatista Movement, the only mestizo (not 100 percent Indian) who was assigned to lead the Zapatista National Liberation Army (EZLN)—as well as the role of their translator or "voice," turned out to be an Althusserian philosopher. He became known as a brilliant thinker and writer.

How was his identity discovered? A huge mobilization geared up to apprehend him through the press and TV, where Marcos's double picture appeared, with and without the ski mask, as "Wanted." But what was astonishing for us was the result of the clipping: *"Rafael Sebastian Guillen* [his supposed name]: *An Althusserian Philosopher."* He had actually studied philosophy at the National Autonomous University of Mexico, and his thesis had been on Althusser's ideological state apparatus, with specific attention to education.

He has also stood out by inaugurating a different language in politics: instead of the dull, flat messages or declarations of the typical politicians, right or left, he wrote short stories, good literature, and invented characters as well, achieving a poetic prose to get his messages across, as well as a brilliant analysis of the country's political and economic situation. He is also known for his sense of humor—something completely absent in all traditional revolutionary leaders, who speak for posterity.

This gave place to a ruthless military invasion, followed by his persecution in the southeastern jungle. Soldiers committed terrible atrocities against the people in the Zapatista liberated zones. There are many

Mexicans, throughout the country, who are Zapatistas. Those who supported them clandestinely, those who fed them, and those who kept their secret—these people suffered. There are videos that show the army's cruelty and destructiveness. In response, thousands of Mexican citizens protested. In Mexico City, within one week there were three huge demonstrations ending up at the main Central Square, or Zócalo (which holds some 120,000 people), filled with people yelling: "Todos somos Marcos [We are all Marcos]." "If you want to apprehend Marcos you must put us all in jail and you will never have enough jails for us."

Many articles in the press also condemned the military invasion, and hundreds of signatures from all over the world (including those of Noam Chomsky, Immanuel Wallerstein, and others from Europe) were published in several newspapers. All this pressure made the government decide to order the withdrawal of troops from the Zapatista area, but not from the state of Chiapas. To this date, they have never been free of military aggressions, due mainly to their triumph in recuperating their original territory, necessary to obtain their complete autonomy, which they finally did achieve in 2003! Since then, although they still face hostilities from the government, they have been able to succeed, astonishingly, in the realms of autonomous education, health, self-government, the status of women, and agro-ecology. There is not enough space to describe how meaningful and dignified this well-organized social and political movement, or interstice, has become, in escaping capitalist domination and becoming an important alternative, in that it truly gathers the population from within and from below, freely and with the light of conscience.

To return to that day: January 1, 1994, marked the time when the armed uprising and their "¡Ya basta! [Enough!]" was heard all over the country, precisely when the North American Free Trade Agreement (NAFTA) between Canada, the United States, and Mexico was to be signed, announcing—in spite of their discourse—more poverty, inequality, and injustice in my country, only strengthening capitalist principles. Needless to say, this shook all Mexico . . . and beyond.

With incredible determination in their struggle for emancipation, "they took arms against a sea of troubles and, by opposing [tried to] end them," as Shakespeare, the greatest poet, put it. Although the fire only lasted twelve days, from then on language, dialogue took its place. This marks an unprecedented case that makes them different from previous guerrillas in South America. From then on, carrying their weapons without using them, they have confronted the war against the State and against the destructive capitalist war machine in a new way. This is how they are resisting globalization from their remote corner, without pretending to be a model or an example to be followed: "We are just an experience . . . from which any other struggle may adopt or adapt whatever it finds useful for its own peculiar geographic conditions." The place of ethics, as in Althusser, is fundamental and goes hand in hand with politics as well as in their daily communitarian life.

The search for autonomy and their fight to recuperate their original territory has been fundamental in order to avoid annihilation, a key struggle in order to build and transform their communities into liberated areas with the right to be treated as human beings. It was in 2003 that they finally achieved their autonomy and made an unprecedented step: having started as an army, at this date the EZLN handed their leadership over to their civilian population. The reason: to be consistent with their values, freedom, justice, and democracy being among the highest. "An army, having a vertical hierarchical structure," they explained, "cannot be democratic. How can we then claim democracy as one of our main goals and practices?" Since then, the army stood aside with the responsibility to defend the movement and all its members and the collective Indian leadership started to organize a different kind of civilian government: the Juntas de Buen Gobierno (JBG), following their traditional communitarian line with no unipersonal hierarchic command, be it a monarch, president, king, governor, or messiah.

How does the JBG function? Once being elected by the community, they must follow the following principles: their posts must be rotating (each three years), revocable, and obliged to render accounts of their tasks and duties, thus fulfilling the three main principles. But there is yet a higher level of authority: the Assembly. A lesson to our actual governments around the *civilized* world!

As regards their philosophical principles and ideas, they also give us lessons, beginning with their language structure—quite distinct from ours, which comes from the Greek-Latin tradition in that there are only subjects in their grammar, no objects at all. Why? Because for them *everything is alive*. Not only human beings but also animals and vegetables, stones and mountains! This entails important consequences that prove that they go far beyond an anthropocentric conception to achieve a true biocentricism.

Their respectful relationship with nature is another trait that leaves our Western civilization far behind. They have a completely different conception of nature, considering it their Mother Earth, a conception that excludes private property. They work the land collectively. This has been a source of conflict ever since with the Mexican authorities, since, following their tradition, it is impossible to think of selling or buying land. "The land (territory) does not belong to us, we belong to it," they say.

Another lesson, coming from their language, is that there exist no antagonistic dichotomies such as body/soul, good/bad, black/white, conqueror/vanquished (this they learned after the Spanish Conquest). Still another philosophical difference comes from the antagonism of monism versus pluralism (which we slightly touched elsewhere). They originally rejected monism even in religion. Before the Conquest they did not believe in a single true God; afterward, this belief was imposed by the sword.

I cannot end this essay without touching one key concept that stands out in the Zapatistas' way of thinking and acting: the reformulation/resignification of the concept of power. What did they mean when, in 1994, they took up arms and at the same time made it clear that their aim was not to seize power?—a statement that enflamed political parties both from the Left as well as from the Right. "What on earth can one do without power?" they asked. The Indians silently responded, "Anything different from barbarism, perchance?" At the same time this position evoked the admiration of many who were looking beyond the traditional political spectrum. They understood that it meant a different way of relating to power. Marcos, among other things, said, "The only virtue of power is that, in the end, it inevitably produces a revolution against itself."

History has taught us that even in the outstanding cases when tyranny or dictatorships were overthrown by revolutionary liberating forces, disillusionment sooner or later followed when the basic principles of justice and freedom, which led the struggle, begin to decay. It is as if there were some dominating traits inherent to power itself that gradually end up in a repetition or reproduction of the rigid, arbitrary governments that were overthrown—not an alternative. Not to speak of the price of anonymous bloodshed this process meant for the human beings who gave their lives!

Marcos also said that "our people taught us that it was not a matter of substituting a domination with another domination; that we should convince, not conquer by vanquishing and destroying" . . . in order to reach a real transformation. Another reason for choosing a different road and saying *no* to the seizure of power is that it is incompatible with real democracy (and not only in electoral terms) since power implies domination, hierarchy, authority, and imposition, and is unable to listen to others. In fact they consider that there are other kinds of democracy, not only the representative electoral one, such as the participative and communitarian form, where the word "we" stands out over the word "I." "Our democracy does not fit in the ballots," they declared, after having discussed it and decided everything in our Assemblies, "where everyone has the right and obligation to speak and be heard."

This was when they revealed a peculiar ancestral slogan: "Mandar obedeciendo," or "Command by obeying," meaning that whoever is elected to be an authority (never a single person, always a group) must obey the needs, claims, and suggestions of the people. They receive no payment, and when their period is over they go back to their usual activity.

After having been with them in the course of shorter and longer visits year after year, I can affirm that after twenty years, the Zapatista movement has proved to be one of the most vital, successful, and exemplary interstices to date; the reason for which I wished to address in this chapter, knowing that it is barely known abroad—by the public in general—due mainly to the state's manipulation of the mass media, since this movement represents everything the powerful ones want to destroy. Many times they have tried. But due to the strong determination and the values they have built in their autonomous self-government, education, and health service as well as the status of women, they have resisted, giving hope to many Mexicans and all those who have visited them from abroad. In their creative, original forums, meetings, and congresses, where they have received thousands of people from the five continents, who after visiting them, have enthusiastically organized solidarity committees in their own hometowns or cities, including some in the United States.

A few examples: From the very beginning there was a group of students from the United States that came to help build the first secondary school (junior high) in a Zapatista community: Oventic. It was highly rewarding to see how language was not a barrier between the two groups: North American and Mexican Indians, working, laughing, playing, and sharing meals together! The same happened with people from Greece, Spain, France, and Italy, this last country rendering an incredible "gift": electricity for a whole community called La Realidad, as well as a doctor who has been in another area for over sixteen years, teaching scientific medicine in combination with the natural herbal tradition. I could go on mentioning other valuable cases, free from all governmental support, since they decided to never again receive one single penny or "charity" from the state, especially the Mexican. They are well known for being proud of their dignity.

Today, twenty years later, there still are many active solidarity committees in many countries that keep returning to their events in Chiapas or elsewhere. For example, June 20, 2015, a "Journée Zapatiste" is being organized by Paris VIII University, to which I was invited. Despite our government's interests in wiping the Zapatistas off our map, they have not been able to do it. This, however, has not stopped the governing class from continuous, violent aggressions with regard to the recuperated territories, without which they could not be autonomous, autonomy being the key to building new human relations and values and to making their famous slogan true: "We want to build a world that holds (includes) many worlds." This shows that even though it is a marginal movement, it is based on universal grounds and values and has been successful in influencing other movements such us the Altermundistas in Seattle (1999), up to the Indignados all over the globe in 2011, including Occupy Wall Street in New York and beyond!

The Zapatistas have addressed and involved people from civil society far beyond the scope of the Left, mainly nonorganized nonmilitants in political parties, common citizens, and intellectuals fed up with traditional politics. This is new. With great creativity and imagination they have organized all kinds of meetings, one of the last of which took place in 2013–14, called "La Escuelita de la Libertad, según los zapatistas [The School of Freedom, according to the Zapatistas]." This gathered, altogether, 5,200 people from the five continents. They generously opened their poor houses for us to share in the course of a whole week, day and night living and working as they do, far from any luxury but satisfying their basic needs, with great dignity. My twenty-seven students and I were astonished by their authenticity and the brotherhood they practice among them—part of their Mayan heritage that stresses the capacity *to listen* to others.

Let me now quote the Zapatistas at the height of a most inhumane experience that happened just last year in May 2014, when armed persons—paid by the local and federal governments—killed a teacher/guide of the "Escuelita de la Libertad." Despite this injustice they answered back with another lesson, far from falling to the provocation of those in power. They kept an unexpected, disciplined, peaceful attitude in saying

"We don't want vengeance, we want justice."

This sentence is more than meaningful today in my country where all politicians, regardless of belonging either to the Left or to the Right, have shown the great degradation of the governing class, acting with an incredible corruption, impunity, and violence. On New Year (2015) we all celebrated with them the First International Festival of Resistance and Rebellion against Capitalism, gathering an even greater number of people all along the long road leading to the southern part of the country before reaching Chiapas, including a great number of Indian groups with millenary heritage as well, willing to gather and take common peaceful steps following the Zapatista's influence in their path toward liberation.

My conclusion is that for a considerable part of our population, this interstice has become an alternative that provides us with some oxygen and hope, and not only rage! How far, then, can we say that this hidden Mexican *interstice* has actually escaped the Hydra of capitalism, giving many of us the hope that a more human society is possible, even if it as yet exists only at a micro scale?

I consider that we must pay close attention to Althusser himself when he said, "These organized minorities or *interstices* that give place to 'possibility' as a category, coexist already at a micro-scale and are working on an alternative platform, seeking a different kind of politics that may allow different kinds of human practice and human relations, while sharing a common goal: to build a more just society, free from ideological manipulation, misery and oppression." The same is true when he concluded that processes should be not centralized but local, not international but regional, finding their unity in objective intersecting lines, by communitarian forms with transversal relations.

Taking a final step, I ask: couldn't we conclude that Althusser would coincide with this approach if he had lived to see it? Knowing that there is no possible answer to it, I go back to my first pages, following this daring line of thought in order to close the circle. Considering what I have stressed above and given his visionary approach couldn't we have enough grounds to announce a different crisis today, in order to repeat, with Althusser, "Vive la Crise!," both in the sense of chaos and catastrophe—since capitalism still prevails—but also in that other meaning, in favor of a new revival or transformation—given that multiple interstices have intertwined within the capitalist/neoliberal stage?

How can this occur? Through an all-embracing glimpse of the interstices or open spaces in widespread geographies across the globe, strengthening them with our support, opening up consciences in the hope they will gradually extend themselves imperceptibly like Deleuze's rhizome, fulfilling Althusser's support of them as not centralized but local, not international but regional. Fortunately, we will always find authorized voices to answer these questions, in either sense: the strengthening or decay of the capitalist system.

In closing, we can agree with Derrida's words at Althusser's funeral: "His work is valuable because it bears witness and takes risks." What he never knew was how far—in those widespread geographies along the globe—his ideas have landed and germinated.

Notes

1. Louis Althusser, *Philosophy of the Encounter: Later Writings*, trans. and ed. G. M. Goshgarian (London: Verso, 2006).

2. In the following pages, I quote extensively from these papers.

Agamben, Giorgio. *Homo Sacer: Sovereign Power and Bare Life*. Translated by Daniel Heller-Roazen. Stanford, CA: Stanford University Press, 1998.

———. *The Open: Man and Animal*. Translated by Kevin Attell. Stanford, CA: Stanford University Press, 2004.

Althusser, Louis. "Avant-propos: Histoire terminée, histoire interminable." In Dominique Lecourt, *Lyssenko: Histoire réelle d'une "science prolétarienne."* Paris: François Maspero, 1976.

———. *Ce qui ne peut plus durer dans le parti communiste*. Paris: François Maspero, 1978.

———. "Correspondence with Jacques Lacan, 1963–1969: Louis Althusser to Jacques Lacan, 11-7-66." In *Writings on Psychoanalysis: Freud and Lacan*. Translated by Jeffrey Mehlman. New York: Columbia University Press, 1996.

———. *Filosofía y marxismo: Entrevista por Fernanda Navarro*. Mexico City: Siglo XXI, 1988.

———. "Finalmente qualcosa di vitale si libera dalla crisi e nella crisi del marxismo." *Il Manifesto*, November 16, 1977; in English, "The Crisis of Marxism," translated by Grahame Lock, *Marxism Today* (July 1978).

———. *For Marx*. Translated by Ben Brewster. London: Allen Lane, 1969.

———. *The Future Lasts Forever: A Memoir*. [1992]. New York: New Press 1993.

———. "The Historical Task of Marxist Philosophy." In *The Humanist Controversy and Other Writings*, edited by François Matheron; translated by G. M. Goshgarian. London: Verso, 2003.

———. *Lenin and Philosophy, and Other Essays*. Translated by Ben Brewster. London: New Left Books, 1971.

———. "Letter to Merab Mardashvili, 16 January 1978." In *Philosophy of the Encounter: Later Writings, 1978–1987*, edited by François Matheron and Oliver Corpet; translated by G. M. Goshgarian. London: Verso, 2006.

———. *Lettres à Franca (1961–1973)*. Edited by François Matheron and Yann Moulier Boutang. Paris: Stock/IMEC, 1998.

———. *Machiavelli and Us*. 2nd ed. Translated and introduced by Gregory Elliott. New York: Verso, 2011.

———. "Marx's Relation to Hegel." *Politics and History: Montesquieu, Rousseau, Marx*. Translated by Ben Brewster. London: Verso, 2007.

———. "On Theoretical Work: Difficulties and Resources." Translated by James H. Kavanagh. *Philosophy and the Spontaneous Philosophy of the Scientists and Other Essays.* London: Verso, 1990.

———. *On the Reproduction of Capitalism: Ideology and Ideological State Apparatuses.* Translated by G. M. Goshgarian. London: Verso, 2014.

———. "Philosophie et Marxisme: Entretiens avec Fernanda Navarro (1984–1987)." *Sur la philosophie.* Paris: Gallimard, 1994.

———. "Philosophy as a Revolutionary Weapon: Interview conducted by Maria Antonietta Macciocchi." *Lenin and Philosophy and Other Essays.* Translated by Ben Brewster. New York: Monthly Review Press, 2001.

———. *Politics and History: Montesquieu, Rousseau, Marx.* Translated by Ben Brewster. London: Verso, 2007.

———. *Por Marx.* Havana: Edición Revolucionaria, 1966.

———. *Pour Marx.* Paris: La Découverte, 1996.

———. "La problématique de l'Histoire dans les œvres de jeunesse de Marx." In *Politique et Histoire de Machiavel à Marx: Cours à l'École normale supérieure de 1955 à 1972,* edited by François Matheron. Paris: Éditions du Seuil, 2006.

———. "Psychanalyse et psychologie." In *Psychanalyse et sciences humaines: Deux conférences (1963–1964),* edited by Olivier Corpet and François Matheron. Paris: Librairie Générale Française/IMEC, 1996.

———. *Reply to John Lewis: Essays in Self-Criticism.* Translated by Grahame Locke. London: New Left Books, 1976.

———. "Réponse à une critique." In *Écrits philosophiques et politiques, Tome II,* edited by François Matheron. Paris: Stock/IMEC, 1995.

———. "Sur le *Contrat Social* (Les décalages)." *Cahiers pour l'analyse* 8 (1967): 5–42; in English, "Rousseau: *The Social Contract* (Discrepancies)," in *Politics and History: Montesquieu, Rousseau, Marx,* translated by Ben Brewster, 111–60. London: Verso, 2007.

———. *Sur le contrat social.* With a study by Patrick Hochart. Houilles, France: Manucius, 2009.

———. "Sur la dialectique matérialiste (De l'inégalité des origines)." In *Pour Marx,* with an avant-propos by Étienne Balibar. Paris: La Découverte, 1996; in English, "On the Materialist Dialectic (On the Unevenness of Origins)." In *For Marx,* translated by Ben Brewster. London: Verso, 2005.

———. "Sur l'objectivité de l'histoire: Lettre à Paul Ricœur." In *Solitude de Machiavel et autres textes,* edited by Yves Sintomer. Paris: Presses Universitaires de France, 1998.

———. "The Transformation of Philosophy." Translated by Thomas E. Lewis. *Philosophy and the Spontaneous Philosophy of the Scientists and Other Essays,* edited by Gregory Elliott. London: Verso, 1990.

———. *22ᵉ congrès.* Paris: François Maspero, 1977.

———. "Une question posée par Louis Althusser." In *Écrits philosophiques et politiques, Tome I,* edited by François Matheron. Paris: Stock/IMEC, 1994.

Althusser, Louis, and Alain Badiou. *Materialismo dialéctico y materialismo histórico*. Translated by Nora Rosenfeld de Pasternac, José Aricó, and Santiago Funes. Mexico City: Siglo XXI/Pasado y Presente, 1969.

Althusser, Louis, and Étienne Balibar. *Reading Capital*. Translated by Ben Brewster. London and New York: New Left Books and Pantheon Books, 1970.

Althusser, Louis, Étienne Balibar, Roger Establet, Pierre Macherey, and Jacques Rancière. *Lire le capital*. Rev. ed. Paris: PUF (Quadrige), 2008.

———. *Lire le capital*. Paris: Maspero, 1969.

———. *Reading Capital: The Complete Edition*. Translated by Ben Brewster and David Fernbach. London: Verso, 2016.

Althusser, Louis, and Jacques Monod. Correspondence. Unpublished dossier, IMEC/Fonds Althusser.

Anderson, Kevin. "The 'Unknown' Marx's *Capital* Volume 1: The French Edition of 1872–75, 100 Years Later." *Review of Radical Political Economics* 15, no. 4 (1983): 71–80.

Aricó, José. *La cola del diablo: Itinerario de Gramsci en América Latina*. Caracas: Nueva Sociedad, 1988.

Aron, Raymond. *Penser la liberté, penser la démocratie*. Paris: Gallimard Quarto, 2005.

Badiou, Alain. *The Century*. Translated by Alberto Toscano. Cambridge: Polity, 2007.

———. *The Communist Hypothesis*. New York: Verso, 2010.

———. "Qu'est-ce que j'entends par 'marxisme'"? Talk presented at the seminar "Lectures de Marx," at the Ecole Normale Supérieure, Paris, April 18, 2016.

———. *Le concept de modèle: Introduction à une épistémologie matérialiste des mathématiques*. Paris: Maspero, 1970.

———. *Logics of Worlds: Being and Event, 2*. Translated by Alberto Toscano. London: Continuum, 2009.

———. "The (Re)commencement of Dialectical Materialism." In *The Adventure of French Philosophy*, translated by Bruno Bosteels. New York: Verso, 2012.

———. *Theory of the Subject*. Translated by Bruno Bosteels. London: Continuum, 2009.

Balibar, Étienne. "Althusser." In *The Columbia History of Twentieth-Century French Thought*, edited by Lawrence D. Kritzman, 380–84. New York: Columbia University Press, 2006.

———. "Althusser and the rue d'Ulm." Translated by David Fernbach. *New Left Review* 58 (July–August 2009).

———. "Eschatology versus Teleology: The Suspended Dialogue between Derrida and Althusser." In *Derrida and the Time of the Political*, edited by Pheng Cheah and Suzanne Guerlac. Durham, NC: Duke University Press, 2000.

———. *La philosophie de Marx*. 1993. Reprint. Paris: La découverte, 2001.

———. "Sur les concepts fondamentaux du matérialisme historique." In Louis Althusser, Étienne Balibar, Roger Establet, Pierre Macherey, and Jacques Rancière,

Lire le Capital, new rev. ed. Paris: Quadrige/PUF, 1996; in English, "The Basic Concepts of Historical Materialism." In Louis Althusser and Étienne Balibar, *Reading Capital*, translated by Ben Brewster. London: Verso, 1997.

Balibar, Étienne, and Yves Duroux. "A Philosophical Conjuncture: An Interview with Étienne Balibar and Yves Duroux." In *Concept and Form*, vol. 2: *Interviews and Essays on the* Cahiers pour l'analyse, edited by Peter Hallward and Knox Peden, 169–86. New York: Verso, 2012.

Benjamin, Walter. "On Language as Such and on the Language of Man" (1916). In *Selected Works*, 4 vols., edited by Marcus Bullock and Michael W. Jennings, 1: 62–74. Cambridge, MA: Harvard University Press, 1996.

Bidet, Jacques. *Exploring Marx's Capital: Philosophical, Economic, and Political Dimensions*. Translated by David Fernbach. Leiden: Brill, 2007.

Bórquez, Zeto, and Marcelo Rodríguez, eds. *Louis Althusser: Filiación y (re)comienzo*. Santiago de Chile: Programa de Magíster en Teoría e Historia del Arte, 2010.

Bosteels, Bruno. *Badiou and Politics*. Durham, NC: Duke University Press, 2011.

Brynjolfsson, Erik, and Andrew Mcafee. *The Second Machine Age: Work, Progress, and Prosperity in a Time of Brilliant Technologies*. New York: W. W. Norton, 2014.

Burgos, Raúl. *Los gramscianos argentinos: Cultura y política en la experiencia de Pasado y presente*. Buenos Aires: Siglo Veintiuno, 2004.

Caletti, Sergio, and Natalia Romé, eds. *La intervención de Althusser: Revisiones y debates*. Buenos Aires: Prometeo, 2011.

———. *Sujeto, política, psicoanálisis: Discusiones althusserianas con Lacan, Foucault, Laclau, Butler y Zizek*. Buenos Aires: Prometeo, 2011.

Caletti, Sergio, Natalia Romé, and Martina Sosa, eds. *Lecturas de Althusser: Proyecciones de un campo problemático*. Buenos Aires: Imago Mundi, 2011.

Čapek, Karel. *Hry*. Prague: Českosovensky spisovatel, 1956.

———. *RUR (Reason's Universal Robots)*. In *Four Plays*. London: Bloomsbury, 1999.

Carchedi, Guglielmo. *Behind the Crisis: Marx's Dialectic of Value and Knowledge*. Leiden: Brill, 2011.

Cavaillès, Jean. *On the Logic and Theory of Science*. Paris: Vrin, 1997.

Cavazzini, Andrea. *Enquête ouvrière et théorie critique*. Liège: Presses Universitaires de Liège, 2013.

Cavazzini, Andrea, and Fabrizio Carlino. "Althusser et l'opéraïsme. Notes pour l'étude d'une 'rencontre manquée.'" *Revue en ligne "Période"* (2014), http://revueperiode.net/althusser-et-loperaisme-notes-pour-letude-dune-rencontre-manquee/.

Claudin, Fernando. *The Communist Movement: From Comintern to Cominform*. Translated by Brian Pearce and Francis MacDonagh. New York: Monthly Review Press, 1975.

Colletti, Lucio. *Marxism and Hegel*. Translated by Lawrence Garner. London: Verso, 1979.

Davis, Angela Y. *Women, Race and Class*. London: Random House, 1981.

Davis, Mike. *Planet of Slums*. New York: Verso, 2007.

Debray, Régis. *Révolution dans la révolution?: Lutte armée et lutte politique en Amérique latine*. Paris: Maspero, 1967.

Deleuze, Gilles, and Félix Guattari. *Anti-Oedipe: Capitalisme et schizophrénie*. Paris: Editions de Minuit, 1972.

———. *A Thousand Plateaus: Capitalism and Schizophrenia*. Translated by Brian Massumi. [1980]. Minneapolis: University of Minnesota Press, 1987.

Derrida, Jacques. *Heidegger: La question de l'Être et l'Histoire. Cours de l'ENS-Ulm 1964–1965*. Edited by Thomas Dutoit with the help of Marguerite Derrida. Paris: Galilée, 2013.

Dmitriev, V. K. *Economic Essays on Value, Competition, and Utility*. [1904]. Cambridge: Cambridge University Press, 1974.

Elliot, Gregory, ed. *Althusser: A Critical Reader*. Oxford: Blackwell, 1994.

———. *Althusser: The Detour of Theory*. [1987]. 2nd ed. Chicago: Haymarket Books, 2009.

Elson, Diane. "The Value Theory of Labor." In *Value: The Representation of Labor in Capitalism*, edited by Diane Elson. London: Verso, 2015.

Endnotes 2: Misery and the Value Form. London: Infoshop, April 2010.

Engels, Friedrich. *Anti-Dühring: Herr Eugen Dühring's Revolution in Science*. 2nd ed. Moscow: Foreign Languages Publishing House, 1959.

———. "Letter to Karl Marx, December 11th or 12th, 1859." www.marxists.org/archive /marx/works/1859/letters/59_12_11.htm.

———. *Ludwig Feuerbach and the Outcome of Classical German Philosophy*. Translated by C. P. Dutt. New York: International Publishers, 1941.

———. "The Part Played by Labour in the Transition from Ape to Man." *Dialectics of Nature*, translated by C. P. Dutt, 279–96. New York: International, 1940.

———. "Speech at the Grave of Karl Marx." March 17, 1883, www.marxists.org/archive /marx/works/1883/death/burial.htm.

Farmer, Paul. *The Uses of Haiti*. Monroe, ME: Common Courage Press, 2005.

Farris, Sara. "Althusser and Tronti: The Primacy of Politics versus the Autonomy of the Political." In *Encountering Althusser: Politics and Materialism in Contemporary Radical Thought*. New York: Bloomsbury Academic, 2013.

Federici, Silvia. "Precarious Labor and Reproductive Work." *Variant*, no. 37 (spring/ summer 2010).

———. *Caliban and the Witch: Women, the Body and Primitive Accumulation*. New York: Autonomedia, 2004.

Filippini, Michele, and Emilio Macchia. *Leaping Forward: Mario Tronti and the History of Political Workerism*. Maastricht: Jan van Eyck Academie, 2012.

Ford, Martin. *The Rise of the Robots: Technology and the Threat of Mass Unemployment*. London: Oneworld, 2015.

Foucault, Michel. *The History of Sexuality*, vol. 1: *An Introduction*. Translated by Robert Hurley. New York: Vintage Books, 1990.

———. *L'ordre du discours*. Paris: Gallimard, 1971.

——. "Society Must Be Defended": Lectures at the Collège de France, 1975–1976, edited by Mauro Bertani and Alessandro Fontana; translated by David Macey. New York: Picador, 2003.

Frey, Carl Benedict, and Michael A. Osborne. "The Future of Employment: How Susceptible Are Jobs to Computerisation?" Oxford, 2013. Accessed January 6, 2015. www.oxfordmartin.ox.ac.uk/downloads/academic/The_Future_of _Employment.pdf.

Frosini, Fabio. "I *Quaderni* tra Mussolini e Croce." *Critica Marxista*, no. 4 (July–August 2012): 60–68.

Gilly, Adolfo. *The Mexican Revolution*. Translated by Patrice Camiller. New York: New Press, 2006.

Gimenez, Martha E. "Capitalism and the Oppression of Women: Marx Revisited." In "Marxist-Feminist Thought Today," special issue, *Science and Society* 69, no. 1 (January 2005): 11–32.

González Rojo, Enrique. *Epistemología y socialismo: La crítica de Sánchez Vázquez a Louis Althusser*. Mexico City: Diógenes, 1985.

——. *Para leer a Althusser*. Mexico City: Diógenes, 1974.

Grossman, Henryk. "The Value-Price Transformation in Marx and the Problem of Crisis." [1932]. *Historical Materialism* 24, no. 1 (2016): 105–34.

Guadarrama González, Pablo. "¿Ciencia o ideología? Estructuralismo y marxismo en Louis Althusser." *Marx ahora* 23 (2007).

Guevara, Ernesto Che. *Apuntes filosóficos*. Edited by María del Carmen Ariet García. Havana: Ocean Sur, 2012.

Hallward, Peter. *Damming the Flood: Haiti and the Politics of Containment*. London: Verso, 2010.

Harnecker, Marta. *Imperialisme en afhankelijkheid*. Translated by Marleen Huybregts. Odijk: Sjaloom, 1974.

——. *Los conceptos elementales del materialismo histórico*. Buenos Aires: Siglo XXI, 1968.

Harvey, David. "Crisis Theory and the Falling Rate of Profit." http://davidharvey.org /2014/12/debating-marxs-crisis-theory-falling-rate-profit/.

——. *Seventeen Contradictions and the End of Capitalism*. Oxford: Oxford University Press, 2014.

Hegel, G. W. F. *The Encyclopedia Logic: Part I of the Encyclopedia of the Philosophical Sciences with the Zusätze*. Translated by T. F. Geraets, W. A. Suchting, and H. S. Harris. Indianapolis: Hackett, 1991.

——. *The Science of Logic*. Translated by George Di Giovani. Cambridge: Cambridge University Press, 2010.

——. *Science of Logic*. Translated by A. V. Miller. London: George Allen and Unwin, 1969.

Heinrich, Michael. "Deconstructing *Capital*: New Insights from Marx's Economic Manuscripts in 'MEGA.'" Summary of the Historical Materialism Annual Conference, 2006, "New Directions in Marxian Theory."

——. *An Introduction to the Three Volumes of Karl Marx's Capital*. New York: Monthly Review Press, 2012.

Hennessy, Rosemary. "Women's Lives/Feminist Knowledge: Feminist Standpoint as Ideology Critique." *Hypatia* 8, no. 1 (winter 1993): 14–34.

Henry, Michel. *Marx*. Paris: Gallimard, 1976.

Hochschild, Arlie Russell. *The Managed Heart: Commercialization of Human Feeling*. Berkeley: University of California Press, 2003.

Ípola, Emilio de. *Althusser, el infinito adiós*, 215. Buenos Aires: Siglo XXI, 2007; in French, *Althusser, l'adieu infini*, translated by Marie Bardet; preface by Étienne Balibar. Paris: PUF, 2012.

James, C. L. R. *State Capitalism and World Revolution*. Oakland, CA: Revolutionary Classics, 1986.

James, C. L. R., and Raya Dunayevskaya. *Invading Socialist Society*. Oakland, CA: PM Press, 2010.

Jappe, Anselm. *Crédit à mort*. Paris: Lignes, 2011.

——. "Kurz: A Journey into Capitalism's Heart of Darkness." *Historical Materialism* 22, nos. 3–4 (2014): 395–407.

Johnston, Adrian. *Adventures in Transcendental Materialism: Dialogues with Contemporary Thinkers*. Edinburgh: Edinburgh University Press, 2014.

——. "Confession of a Weak Reductionist: Responses to Some Recent Criticisms of My Materialism." *Neuroscience and Critique*, edited by Jan De Vos and Ed Pluth. New York: Routledge, 2015.

——. "Drive between Brain and Subject: An Immanent Critique of Lacanian Neuro-psychoanalysis." In "Spindel supplement: Freudian Future(s)," special issue, *Southern Journal of Philosophy* 51 (September 2013): 48–84.

——. "From Scientific Socialism to Socialist Science: *Naturdialektik* Then and Now." In *The Idea of Communism 2: The New York Conference*, edited by Slavoj Žižek, 103–36. London: Verso, 2013.

——. "An Interview with Adrian Johnston on Transcendental Materialism (with Peter Gratton)." *Society and Space*, 2013, http://societyandspace.com/2013/10/07/interview-with-adrian-johnston-on-transcendental-materialism/.

——. "Interview about *Adventures in Transcendental Materialism: Dialogues with Contemporary Thinkers*, with Graham Harman for Edinburgh University Press." Edinburgh: Edinburgh University Press, April 2014. www.euppublishing.com/userimages/ContentEditor/1397840563624/Adventures%20in%20Transcendental%20Realism%20-%20Author%20Q%26A.pdf.

——. "Man, That Sickness: The Helplessness of Hegelian Philosophy, Lacanian Psychoanalysis, and Althusserian Marxism." *Crisis and Critique* (2015).

——. "Points of Forced Freedom: Eleven (More) Theses on Materialism." *Speculations: A Journal of Speculative Realism*, no. 4 (June 2013): 91–99.

——. *Prolegomena to Any Future Materialism*, vol. 1: *The Outcome of Contemporary French Philosophy*. Evanston, IL: Northwestern University Press, 2013.

———. *Prolegomena to Any Future Materialism*, vol. 2: *A Weak Nature Alone*. Evanston, IL: Northwestern University Press, 2016.

———. "Reflections of a Rotten Nature: Hegel, Lacan, and Material Negativity." In "Science and Thought," edited by Frank Ruda and Jan Voelker, special issue, *Filozofski Vestnik* 33, no. 2 (2012): 23–52.

———. "Repeating Engels: Renewing the Cause of the Materialist Wager for the Twenty-First Century." In "animal.machine.sovereign," special issue, *Theory @ Buffalo*, no. 15 (2011): 141–82.

———. "This *Is* Orthodox Marxism: The Shared Materialist *Weltanschauung* of Marx and Engels." In "On Sebastiano Timpanaro," special issue, *Quaderni materialisti* (2015).

———. *Time Driven: Metapsychology and the Splitting of the Drive*. Evanston, IL: Northwestern University Press, 2005.

———. "Transcendentalism in Hegel's Wake: A Reply to Timothy M. Hackett and Benjamin Berger." "Schelling: Powers of the Idea," edited by Benjamin Berger, special issue, *Pli: The Warwick Journal of Philosophy*, no. 26 (fall 2014): 204–37.

———. "The Weakness of Nature: Hegel, Freud, Lacan, and Negativity Materialized." *Hegel and the Infinite: Religion, Politics, and Dialectic*, edited by Slavoj Žižek, Clayton Crockett, and Creston Davis. New York: Columbia University Press, 2011.

———. *Žižek's Ontology: A Transcendental Materialist Theory of Subjectivity*. Evanston, IL: Northwestern University Press, 2008.

Kaplan, E. Ann, and Michael Sprinker, eds. *The Althusserian Legacy*. London: Verso, 1993.

Kaser, Michael. "The Debate on the Law of Value in USSR, 1941–53." In *Economics in Russia: Studies in Intellectual History*, edited by Vincent Barnett and Joachim Zweynert. New York: Ashgate, 2008.

Kliman, Andrew. *The Failure of Capitalist Production: Underlying Causes of the Great Recession*. London: Pluto, 2012.

———. "Harvey vs. Marx on Capitalism's Crises Part 1: Getting Marx Wrong," March 10, 2015. www.newleftproject.org/index.php/site/article_comments/harvey_versus_marx_on_capitalisms_crises_part_1_getting_marx_wrong.

———. *Reclaiming Marx's "Capital": A Refutation of the Myth of Inconsistency*. Lanham, MD: Lexington Books, 2007.

Koyré, Alexandre. *From the Closed World to the Infinite Universe*. New York: Harper Torchbooks, 1958.

Kritzman, Lawrence, ed. *The Columbia History of Twentieth-Century French Thought*. New York: Columbia University Press, 2006.

Kurz, Robert. *Vies et mort du capitalisme*. Paris: Lignes, 2011.

———. *Dinheiro sem valor: Linhas gerais para uma transformação da critica da economia política*. Translated by Lumir Nahodil. Lisboa: Antígona, 2014. In German, *Geld Ohne Wert: Grundrisse zu einer Transformation der Kritik der politischen Ökonomie*. Andermunde, Germany: Horlemann, 2012.

Kurz, Robert, Ernst Lohoff, and Norbert Trenkle. *Manifese contre le travail*. Paris: Editions Léo Scheer, 2002.

Lacan, Jacques. *Ecrits: The First Complete Edition in English*. Translated by Bruce Fink. New York: W. W. Norton, 2006.

———. *Le Séminaire de Jacques Lacan*, livre 16: *D'un Autre à l'autre, 1968–1969*, edited by Jacques-Alain Miller. Paris: Éditions du Seuil, 2006.

———. *The Seminar of Jacques Lacan*, book 7: *The Ethics of Psychoanalysis, 1959–1960*, edited by Jacques-Alain Miller, translated by Dennis Porter. New York: W. W. Norton, 1992.

———. *The Seminar of Jacques Lacan*, book 11: *The Four Fundamental Concepts of Psychoanalysis, 1964*, edited by Jacques-Alain Miller, translated by Alan Sheridan. New York: W. W. Norton, 1977.

Laclau, Ernesto. *Politics and Ideology in Marxist Theory: Capitalism-Fascism-Populism*. London: New Left Books, 1977. In Spanish, *Política e ideología en la teoría marxista: Capitalismo, fascismo, populismo*. Mexico City: Siglo XXI, 1978.

Laclau, Ernesto, and Chantal Mouffe. *Hegemony and Socialist Strategy: Towards a Radical Democratic Politics*. [1985]. London: Verso, 2001.

Larsen, Neil, et al., eds. *Marxism and the Critique of Value*. Phoenix, AZ: MCM, 2014.

Lasowski, Aliocha Wald. *Althusser et nous*. Paris: PUF, 2016.

Lenin, V. I. *The Lenin Anthology*. Edited by Robert C. Tucker. New York: W. W. Norton, 1975.

———. "Conspectus of Hegel's Book *The Science of Logic*." In *Collected Works*, vol. 38: *Philosophical Notebooks*, edited by Stewart Smith; translated by Clemence Dutt, 122–25. Moscow: Progress, 1976.

Lewis, William S. "The Under-theorization of Overdetermination in *Hegemony and Socialist Strategy*." In "Althusser and Us," edited by David McInerney, special issue, *borderlands e-journal* 4, no. 2 (2005).

Lohoff, Ernst, and Norbert Trenkle. *La grande dévalorisation: Pourquoi la speculation et la dette de l'état ne sont pas les causes de la crise*. Paris: Post-éditions, 2014. In German, *Die große Entwertung: Warum Spekulation Und Staatsschulden Sind Nicht Die Ursachen Der Krisee*. Münster: Unrast, 2012.

Löwy, Michael. *The Politics of Combined and Uneven Development*. New York: Verso, 1981.

———. *The Politics of Combined and Uneven Development: The Theory of Permanent Revolution*. Chicago: Haymarket Books, 2010.

Lukács, Georg. "Karl August Wittfogel: The Science of Bourgeois Society." In *Tactics and Ethics: Political Writings, 1919–1929*, edited by Rodney Livingstone; translated by Michael McColgan, 144–45. London: New Left Books, 1972.

———. "N. Bukharin: Historical Materialism." *Tactics and Ethics: Political Writings, 1919–1929*, edited by Rodney Livingstone; translated by Michael McColgan, 136, 139–42. London: New Left Books, 1972.

———. "Tailism and the Dialectic." In *A Defense of History and Class Consciousness: Tailism and the Dialectic*, translated by Esther Leslie, 100, 102. London: Verso, 2000.

———. "What Is Orthodox Marxism?" In *History and Class Consciousness: Studies in Marxist Dialectics*, translated by Rodney Livingstone. Cambridge, MA: MIT Press, 1971.

Luxemburg, Rosa. *The Accumulation of Capital*. London: Routledge, 2003.

Malabou, Catherine. "Whither Materialism? Althusser/Darwin." In *Plastic Materialities: Politics, Legality, and Metamorphosis in the Work of Catherine Malabou*, edited by Brenna Bhandar and Jonathan Goldberg-Hiller, 47–60. Durham, NC: Duke University Press, 2015.

Mandel, Ernest. *Late Capitalism*. London: New Left Books, 1975.

Marini, Ruy Mauro. *Sous-développement et révolution en Amérique Latine*. Paris: François Maspero, 1972.

Martínez, Fernando. "Althusser y el marxismo." *Pensamiento crítico* 37 (1970): 210–18.

Marx, Karl. *Capital*. Vol. 1. New York: Penguin, 2004.

———. *Capital*. Vol. 3. London: Penguin, 1991.

———. "Critique of the Gotha Programme." Translated by Joris de Bres. *The First International and After: Political Writings*, vol. 3, edited by David Fernbach. Harmondsworth, UK: Penguin, 1974.

———. "Critique of the Gotha Program." Accessed May 14, 2015. https://www.marxists.org/archive/marx/works/1875/gotha/ch01.htm.

———. *Le Capital*. Translated by M. J. Roy. Paris: Éditeurs Maurice Lachatre, 1872–1875.

———. *Le Capital: Critique de l'économie politique*. 4th ed. Translated by Jean-Pierre Lefebvre. Paris: Éditions sociales, 1983.

———. *Capital*. 3 vols. Translated by Ben Fowkes and David Fernbach. Harmondsworth, UK: Penguin Books, 1976–81.

———. *Economic and Philosophical Manuscripts, Early Writings*. Translated by Rodney Livingstone and Gregor Benton. New York: Penguin, 1992.

———. "Einleiting." In *Grundrisse der Kritik der politischen Ökonomie*. Karl Marx and Friedrich Engels, *Werke*, vol. 42. Berlin: Dietz, 1983.

———. *Grundrisse: Introduction to the Critique of Political Economy*. Translated by Martin Nicolaus. New York: Vintage, 1973.

———. "Letter to Ferdinand Lassalle, January 16th, 1861." www.marxists.org/archive/marx/works/1861/letters/61_01_16.htm.

———. "Letter to Frederick Engels, December 7th, 1867." www.marxists.org/archive/marx/works/1867/letters/67_12_07.htm.

———. *Marx's Economic Manuscript of 1864–65*. [1864–65]. Translated by Ben Fowkes. Leiden: Brill 2016.

———. "Theses on Feuerbach." Translated by S. Ryazanskaya. In Karl Marx, *Karl Marx: Selected Writings*, edited by David McLellan, 156–58. Oxford: Oxford University Press, 1977.

Marx, Karl, and Friedrich Engels. *The German Ideology*, edited by C. J. Arthur. New York: International Publishers, 1970.

──── . *The German Ideology*, including *Theses on Feuerbach* and *Introduction to the Critique of Political Economy*. Amherst, NY: Prometheus Books, 1998.

──── . *Gesamtausgabe (MEGA)/herausgegeben vom Institut für Marxismus-Leninismus beim Zentralkomitee der Kommunistischen Partei der Sowjetunion und vom Institut für Marxismus-Leninismus beim Zentralkomitee der Sozialistischen Einheitspartei Deutschlands*. Berlin: Dietz, 1972.

Milios, John. "Rethinking Marx's Value-Form Analysis from an Althusserian Perspective." *Rethinking Marxism* 21, no. 2 (April 2009): 260–74.

Monod, Jacques. *Chance and Necessity: An Essay on the Natural Philosophy of Modern Biology*. Translated by Austryn Wainhouse. New York: Alfred A. Knopf, 1971.

Montag, Warren. *Althusser and His Contemporaries*. Durham, NC: Duke University Press, 2013.

──── . "Althusser's Lenin." *Diacritics* 43, no. 2 (2015): 48–66.

──── . *Louis Althusser*. London: Palgrave, 2003.

Moseley, Fred. *Money and Totality: A Macro-Monetary Interpretation of Marx's Logic in Capital and the End of the "Transformation Problem."* Leiden: Brill, 2016.

Nesbitt, Nick. "From Louverture to Lenin: Aimé Césaire and Anticolonial Marxism." *Smallaxe* 48 (fall 2015): 129–44.

Nietzsche, Friedrich. *The Gay Science: With a Prelude in German Rhymes and an Appendix of Songs*, edited by Bernard Williams. Cambridge: Cambridge University Press, 2001.

Peden, Knox. *Spinoza contra Phenomenology*. Stanford, CA: Stanford University Press, 2014.

Peeters, Benoît. *Derrida: A Biography*. Translated by Andrew Brown. Cambridge: Polity, 2013.

Pico della Mirandola, Giovanni. "On the Dignity of Man." In *On the Dignity of Man*, translated by Charles Glenn Wallis, Paul J. W. Miller, and Douglas Carmichael. Indianapolis: Hackett, 1998.

Pippa, Stefano. "The Necessity of Contingency: Reading Althusser on Structural Causality." *Radical Philosophy* 199 (September–October 2016): 15–25.

Postone, Moishe. *Time, Labor, and Social Domination: A Reinterpretation of Marx's Critical Theory*. Oxford: Oxford University Press, 1996.

Rancière, Jacques. "Dissenting Words: A Conversation with Jacques Rancière" (interview by Davide Panagia). *Diacritics* 30, no. 2 (2000): 113–26.

──── . *La leçon d'Althusser*. Paris: Gallimard, 1974.

──── . Preface to the English edition. *Staging the People: The Proletarian and His Double*. Translated by David Fernbach. London: Verso, 2011.

──── . "Sobre la teoría de la ideología (La política de Althusser)." In *Lectura de Althusser*, edited by Saúl Karsz. Buenos Aires: Galerna, 1970.

Ricardo, David. *On the Principles of Political Economy, and Taxation*. 3rd ed. London: John Murray, 1821.

Rodrick, Dani. "Premature Deindustrialization." NBER Working Paper No. 20935, February 2015. Accessed April 28, 2015, www.nber.org/papers/w20935.

Rooney, Ellen. "Better Read Than Dead: Althusser and the Fetish of Ideology." In "Depositions: Althusser, Balibar, Macherey, and the Labor of Reading." *Yale French Studies*, no. 88 (1995): 183–200.

Roth, Regina. "Karl Marx's Original Manuscripts in the Marx-Engels-Gesamtausgabe (MEGA): Another View on *Capital*." In *Re-Reading Marx: New Perspectives after the Critical Edition*, edited by Riccardo Bellofiore and Roberto Fineschi, 27–49. Basingstoke, UK: Palgrave Macmillan, 2009.

Rozitchner, León. "La tragedia del althusserismo teórico." *El Ojo Mocho* 17 (2003).

Rubin, I. I. *Essays on Marx's Theory of Value*. Delhi: Aakar Books, 2008.

Sánchez Vázquez, Adolfo. "Sobre la teoría althusseriana de la ideología." In *Ideología y ciencias sociales*, edited by Mario H. Otero. Mexico City: UNAM, 1979.

———. *Ciencia y revolución (El marxismo de Althusser)*. Madrid: Alianza, 1978; new ed., Mexico City: Grijalbo, 1983.

———. "El teoricismo de Althusser (Notas críticas sobre una autocrítica)." *Cuadernos políticos* 3 (1975).

Schmitt, Carl. *Crisis of Parliamentary Democracy*. Translated by Ellen Kennedy. Studies in Contemporary German Social Thought. Cambridge, MA: MIT Press, 1985.

Smith, Jason. "Jacques Derrida, Crypto-Communist?" In *Critical Companion to Contemporary Marxism*, edited by Jacques Bidet and Stathis Kouvelakis. Chicago: Haymarket, 2006.

Smith, John. *Imperialism in the Twenty-First Century*. New York: Monthly Review Press, 2016.

Stedman Jones, Gareth. *Karl Marx: Greatness and Illusion*. Cambridge, MA: Harvard University Press, 2016.

Taylor, Christopher. "The Refusal of Work: From the Postemancipation Caribbean to Post-Fordist Empire." *Smallaxe* 44 (July 2014): 1–17.

Tirard, Stéphane. "Monod, Althusser et le marxisme." In *Une nouvelle connaissance du vivant: François Jacob, André Wolff et Jacques Monod*, edited by Claude Debru, Michel Morange, and Frédéric Worms, 75–88. Paris: Éditions Rue d'Ulm, 2012.

Tomba, Massimiliano, and Ricardo Bellofiore. "The 'Fragment on the Machines' and the *Grundrisse*: The Workerist Reading in Question." In *Beyond Marx: Theorising the Global Labour Relations of the Twenty-First Century*, edited by Marcel van der Linden and Karl Heinz Roth, 345–67. London: Brill, 2014.

Toscano, Alberto. "From the State to the World?: Badiou and Anti-capitalism." *Communication and Cognition* 37, nos. 3–4 (2004): 199–224.

———. "Transition Deprogrammed." In "Communist Currents," edited by Bruno Bosteels and Jodi Dean, special issue. *South Atlantic Quarterly* 113, no. 4 (fall 2014).

Trenkle, Norbert, and Ernst Lohoff. *La grande dévalorisation: Pourquoi la speculation et la dette de l'état ne sont pas les causes de la crise*. Fécamp, France: Post-éditions, 2014.

Tronti, Mario. *Noi operaisti*. Rome: Derive approdi, 2009.

———. *Operai e capitale* (1966). 2nd ed., enlarged. Torino: Einaudi Editore, 1971; new ed., Rome: Derive approdi, 2006.

———. *Ouvriers et capital.* Translated by Yann Moulier-Boutang. Paris: Editions Christian Bourgois, 1977. www.multitudes.net/category/archives-revues-futur -anterieur-et/bibliotheque-diffuse/operaisme-autonomie/tronti-ouvriers-et -capital/.

———. *Workers and Capital.* English translation of *Operai e capitale*, 2011. http:// operaismoinenglish.wordpress.com/2011/05/11/workers-and-capital-contents/.

Trotsky, Leon. *The History of the Russian Revolution.* Translated by Max Eastman. Atlanta: Pathfinder, 2010.

Turchetto, Maria. "Althusser and Monod: A 'New Alliance'?" Translated by Peter Thomas. *Historical Materialism*, no. 17 (2009): 61–79.

Vacca, Giuseppe. *Vita e pensieri di Antonio Gramsci (1926–1937).* Torino: Einaudi Editore, 2012.

Weeks, Kathi. *The Problem with Work: Feminism, Marxism, Antiwork Politics, and Postwork Imaginaries.* Durham, NC: Duke University Press, 2011.

Young, Robert J. C. *Postcolonialism: An Historical Introduction.* Malden, MA: Blackwell, 2001.

Zedong, Mao. *Acerca de la práctica.* Havana: Editora Política, 1963.

CONTRIBUTORS

EMILY APTER is Professor of French and Comparative Literature and Chair of Comparative Literature at New York University. Her most recent books books include: *Against World Literature: On The Politics of Untranslatability* (2013), *Dictionary of Untranslatables: A Philosophical Lexicon* (co-edited with Barbara Cassin, Jacques Lezra, and Michael Wood) (2014); and *The Translation Zone: A New Comparative Literature* (2006). A French translation of *The Translation Zone: A New Comparative Literature* was published in 2016 by Fayard in the series "Ouvertures" edited by Barbara Cassin and Alain Badiou. Together with Bruno Bosteels she co-edited Alain Badiou's *The Age of the Poets and Other Writings on Poetry and Prose* (Verso 2014). Her most recent project is *Unexceptional Politics: A Glossary of Obstruction* (forthcoming, Verso, 2017). She edits the book series *Translation/Transnation* for Princeton University Press.

ALAIN BADIOU has taught philosophy at the École Normale Supérieure and the Collège international de philosophie in Paris. He is the author of over seventy books, including *Theory of the Subject, Being and Event*, and *Logics of Worlds*. Among his more recent books are *The Communist Hypothesis*; *The Age of Poets*; and *The Adventure of French Philosophy*.

ÉTIENNE BALIBAR is professor emeritus of moral and political philosophy at Université de Paris X–Nanterre and Anniversary Chair of Modern European Philosophy at Kingston University, London. He has published widely in the area of Marxist philosophy and moral and political philosophy in general. His many works include (with Louis Althusser, Pierre Macherey, Jacques Rancière, Roger Establet, and F. Maspero) *Lire le Capital* (1965); *Spinoza et la politique* (1985); *Nous, citoyens d'Europe? Les frontières, l'État, le peuple* (2001); *Politics and the Other Scene* (2002); *L'Europe, l'Amérique, la Guerre: Réflexions sur la mediation européenne* (2003); and *Europe, Constitution, Frontière* (2005).

BRUNO BOSTEELS, a professor of Romance studies at Cornell University, holds a PhD in Romance languages and literatures from the University of Pennsylvania (1995; MA 1992) and an AB in Romance Philology from the Katholieke Universiteit Leuven, Belgium (1989). Before Cornell, he held positions at Harvard University and at Columbia University. He is the author of *Alain Badiou, une trajectoire polémique* (2009); *Badiou and Politics* (Duke University Press, 2011); *The Actuality of Communism* (2011); and

Marx and Freud in Latin America (2012). He has translated Alain Badiou's *Theory of the Subject* (2009); *Wittgenstein's Antiphilosophy* (2011); *The Adventure of French Philosophy* (2012); *Philosophy for Militants* (2012); *Rhapsody for the Theatre* (2013); and *The Age of the Poets and Other Writings on Poetry and Prose* (2014). He is the author of dozens of articles on modern Latin American literature and culture and on contemporary European philosophy and political theory. Between 2006 and 2011 he also served as the general editor of *Diacritics*. He is currently working on two new book projects, *Philosophies of Defeat: The Jargon of Finitude* and *The Mexican Commune*.

ADRIAN JOHNSTON is a Professor in the Department of Philosophy at the University of New Mexico at Albuquerque and a faculty member at the Emory Psychoanalytic Institute in Atlanta. He is the author of *Time Driven: Metapsychology and the Splitting of the Drive* (2005); *Žižek's Ontology: A Transcendental Materialist Theory of Subjectivity* (2008); *Badiou, Žižek, and Political Transformations: The Cadence of Change* (2009); and *Prolegomena to Any Future Materialism, Volume One: The Outcome of Contemporary French Philosophy* (2013), all published by Northwestern University Press. He is the co-author, with Catherine Malabou, of *Self and Emotional Life: Philosophy, Psychoanalysis, and Neuroscience* (Columbia University Press, 2013). His most recent book is *Adventures in Transcendental Materialism: Dialogues with Contemporary Thinkers* (Edinburgh University Press, 2014). In 2017, Columbia University Press will be publishing by him *A New German Idealism: Hegel, Žižek, and Dialectical Materialism*. Moreover, he currently is finishing two new book manuscripts: *Prolegomena to Any Future Materialism, Volume Two: A Weak Nature Alone* and *Irrepressible Truth: On Lacan's "The Freudian Thing."* With Todd McGowan and Slavoj Žižek, he is a co-editor of the book series *Diaeresis* at Northwestern University Press.

WARREN MONTAG is Brown Family Professor in Literature, English, and Comparative Literary Studies at Occidental College. Montag teaches eighteenth-century British and European literature with particular reference to political philosophy; he also teaches twentieth-century European critical theory. His publications include *Philosophy's Perpetual War: Althusser and His Contemporaries* (Duke University Press, 2013); *Louis Althusser* (2003); *Bodies, Masses, Power: Spinoza and His Contemporaries* (1999); *The Unthinkable Swift: The Spontaneous Philosophy of a Church of England Man* (1994); (coeditor) *Masses, Classes and the Public Sphere* (2001); (editor) *In a Materialist Way: Selected Essays by Pierre Macherey* (1998); and (coeditor) *The New Spinoza* (1997).

FERNANDA NAVARRO (UMSNH-UNAM, Mexico) is the author of numerous books and articles on modern European philosophy, including *Ethics and Politics* (Siglo XXI) and *Existence, Encounter and Hazard*. Between 1983 and 1984 she traveled to Paris at the Collège International de la Philosophie. That same year she met Louis Althusser, marking the beginning of a fruitful relationship that resulted in the publication, four years later of *Philosophy and Marxism, Interviews with L. Althusser*, subsequently translated into Japanese, French, English, Italian, and in 2012, Chinese. These interviews constitute the definitive statement of the "last Althusser."

NICK NESBITT is a professor in the Department of French and Italian at Princeton University. He received his PhD in Romance Languages and Literatures (French) with a minor in Brazilian Portuguese from Harvard University. He has previously taught at the University of Aberdeen (Scotland) and at Miami University (Ohio), and in 2003–2004 he was a Mellon Fellow at the Cornell University Society for the Humanities. He is the author of *Caribbean Critique: Antillean Critical Theory from Toussaint to Glissant* (2013); *Universal Emancipation: The Haitian Revolution and the Radical Enlightenment* (2008); and *Voicing Memory: History and Subjectivity in French Caribbean Literature* (2003). He is also the editor of *Toussaint Louverture: The Haitian Revolution* (2008) and coeditor, with Brian Hulse, of *Sounding the Virtual: Gilles Deleuze and the Philosophy of Music* (2010).

KNOX PEDEN is an ARC Research Fellow in the School of Philosophy, Research School of the Social Sciences, at the Australian National University. He is the author of *Spinoza Contra Phenomenology: French Rationalism from Cavaillès to Deleuze* (2014) and the coeditor, with Peter Hallward, of a two-volume work devoted to the *Cahiers pour l'Analyse* (2012). His work has also appeared in *Modern Intellectual History*, *History and Theory*, *Radical Philosophy*, *History of European Ideas*, and *Continental Philosophy Review*.

NINA POWER is a senior lecturer in philosophy at Roehampton University. She is the coeditor of Alain Badiou's *On Beckett*, and the author of several articles on European philosophy, atomism, pedagogy, art, and politics. Her book *One-Dimensional Woman* was published in 2009. She is based in London.

ROBERT J. C. YOUNG is the Silver Professor of English at NYU, where he writes on topics including postcolonial literatures and cultures; the history of colonialism and anticolonialism; cultural history of the nineteenth and twentieth centuries; and literary and cultural theory. His publications include *The Idea of English Ethnicity* (2008); *Postcolonialism: A Very Short Introduction* (2003); *Postcolonialism: An Historical Introduction* (2001); *Torn Halves: Political Conflict in Literary and Cultural Theory* (1996); *Colonial Desire: Hybridity in Culture, Theory, and Race* (1995); and *White Mythologies: Writing History and the West* (1990), and he is General Editor of *Interventions: International Journal of Postcolonial Studies*.

INDEX